TERRORISM IN INDIA

TERRORISM IN INDIA

(Volume-II)

Col. Ved Prakash

KALPAZ

Terrorism in India (Volume II)

Rs. 900

ISBN: 978-81-7835-747-8 (Set)
ISBN: 978-81-7835-749-2 (Vol. 2)

Published in 2010 in India by
Kalpaz Publications
C-30, Satyawati Nagar,
Delhi-110052
E-mail: kalpaz@hotmail.com
Phone : 9212729499

Lasser Type Setting by: Quick Media, Delhi
Printed at : Young Art Press, Delhi

Contents

8

Need for Counter-Terrorism Policy and Allied Issues : Part 3

Diwali Eve Arrests 2006 Save Situation

Police on the lookout for militants out to unleash death and destruction before Diwali 2006, succeeded in arresting on 23 Oct. 2006, Jaish-E-Mohammad (JEM) ultra Parvez Ahmed Radoo, 29, alias Raju from Azadpur in north-west Delhi. The Delhi Police Special Cell team recovered from him three kg of RDX, a detonator, a timer and Rs. 10 lakhs.

The investigations showed Radoo was just the "hand on the button" while the mastermind behind this civil plot was one Shergill, who is still at large, the press learnt on 29 Oct.

Shergill is said to be the JEM Avantipora 'commander'. A special cell team had raided his Avantipora (in Jammu and Kashmir) hide-out at midnight 27 Oct but he had left earlier.

"Shergill had directed Parvez to carry out blasts in the capital on Diwali..It was he who gave the explosives and cash to Parvez belongs to Sopore in Baramulla district of Jammu and Kashmir.

Shergill is a Pakistani and gets his orders from JEM bosses in Pakistan. He was asked to set up a JEM base in Delhi. Parvez has disclosed to police the Avantipora hideout of Shergill where a raid proved abortive. "The police is still looking for Shergill as he can tell more on Jaish's future plan for Delhi (and India)."

A source said: "As the festival reason is on and will continue till the New Year (2007), terrorists have mobilized themselves as several arrests this month (October) indicate."

The police feels "situation is still sensitive as the International Trade Fair is scheduled for Nov." The intelligence has also warned that "JEM would try to sneak into the city, with the sole aim of spreading terror on their minds."

Ordinary laws not Enough to Fight Terrorism: Nov 2006

Prime Minister Man Mohan Singh in Nov 2006 reiterated the nation's commitment to zero tolerance for terrorism but within the framework of existing laws. He hastened to add that no community or religion should be blamed for terrorist act. Democracy has its own compulsions (perhaps including the vote-bank considerations), more so in a caste and community-ridden political environment.

May be, Prime Minister spoke out of conviction, but it would also be ideal if existing laws could take care of acts of terrorism in our country. The nation has taken these hits with great forbearance, maturity and resilience. Some analysts feel these qualities in the face of terrorism are not to be lauded unduly, because these are indicative of people's helplessness—perhaps cowardice. They are unable to force the government to adopt tough stance against terrorism. They are unable to understand why India can not adopt a series of tough measures a la the US to contain the US. Interestingly, these measures annoyed quite a few people in America but the Government want ahead and implemented them.

Prime Minister Man Mohan Singh is an honest man, accept the analysts but he has his compulsions as head of a coalition government. His compulsions to caution his countrymen not to blame any community or religion are also understood. There is no point in labouring on the point time and again.

But on one point, security experts the world over agree that terrorism cannot be contained by ordinary laws and for that are required both tough measures and enabling environment. Director, Intelligence Bureau Narasimhan during his "recent speech at the DGP's conference" was frank enough to articulate the need for an enabling legal architecture. The IB Chief who is more information than anyone else in the country, must be having, analysts feel, enough reasons to say what he did. The Government will be well-advised to take his articulation seriously.

Any law is likely to be abused occasionally by a few in power but that cannot be allowed to be quoted/cited as a reason to negate instituting strict laws. If the security establishment feels that the Unlawful Activities (Prevention) Act which replaced POTA is not potent enough, the Government must listen to the advice and consider the possibility of restoring the status quo. When a nation's security is at stake, there is no scope for compromises.

An analyst sees an opportunity provided by the Supreme Court to strengthen and professionalise the police forces across the country. Law and order being a state subject is after cited as an excuse to ignore Centre's advise or suggestions under all circumstances. With the Supreme Court backing the reforms, the states have little option but to implement the court directives. The UPA should take advantage of the situation and bring about a consensus between various states for complete uniformity of action against terrorist acts.

Countering terrorism is a serious business. "Merely chanting peace hymns and the slogan, 'Vasudeva Kutumbkam' will not do".[1]

"Sonia Gandhi is the Target," Says Intelligence: Dec. 2006

Vandana Kini, incharge of VIP security in the Union Home Ministry, has warned UP and Rajasthan government and the authorities in the capital that the UPA chairperson and Congress president Sonia Gandhi is likely to be targeted by the United Jihad Council, an anti-India jihadi outfit set up recently in Bangladesh by Al Qaeda. A daily (*Times of India*) reported this on 21 Dec 2006.

Kini's letter even provides physical description of Sajjad, detailed here:

- Sajjad—Pak national, leader of jihadi squad targeting Sonia Gandhi
- Age—About 35 years
- Height-5 feet 6 inches
- Last seen—In Meerut, wearing a jacket and a muffler
- Aides—Sajjad has at least five aides, four Bijnor-based and one in Rajasthan.
- Route to India –Sneaked in from Bangladesh

Sajjad is heading the fidayeen squad to target Sonia, says the Ministry letter.

As a result of this heightened concern, a fresh massive hunt for Pakistani nationals, those who entered illegally or those who came on valid papers but stayed on beyond the visa period, "is also expected to be launched shortly."

Al Qaeda is seen the moving hand behind this UJC threat. The UJC was formed by Al Qaeda with support from ISI.

Sajjad has been collaborating with Mohd Salim, head of a Lashkar cell holed up in Meerut.

"Diologue cannot Replace Guns": LET : 19 Jan 2007

Even as the visiting Umar Farooq-led APHC team met Gen Musharraf and made appropriate 'peace-noises', the main driver of terrorists violence in Jammu and Kashmir, LET, was not prepared to buy the argument that dialogue can replace the guns. LET Chief Hafiz Saeed said, speaking to the gathering after Friday prayers in Lahore, "It is a historical fact that nations have always achieved their independence through sacrifices on battle front."

It is clear that Umar Farooq's peace-exertions not withstanding, the jihadis continue to see Kashmir as a religious and political cause that the our determined to achieve. Contrary to Musharraf's statements that elements hostile to peace process should be discouraged and dealt with, the LET Supremo said: "The Kashmir issue cannot be resolved through back channel diplomacy.

The LET founder even warned Musharraf "to desist from stabbing the Kashmiris in the back in exchange of better relations with India."

Arms haul in Kochi from Dubai Container: 9 Jan. 2007

Kochi customs stumbled upon a huge cache of sophisticated arms from a container stored in a Kochi port godown owned by brother of a controversial senior IPS officer, Tomin J. Thachankery. The container was shipped to Kochi from Dubai on 4 Jan 2007.

110 of the 810 boxes, opened till the 8th, yielded 97 guns. Of which 49 are meant for training and 38 are rifles. The guns were shipped along with knocked out furniture.

The seized guns are manufactured by Beretta, Walther and Gamo in Germany, Spain, and Italy. Experts assert that a person who receives training on these guns can operate any sophisticated rifle.

Sources said the role of Islamists is suspected in this attempt to smuggle guns in the country.

New Delhi may Issue Goa Terror Alert: 26 Dec. 2006

The Centre is considering issuing a New Year terror alert to Goa to keep the tourist destination—particularly beaches and night clubs—secure during the festivities leading up to and including New Year's Day.

The decision comes after Indian missions in West Asia (Yemen, Saudi Arabia etc) and North Africa (Algeria) reported that intelligence inputs warning of a terrorist strike in Goa tallied with information obtained from interrogation of members of Islamic militant groups arrested in these regions.

Sources said Indian missions in Yemen, Algeria and Saudi Arabia had been asked to follow up intelligence inputs after "Israel's advisory on Goa earlier this month" (13 December). These inputs were based on information after the arrest of Yemenese and Algerian militants in Jeddah, which showed that militant groups had done a recce of popular Goa spots.

A laptop with them had detailed plans of a possible militant strike, intelligence sources said.

IDPs are also Victims of Terrorism: Feb. 2007

Policy Needed for their Rehabilitations

With the situation of Internally Displaced Persons (IDPs) assuming worrying proportions, Human Rights groups have stepped up pressure on the government to evolve a national policy on the subject. Of India's one billion population, IDPs currently—Feb 2007—aggregate more than half a million, according to the draft report of the Asian Centre for Human Rights (ACHR).

The draft report says 6,00,000 conflict-induced IDPs, 80 per cent of whom constitute tribals 1,07,485 Bodos and Santhals in Kokrajhar and Gosaigaon districts of Assam and about 35,000 Brus (also called Reangs) in Tripura. Other groups include

43,740 displaced Advasis living in the anti-Naxalite 'Salwa Judum' camps in Chhattisgarh and 10,000 Muslims of Gujarat living in 34 camps.

Ongoing fencing activities on the Indo-Bangla border will also displace an additional 35,438 persons, said ACHR Director Suhas Chakma. Kashmir Pandits, numbering over 300,000, constitute the largest community of IDPs in India. In view of this figure, the tribals can not form 80 per cent of the total IDPs in India, as claimed by the ACHR report.

It is a huge problem and the Union Government has been readily providing financial and other forms of assistance, "but it is essentially for the state governments to deal with the problem" says Minister of State for Home Affairs Sriprakash Jaiswal. "Given the federal structure of the Constitution, the Centre can not directly intervene in such matters."

There is other view from Shabnam Hashmi of Act Now for Harmony and Democracy (ANHAD). Warns she: "The Centre is unwilling to take responsibility, but can continue to neglect the issue only at great peril. The ANHAD organized the first ever conclave of the IDPs in New Delhi in Apr 2007. Activist/ journalist Farah Naqvi reinforces the same postulation through a loaded question: "If the Union Government can formulate a draft national rehabilitation policy (covering the individuals displaced by mega projects) why is it not possible for it to evolve an over all policy that covers all categories of IDPs ?"

The UN's "Guiding Principle's" on the IDPs—not legally binding international document—are irrelevant in the Indian context in any case, because as for the IDPs are concerned, the UN gets in the picture only when specifically requested by the host country. In the absence of any request from India, "our concern is only with the refugees," said the UNHCR's associate external relations officer Nayana Bose.

Prof. Zoya Hasan of National Commission for Minorities said, "I can only reiterate what we said in Nov. 2006 : There is a used for a national policy on the IDPs."

Acting NHRC Chairperson Justice Shivraj Patil agreed with the sentiments expressed by Zoya Hasan. (Srinand Jha, *Hindustan Times*, 27 March 2007; srinandjha@hindustan-times.com)

Location of IDPs in India

1.	Kashmiri Pandits (Jammu and Kashmir, Delhi and South India)	300,000
2.	Bodo, Santhal, Karbi and Dimasa tribals (Assam)	1,51,485
3.	Adivasis, Bodos and Muslims (Bodoland)	2,00,000
4.	Hmar tribals (Manipur)	690
5.	Brus/Reangs (Tripura)	35,000
6.	Assamese (Hindus and Muslims) (Indo Bangla border)	35,438
7.	Salwa Judum Adivasis (Chhattisgarh)	43,740
8.	Muslims (Gujarat)	10,000

Terrorists Manipulating Stock Markets: 9 Feb., 2007 : MK Narayanan

Manipulation of stock exchanges is the new modus operandi used by terrorist groups to raise funds for their operations, and fictitious companies have operated in the Mumbai and Chennai stock changes.

Revealing this, National Security Advisor MK Narayanan has said some of the companies were later traced to terrorist groups. Stock exchanges in these two metros have, on occasions, reported that fictitious or national companies were engaging in the stock market operations.

The NASH revealed these disturbing news, directly impacting the national security, while addressing the 43rd Conference on Security Policy in Munich on 9 Feb 2007.

Calling for the lifting of banking secrecy and the corporate veil in terrorist-related cases, he said security agencies had detected many instances of funds received via banking channels from so-called safe locations like Dubai and UAE that were intended for terrorist groups.

A belt bomb 'almost' Smuggled into India : 13 Feb., 2007

"The last time a belt bomb entered India, it claimed the life of Rajiv Gandhi in May 1991. On 13 Feb 2007 afternoon the

Coast Guard intercepted a fibreglass fishing boat off Tamil Nadu coast and among its deadly consignment was a belt bomb and (omenously) its destination was India". (GC Shekhar, *Hindustan Times*, 15 Feb 2007).

There was no doubt or uncertainty about the intent of the consignor. Made of black nylon material, the 7-kg belt bomb had been packed with explosives and the small sockets meant for placing detonators were filled with wheat dough. The trigger mechanism consisting of a battery, wires and clips and a switch was also seized. The other items seized were:

1. AK-56 rifle with 12 rounds.
2. Hand grenades 5
3. Ammonia Powder 7kg
4. Liquid chemical 8 drums
5. Small bottles rebelled as retro pen.
6. A hand-held GPS device
7. A satellite phone.

The seizure, by personnel of Coast Guard Ship Ramadevi, was made during a regular patrol, 20 nautical miles off Kodiakaral along the Tamil Nadu coast.

Coast Guard Regional Commander Rajendre Singh told the Press: "It is a significant catch since the boat, carrying three Sri Lankan Tamils and two local Tamils, was heading towards India. The crew was planning to deliver the consignment at the Indian coast as our preliminary investigation revealed. The complete picture would be clear after the state and central agencies question them. It is not clear if any of the Lankan Tamils belonged to the LTTE."

Incidentally, it was at Kodiakaral that the Rajiv Gandhi hit team had landed in two groups: in Oct 1990 and Mar 1991. The present catch has set off alarm bells if the LTTE was planning another hit job in India.

TERRORIST TRADING ENDANGERS INDIAN ECONOMY: FEB., 2007

There were dark rumours during 2006 and early 2007 that the share markets were having a bull run partly because terrorist groups were operating on the stock exchanges. These fears and allegations stood confirmed following an assertion in this regard made by none less than the National Security Advisor (NSA), Mr. MK Narayanan.

Speaking at the 43rd Conference on Security Policy in Munich, Germany on 12 Feb 2007, he not only revealed that terrorist groups were raising funds for their operations through fictitious companies, he also disclosed a conspiracy by "official agencies" in Pakistan, a euphemism by the ISI", to carry out "economic subversion."

It is obvious that the operation is being carried out in a deliberate, well-planned and systematic manner. The consequences can be extremely damaging. One, the share market may rise and fall at the beck and call of the enemies of the nation. Then, the money that they make through "legitimate" means may be deployed to wage a low-intensity or/and clandestine war against India.

This is the first time that the NSA has disclosed the use of the stock exchange operations to fund terrorism in India. Earlier, he had shaken the strategic community by revealing the existence of a jihadi plot against Indian nuclear plants.

While it is good that he has taken the public into confidence on these sensitive issues, but what the nation wants to know is what the government is doing/has done to counter the threat. In the absence of the latter, he can be accused of scare-mongering.

It is a known fact that this slush money follows a complex funding route. But surely, there are enough means at the command of the government to defeat these ugly designs which pose a serious security threat to India. People demand a reassurance to this effect from the Prime Minister, or the NSA himself at the very least.

It is not only the local terrorist modules which are engaged in clandestine operations. "Security agencies have detected many instances of funds received via banking channels from the so-called safe locations like Dubai and the UAE that were meant for terrorist groups" (Editorial, *Tribune*, 14 Feb 2007).

Then there is also an equally sinister plan aimed at economic subversion of India, namely, huge amounts of fake currency routed to India through Nepal and Bangladesh. For an effective curb on such practices, India will need to forge better cooperation with these neighbours.

Serious Issues of Government is Culpability

It must be accepted that these dangerous disclosures have created ripples in the security and political circles, with the questions being immediately raised about the Government's failure to secure the Indian financial institutions. Expectedly, the BJP came out with a full-throated attack on Narayanan, asking what the government has done in the past three years. "Was the NSA not privy to such vital national security information?"

3-4 years back, the US had initiated some effective action against terrorist funding operations through banking channels and charitable institutions. But Narayanan's assertion that terrorist groups were involved in restaurants, real estate and shipping, however, appears to indicate a fresh burst of terrorist financing activity even if he has not backed it up with evidence, or with any idea of what action Government of India has taken to cripple this nexus, if it exists in such sinister shape.

The BJP statement pointed out that Narayanan is in the "habit of springing surprises" as he had earlier by stating that Indian atomic energy installations were under threat of terrorist attacks and the LET and Al Qaeda elements had infiltrated the Indian Army. The last was hotly denied by the defence services.

During its three years in power, the UPA has never touched upon terror funding. And now, its NSA comes out with a dramatic disclosures in Munich. His detailed report appears to suggest infiltration of terrorist groups in Indian financial institutions in a big way. But why this hugely damaging disclosure had to wait a security conference in a foreign land?

The only specific consequence of the NSA's information, which has regularly appeared in newspapers and state Department briefings over the past several years, has been a demand from the BJP for more stringent laws, and restoration of the Prevention of Terrorism Act (POTA), which was repealed by the UPA Government in 2004 without a mechanism for controlling the foreign funding. If "official agencies" in Pakistan were using a parallel banking system to send money for militancy in India, as Narayanan claimed, BJP pointed out it was a failure of the intelligence system. As far as the BJP reaction and its faulting the government for its policy failures go, there is nothing exceptionable in it. It has behaved like any opposition party in a democracy would.

But the Government's silence on the issue is inexplicable. It may not explain its side in public, but it can certainly take some opposition leaders in confidence.

US Action on Terrorist Funding

Terrorism financing came up as a big issue some three to four years back. The US had taken action then against funding organizations like Al Rashid. As far back as 2002, it froze over $112 million in 500 accounts world wide as part of its "war on terrorist financing". The international community must learn to respect the US for its through going ways.

Narayanan's referernce to Habib Bank (a Pakistani bank) appears to be linked to an investigative report in the Pakistani newspaper *Daily Times* which found that a Muslim charity based in the UK had remitted a big amount of money as "earth quake relief" to the accounts of three individuals in the Saudi Pak Bank, Standard Chartered and Habil Bank Ltd. The money was transferred from the UK through the Barclays PLC. Two of the recepients were British citizens of Kashmir origin and the third was based in Islamabad and was also of Kashmir origin.

All three of them were arrested and reportedly connected to an "aircraft bombing plan" that was effectively countered. Bank sources admitted that individual accounts were likely to be used for such purposes but that now "a close watch is kept on individual and other accounts to detect any unusual movement of finances."

The question remains: what has India done to check such malicious and dangerous transfers? Should n't New Delhi take a leaf out of the US book? The US had earlier taken action against Pakistan-based charities that had been found to have links to terrorist outfits. The US Treasury designated the Al Akhtar Trust as a Terrorist support organisation linked to Al Qaeda, and said it was reportedly carrying out the activities of the better known Al Rashid Trust, which had been designated by the US earlier. The trust had reportedly deposited funds in Habib Bank Ltd, Habib Bank AG Zurich and the Muslims, Commercial Bank.[2]

The US State Department had designated 236 individuals, entities and organisations under the President's Executive Order as supporters of terrorism. It had also identified and designated 34 entities as foreign terrorist organizations with 166 countries, having issued blocking orders against the assets of terrorists at least five years ago.

The US has taken effective steps in the field of anti-terrorism. India, too, must go beyond those high-sounding and sanctimonious pronouncements mouthed so routinely after every act of terrorism and forgotten soon after. Nation must show some resolve to fight terrorism, which today threatens not only its sovereignty but also some other aspects like disrupting social harmony, threatening economy and sneaking into the country through its sea shores. Restoration of POTA may be the first step.

7 Accused of Terrorist Activities Acquitted: 1 March, 2007

Pulling up the Punjab police for framing seven innocent persons, the local fast track (Amritsar) court of Additional sessions Judge Hardip Singh, on 1 Mar 2007 acquitted all the seven accused in a case registered in 1998.

Delivering the significant order, the Judge observed that the prosecution failed to produce cogent evidences to prove the case against the accused. The court also reprimanded the police officials involved in the case for acting as extra-constitutional authorities.

The respite for the accused has come for the second time as earlier the Punjab State Human Rights Commission (PSHRC) had found the case a "frame up". The PSHRC even recommended the cancellation of the FIR registered against them and a compensation of Rs. 50,000 to the three accused.

The police, however, did not comply with the orders of the PSHRC and went ahead to file a challan against the accused, though a case related to the judicial purview of the Commission into the matter was still pending in the Punjab and Haryana High Court.

ULFA Deserves a Tough handling: May, 2007

ULFA is determined to intensify its terror tactics in Assam. It has claimed 130 lives in the state since Jan 2007 (till 25 May). The chain of low-intensity blasts has created a sense of insecurity and public anger. Analysts feel the outfit took advantage of scaled down security during the UP Assembly polls, which necessitated the shifting of 40 companies of central paramilitary forces to that State. Elections over, these forces should have been returned to Assam, as the state government had wanted it. Taking advantage of the situation, ULFA struck on 25 May. It jolted the Centre to send in additional forces.

Hitting economy of the state seems to be the current strategy of ULFA. That is ironical since its constant refrain was that New Delhi took away Assam's resources and gave little in return—neglecting its economic development and infrastructural requirements. Its renewed vicious targeting of Hindi-speaking people not only hits Assam's economy as they contribute substantially to it but also creates a societal rift.

The popular sentiment favouring peace manifests in various ways: Not too many recruits are willing to join its ranks; there is ground-level disenchantment against its violent and disruptive ways; and dissensions within its ranks leading to large scale surrender by its cadres. Notwithstanding all this, it still has potential for inflicting terror strike at a place and time of its own choosing.

Critics fault the Central Government for refusing to learn from ULFA's past: making use of all peace interregnums to reequip itself and reinforce its capabilities. It made good use of the 6 weeks New Delhi provided it by holding its fire in 2006 as it was holding unsuccessful rounds of talks with the People's Consultative Groups constituted by ULFA for the purpose.

It is time the Centre and Guwahati took a tough stance against ULFA to instill confidence among the common men against its atrocities and terrorist strikes. First thing New Delhi must do is to issue instructions to Assam Minister Gogoi to stop making repeated fervent appeals to ULFA, offering it unconditional talks. They are counter productive. Choking its supply and communications networks and staunching its income from extortions should be Government's priorities. India must step up diplomatic and political pressure on both Bangladesh and Myanmar to act more vigorously and sincerely to end cross-border support Indian terrorist outfits, including ULFA. Dhaka, in particular, must shut ULFA's money-making enterprises in various spheres of its economic life. A democratic transition in Dhaka is likely to help, but it may be as yet far away.

Internally, there is an urgent need to eliminate ULFA's linkages and bases in neighbouring North-Eastern States. The 25 May terrorist attack must persuade New Delhi that the time for final push against Assam's and North-East's strongest secessionist outfits has come. The time for restraint has long past.

Jammu and Kashmir: Terrorists Try not-so-common Routes: May 2007

The militants are never short of ingenuity or innovative skills. This was once again proved by their exploring new and not-so-common routes to infiltrate into India across the LOC in May 2007 since the security forces have plugged the traditional routes of ingress used by them in the recent years.

The militants infiltrating through not-so-common routes in the border districts of Rajouri and Poonch was indicative of their new strategy. The first instance of their changing tack was on 25 May 2007 when a group of militants chose not-so-common' route of Chakla in Sunderbani tehsil of Rajouri to infiltrate across the LOC. The very next day, the 26th, they tried infiltration through the Mankote area of Poonch district—again not among their favourite routes for ingress.

Defence sources disclosed that when the snows melt in April/ May (or so) every year on the mountains, militants mostly used the traditional routes of Uri, Gurez and Kupwara in Kashmir to cross over to Indian side. But since the traditional routes have been plugged, militants are switching over to the alternative, not-so-common routes in Rajouri and Poonch districts. The shift in strategy was dictated by the militants' plans to suffer minimum casualties, if not eliminate them altogether.

A Defence source explained the details:

> "Previously, they used the routes like Mendhar, Balnoi, Bhimber Gali, Balakote and Krishna Ghati in Poonch, and Keeri, some border areas in Sunderbani and Laam Ladoka in Rajouri. But these routes were not frequently used for infiltration. The shift their strategy can also be gauged from the fact that the militants mainly used Kupwara, Uri and Gurez for infiltration in in April—May period, while the roots in Poonch and Rajouri were being used during the winter months."

Defence spokesperson for 9 and 16 Corps Col SD Goswami told a daily that all traditional routes plugged in a big way, militants now were trying "not-so-common routes" for infiltration. "As part of their changed strategy, they are emphasizing on lesser important routes for infiltration. We were expecting this was going to happen after the melting of snows in the mountains. We are taking preventive measures and have been successful in foiling all infiltration attempts through Rajouri and Poonch sectors."[3]

He said till the militant camps in the POK were intact, these types of infiltration attempts would always be tried by the militants.

In 2006, from January to June, the number of infiltration attempts was 74, whereas the number of militants who actually crossed the LOC was 35. How the respective figures for the equivalent period for this year (2007, till May) are 97 and 56.

Deceitful ULFA: A Criminal Outfit for Long

The abduction and killing in June 2007 of the Food Corporation of India (FCI) Regional Director, Phul Chand Ram, was only the last of the periodical outrages committed so blatantly by ULFA. It caused disquiet within and outside Assam.

A considerable public anger came to be focused on the outfit. Since a substantial amount of money had been paid to his abductors, many had hoped the ULFA would have kept the official, for additional lucre, if for no other reasons. But such postulations, obviously, tended to appear to ignore the fundamental character of the militant outfit. The ULFA's transformation into a criminal entity has long been completed.[4]

But it should not come as a surprise that ULFA has eliminated a hostage after abduction. There are a number of such examples in its history but two are specifically mentioned since they pertained to the high-profile individuals and had received considerable contemporary media attention.

1. On 9 July 1991, ULFA cadres killed a Russian coal expert, Sergei Gritchenko, who was working on a project in Assam and held for a long period, because he was alleged to have made an escape bid.
2. AVARD (North-East) General Secretary Sanjay Ghose was abducted on 8 July 1997 from Majuli, the world's largest river island by the ULFA. After a number of conflicting stories, he had been done to death. But the outfit claimed that he died after falling off a cliff in Arunachal Pradesh.

It should also be in order here to cite an equally high-profile case of abduction of B. Bordoloi, president of a major tea estate company. But he was released after months of detention after receiving a ransom that reportedly ran into seven figures. ULFA was believed to have baulked at killing him since it would have been on the receiving end of too much adverse publicity because the hostage was the younger son of Assam's popular first Chief Minister (Lokpriya) Gopinath Bordoloi.

But abduction as a strategy to put pressure on the state and its agencies, or even to extract financial benefits is somewhat on the decline in the North-East. Some details follow:

1. Tripura, known some years back as the abduction center of the North-East, records only a handful of such cases presently.
2. Likewise, there has been decline in number of abduction cases in Assam since 2001. Compared to 82, 97 and 89 abductions in 2001, 2002 and 2003 respectively, figure for 2004 was only 27.

3. In recent years, fringe tribal outfits, rather than the major ones like ULFA, have been responsible for most of the abductions.

There could be more than one reason for this decline. One, media focus on them earns the outfits adverse publicity, disproportionate to any likely gains. Two, a wide-ranging undisrupted extortion network has rendered abduction and subsequent ransom money amounts far less attractive.

Reverting to Ram's abduction, the initial demand of Rs. 21 crore for his release was rather too steep. In a manner of speaking, this staggering sum was a record of sorts for a ransom demand made by any militant outfit in the country. Later, it was reportedly brought down to Rs. 3 crore. The ULFA was believed to have been paid Rs. 12 lakh. Before more money could change hands, Ram was done away with—something totally unexpected.

But ULFA, obviously, had its reasons. There are indication that it wanted to use Ram as a bargaining chip. It linked the release of Ram with that of its jailed leaders in one of the issues of its mouth piece, *Freedom*. Since such a precondition had little chance of ever being entertained by New Delhi, Ram's killing seemed to have become necessary to send an unambiguous message across to the powers that be. But Ram's killing was this time accompanied by certain unprecedented actions/policy changes by the outfits.

It needs to be noted that the periodic strikes by the ULFA have all been similar, rather familiar, attempts at reinventing itself, not only for its own cadres but also for the people who have written it off. But such measures so far have been blended with a policy of denial. While the ULFA has followed a practice of not owning up to civilian deaths, this time around a statement expressing its willingness to start a process dialogue with the government followed the discovery of Ram's body. The ploy was apparently aimed at diverting attention from the killing.

Ram's death—rather murder—raised some questions about the functional aspects of Assam police, and its competence. Not only did the state police have almost two and a half months spanning the dates of his abduction and his possible killing, it also appeared to have failed to take action on the available information that Ram was being held in/confined to Baska district, one of the smallest in Assam, on the Bhutam border. Ram's body was dug out of a pit there. The primacy of the safety of the hostage is believed to have been the reason behind the police's reluctance to adopt harsh measures for his release from his abductors. But analysts aver that it is doubtful if the police at any time came anywhere close to rescuing him.

In fact, there were reports of police officials speaking openly to the media about how they had almost nabbed his abductors. It is unimaginable how operational details could be "willfully disclosed (to the media) in this fashion, stripping such operations of their vital element of surprise". Now enter even more confusing news on the issue that appeared in the media. One story said that Ram was killed in the cross-fire between the police and Ram's ULFA abductors/cadres. If that be so, ULFA gets acquitted of any suspicion/charge of killing Ram. Police officials who disclosed such "news" to the media are obviously unaware of the significance and implications of such 'smart' stories planted in the media. It seems a case of free-for-all situation in the police hierarchy. They could bar any unauthorized person talking to the media. Assam police, obviously, needs the services of an intelligent spokesperson to cover such situations.

Now comes the crunch question: will ruthless killing of Ram by ULFA foment certain feelings of revulsion against the outfit? Empirical experience and widely-shared belief across spectrum of the cognescenti suggest emphatic "unlikely" as an answer. An analyst says, speaking for the vast majority, "Ram's death, in spite of the anger and frustration it has evoked, will not snowball into a movement against the ULFA." As many as "156 civilians have already been killed (this year) in 2007 (till June)" in Assam in terrorist violence and there is a little hope that Ram's (death) case will be remembered for long. Anger against the ULFA has always been short-lived in Assam. And there is reason for this:

> "It is mostly, and essentially, because certain power centers in the state have been able to advocate their cause rather successfully. To them, killings, abduction, extortion by the

outfit—while avoidable—still represent the means to coerce New Delhi into listening."

With such influential intellectual friends and an army of over ground sympathizers, ULFA will not be tamed in a hurry. Much more work needs to be done by the state Government and civil society to bring this 'criminal' outfit to a path of reason. Till then, it is a long haul of occasional gore and blood letting for Assam and its inhabitants, notwithstanding all the valiant efforts of the authorities to mend the situation.

Three Arrested with Fake Currency

A father-son duo, Asghar Ali, 61 and Vakil Ahmad, 21, were arrested at New Delhi Railway Station on 26 May 2007. The Inter-State cell of the crime Branch of Delhi Police had received the information that the duo would arrive at New Delhi by Mumbai—Ferozepur Janata Express on the 26th with a large consignment of fake currency.

The police laid a trap. When the train arrived at 1.20 pm, the duo with a woman, later identified as Meena Begum, alighted from it. The three were arrested and counterfeit currency notes of Rs. 500 denomination worth Rs. 5.10 lakh were seized from their possession.

The accused had allegedly procured the consignment from Mumbai and were on their way to Muzaffarnagar, UP. The police disclosed that Asghar Ali, a vegetable shop owner in Muzaffar Nagar, had been running the fake currency racket for the past four years. In Jan 2006, he sent Vakil Ahmad, one of his nine children to Pakistan to establish direct contact with fake currency racketeers in the country. When Vakil failed to do the job. Asghar himself visited Pakistan twice in the past four months, and met one Iqbal alias 'Kana' (=one-eyed) in Lahore. He was asked to wait for the currency. He returned to India in Apr 2007.

As directed, he came to Delhi on 23 May with Rs. 3.5 lakh in cash as payment against a consignment of fake currency worth Rs. 6 lakh. After handing over the money to a man outside a 'paan' kiosk in the capital, he and his son were asked to reach Mumbai, with a women. Accordingly, the three reached there on 24 May and checked in a hotel near Victoria Terminus (VT). Then he was called near a patrol pump near the VT, through a message on his mobile phone. It was at this spot that he was handed over a bag with the promised fake currency. The next day, the three returned to New Delhi where they were arrested, as narrated above.

The accused are now being jointly interrogated by the IB and Military Intelligence. Both men were also found wanted in an 'attempt to murder' case registered at Muzaffarabad.

Mumbai Women held with Fake Currency: 7 June, 2007

(She had made a delivery last week too)

The Delhi Police's Special Cell on 7 June 2007 arrested a Mumbai women, Tabassum Abdullah, a 26-year-old BSc graduate, for carrying fake currency amounting to Rs. 5 lakh.

Abdullah was arrested from Diamond Hotel, near Daryaganj, while she was waiting for an intermediary to take over the consignment. The police are hunting for the latter.

She had delivered a consignment of similar amount of fake currency in the Capital even on 4 June, police said.

The police told the press: "Abdullah, based in western Mumbai suburb of Jogeshwari, had been working for a Dhaka-based operator for the past several months. She has made several trips to Kolkata, Karachi and Dubai with consignment."

The officer said she delivered fake "amounting to Rs. 10 lakh in Kolkata last week and then came to Delhi last Monday (4 June) with a consignment of Rs. 5 lakh. She had then stayed in a hotel in Karol Bagh."

The police disclosed she acted as a courier, and was paid for delivering the consignments though hawala. "The master mind in Dhaka zeroed in on her possibly since, being a women, she would have escaped suspicion." She reportedly escaped with mild security checks at airport during all her previous transactions.

"The currency notes were concealed in a cavity at the bottom of her bag, which was stuffed with clothes and cosmetics to avoid suspicions", the officer said.

3 ISI Men held with Huge Fake Currency: 25 June, 2007

In one of the biggest hauls ever of fake currency notes, the Special Cell of the Delhi Police claimed to have arrested three ISI agents from Delhi on 25 June 2007 and seized fake currency notes worth Rs. 33 lakhs about 5.30 pm.

These youths belong to Ghaziabad in the neighbouring UP. Mohd Nayeem, one of the accused, had come to deliver the consignment to his two associates, Mohd Muslim and Wasim in the capital. The police had prior information about his trip and its purpose and conducted the raid at the Comesum Restaurant at Nizamuddin railway station. They were nabbed in this raid.

The police disclosed they had the notes inside the bundles of the resham (=silk) treads they were carrying. Several notes of Rs. 500 and Rs. 1000 denomination were found in their possession.

Sources disclosed Nayeem came from Pakistan and arrived in the capital via Rajastan on 25 June, traveling on Inter-City Jodhpur—Delhi Express. "The special sleuths interrogated them for further tip-offs."

Initial interrogation revealed that fake currency was meant to be circulated in several connected circles of Delhi

Meghalaya Hopes Peace as HNLC Chief Surrenders: July 2007

In a major impetus to the peace process in Meghalaya, Hynniewtrep National Liberation Council (HNLC) Chairman Julius K Dorphang on 23 July 2007 surrendered before the Chief Minister DD Lapang. Four of his PSOs—Teilang Wanniang Salonsar Thongni, Bima Suting and Rit Lakashiang—also surrendered along with him.

Dorphang arrived in Shillong on the 23rd night itself from Bangladesh with his four colleagues. He came through Lyngkhat village near the international border and traveled by road to Pynursla, whence he came to Shillong. He was provided heavy security cover by the state police.

According to Lapang, negotiations with Dorphang had been on for the last two years. On 24 July morning when the Chief Minister's Secretariat informed newspaper offices that Lapang would be meeting reporters, no body know that Dorphang would be surrendering.

Dorphang was one of the founding members of the HNLC along with Cherishsterfield Thangkiew and Bobby Marwein. It came into existence in 1988. The underground outfit came into prominence in the early 1990s when it unleashed a reign of terror. The three became leading lights of the HNLC as chairman (Dorphang), General Secretary (Thangkiew) and Commander-in-Chief (Marwein), and were household names in the Khasi and Jaintia Hills District as the HNLC waged a war against the State Government for the cause of Khasi nationalism.

Incidentally, the four colleagues who accompanied Dorphang surrendered without any arms and weapons. The reasons behind this surrender are not known for certain. But police intelligence has its own on the question: The Chairman had been sidelined by the General Secretary and the C-in-C.

The growth of the HNLC was on the line of growth of other such outfits. As its coffers filled with money-garnered through extortion, looting, levies and kidnapping for ransom—the outfit started equipping its cadres with sophisticated weapons, mainly sourced/purchased from the NSCN(I-M). Subsequently, it established training camps inside Bangladesh and as in case of other smaller outfits, its cadre too were trained by NSCN(I-M) and other regional insurgent groups.

Again, on the expected lines, as the HNLC grew it forged ties with various north-eastern insurgent and terrorist group, in particular with the NSCN(I-M), which had helped it grow for so many years.

But the HNLC fire power started declining from 2000 onwards when RG Lyngdoh took over as Home Minister of Meghalaya. He cracked down on businessmen and government officials who gave in to extortion demands. As its funds dried up, the HNLC started losing its stranglehold. At the same time, Lyngdoh also offered the outfit an olive branch—an invitation for talks. The Church also pitched in and started negotiations with the tree leaders.

As mentioned above, the talks had been going on over the past two years. Only the Chairman has relented so far. The other two of the top trio—Thangkiew and Marwein—have given no indications of their intention to emergeover ground.

Whether Dorphang has surrendered to test waters for the HNLC and also on behalf of the remaining two members of the leadership trio, or he has really been sidelined by them, only time will tell. For the time being, it is only 'wait and watch' for the State Government as also for the common citizens.

Is the Fake Currency Flooding the Market? July 2007

Here is a well-meaning advice to the inhabitants of the nation's capital which is not only timely but more importantly, is also indicative of serious threat a large amount of fake currency in circulation in the country is posing to India economy and economic health: "Next time when you are counting your cash check twice, your hard-earned money may turn out to be fake". With more than Rs. One crore fake currency being circulated in and around Delhi, a large number of people are making use of it without knowing that it is fake.

Senior officials, including those from police, who had experience of dealing and have gone through with fake currency, explain the problems faced by unsuspecting and innocent citizens:

> "It is impossible to distinguish the original and counterfeit currency with the naked eye."
>
> "the only difference is the quality of paper of the fake currency is inferior compared to the original one. Besides this the font size of the serial number printed on the fake note is also smaller."

Besides risks the circulation of fake currency involves for the individual citizens, its adverse implications for economic security of India are not to be dismissed lightly. Special Cell, Delhi Police busted the biggest racket of counterfeit currency in the last week of June 2007—recovering a haul of Rs. 33 lakh. More significantly, the persons arrested with this amount disclosed in their interrogation that "they have so far successfully brought in Rs. 2 crore worth of fake currency from Pakistan."

It will be realistic to underscore the fact right away that this recovery and the amount represent but the proverbial tip of the iceberg. The conventional wisdom is that against one detection made by police on tip-offs, 10 to 20 go undetected. And this detection pertains to one particular place only. And of even greater concern is our ignorance on the dimensions of this threat: How many gangs of such racketeers are operating in how many areas and in how many states? It is mind. boggling exercise. One however prays fervently that Indian intelligence has a rough idea of total fake currency flooding the Indian market—courtesy Pakistan and its agencies like the ISI.

After the recovery, fake currency notes were sent to the experts at the Indian Security Press, Nasik, Maharashtra. In the post-recovery period, Reserve Bank of India also contacted the Special Cell sleuth for relevant inquiry and details.

The going rate for one lakh worth of fake currency is Rs. 40,000 worth of its genuine counterpart. "Three persons—Mohd Naeem, Mohd Muslim and Mohd Wasim—had pooled the money to buy the fake currency from Iqbal Kana (=one eyed) and they had planned to distribute it accordinly",[5] an officer disclosed. He further added it was only a small part of the racket that the Special Cell was able to crack.

"Iqbal cheema is the mastermind of this whole racket". His various agents illegally sneaked in fake currency into India through Nepal, Bangladesh, Sri Lanka, Malaysia and Thailand. The three Indians, named above and who were arrested on 25 June, were involved in buying fake currency in bulk. Police still were to arrest persons who are involved in the retail network of this whole racket. A Special Cell officer said: "We have got some clues and we expect to arrest persons who brought the fake currency in the market."

Sources disclosed that the retail network is more active in districts of the western UP like Hapur, Muzaffarnagar, and Saharanpur compared to the National Capital as chances of being caught/arrested are far greater in Delhi.

Investigations have revealed a trend of young women being involved in money trafficking rackets. The reasoning behind the masterminds of this trade wanting to employ women for this task is that the latter do not arouse too many suspicions, and consequently would not be checked too much and too often.

Last time also, the fake money was brought to India by two female sawaris—Rashida and Mehrunisha. The money was concealed in the cavity of bundle of thread. Police sources disclosed that in each bundle, 18 to 20 notes of Rs. 500 and Rs. 1000 denominations were concealed.

Recoverics/Seizures during 2007 alone

Date	*Fake currency (Amount)*	*Details*
23 Feb	2,90,000	One Rajkumar alias Vikki arrested with the amount.
28 Feb	10,00,000	A 75-year-old women arrested at IGI Airport, Delhi.
7 Apr	50,000	One Shamim was arrested with the amount, which was brought into India through Delhi-Lahore Bus service.
25 May	50,50,000	A women arrested with the said amount of counterfeit currency.
7 June	5,00,000	Two arrested, including a women with this fake currency.
25 June	33,00,000	Three persons (Mohd Naeem, Mohd Muslim and Mohd Wasim) arrested.

Jihadis Attack and Kill Tourists in Jammu and Kashmir: July, 2007

Four tourists from Gujarat and two local women were killed in a blast that also 22 others in a tourist but near Shalimar Gardens on the banks of the Dal Lake in Srinagar on 29 July 2007.

Police believed a gas cylinder had burst inside the bus. IGP, Kashmir Range SM Sahai said the cause of the blast was under investigation. But a CRPF spokesman said the blast was triggered by an Improved Explosive Device (IED) fitted under seat No. 3 of the bus".

The tourists were guests of a local family at Navakadal in old Srinagar. They offered afternoon prayers at the Hazratbal Mosque, lunched there and went to see the Mughal Gardens in a bus.

"As they reached Shalimar, a low-intensity blast took place killing five persons and injuring eight others", said the police spokesman.[6]

He identified the dead as Razia, Rabia, Amina Bi and Mossa Shaikh of village Rajpipla Narbada in Gujarat. The local women was identified as Nusrat. One of the 23 injured, Shazia Wazir, a resident of Budshah Chowk in Srinagar, died in the hospital, raising the toll to six.

During 2006, 15 tourists had been killed and over 100 injured in a series of grenade attacks in various places across the valley.

Previous Attacks

Date	*Killed/injured*	*Details*
12 June, 2004	4/28	In a grenade attack on a tourist hotel in Pahalgam
22 May, 2006	2/5	Grenade attack on tourist bus near Soura.
25 May, 2006	5/14	In a grenade attack on a tourist bus carrying Gujaratis at Habakadal near Hazratbal in Srinagar.
31 May, 2006	2/30	In separate grenade attacks on two tourist buses from West Bengal at Dal Gate in Srinagar.
21 June, 2006	—	Five Amarnath pilgrims injured in grenade attack at Ganderbal.
11 July, 2006	9/43	In five grenade attacks at separate locations in Srinagar's Dal Gate, Lal Chowk and Boulevard areas.
23 Nov., 2006	Nil/11	Five tourists besides six locals injured in a grenade attack near Gulmarg.

Foreign Tourists on Hit List in Jammu and Kashmir: Oct., 2006

Vital installations, communications links, places of worships, commercial, industrial and scientific centres. There is an addition to this list of potential targets of Pakistan-based terrorist outfits—tourists. This is a Union Home Ministry official speaking in a daily dated 30 Oct. 2006.

The list of potential targets has been expanded by the Ministry "in view of recent intelligence inputs that the tourism sector, especially in Goa, is on the radar of terror groups."

Over the last five years, foreign tourist arrival is estimated to have grown at 75 per cent, increasing foreign exchange earnings by 122 per cent and creating nearly three million additional jobs annually. The militants' objective is to gradually undermine international confidence and create an atmosphere of pervasive terror that will dampen the country's capacity to attract foreign investment.

It is obvious from the above that the terrorists are no longer led by brawny half-wits any more. They have 'thinking' leadership which wants to destroy India's political and strategic stability? But also its economy.

"The moment you target foreigners, it has an impact on foreign perceptions at an escalated level", said Ajai Sahni, Executive Director, Institute for Conflict Management, New Delhi. But this is not unique: a direct attack on a financial centre, a direct attack on industry like multi-national companies will have comparable consequences, he added.

A Goa police officer said that the intelligence inputs were shared in detail with police chief BS Brar, when he was in Delhi last week, and he was also advised on preventive measures.[7]

Goa is scheduled to play host to the high-profile International Film Festival of India starting 23 Nov 2006. "The inputs are being factored into the arrangements for the film festival which are presently under way."

The Man who Killed Jammu and Kashmir Tourism

Mohd Ali Hussain—better known in Kashmir by his alias Qasim—the Al Badr militant arrested in Mysore for the alleged plot to attack the Karnataka Assembly, is also the man who masterminded a series of grenade attacks on tourists in Kashmir in May and June (2006).

The attacks expectedly created panic in the Valley, which was just waking up to the rush of tourists. But following the blasts, tourists are shying away from visiting the State; in fact, they are yet to return.

Initial investigations by the Jammu and Kashmir police after the arrest of Hussain and his associate Fahad in Mysore, revealed that Hussain had orchestrated most of the attacks on tourists. He was operating in the Harwan area of Srinagar.

"He was involved in 12 killings and there are as many FIRs against him in different police stations in Srinagar and other places in the Valley", IG, Kashmir Zone, SM Sahai told a daily.[8] "Next week will be sending a team to bring him here for interrogation."

20 tourists, mostly from West Bengal, Gujarat and Madhya Pradesh, were killed in the grenade attacks and several were wounded. Sahai said investigations revealed that Qasim used to hire young men to hurl the grenades. He would lure them with money, or threaten them into it.

"We were looking for him. Now that he has been arrested in Mysore, we would bring him here and find out how he traveled. We suspect that he might be involved in many more violent acts", said Sahai.

Mysore Mastermind's Kashmir Link

Mohd Ali Hussain, an Al Badr militant arrested in Mysore, is also the man who masterminded the vicious grenade attacks on tourists in Jammu and Kashmir during tourist season, 2006.

The Man

Hussain, also known as Qasim in the Valley, hails from Manshera in Pakistan.

His Crime

Arrested in Mysore for allegedly plotting to attack the Karnataka Assembly, he also masterminded a series of grenade attacks on tourists in the Valley in May and June (2006). He is involved in 12 killings with as many FIRs against him in various police stations in the State. He outsourced the job of throwing grendes at the unsuspecting tourists to the youth—luring or threatening them into the crime.

How Tourism Suffered

- Tourist inflow immediately declined by 15-20 per cent.
- House boats, hotels and travel agencies received calls for cancellation of bookings.
- The attack on tourists has an impact on foreign perception at an escalated level. It undermines international confidence in India's tourism industry and creates an atmosphere of pervasive terror that will dampen the country's capacity to attract foreign investment.

Govt-NSCN(IK) Ceasefire Extended Indefinitely: 31 July, 2007

The ceasefire between the NSCN(IM) and the Central Government, which was to expire on the 31 July night, has been extended for an indefinite period on the day during discussion that lasted four hour between the two sides.

A joint press statement, issued by Thuigaleng Muivah, General Secretary of the NSCN (IK) and K Padmanabhaiah, representative of the Central Government, said it was decided to extend the ceasefire indefinitely, with effect from 1 Aug 2007, subject to progress in the talks.

On 31 July (2007), the tenth anniversary of the ceasefire, representatives of the two sides engaged in a marathon four-hour discussion in Dimapur. It was for the first time that such a meeting between the two side took place outside New Delhi.

Speaking to the media, Lt Gen (Retd) VS Atem, the representative of the NSCN in the Monitoring Commission, said: "Both sides also agreed to strengthen the monitoring mechanism to ensure that the ground situation remains conducive for the continuation of the ceasefire." With the ceasefire extended for an indefinite period, it was now also become easier to discuss the basic issues, Atem said.

Padmanabhaiah said: "It is a good thing that has happened. Now we do not have to meet every time just to extend the ceasefire."

The NSCN in understood to have told the Government that over 100 of its cadres have lost their lives at the hands of the security forces during the past 10 years. With the ceasefire extension problem over, the stage is now set for talks on hard politics between the two sides.

While central minister Oscar Fernandes led the Government delegation, Chairman Isaac Chishi Swu led the NSCNs.

Some of the poster, displayed/held by some Naga organizations outside the talks venue, read: "Enough of 10 years' negotiations...", "we want peace and solution," "Do not try our patience," etc.

Real Problem: Fratricidal Wars between Two (IM) and (Khaplang) Factions

The real problem here is the enemity between the two factions of the NSCN. This was one of the issues Muivah discussed with Congress President Sonia Gandhi he met at New Delhi on 6 Jan 2007. He was obviously looking for a political solution to the vexed Naga problem.

Sources disclosed that Muivah sought her intervention on repeated attacks on NSCN(I-M) cadres by the rival Khaplang faction in Nagaland. In the past also, NSCN (I-M) accused the state machineries of helping the Khaplang faction in the fratricidal wars that has claimed several lives.

It is known that during his two-month stay in India he met various leaders to see a crackdown on Khaplang faction. Muivah also heads the group of ministers engaged in the talks with the NSCN(I-M) leaders, and sought a meeting with the Prime Minister. "After a week's stay in the capital, he plans to return to Nagaland to join Chairman Swu, who is already camping there." Security for both the leaders was enhanced during their stay in India in view of the serious threat posed by the rival faction.

Muivah's meetings with political leaders assume significance "in view of the Assembly polls due next month (Feb 2007) in Manipur". Four northern (hill) districts of Manipur are dominated by Naga tribes, including Tangkhul Muivah himself belongs to.

It may be apt here to point not one but two ironies of the situation. Muivah is not a Naga from Naga land as of today. He is a Manipuri Naga fighting for hill districts of his State to be merged with Nagaland. Yet again, Khaplang is a Myanmarese Naga fighting for Greater Nagaland in India, like his 'enemy', viz Muivah. Some Unity, this, of Nagas straddling the Indo-Myanmar border!

The sources said the NSCN(I-M) had also expressed "utmost surprise" at attacks on its cadres by the NPP, the organization which dominated the Naga movement in its early stages but had become virtually defunct over the decades. So, it is a case of wheels within wheels in the Naga conundrum.

The only sticking point in the long while in the talks the NSCN (I-M) is having with the Centre has been its demand for integration of Naga-inhabited areas of Manipur, Arunachal Pradesh and Assam with the existing state of Nagaland.

This is the knot the Centre cannot even attempt unentangling. A mere hint from it just to 'consider' the demand will have these three states going up in flames!

BEANT SINGH CASE: DEATH FOR TWO: 31 JULY 2007

The Beant Singh Assassination case finally drew to a close on 31 July 2007 with the Additional District and Sessions Judge (ADJ), Ravi Kumar Sondhi, awarding death sentence to Jagtar Singh Hawara nd Balwant Singh, two of the six declared guilty in the case, amidst pro-Khalistan slogans. Three of the rest were given life imprisonment, while Naseeb Singh, the oldest of the accused at 72, was released after being awarded 10 years in prison.

Chronology of Events

- 31 Aug 1995. Punjab Chief Minister Beant Singh and 17 others assassinated by human bomb Dilawar Singh outside Punjab and Haryana Civil Secretariat.
- Sep 1995. Chandigharh police recovered an abandoned Ambassador car with Delhi registration number, which leads to arrest of Lakhwinder Singh, following a clue given by a painter.

- Sep 1995. Gurmeet Singh, an engineer with BPL, arrested following disclosure of Lakhwinder Singh.
- 19 Feb 1996. Challan to Sessions Court Chandigarh, against 12 persons, including three absconders.
- 19 Feb 1996. 3 NRIs declared proclaimed offenders. They are named here:
    1. Manjinder Singh Grewal (England)
    2. Resham Singh (Germany)
    3. Harjit Singh (USA)
- 30 April 1996. Charges framed in the Court of District and Sessions Judge, Chandigarh against nine persons, named here:
    1. Gurmit Singh (BPL Engineer), Mohali
    2. Nasib Singh (Agriculturist), Jhingara Kalan.
    3. Lakhwinder Singh, Punjab Police Constable.
    4. Navjot Singh (Ranbaxy), Mohali
    5. Jagtar Singh Tara (Taxi driver)
    6. Shamsher Singh (Truck driver)
    7. Jagtar Singh Howara (Babbar Khalsa International)
    8. Balwant Singh, Punjab Police Constable, Patiala.
    9. Paramjit Singh Bheora.
- 31 July 2007. The case comes to a close with the announcement of the sentences.

The mastermind behind the assassination, Hawara, had reported to have arranged finances and explosives for the human bomb Dilawar Singh who blew himself up near the then Chief Minister, Beant Singh, while Balwant Singh, a police man, had smuggled the human bomb into the secretariat building. Hawara also masterminded the escape of four accused from the Burail jail in 2004. He was later re-arrested on 8 June 2005.

Reacting to the death sentence with the permission of the judge, Balwant Singh said: "Judge Saab, I do not have any grudge against you for the sentence you have awarded me. I won't move any court challenging your order." Hawara reportedly also nodded in agreement.

Three others convicted in the case—Gurmeet, Lakhwinder and Shamsher—were awarded life imprisonment for their involvement in the criminal conspiracy, while the sixth accused, Naseeb Singh, was awarded 10 years of imprisonment under the Explosives Act along with a fine of Rs. 10,000. As Naseeb had already undergone more than the sentence awarded to him, he was set free soon after sentencing.

The Judge began by placing the five accused into two categories according to the role played by them in the assassination. "As per the principles laid down by the Hon'able Apex Court in the state of Tamil Nadu versus Nalini the accused can be divided into two categories keeping in mind their role in planning and execution", declared the ADSJ.

The court placed in the first category Jagtar Singh Hamara and Balwant Singh for being part of the nucleus which took the decision to assassinate Beant Singh and mastermind it. The rest of the accused were placed in the second category of those who joined the conspiracy by inducements or instigation.

The court said Hawara and Balwant first decided to kill the Chief Minister and then made use of the remaining accused by playing with their religious sentiments in the backdrop of the prevailing situation in Punjab at the time.

The Aftermath

Some events and observations connected with the case and this conviction are mentioned here.

- Sikh bodies such as the Dal Khalsa, Akal Federation, etc decided to assemble at Akal Takht on 4 August to offer their prayers to those convicted.
- The nib of the pen which was used in writing the judgment of death sentence was not broken in the open court as is the convention since the Judge had to pen down certain other observations.
- Defense counsels challenged MS Bitta, President of All-India Anti—Terrorist Front, to an open debate accusing him of leveling false allegations against them.

- Relatives of the guilty were allowed to meet them before the sentencing as per the direction of the Judge.[9]

Ayodhya 'Master-mind' Killed in Jammu and Kashmir: Aug. 2007

Jammu and Kashmir police claimed a major achievement when it killed a senior JEM commander, incharge of its India operations, who had masterminded the 2005 attack on the Ram Mandir in Ayodhya, in a gunbattle in the heart of Jammu city on 11 Aug. 2007.

The breakthrough came when in a joint operation carried out by the Jammu and Kashmir police and Delhi police, Saifulah Qari was killed and his associate arrested.

Acting on the intelligence reports that three JEM terrorists including Qari were planning to disrupt Independence Day celebrations and putting up in a house in the Janipur area of the city, the joint them cordoned off the house on the 11th morning.

Seeing the police, the outlaws opened fire and in the ensuing fire fight that last for over three hours, Qari, a Pakistani terrorist, was killed and his associate, Zaffar Iqbal of POK's Tradkhan area, was injured. Delhi police Sub-Inspector Devinder Singh was also injured in firing.

IGP Jammu Range SP Vaid said Qari was one of the most active militants in his State and his elimination was a major success, adding, "Qari was incharge operations in India and was monitoring its activities throughout the country."

In the Valley, Qari mostly operated from militancy-hit Mendhar area of Poonch district. "A Rajouri to Jammu in a bus and rented a house in Janipur." Police rounded up the wife of the house owner and three others, including a college girl at Jammu and a Government employee of Medhar in this connection.

Before joining the JEM, Qari was Deputy Operational Commander of Harkat-ul-Mujahideen and deemed as the right-hand man of its FATA (Federally Administered Tribal Area of Pakistan)—based Chief Abu Khalil, who had formed the outfit after breaking away from Harkat-ul-Jihad-e-Islami.

Police recovered on Chinese-made pistol, two grenades, one satellite phone, seven mobile phones, four SIM cards, three matrix sheets and Rs. 30,000 in cash. A voter identity card was also recovered from Qari, which identified him as Mohd Raqeeb of Gursai, Mendhar.[10]

Qari was responsible for recruiting youths and leading them into militancy. The finances to the outfit were routed through him. He had been active in the Jammu division for the past six years.

Al-Qaeda Identifies New Delhi as Target: Aug 2007

With the Al-Qaeda mentioning Kashmir in its latest video, which put US embassies on top of its hit list, separatists in the Valley are desperately struggling to formulate a response to the association of their campaign with a pan-Islamic jihadi outfit. The former are extremely uncomfortable with such an association, so strongly suggested by an Al-Qaeda spokesman Adam Gaddahn aka. Azzam al Amriki, in a video message on 5 Aug 2007.

Gaddahn in the video also identified Indo-US diplomatic mission and New Delhi as legitimate targets for the terror outfit. He also accused India of killing one lakh Kashmiris, suddenly bringing the state on the compass of the outfit's jihadi discourse.

Though none of the major separatist conglomerates has rushed to deny—till 7 Aug—an Al-Qaeda role in the state, they view the development as very serious. In fact, the Al-Qaeda's reference to Kashmir has put the separatists in hot spot, denying contradicting all the tall claims about theirs being totally indigenous struggle.

Ayaz Akbar, the spokesman of the hardline Hurriyat led by Syed Ali Shah Geelani, was rather cautious in his comment on the Al-Qaeda video. He told a daily on 7 August: "We are still going through the statement. They have incidentally mentioned Kashmir. It does not mean they are operating from the state."[11] At the same time, Akbar underlined that his outfit's position on the Al-Qaeda was well-known: "We are against any role for them in Kashmir. Our struggle is purely indigenous."

The moderate Hurriyat faction led by Mirwaiz Umar Forooq also insisted Kashmir struggle was political in nature and rooted in the troubled history of the past six decades. "Kashmir solution is not a part of the pan-Islamic agenda", its spokesman Shahidul Islam said, adding that they had always opposed the presence of the Al-Qaeda in the state. "This has been our official line."

Incidentally, the statements came two months after a locally generated video in Kashmir announced the entry of the Al—Qaeda into the state. However, the video which accused all Kashmiri separatist and militant outfits of selling out on Kashmir and slammed the talks process between India and Pakistan, was soon dismissed as fake.

The United Jihad Council—an amalgam of Kashmiri militant groups—had, at the time, questioned both the existence and need for Al-Qaeda in the state.

Calling it a conspiracy of the "Indian agencies", the Hizbul Mujahideen had said Al-Qaeda video was "aimed at destroying the indigenous character of the separatist movement and label it international terrorism." It had also urged the people to make it clear to the world that Kashmiris can wage their own struggle and do not need the Al-Qaeda.

With Gaddahn making a mention of the state in an Al-Qaeda broadcast, the separatists fear they have a harder time convincing others of the "indigenous" nature of their "azadi movement."

KL-NLF Joins ULFA to Kill Hindi Speakers in Asam: Aug., 2007

A combined group of ULFA and the lesser-known Karbi Longri National Liberation Front (KL-NLF) armed ultras attacked Hindi-speaking Biharis in Assam for the second time in less than 48 hours, gunning down 14 of them in trouble-torn Karbi Anglong Hill District late on 10 Aug 2007 night. Eight of those killed are children, one a baby boy just two months old. The incident occurred at Dolamora Rongteron under Bokajan police station, around 10 pm, with police reaching the spot next-morning only.

The village is some 140 km from the nearest police station in the hill district, but hardly 30 km from Bokakhat police station in Golaghat district.

Karli Anglong SP Anurag Tangkha said the attackers, numbering about 20, first set on fire the house belonging to one

Dilip Sahu and fired upon the inmates, killing six members of the family. The outlaws also set on fire the rice mill belonging to Sahu.

They then attacked three more houses, and killed eight more, taking to the toll to 14.

Tangkha said the ultras used AK-47 and AK-56 rifles and they were a combined group of the two outfits named above, just like the one that had attacked a cluster of houses belonging again to Biharis at village Ampahar under Howraghat police station on 8 August. Eight migrants were killed in that attack.

Assam Hills Districts (Karbi Anglong and North Cachar) DIG LR Bishnoi said the KLNLF and ULRA had come close in recent months with the former providing the larger outfit shelter in the Karbi Anglong forests and help it (the ULFA) regroup its 709 Battalion in Central Assam. "It has always been ULFA's strategy to target Hindi-speaking people to attract attention, especially around the Independence and Republic Days", he said.[12]

Quiet Law College Student turns out to be a 'Terror Girl'

21-year old Nahida Altaf, a law college student in Jammu was arrested on 7 Sep 2007 by special Operation Group (SOG) of Jammu and Kashmir police along with a consignment of eight live grenades and one UBGL from near Akhnoor.

It sent shock wave among the college students and faculty life. Because before her arrest, she was a quiet person, having few friends. For the last two years, Nahida lived a very private college life. "When she walked through the corridors of her law college building, head covered with scarf and eyes down cast, very few around her spared her a second glance or noticed her". In the class, she remained silent most of the time. She never scored enough marks to pass her semester examinations in one go. She was last seen in the college campus on 22 August, the last day of her fourth semester examination. This is the information gathered about her pre-arrest days by a journalist.[13]

It is the story of a small town girl whose parents are government servants, including one in police. A little probing in her college resulted in many more startling revelations. "The transformation started happening in the last three months". It is believed it was around this time that she came in contact with one of the Hizbul Mujahideen (HM) militants Altaf Ahmad, who had been released from the Kot Bhalwal Jail, near Jammu, after eight years of imprisonment. "Since then she did not attend her classes regularly and maintained a low profile in the class room", a professor said.

She was living in Janipur area of the Jammu city and was in contact with some more HM ultras through Altaf Ahmad.

A senior college authority disclosed: "We were shocked that such an incident could happen with one of our students. Later when I checked her academic record and interacted with her class teachers, they convinced me there was nothing exceptional about Nahida as she was an average girl who avoided mixing up too much with the other students in the class. Her academic class is no brilliant either. She failed successively in all her three semester examinations."

It is obvious that she avoided friendships as a calculated move: To keep her secret contacts secret—away from the prying eyes. Attending the college was a façade, as she was engaged in more serious 'business'. Her successive failures and none-too-brilliant academic record are quite understandable in view of her more pressing assignments and mission—as revealed by her arrest and reasons behind it! It is also obvious that the 'association' with terror brigade might not be just three-month old—as stated above. It could be older, much older.

Two days after her arrest, the 'silent girl' had already acquired a new acronym/alias for herself, 'terror girl', in her own backyard.

The said college teacher expressed serious apprehensions: "Another disturbing trend that came to my knowledge is really an eye opener. She was attempting to widen the network of militants with whom she was associated due to her personal reasons by bringing more college students into the loop. Now we are alert and keep a regular check on the activities of our students."

"Behind her silent face, Nahida was full of anger and revenge", said one of her class mates, who had once 'tasted' her anger.

Pages of local newspapers that carried her pictures and news story were still making rounds of almost all the tables in the canteen and an eerie calm prevailed, found, a reporter visiting the college two days after her arrest. Students huddled in small groups could be seen discussing her in hushed voices: "Did you ever see her earlier? She was so quiet and never looked like she could be moving around in the company of hardened militants and anti-national elements."

Sums up this reporter: "What all I could gather from listening to various friends in the college canteen is that she was headstrong and a tough nut to crack and even attempted to rope in a few others to make her task easier."

In order to crack the network of militants in the region, the interrogators at the Joint Interrogation Centre in Jammu worked hard to piece together the bigger game plan of terrorist outfits who have started targeting college students, especially girls from remote areas.

According to Nahida's claims, HM militants had already built a strong network of sympathizers to strike big in the city and have amassed arms and ammunition for the purpose.

IGP Jammu Range SP Vaid, while addressing a press conference in early Sep 2007, had also admitted that they were shocked over the use of girls and women by militant cadres to transport arms and ammunition and setting up the secret hideouts.

By now nothing should surprise the police and intelligence: The terrorists aided by the mullahs and maulvis can convert any one to join their ranks and do their biddings—from illiterate unemployed, drug addicts, students from schools and colleges including girls to technical graduates and highly qualified IT professionals.

Entrepreneurs find the Going tough in Jharkhand

Chief Minister Madhu Koda may be getting ready to celebrate one year in office on 18 Sep 2007, but the businessmen in his state has little to cheer about, says a daily on 12 Sep.

Rattled by frequent attacks on businessmen and industrial units in the recent past, entrepreneurs under the banner of

Federation of Jharkhand Chamber of Commerce and Industry (FJCI) have now been forced to resort to dharnas and bandhs to voice their protests. As these such measures seem to be achieving little by way of a positive response from the Government, FJCI members have also taken to "boycotting ministers". They have neither been attending any Government function, nor have they been inviting any minister of the Koda Government to events organized by them. Rues FSJI president Arun Budhia: "What else can we do? For us there is no way out but to take to Gandhigiri",

Just one example should suffice to explain that the businessmen have a right to be frustrated and even angry. Kolkata-based entrepreneur Vijat Bothra's Kohinoor Steel Company (KSC) signed a MoU to set up a quarter million tonne capacity integrated steel plant with a 17 mw capacity power unit at a cost of Rs. 505 crore in the state.

Bothra invested more than Rs. 200 crore, purchasing and setting up the unit with machinery imported from China. He kicked off the production process, by purchasing coal and iron ire, on 5 April, 2006. It was a short-lived joy. On 4 July, 2007, 150 armed men led by Jharkhand Mukti Morcha's (JMM) Sukhram Hembrom entered his factory and ran amok—damaging the machinery and breaking furniture.

Presently, his plant's premises are under lock and key. He is victim of state's politics. The ruling coalition perceives Bothra as a "friend" of former Chief Minister Arjun Munda, and so he was targeted by the former.

But his is not an isolated case. Many more can be cited. Some are mentioned briefly here.

Victims of Crime: 2007

- 31 August: Cloth merchant Manohar Agrawal shot dead in Gumla.
- 1 Sep: Petrol pump owner Sudhanshu Sarawagi assaulted by a band of JMM cadres.
- 2 Sep: Milk vendor Rohit Yadav lynched by alleged JMM cadres in Jamshedpur.

- 10 Sep: Businessman Kishore Kumar Poddar's son kidnapped for ransom. His body was later found near Potni Hill.

First Maharashtrian Muslim Killed in Kashmir: Kolhapur Shamed

"He was dedicated to God by a childless couple in Kolhapur after his birth. But 18 years later, Attar's parents had to see their God's gift turn into one of the country's biggest traitor and gunned down like a dog in Kashmir."

This is the way a daily dated 8 June 2006 put it, depicting the anguish and pain of a Muslim couple. This is an inglorious end of an 18-year-long life. And it brought shame to the community he belonged to and to the state he came from!

Irfan Attar, a student of a Madrassa in Gujarat's Bharanch district, was shot dead in Kashmir in the first weak of June. His body was charred beyond recognition in a fire-fight with the troops. Irfan earned the infamy of being the first Maharashtra—Muslim to be killed as a traitor/terrorist. Kolhapur stood shamed!

Officers from the ATS (Anti-Terrorist Squad) from Mumbai reached Kolhapur to find if there are others like him studying in Gujarat's Islamic seminaries (= *Madrassas)*, or having returned from there. They are already believed to be keeping tabs on four more youths studying in Gujarat.

Anguish and disbelief grips the mind of the Muslim community in Kolhapur—the little sugarcane town tucked away in the Sahyadris. It is uneary, and unwilling to believe that Attar let down his community and his country. And the Muslims are feeling concerned and their religious leaders have refused land for Attar's burial. "We will not allow his burial here as he has brought bad name to the city", said Kadar Molhari, Chairman of the Muslim Boarding, the local Muslim body which manages community's religious affairs. Other Muslim organizations such as the Muslim *Satyashodhak* Mandal and Mohammedan Education Society also supported the move. The growing hostility "may prevent the police from bringing the body of the slain terrorist home."[14]

"In view of the prevailing tension, we cannot bring Irfan's body. It is still with the Jammu and Kashmir police", said the Superintendent of Police, Kolhapur district, Sukhwinder Singh.

In Tarabai, an upper middle class locality, government engineer Mohiuddin Gajbhar Saheb Attar and his wife Shabira are finding it difficult to live with the stigma. The Kolhapur police, which grilled Attar's family, suspect that it held back information on their son's terrorist links.

The preliminary investigations revealed that Irfan studied at madrassa for less than six months. Madrassa Principal Maulana Surati told Irfan's parents that their son had been absent from the school for a long time and had, therefore, been barred from classed. Parents used to send Rs. 10,000 every year to Irfan.

But how did Irfan become a *jihadi*? The question continues to baffle the town, which believed he was studying in a Bharauch madrassa. In any case, they learnt about his links with the terrorism when it was already too late. Because they, like the rest of Maharashtra, including its police, learnt about his terror links after a spokesman of the Hizb-ul-Mujahideen declared that "one of their 'martyrs' in the recent spate of violence that rocked the Valley was a Muslim from Kolhapur (Maharashtra)." In was only then that the Jammu and Kashmir police contacted Kolhapur police.

Kolhapur SP told the police that his men sent to the *madrassa* in question could not trace Irfan there. Raids at Attar's home yielded some Urdu books and maps of India and Pakistan "with some markings." Sources in police say it is likely "that the teenager Irafan was indoctrinated by extremists in Gujarat."

Since the Attars went childless for years after their marriage, they, on the advice of the clergy, dedicated their first born, Irfan, to the Almighty. They have two other children.

Irfan received his preliminary education in the madrassas of Kolhapur's Kagal and Uchagaon towns. The Attars told the police that Irfan visited them on Eid every year and his last trip home was in Nov 2006.

The police is yet to identify the terrorism chain in western Maharashtra.

SIMI 'Friend' Bags Top Seminary Post: June, 2006

In a significant, if intriguing, development after the UP government refused to accept the centres proposed extension of the ban on the Students Islamic Movement of India (SIMI), the Sunni Central Waqf Board has appointed a Sunni sympathizer, Mohd Ismail Syed Shareef, a leather industrialist, as caretaker—manager of Kanpur's biggest and oldest seminary, Jaam-e-Uloom (*Hindustan Times*, 11 June 2006).

Earlier, helped by Mulayam Singh's Samajwadi Party (SP) leaders, former (UP) state SIMI chief Mohd Amir had surrendered in a clandestine manner in an attempt to invite milder charges than those relating to treason.

Shareef is learnt to have helped the SIMI considerably in 1999, at a times when the organisation began to be noticed for its subversive activities. Shareef's "generosity" toward the SIMI had him placed on the intelligence watch list among 100 "sleeping agents." The agencies "are now trying to ascertain the reason for Shareef's appointment. An intelligence officer is rightly surprised, perhaps intrigued: "He has never been involved with the seminary or its activities. His emergence out of the blue is baffling."

But Shareef denies any links with the SIMI: "My only association is with the Jamaat-e-Islami. My father was the Ameer (=Chief) of Jamaat, and I am inclined towards it". The constitution of Jaam-e-Uloom, however, clearly bars anyone associated with political outfits like the Jamaat-e-Islami from taking up any of seminary posts.

UP's refusal to accept the Centre's advice to ban the SIMI and now appointment of a SIMI sympathizer to a seminary's top post are not the happenings that can be easily accepted, or explained. Politics obviously seems to be playing a part in these events. Worst still, it is the politics of the vote-bank that seems to be affecting the decisions directly impinging on the nation's security and its fight against the curse of terrorism.

It is such happenings that make the serious analysts cry foul and creates doubts in their minds about some individuals in ability to rise above their vested interests—political or personal—while dealing with the issues of national interests. Authorities at the Jaam-e-Uloom can't be taken to be innocent of implications of such decisions taken by them.

The stories made of such stuff are the archetype that convinces people that India will have to go a long distance before it can be deemed serious about fighting terrorism on its territory. As of today, it remains a soft state!

The Students Islamic Movement for India (SIMI) was founded in Aligarh in 1977 by Mohd Ahmadullah Siddiqui, professor of journalism and public relations at Western Illinois University, Macomb, Illinois. An offshoot of Jammat-e-Islami Hind, SIMI's members are young extremist students, whose aim is to declare Jihad against India and establish an Islamic state. While its original bases are in UP, it has spread its tentacles in Delhi, Bihar, Madhya Pradesh, West Bengal, Kerala, Gujarat and Maharashtra over the years. In Maharashtra, it has strong presence in Aurangabad, Malegaon, Jalgaon and Thane.

'Vote bank' Politics of certain political formations has helped SIMI to survive the 2001 ban and to continue its anti-national activities. Here is an apt example of political opportunism on display. In the wake of July 2006 terrorist attacks on commuter trains in Mumbai, SIMI along with the LET was found to have been the main provider of logistical support for seven train bombings. The very next day, we have UP Chief Minister Mulayam Singh publicly declaring that "the SIMI is not a terrorist organization", simply because his government has found no proof about its anti-national activity.

Intelligence sources claim that SIMI has managed to stay alive because of its political connections, particularly in the Samajwadi Party[15] (SP) headed by Mulayam Singh. SP Rajya Sabha MP Abu Azmi has been accused of being a SIMI sympathizer. Some sources even claim "the UP government recently sought legal opinion on whether (criminal) cases against SIMI activists in the State can be withdrawn."

The alleged role of SIMI 'ansars' (full time cadres) has come to light in several attacks, including the 7 March 2006 Varanasi blasts, which killed 15. The group was also said to be behind the explosion in the Shramjeevi Express near Jaunpur, UP, on 28 July 2005, which claimed 10 lives. The Oct 2005 blasts in Delhi are also believed to be the handiwork of the SIMI.

It is a strong outfit, with estimated 700 ansars and 40,000 ordinary members.

The outfit had been banned and declared unlawful under the

Prevention of Terrorism Act in 2001. The ban was reinforced by the Union Home Ministry on 8 Feb 2006. And just 5 days before the Mumbai blasts, the Supreme Court had rejected the plea to lift the ban.

The investigation had nearly established that the Mumbai blasts were planned and executed by the LET with local support and logistical wherewithals provided by the SIMI cadres. This role was confirmed when on 16 Sep 2006 the Meharashtra police top brass briefed the media on their cracking the 11 July train bombings case. What is really worrying the police and intelligence agencies is the fact of the SIMI providing logistic and local support to the foreign terrorist groups. For the Varanasi blast, it had teamed up with the Harkat-ul-Jihad-al-Islami, Bangladesh, for the Delhi blasts, it chose to help the Jaish-e-Mohammad; and for the Mumbai blasts, it helped the LET. Most believe SIMI is giving a local face to the unknown terrorist. On the flip side, critics say they are handy names when the intelligence agencies have nothing to show for their exertions. Leaving such critics aside for a moment, it must be self-obvious that an operation of the scale of Mumbai's could not have been mounted sans local help.

Like so many other outfits have done/are doing in Pakistan/PoK, the SIMI after it was banned in 2001 had taken a new form and assumed a new name to hoodwink the authorities. Intelligence believes it is functioning presently as Tehbaz-e-Fasche Islam (TEFI), having joined hands with outfits like LET and the ISI.

Originally set up as students' organisation nearly three decades back, SIMI soon got embroiled in allegation of involvement in the riots across Maharasthra. In specific terms, the group engaged in street fighting with the RSS cadres and policemen during the 1992 Mumbai Riots and later in Malegaon and Beed. Such militant activities led to its ban in 2001. "Today, SIMI is a nagging threat to the security of the country. The state government maintains a list of former SIMI members who are being monitored constantly, a police officer told a weekly.[16] Apparently, SIMI has been growing in strength working in tandem with various pseudo-religious and terror outfits, rendering its detection difficult.

A police officer who investigated the 2002 Ghatkopar bomb blast talks about a former secretary of SIMI, Saquib Nachan, arrested in connection with various blasts, who studied the charge sheets and cleverly pointed out the legal infirmities in them. Such loopholes are then exploited by the defence to damage the police credibility. "Despite the ban, they have kept the organization active and continue to espouse the cause of *jihad* in one way or the other", he said.

The deeper concern is that SIMI has solid foreign funding and maintains local bases in various parts of country through a network of sleeper cell/modules.

"What became of the SIMI I Knew?"

This is the heading of a piece penned by a serving police officer[17] for an Indian[18] daily in Oct 2006. The second head-line is more revelatory : "The organization of old, dominated by intellectuals, had metamorphosed into a Mr. Hyde-like variation." Most of the story is told in author's words, all be it paraphrased, for its integrity and intrinsic value.

"In the early 1980s, as a young student in Uttar Pradesh, I had heard about SIMI. But is was only when I joined Aligarh Muslim University (AMU), Aligarh that I came across some of its members: solemn, bearded boys who would tell you to *salaam* a senior when he passed by. Clad mostly in Aligarh-style ankle-high pyjamas and crushed sherwanis, some of them had rosaries in their hands. My class follow and a good friend, a Maulana from Bihar, was a staunch SIMI worker. Skipping classes on Saturday afternoons, he would work in the rural areas, making a 'Muslim a Muslim', as he put it. Once as I was at the house of a Muslim friend, his mother suddenly switched off all the lights. She had obviously spotted a group of such propagators approaching her home. That was the response of many educated Muslims to this groups.

"Many SIMI volunteers were ready to freely discuss issues related to Islam one of the best discussions I had on the topic was with my Maulana friend. I told him he would drag the Muslim Community back by being too driven by religion, an agenda contrary to the dreams of Sir Syed, founder the AMU. But the Maulana had the last word: 'I will change your heart. A drop of water dripping at the same point makes a mark.

"I later joined the IPS and almost forgot about SIMI. One day, during discussions on internal security before Kumbh Mela, some intelligence officers talked at length about SIMI's new dimensions. I instinctively wanted to question their theories, almost certain that my Maulana friend of the yore would be the last one to espouse violence. But soon, credible evidence started surfacing, linking SIMI to ISI-sponsored terrorist violence and to groups like Hizbul. It slowly dawned upon me that SIMI of yore, dominated by intellectual, had metamorphosed into a new, Mr. Hyde-like SIMI, which fed on the (insecurities and) alienations of Muslims in the early 1990s. The group seemed to have fallen a prey to the designs of the perpetrators of terror from across the border. The ultimate target of the terrorist masterminds sitting across the border is to make the minority community in India feel the way its counterpart do back home.

"The maturity shown by the citizens of our own citizens in the face of grave acts of terror is a slap on the face of these evil forces. They have failed *so far* in their designs. I also miss the voices of many broad-minded, forward-looking Muslims I knew. They would do well to counter the designs of those from within the community who work to unravel the secular ties that bind this country. I, in fact, would have wished that my Maulana friend of yore had come out and decried recent acts of jihadi terror."

One must welcome such transparently honest pieces/articles from police officers, particularly the ones still in uniform. The words 'so far' in line three of the last paragraph of his piece must be noted. Being in service, he could not have expressed himself more explicitely or more directly. It is for senior police officers or the ruling politicians to understand the implications of these two words and the dire consequences. They all must act in time and with due resolve to see that the communal situation and the so called secularism that hold the nation together are not stretched or tried beyond a point. Some hold the view that it is not secularism that has held the communal peace in India but in pure and simple terms, it is the tolerance or cowardice—you may take your pick—of the Hindu Majority that accounts for continued peace in the country, repeated and increasingly vicious terrorist attacks on them and their institutions notwithstanding. Finally, a word on his wishing that his "Maulana friend of yore had come out and decried recent acts of jihadi terror." His wish fulfillment apart, it is more likely that his Maulana friend is today a leading jihadi himself, changing the heart of people, with constant hammering of the innocent victims and "making a mark", as he had told his friend during his AMU days, in the manner of "a drop of water dripping at the same point."

A word on this police officer missing "the voices of the many broad-minded, forward-looking Muslims I knew." There are undoubtedly such Muslims in the community. But very few among them—like Shabana Azmi and Javed Akhtar, Farooq Sheikh, and Maulana Wahiduddin—come forward to voice liberal and moderate views on the issues concerning the world of Islam. Islam no doubt is a religion of peace and tolerance but this is not the image one gets seeing a plethora of terrorist attacks by its followers all over the globe. It is an accepted proposition that vast—rather preponderously huge—majority of Muslims are peace loving. It is possibly less than one per cent, including the mullahs, of the Muslims who propagate extremist and fundamentalist ideology and perpetrate untold terrorist violence on the innocent human beings. If Islamist terrorists are to be reformed and brought within the peaceful fold of Islam, it can only be done by their moderate brethren. As for the non-Muslim victims of the terrorism are concerned, they can only adopt counter-terrorism as best as they can, they can not persuade the terrorist to become peaceable. This task can only be performed from within. Presently, it is this miniscule minority within that is dictating terms to the community and bringing all the opprobrium to it.

A Larger Bench to Hear SIMI plea Against Ban: March, 2007

The petition filed by Students Islamic Movement of India (SIMI), challenging the ban imposed on it by the Central Government, will be heard by a larger Bench of the Supreme Court, a Bench comprising Justices SB Sinha and Markandeya Katju ruled on 7 Mar 2007.

Announcing the decision, the judges said that the matter needs to be referred to a larger bench, which shall decide whether or not the organisation's plea holds any merit. Representing the SIMI, advocate Kamini Jaiswal contended that the ban imposed is devoid of any merit, as it is unconstitutional and illegal.

SIMI was banned for its anti-national activities by the Centre on 27 Sep 2001, and again on 27 Sep 2003. In the last hearing the Court had observed that it was still continuing with the anti-national activities. "You continue to be a secessionist movement and have not stopped your activities till now," the Bench had remarked.

Al-Badr (ABDR)

Named after the 624 AD battle in which Prophet Muhammad registered a historic victory over the superior forces of the Meccan tribe of Quraish, the Al-Badr traces its origins to a quasi-fascist militia group set up by Pakistan's armed forces in 1970.

Made up of cadre of the Jamat-e-Islami and its student wing, the Islami-Jamiat-e-Tulba, the terror groups was responsible for large-scale massacres of nationalists, communists and members of the religious minorities during the Bangladesh War of Liberation.

An analysts whote on 28 Oct 2006[18] : "For most people in India, the Al-Badr was till yesterday an unknown name. But for the counter-terrorism services, it has, for over a year, been an emerging nightmare."

Reinvented Role

After 1979, the ABDR re-invented itself as a part of the jihad funded by the US against the Soviet forces in Afghanistan. Then, from 1998, its infrastructure was used to train ethnic Kashmiri (Muslim) youth. By mid-1990s, it was operating as part of the Hizb-ul-Mujahideen (HM), then a 7-group coalition. Under its early commanders, who included Afghan jihad veterans Masood Sarfaraz, Syed Saleem Gardezi, Abdul Hamid Fayyaz and Saifullah Khalid, the ABRD built up a significant operational presence in the Jammu region, notably Rajouri and Poonch. But it parted with the HM after the non-combatant Badership of the Jamaat-e-Islami in Pakistan attempted to impose its authority over ABDR commanders. In 1997, the cadre of the two groups engaged in a bloody firefight near Muzaffarabad, which claimed five lives.

After these clashes, the ABDR allied with the Tehreek-I-Islami, a breakaway Jamaat-e-Islami faction, and the Afghan warlord, Gulbuddin Hekmatyar.

In 1999, the Reuters news agency reported that ABDR commander Mohd Nasiruddin held a meeting with Al-Qaeda chief Osama bin Laden near Jalalabad to discuss joint operational strategies. Many Arab cadres expanding its base.

Pakistani analyst Mohd Amir Rana says "the ABDR includes a number of Arab cadre. It has lost 18 Arab mujahideen, coming from Sudan, Saudi Arabia, Yemen, Algeria and Egypt, in occupied Kashmir."[20]

Under the leadership of its present Chief, Bakht Zamin Khan, the ABDR has sought to expand its over ground infrastructure as well. It has built a large seminary and welfare complex on the Rawalpindi-Islamabad road, and played an active role in emergency relief work after the great Kashmir earthquake of 2005.

The Al Badr is known to have been seeking all-India capabilities for some time. In Dec 2005, the Jammu and Kashmir police eliminated its central-Kashmir commander, Mohd Wasim. Possibly the longest-serving Pakistani national among jihadi groups in the State, Wasim was in the process of setting up terror cells outside the State. Using document identifying him as Fayyaz ahmad Rather, a Srinagar resident with interests in wholesale trade, Wasim had been attempting to set up safe houses and front businesses for the organization in New Delhi. "Wasim, *The Hindu* exclusively reported late last year (2005), hoped to use these assets to route funds from Pakistan and shelter operatives sent in for specific missions."

Soon after this exclusive in *The Hindu*, the Delhi police in Feb 2006 arrested (alleged) Al—Badr operatives Irshad Ali and Mohd Qamar. The police claimed that these two operatives, Delhi residents of Kashmiri origin, had been paid Rs. 90,000 to carry out a series of bombings in the capital. Even explosives were recovered from their home in north-west Delhi, that seemed to prove the police suspicions.

Hawala Funding and Pak-Based Outfits' Cooperation

As by so many other terror groups, *Hawala* routes have long been used by the Al-Badr to funnel funds to its units in Jammu and Kashmir. In 2000, for example, authorities in Srinagar held the well-known city businessman, Wasim Khatib, on the charge of funneling *hawala* funds to Al-Badr units in the State. Much of this outfit's funds is believed to be raised form the ethnic—

Mirpuri diaspora in the UK, as well as members of the community who have large businesses in Karachi.

The Al-Badr closely cooperates with other Pakistan-based jihadi groups operating against India. In Mar 2006, Bakht Zamin Khan joined HM Supreme Commander Mohd Yusuf Shah's protests against Pakistan's decision to cut off direct funding to terrorist groups. According to a report in Pakistan's Herald magazine, the Al-Badr till recently received monthly *subsidies* of Rs. 3,00,000 from the ISI Directorate.

Are Madrassas Spreading Islamist Extremism?

Madrassas—more accurately 'madris' (plural for *madrassa*, or an Islamic seminary)—have for long been accused of spreading extremist ideology among the Muslims. At least, some people are convinced of it. On the other hand, most people feel it is a small number among them who can be doing that—certainly not not all of them. What follows concerns some *madaris* of Gujarat.

Dar-ul-Uloom Islamia Arabiyya in Bharuch is situated along a busy highway and has some sprawling factories around its premises. The impressive madrassa complex has been built to fitter out the sights and sounds of the world around it. "From the outside, this madrassa resembles nothing so much as a fortress. Its elaborate battlements and massive iron gate seem wilfully designed to illustrate the entrenched myth that Islamic seminaries are nurseries of hatred, not centers of learning."[21]

In mid-Sep. 2006, police in Ahmedabad arrested four men from two of Gujarat's most famous *madaris* for their links to the LET. They were:

1. Khalid Sardana, the brother of a top Rajouri—based recruiter
2. Illyas Memon
3. Siraj Ansari
4. Qari Mufidul

The two *madaris* in question were: Dar-ul-Uloom Islamia and its sister madrassa, the Dar-ul-Uloom Falah-e-Darain at Tarkeshwar. All that was recovered from them was nothing more than inflammatory Islamist literature and videos, but the police claim they have hard evidence that the men were linked to

Lashkar cells responsible for a string of terror strikes in western India.

Ever since these arrests, Gujarat's *madaris* came under serious criticism by both politicians and the press. Much of the criticism flows from the fact that all four were linked to the said two *madaris*.

A nuanced examination is called for to see just how the Lashkar cell came into being, and precisely what role was played by the *madaris* in that denouement.

It all Started from Kashmir

In Sep 2006, troops raided the small mountain hamlet of Hanslot, near Thana Mandi in Rajouri district of Jammu and Kashmir. Moh Aslam Mohd Latif Sardana they were looking for was not at home. If the troops had reasons to hunt him, the villagers were not surprised either. After all, Sardana, using the code name 'Aslam Kashmiri', is believed to have recruited at least 20 men from the neighbouring states of Gujarat and Maharashtra to the LET—including several members of the cell that executed the July 2006 serial bombings in Mumbai.

His family sent Sardana to Dar-ul-Uloom Falah-e-Darain at Tarkeshwar in 1993, hoping the rigours of a madrassa education would help still his teenage rebelliousness and, consequently, ensuring that he stayed clear of the terrorist groups which were by then beginning to make their presence felt in the mountains south of the Pir Panjal range. Over the next nine years, he acquired the titles Hafiz (= individuals who know the Quran by memory) and Qari (= individuals skilled in the rules that govern the recitation of Quran"). Thence in 2002, he left for a 2-year stint at a madrassa in Lucknow, and then returned to Tarkeshwar.

During his first stint at "Tarkeshwar, Sardana met Mohd Amir Shakeel Ahmed Sheikh, one of the 11 Lashkar operatives arrested at Aurangabad and Beed in Maharashtra in May 2006 for their role in handling a massive consignment of explosives and arms that was intended for major strikes in Gujarat and Maharashtra. Sheikh fell ill after just six months at Tarkeshwar and returned to Aurangabad. However, the two met again in 2001 at the Khatm-e-Bukhari Sharif, a convocation held to felicitate students who have mastered the nine volumes of Hadith—compilations of the words and deeds of Prophet Muhammad authored by Imam Mohd al-Bukhari.

Soon after the convocation, Sardana and Amir traveled to Aurangabad to meet with members of the proscribed SIMI, who had regrouped under the flag of the local Jamaat Ahle-e-Hadis, a far-right religious order. Zabiuddin Ansari, the operational head of the LET cell that carried out the Mumbai train bombings, was one of the men Sardana persuaded to join the LET. The other was Zulfikar Fayyaz Ahmad 'Kagzi', the author of the abortive 19 Feb 2006 bombing of a Mumbai Ahmedabad train and one of Ansari's principal lieutenants.

Sardana left Aurangabad for Poonch with three Beed residents Sheikh and Ahmad had selected for training with a LET unit active in the Hil Kaka area of Jammu and Kashmir. One of them, Fahd Sheikh, is thought to have been killed in the course of a fighting with Indian troops; the two others Nisar Ansari and Asad Ansari, were never heard of again. Not surprisingly, Sheikh and Ahmad became increasingly suspicious that Sardana might be an Indian covert agent, who was leading members of the Aurangabad SIMI cell into jail, or even death. To reassure the group, Bilal Ansari, a calligraphist turned-terrorist who was arrested for his role in the Aurangabad LET cell, was despatched along with Sheikh to meet with top LET commanders in Poonch. A similar meeting was arranged with the LET commander responsible for all cells active out of Jammu and Kashmir, a Pakistani national so far identified only by the code name 'Junaid'.

By late 2004, the Aurangabad-Beed cell was operating independently of Sardana. Of the precise workings, though, relatively little is known. Rahil Abdul Rehman Sheikh, a Mumbai resident who is thought to have had over-all operational command of the multiple cells that executed the July 2006 bombings, fled for Dhaka after a botched raid on his home by the Delhi Police.

Fayyaz 'Kagzi', for his part, flew to Teheran on an Iran Air flight on the morning of 9 May (2006)—hours before the IB and Maharashtra police personnel began making arrests in

Aurangabad, and is then believed to have then traveled by road through the Zahedan border into Pakistan. Zabiuddin Ansari dodged a high-speed car chase by the Maharashtra police, and is believed to have found sanctuary in a LET safe house in Bangladesh. Even as this drama was unfolding, Sardana had begun work on his next project: building the new LET cell in Gujarat using his contacts at the Dar-ul-Uloom Islamia.

Training Ideologues at Madrassa

When the madrassa, Dar-ul-Uloom Islamia, opened after Ramzan, vacation in Oct 2006, some 1600 students 95 per cent of whose families can not afford to pay their fees—resumed their studies. After obtaining the degrees offered by the institution—those of Alim and Qari, which take an average of nine years to complete—most will go on to be small-town clerics, on salaries ranging from Rs. 1500 to Rs. 2000 a month. Although the Dar-ul-Uloom offers classes in English, "will open a computer course in Nov 2006.)" Most faculty sees these is distractions from its core project rather than as an integral part of a well-rounded theological education.

An important question: is madrassa training terrorists? "It is ridiculous to blame the whole institution for the crimes of a few pople", says madrassa spokesperson Maulana Wali Surati. He points out each of the 122 students from Jammu and Kashmir was admitted only after they produced a certificate from the local authorities declaring them to be uninvolved in terrorism. These certificates were then cross-checked with the State government.

Although madrassa is contemplating ending admissions from Jammu and Kashmir, Surati points out the flaws in the idea. "Jammu and Kashmir is a part of our country," he argues, "so it would be tragic if children from the State is denied an education just because of suspicion." Then he adds: "I know young people are not what they used to be and we have even been compelled to post a watch man outside the local cinema theatre to stop our students from sneaking in there. But I cannot spy on my students round the clock."

The protagonists claim there is no evidence to show that the majority of Islamist terrorists studied at *madaris*, or that their curriculum breeds hate. Many of the ethnic Kashmiri students there, Sardana's own story shows, were sent because their parents feared they would be recruited by the Islamists. If the parents were intent that their wards join the terror brigade, they could simply let them to stay at home.

Up the road, at Dar-ul-Banat madrassa for girls, most of the pupils came because their parents were wary of sexual harassment in the wake of terrorist violence brings in its wake. Thousands of middle class and elite families from that state send their children to institutions across India, but Gujarats' *madaris* attract only those who can afford nothing better.

It may not be right to see Gujarat's *madaris* solely as bastions of an inward-looking orthodoxy. The case of Ahmed Deedad, a Gujarat born South African evangelist who built an enormous reputation for his aggressive proselytisation campaign, is instructive. The winner of the 1986 King Faisal Award for services to Islam, Deedad's followers, often immigrants from the sub-continent, helped finance campaigns across Gujarat focusing on spreading neo-conservative practices among liminal sects whose religious practices included elements of Hindu tradition, like the Sunni Vohras. Tablighi Jamaat preachers inspired by Deedad focussed on spreading what they saw as piety and correct practice—not terrorism.

But Deedad's work also contained the seeds of violence praxis. A 2004 investigation by the *New York Times* found that his Durban-based Islamic Propagation Center International had received large financial contribution from Al Qaeda leader Osama bin Laden, a figure for whom the cleric made no secret of his admiration. In 2001, South Africa's well-respected *Sunday Times* reported that Deedad's son and successor, Yusuf Deedad, has distributed anti-Jewish literature emblazoned with pictures of Adolf Hitler at the World Conference Against Racism. While the elder Deedad traveled across the world before his death in 2005, his incendiary attacks on Christianity often caused trouble. Singapore, France and Nigeria all refused him entry, while Australia on one occasion threatened to deport him.

Most of Gujarat's *madaris* frown on such discourses. Dar-ul-Uloom Islamia's widely circulated Gujarati-language magazine as well as its text books are studiously, even self-consciously, apolitical. Clerics like Surati, for their part, are at great pains to emphasise importance of inter-faith dialogue and tolerance.

Madrassa: Places for Networking of Terrorism?

But madrassas, in practice, have acted as centers where Islamists may meet, network and obtain access to individuals connected with terrorist groups. Loose, personalized networks often emerge cutting across States.

Among Khalid Sardana's friends at Tarkeshwar was Bashir Ahmed Bhat, a HUJI terrorist who returned to active field service in the Kulgam area of Jammu and Kashmir soon after Mumbai serial bombings. "Bhat was recently killed in on encounter with Jammu and Kashmir police, but is thought to have left behind a network of associates that other HUJI operatives will be able to tap in the future.

Such networks are not new. Earlier in 2006, an Ahmedabad court convicted three students of the Dar-ul-Uloom Anwar-e-Raza, near Navsari, for their role in a HUJI terror plot targeting the city. 4 kg of an RDX-PETN cocktail and nine 30-MM pistols were recovered from the men on 15 Feb 2002, less than a fortnight before the Godhra tragedy.

One of the three, Imam-ul-Haq Banarasi, was the son of a cleric and had been schooled in *madaris* all his life—the stereotype of a likely terror recruit. The other two, Asad Ahmad Munshi and Husain Alibhai Maniar, though, were children of affluent business families, who had chosen to undertake studies in madaris—rejecting the world their parents had built for them. Many of the estimated two dozen men who joined Jihadi organizations after the 2002 pogrom in Gujarat also came from affluent homes, one, Ayub Damarwala, is known to have been killed in combat in Jammu and Kashmir.

An analyst, obviously sympathetic to the world of Islam and the problems it faces, writes:

> "perhaps, clues to what is going on lie in the Dar-ul-Uloom Islamia Arabiyya's fortress-like architecture: walls designed not to hid secret armies but defend what lies inside from a hostile world. Despite its enormous and evident liberating possibilities, modernity has spoken to Gujarat's Muslims mostly through economic marginalization and communalization. No serious assessment of Islamist

terrorism in Gujarat can ignore, for example, the role the closure of Ahmedabad's textile mills and the consequent displacement of Muslim workers had in the empowerment of reactionary clerics. Although ultra right tendencies in Islam long predate the pogrom of 2002? There is little doubt that large-scale communal violence has stoked them".[22]

Being sympathetic to Islamist world of right extremism and make a sincere effort to understand their problems is one thing but to find reasons, explanations and even justification for the terrorism perpetrated by them, in whatsoever may, directly or indirectly, is quite a different kettle of fish—and totally unacceptable. Muslims were not the only employees affected by the closure of textile mills. How did the non-Muslims cope with this blow to their livelihood? Did they resort to terrorism? Empowerment of Muslim clerics is the real problem facing the world of Islam. It is these "low-paid and semi-illiterate clerics" produced by the *madaris* like the ones named above, who interpret the Quran for the mofussil Muslims in most illiberal ways. Even educated Muslim of urban areas fall prey to their illiberal interpretation of the Quran. As Aref Mohd Khan wrote: "Islam has to be rescued from the stranglehold of these mullahs and maulvis".

To justify any Islamist extremism in the name of the so-called 2002 pogrom is an utterly irresponsible act of academics, which will only encourage such extremist violence/terrorism. How will modernity talk to the students of such *madaris* if they are not even allowed to watch a movie? Why should the world outside the fortress-like walls of this *madrassa* be hostile to what lies behind them? These walls do not defend anything. They are a loud declaration of Muslim separateness. In fact, they promote it in the first place. Yet again, these walls are not only indicative of ghettoisation of the community, but they promote it in the first place.

Ultra right tendencies not only long predate the 2002 'pogrom', these are the part of the Islamic world almost from the day Islam was born. Anyway, this is not the place for a bong, detailed debate on the issue. Hence the need to let the case rest here.

Conservatives like Maulani Surati hope the walls around the madrasa will protect its students and the traditions they represent from the dangers outside. At least, some of his students, though, see offence as a more effective form of defence and seek to blow up the hostile world.

Now comes the most important observation of this analyst, suggesting ways to end Islamist terrorism: "Gujarat's *madaris* are neither victims nor villains, but sites of complex contestations. *Madaris* in themselves are not the problem; it is India's civil society that must instead undertake the more difficult task of engaging with the ideas and ideologies that make Islamists engender violence".

This advice to India's civil society is rather quiaint, to put it mildly. In any case, what constitutes the civil society? More importantly, will the Islamist terrorists, or even the Muslim community at large, be willing to interact with this civil society? The answer is emphatic 'no'. Any action or initiative by civil society in this respect will be straight away dubbed as 'blatant interference' in religious matters of the Muslims and rejected out of hand.

This question of civil society engaging with the ideas and ideologies that make Islamists engender violence is a cliché. It is at par with another fovourite cliché: non-Muslims must understand Islam.

The truth is only Muslims can find a solution to the problem of Islamist terrorism. Only they can bring them to the path of reason. But it is also clear that they are either unwilling or unable to undertake the task. The extremist fringe is ruling over the Muslim majority—huge majority of 99.99. A contradiction but true one.

Muslims must Join the Others to Fight Terrorism

Malegaon was not the first instance when a mosque or a Muslim shrine was targeted by Islamic terrorists in India. Yet when it happened, the media, certainly a majority among its ranks, and Delhi's *Chatterati* club pretended as if Muslim terrorists can never quite be atrocious and demented enough to kill fellow Muslims.

They, in particular Left-liberal combine, had convinced themselves that long last, they had some non-Islamist terrorists to blame for the mindless violence. Curiously, they argued so after having grudgingly conceding that Muslim terrorists may kill just about anybody. To this combine, Godhara was a case of mass suicide. Terrorist attack on Delhi's Jama Masjid and Malegaon's Friday Muslim Congregations were obviously the work of some vicious Hindu terrorists. One particularly visceral anti-Hindu—he prefers to call it anti-Hindutva bigot of a journalist of the Left variety could hardly conceal his gleeful reaction: oh, long last, he could target his poison—filled barbs at Hindu terrorist! Long last, he could say that Muslims were not the only terrorists in India. The dementia that gripped India's Secularist Communist groupies encompasses too many processes of "diseased thinking" to recall and dilate. But what needs to be addressed urgently is that due to India's fractured polity and compulsions of coalition governance is that this "lopsidedly argumentative" 'mafia' has actually become the *Establishment*.

By now it must be clear to these partisan and biased minds that Islamist jihadis/fascists it do not spare the innocents within the faithfuls. An academician Khwaja Ekram put it more realistically: Terror knows no religion.

The SIMI, found guilty of masterminding the attack on the faithfulls near the Malegaon mosque, is not the only disruptive outfit indulging in such attacks. Various other Islamic and jihadi organizations with support from ISI and terror groups in Pakistan, have shown scant regard for religious places of any religion and lives of innocent devotees. Terrorists attacks on Varanasi temples, Akshardham temple, and Jama Masjid, Delhi only prove that postulation. Such mindless attacks cannot be described as jihad and no religion justifies, and sanction such blood shood. As a corollary, all religions, including Islam, must condemn them unequivocally.

Be it Hazaratbal in Jammu and Kashmir, Delhi's Jama Masjid, or the mosque at Malegaon, none are immune to terror groups. This is the situation as it stands today. At Malegaon, those who masterminded the blasts timed the attacks to have maximum impact possible in two ways: in terms of casualties and inflamed Muslim sensitivities. The day chosen for attacks was Friday and *Shab-e-Baraat* (Night of Salvation), a festival occasion when Muslims visit graveyards to offer nightlong prayers for their dead relatives. The brains behind the blasts also chose their targets carefully. The bombs went off in the Noorani Masjid in the Bada Qabrastan (Main or larger Graveyard) area at Malegaon where people had come to pray for the dead. The attack was aimed at creating communal tension, which fortunately did not occur.

SIMI has a wide network across Indian States. Almost all terrorists arrested recently have links with SIMI, an organization set up in the late 1970s in Aligarh Muslim University. It had begun as a student wing of the Jamat-e-Islami, but under the influence of the Wahabis the groups adopted an extremist ideology and broke away from the parent body. Before the ban on it, SIMI boasted of an active membership of 10,000 all over India.[22]

Investigations into the recent terrorist attacks have revealed a growing understanding, cooperation and alliance between jihadi groups operating from Pakistan and Bangladesh with the help of ideological allies. This development signals a new phase of terrorism in India, where international terrorist groups like LET and HUJI are likely to exert/exercise influence over a small and diffused groups of individuals to take up arms against the state in the name of religion.

Terror is not the only agenda these groups profess. As revealed in attacks on Jama Masjid, Delhi and also at Hindu pilgrim site in Varanasi and Ayodhya, the primary objective was to trigger communal riots and widen the historical divide and suspicion between the communities. The worst manifestation of this policy was the Divali bombings in Delhi in Oct. 2005. The bombs were turned to go off during the hour of *iftar* when everybody known that the Muslims would be indoors and only Hindu shoppers and revelers will be hit.

On 14 Apr 2006, again a Friday, two blasts immediately after the *Arsa namaz* injured more than 15 people at Jama Masjid, Delhi. Although, it created initial panic and sent the security apparatus into a tizzy, the *Magrib namaz* which followed saw undeterred devotees offer their prayers, and the next day was no exception when there was usual attendance to offer prayers Shahi Iamam Syed Ahmad Shah Bukhari's statement, "Emulate the people of Varanasi, who did not react in anger and defeated the plans of communal forces", helped calm the feelings of the devotees.

The misguided Muslims who claim that their version of jihad is "true" Islam are proving a burden for the Muslim world in general. After the recent terror strikes across India, there have been demonstrations against terrorism by various Muslim groups. In Delhi, the activists of Shia-Sunni Muslim Front protested against terrorism by signing with their blood. But Indian Muslims need to do more. They should maintain a strict vigil over members of their community who are increasingly getting influenced by external *jihadi* elements. Non-Muslims should encourage the liberal Muslims, to come out boldly against Islamist terrorists and criticize the trend of misusing religious freedom and public places of worship for spreading extremism.

According to National Security Advisor M.K. Narayanan, "faith-based" terrorism was the biggest challenge facing the international community as most groups engaged in violent conflicts "tend to have a radical Islamic visage". It should be clear that under such circumstances, mere force would not be enough to crush terror.

But is should also be equally clear to the advocates of the above postulation that reason and reasonableness alone will never convince the mindless murderers, who are convinced that they are defending their faith through the so-called jihad, to abjure their violent and murderous ways. Unless they are defeated on the 'battle field' by the State and its security forces and some even eliminated in the process, there is no hope ever of their listening to reason or coming to the negotiating table. So if at all we are to succeed against them, it has to be a combination of force and the negotiations, and in the same order. There just are no other options.

Civil society comes into picture only at the second stage. All sections of civil society, and particularly the Muslims because most violent groups "tend to have a radical Islamic visage", must convince the terrorist jihadis about the futility of their violent, murderous ways.

N-E border madrassa wory MHA: Feb. 2007

Sprouting of madrassas along the country's international borders and presence of jihadi modules in the North-Eastern states has emerged as major challenges on the internal security front. Besides, coastal security has also been raising serious concerns in the Ministry of Home Affairs (MHA).

The issues were reviewed on 8 Feb 2007 at a meeting chaired by Home Secretary VK Duggal. The following issues came up for scrutiny:

- Situation in Jammu and Kashmir
- Situation in the North-Eastern states.
- Situation vis-à-vis internal security in the hinterland
- Naxalite violence
- Communal violence and conflict

There are reports of infiltration through the coastal belt in Kerala. Home Minister Shivraj Patil has already cautioned the security forces about the possibility of infiltration through the seashores as the terrorists could use uninhabited islands as their hideouts. Some terror outfits are attempting to sneak into India through eastern and western coasts, after testing waters against the strict vigilance against the LOC and international borders.

The situation along the international borders in the context of a large number of madrassas coming up there was also reviewed. It was also decided to keep a close watch on the unregistered madrassas.

A meeting of the task force on Naxalism followed by a meeting of the Empowered Group of Ministers (EGOM) "is scheduled for later this month (Feb)".

The border forces were asked to increase the vigilance along the Indo-Nepal and Indo-Bangla borders, besides erecting additional floodlights and completing the fencing work at the earliest.

It was an important internal security review meeting, which is obvious from the list of high-ups who attended it:

1. DG, CRPF
2. Senior officers from Directorate Generals of Military Intelligence and Military Operations.
3. DG BSF, DG SSB and DG ITBP.
4. Officials of the Border Management Division of the MHA.

West Bengal: No Recognition for Private Madrassas: April 2007

The West Bengal Government is planning to set up 100 new madrassas in the state, but it has ruled out any chances of government recognition and affiliation to the West Bengal Board of Madrassa Education for the hundreds of existing unrecognized (private) madrassas.

Sources on 30 Apr 2007 disclosed that the Madrassa Education Department is in the process of formulating a "uniform policy", parallel to school education, that will make it possible to set up new madrassas across the state. It was made clear that the madrass run privately in the state should not hope for anything substantial in the near future.

Sources in the West Bengal Madrassa Board inform that over 400 applications from madrassas seeking recognition have been lying unattended. Madrassa Board president Sohrab Hossain confired "there are 425 to 430 applications with the Board".

Sources in the Ministry told a dailly[24] that there is no thought, at present, on what is the Department supposed to do with the private madrassas being run across the State. An official, echoeing the same averments, said, "We have no direction from the Ministry on what should be done with the madrassas seeking recognition."

The private madrassas have for years been accused by various governments of harbouring fundamentalism in Children. Chief Minister Buddhadeb Bhattacharjee had once questioned the curriculum of the private madrassas. Despite this, the administration has not done much to help the financially crippled institutions to join the "mainstream".

On the other hands, hundreds of private madrassas that are financially sound, have stayed away from the government funding, as that will force them to accept government appointed teachers and follow the government sanctioned/declared syllabus.

Madrassa Students Can Join Government Schools: May 2007

In a move to bring madrassa students into mainstream education, the UT Administration, Chandigarh, has decided to give these students a one-time option of taking admission in government schools. These students would not be required to show their last year's pass mark-sheet while seeking admission in any government school.

The Administration, after inspecting madrassas in Mani Majra and Bapu Dham, has decided to shift madrassa students to government school in Sector 26.

After inspecting madrassa in Mani Majra, the two officials—UT Deputy Commissioner RK Rao and Municipal Commissioner PS Aujla—said in their report that its building was not habitable and suggested immediate corrective measures.

United Progressive Muslim Front, a local Muslim body, had been demanding bringing of madrassa students into the mainstream system for very long. The Front President Arshad Khan told a daily: 'In a madrassa, a student is provided education only till the secondary level and later these students find it difficult to get admission in government schools. This step by education department really needs to be appreciated as these students will now get better educational facilities in terms of qualified teachers and better infrastructure".[25]

This opportunity is not only for madrassa students but for those students as well who had dropped out of school and want to get back to studies. District Education Officer Kamal Bains gave this information, clarifying "all such students are free to contact us".

Besides, the Administration is also worling on the proposal to have Muslim academics/administrators on the board of schools where the madrassa students will be shifted.

Veil Debate in India

Even as the veil debate in Britain refuses to die down, Muslim clerics in India have sharply reacted to veteran Indian actress Shabana Azami's statement in London that the *Koran* does not make it mandatory for a women to cover her face.

"Is has become a fashion of sorts for some Indian Muslims to criticize the teachings of the holy *Koran* and *Hadees*", said Maulana Khalid Rashid Firangimahali, a senior member of all India Muslim Personal Law Board (AIMPLB) and *imam* of the historic Tilewali Masjid at Lucknow. He was reacting on 29 Oct 2006 to Shabana Azmi's assertion earlier in the week when she was in London to receive the Gandhi Foundation's International Peace Award. The actress, a former MP (Rajya Sabha), had called for a debate on the Muslim women wearing the veil, saying the *Koran* speaks about women wearing clothes to cover their modesty and that they need not cover their faces.

Commenting further on Shabana, Firangimahali said: "Some Muslims in the country think they will be considered modern only when they criticize the *Koran* and *Hadees*. The *Koran* has clearly instructed the women to wear veil. But this does not mean they should not go to college or work and remain confined to their homes.

On the controversy over Muslim women wearing veils that was sparked by Commons' leader Jack Straw in Britain, the Maulana said asking Muslim women not to wear veils was tantamount to a "violation of their fundamental rights."

It is important to note that both sides, Shabana and Maulana, are quoting Kuran for their diametrically opposite views on the issue of veil, but the Muslims, especially the clerics and hard-liners do not ever welcome the idea of debate as to what exactly Koran says on it. Liberals have often demanded, as Shabana has done in the instant case, a debate but it all falls by the way due to reluctance of the hard-liners because they are scared of any other interpretation of the Kuran's contents except their own, which some analysts feel is meant to keep Muslim women under subjugation in perpetuity!

NSCN factions' fierce fire-fight: 26-27 Oct. 2006

About 160 cadres of NSCN (I-M) and 100 of the Khaplang

faction engaged in two-day long fierce gun battle, as detailed below, at Amiphoto Colony in Nagaland's Zunheboto district.

26 Oct	9 AM to 6.30 PM
27 Oct	8 AM to 6.00 PM

The Deputy Commissioner told the press on the 27th that "if the ongoing efforts to end the battle peacefully and amicably failed, the district administration will use force on the 28th to flush out the militants".

The militants used rocket launchers, mortars, AK-47, AK-56 and snipers in the heavy exchanges of fire, in which two Khaplang faction fighters were killed. Only one of these has been identified: Abol Zeliang of Tamenglong district of Manipur.

Although no civilian was injured, around 4,000 people fled the area, taking shelter in relatives' houses elsewhere in the district.

The Deputy Commissioner said: "It is a systematic violation of the ground rules of ceasefire by both the factions....Three companies of the Assam Rifles and two of the India Reserve Battalion have been kept ready for intervention". It was not found necessary subsequently Chief Minister Nephiu Rio was kept informed of the situation.

Arrested ULFA leader claims Split: Sep 2007

Self-styled commander ULFA's 28th Battalion, Prabal Neog, captured on 17 Sep 2007 while traveling from Tezpur in Northern Assam to Itanagar, Arunachal Pradesh's capital, reportedly "confessed to the police—19 Sep—that the order to attack Hindi-speaking people in the State (Assam) came from the outfit's top leaders presently hiding in Bangladesh".

Neog made an interesting claim that he was not in favour of carrying out these killings. "He said there was a strong division of opinion within ULFA over launching an attack on Hindi-speaking people", said a police officer involved in Neog's interrogation.

Interestingly, in Jan 2007 when most of the migrant killings were carried out, a section of the local media in Guwahati published a statement attributed to Neog in which he said he was not in favour of attacking Hindi-speaking people. However, another statement also attributed to him soon surface denying this.

Neog on 19 Sep was remanded to 10-day police custody by a city court.

Although all three top leader of ULFA—Paresh Baruah, C-in-C of ULFA's armed wing, Chairman Arbinda Raj Khowa and General Secretary Anup Chetia—are ensconced in the safety of Bangladesh base/headquaters, it is the former who is said to call the shots, including deciding about holding talks with New Delhi.

71 Hindi-speaking people were killed in the Upper Assam districts over a period of two weeks in Jan 2007 ranging from petty traders and seasonal brick kiln labourers to domiciled farmers. It is believed 28th Battalion men had carried out the dastardly task. ULFA was also believed to be involved in the gunning down of 31 Hindi-speaking people in Karbi Anglong district in Aug 2007 in collaboration with the Karbi-Longri National Liberation Front (KL-NLF).

But police are taking Neog's claims of a split in ULFA over migrant killings with a pinch of salt. "That ULFA is the most unreliable of all insurgent outfits has been proved time and again", noted the police officer, though it remains a fact that for sometime after the killings, Neog was sent off to look after ULFA camps in Myanmar across Tirap and Changlang in Arunachal Pradesh, and was subsequently assigned the task of reorganizing the almost defunct 709 Battalion of the outfit in central Assam.

Important Information

9/11 has become a landmark in the international fight against terrorism. The following pages have some post-9/11 information about terrorism in India.

At the end there is an appendix, containing brief details on some cases of terrorist incidents selected at random.

Post-9/11: Terror Timeline: India

Date	Place of Incident / Attack	Killed
1 Oct 2001	Attack on Jammu and Kashmir Assembly complex	35
13 Dec 2001	Attack on the Parliament Complex in New Delhi	7
24 Sep 2002	Attack on Akshardham Temple in Gandhi Nagar, Gujarat	31
14 May 2003	Attack on the Army camp, near Jammu.	30
25 Aug 2003	Serial blasts in Mumbai	52
15 Aug 2004	Blasts in Assam	16
5 July 2005	Ram Janmabhoomi Temple attack in Ayodha	2
29 Oct 2005	Three blasts in New Delhi	70
7 Mar 2006	Blasts in Varanasi	21
11 July 2006	Seven blasts in Mumbai local trains	21
8 Sep 2006	Blasts in Malegaon Mosque	37
18 May 2007	Mecca Masjid blasts, Hyderabad	13
25 Aug 2007	Twin blasts in Hyderabad	43

Jammu and Kashmir: Post-9/11 Timeline

Year	*Incidents*	*Civilians*	Fatalities *Security Forces*	*Terrorists*	*Total*
2001	4,522	919	536	2,020	3,475
2002	4,038	1008	453	1,707	3,168
2003	3,401	795	314	1,494	2,003
2004	2,565	707	281	976	1,964
2005	1,990	557	189	917	1,663
2006	1,667	389	151	593	1,133

Post-9-11 Terror Timeline: Delhi

2001

Arrests	4
Encounter deaths	5
Injured	30
Deaths	6 (Parliament attack)
Groups	LET, IIM

2002

Arrests	12
Groups	LET, ISI

2003

Arrests	26
Encounter deaths	2
Groups	LET, JEM, BKI, ISI

2004

Arrests	13
Encounter death	1
Groups	LET, Al Jehad, HM

2005

Arrests	23
Encounter deaths	5
Injured	215 (155 in Sarojini Nager blasts and 60 in Liberty blast)

Deaths	63 (62 in Sarojini Nagar blasts, and one in Liberty blasts)
Blasts	5 (3 in Sarojini Nagar, Paharganj and Govindpuri, 2 in Liberty and Satyam Cinema)
Groups	LET, JEM, ISI, HM, BKI
2006	
Arrests	25
Encounter deaths	1
Injured	14
Blasts	2
Groups	LET, Al Badr, HM
2007 (till 1 August)	
Arrests	16
Groups	LET (6), ISI, HUJI, JEM, ISI

(*Source: Pioneer,* 9 Sep. 2007)

Post-9/11 Maharashtra Timeline

Date	*Attack / Blasts: Place*	*Killed / Injured*
2 Dec., 2002	Ghatkopar	2/49
6 Dec., 2002	Mumbai Central Station	Nil/22
27 Jan., 2003	Vile Parle Station	Nil/30
13 Mar., 2003	Mulund	13/83
29 July, 2003	Ghatkopar	3/31
25 Aug., 2003	Javeri Bazar	55/157
3 May, 2006	Ghatkopar	1/Nil
11 July, 2006	Serial blasts in Mumbai suburban trains	187/824
8 Sep., 2006	Three blasts at Malegaon	31/153

Some Cases Related at Random

Date	*Killed/Injured*	*Details*
26 Oct., 2006	6/9	**Terrorists disrupt rail work in Tripura.** Outlawed groups of insurgents in the North-East are hell bent on disrupting work on railway extension undertaken by the Centre to link all the state capitals by railway within 2011. The National Liberation Front ultras fired at Tripura State Rifles (TSR) personnel who were protecting workers engaged in construction of railway up to the state capital near Sindhu Kumar in North Tripura's Longthorai Valley region. Two TSR men were killed on the spot and their arms were looted. "Six security men have been killed by militants in separate attacks in the last five days."
26 Oct., 2006		**Clashes between two factions of NSCN** Heavy clashes broke out between the two rival factions of the National Socialist Council of Nagaland at Zunheboto town, reportedly causing the death of some cadres of both groups. The clashes took place at a residential colony of the district head-quarters, forcing some people to vacate their homes.
20 Mar., 2007	6/Nil	**Army captain, 5 others killed in Jammu and Kashmir** Six people, including an Army captain from Kerala and his soldier, were

Date	Killed/Injured	Details
		killed in an encounter with four militant holed up in a house in village Chontimarg of Kupwara district, some 120 km from Srinagar. Acting on a tip-off, troops had surrounded the village as LET militants were reported to be hiding there. Capt R Harshkan and his soldier were killed when they entered the house where the four militants were found to be hiding. All the four militants were killed in a three-hour encounter that ensued the arrival of reinforcements from their camps. "Captain's parents and his two brothers were incoherent with the enormity of the tragedy that had struck tiem—so suddenly and so brutally. And just two days before he was to come home for a holiday".
13 Apr., 2007	4/Nil	**4 JEM ultras killed in Jammu and Kashmir** Four militants, including district commander of Jaish-e-Mohammad (JEM) were killed by 11 Rashtriya Rifles (RR) troops in an ambush in the snow-clad remote Navapachhi area in Kishtwar. The Defence spokesperson said a group of militants led by district commander of JEM were riding mules while passing through Zaban area, 10 km east of Navapachhi when the troops of 11 RR ambushed them, killing all the ultras on the spot in an exchange of fire. The militants may have been moving towards Kashmir Valley through the area.

Date	*Killed / Injured*	*Details*
		The identity of one terrorist, Fayaz Ahmed, District Commander, JEM, has been ascertained. The three bodies remain to be identified. The troops recovered two AK-47 rifles, one sophisticated radio set and some magazines.
18 May, 2007	0/20	**ULFA explosion: Guwahati** At least 20 people were injured when a powerful IED hidden in a rikshaw by suspected ULFA militants exploded at the Fancy Bazaar in Guwahati.
5 June, 2007		**ULFA's Nepal Coordinator surrenders** For long, the ULFA was believed to have established camps in Nepal under the Maoists' patronage. On 5 June 2007, Security forces came to know it for certain after the man, senior ULFA leader and self-styled Lieutenant, Ghanakanta Bora alias Jagadish Phukan, surrendered before the 19 Kumaon at Laipuli army camp in Tinsukia district. Bora, who helped the outfit expand to the erstwhile Himalayan kingdom, came with his wife, 'Seargent Major' Tulsi Bora Gohain, alias Archana Phukan. Bora is a major catch as he was known to be ULFA's front man in Nepal besides being a coordinator for the outfit's dreaded 28th Battalion. He confessed to having helped ULFA set up Maoist-aided camps in

Date	*Killed / Injured*	*Details*
		southern and eastern Nepal. He was also the interface between the ULFA and Nepali Maoists. Bora was among the ULFA's earliest recruits. Joining it in 1988, he graduated to become ULFA's PRO, and specialized in procuring arms and ammunition. He also oversaw operations from Myanmar before moving to Bhutan. He was caught during the Royal Bhutan Army's 'Operation All-clear' in Dec 2003 and vanished after securing bail a couple of months later. (Rahul Karmaker, *Hindustan Times,* 6 June 2007. rahconteour@rediffmail.com)
June, 2007		**Lining up to return home** "My name is Nasir Ahmad Pathan" shouted the bedraggled figure from across the rolls of barbed wire that mark the LOC, "and want to come home". For over an hour one June 2007 afternoon, troops at the Nanak post had peered out at the four specks winding their way towards the LOC. First thought was they are terrorists, but later when they espied a women with two infants in her arms, it was something unusual for the soldiers; and the man was urging two exhausted children to take the last slaps up the mountains that rise up along the Jhelum Valley.

Date	*Killed/Injured*	*Details*
		Like the Pathan family, at least 138 Jammu and Kashmir residents have returned home from across the LOC since the Kashmir earthquake of Oct 2005—five of them with the families they built during their time in Pakistan.
		Most had left to train at camps run by Islamist terror groups; others were among the estimated 35,000 refugees, who fled the State, fearing war and ethnic cleansing when the jihad broke out in 1989.
		Ever since 2002, however, Pakistan's ISI started squeezing funding to terror groups, and the jihad in Jammu and Kashmir began to disintegrate. Now hundreds of men are thought to be waiting in jihad camps for a chance to come in from the cold. Thousands of refugees, too, believe the time has come to resume their war-interrupted lives.
		Pathan was a school student when he began his journey from the impoverished mountain hamlet Sultan Dhakki to Pakistan. His brothers, Javed and Mubassir, would join the Indian Army; Pathan turned to join jihad in search of adventure, self-esteem—and a living.
		One summer evening in 1989, Pathan traversed the minefield along the LOC with the help of a HM recruiter. By that evening, he was on a truck to a training camp near Muzaffarabad.

Date	*Killed / Injured*	*Details*
		A report says "upward of a thousand more are waiting to come in" like the 138 who have already done so. (Praveen Swami, *Hindu*, 25 June 2007)
23 June, 2007		**Two more HUJI militants held** UP's Special Task Force (STF) arrested two Pakistan-trained militants of the banned Harkat-ul-Jihadi Islami (HUJI) with 9 kg of RDX and other ammunition. The militants (Babu, the area commander of HUJI in the area and a resident of 24 Parganas south district in West Bengal, and Naushad who belongs to Chak Uday Chand village of Bijnor district of UP) were arrested from outside the Residency in Wazirganj locality of Lucknow around 2.40 AM. One AK-47, one pistol, some grenades and materials used for making IEDs were recovered from their persons. UP DGP GL Sharma said that Babu aka Jalaluddin was the mastermind behind the Varanasi blasts in July 2006. Police was silent on whether Lucknow was the target or a were base for the HUJI militants. (*Asian Age*, 24 June 2007) Babu, with another alias Amanullah Mandal, belongs to Bangladesh-based HUJI. Another daily (*Indian Express*, 24 June 2007) does give more details. Babu confessed to have supplied

Date	*Killed/Injured*	*Details*
		explosives for the 2005 blasts in Varanasi, Delhi and Mumbai. The names of both the militants had figured in the confessional statements of two others (Yaqub and Nasir) who were arrested by the STF on 21 June. While Babu was described as an "international terrorist", it was Naushad who motivated both Yaqub and Nasir to join terror training camps in Pakistan. Detailed list of seizures from Babu and Naushad follows: • High explosives 9 kg • Detonators 10 • Timers 4 • Hand grenades 20 • Chinese-made 7.62 rifle 1 • AK-47 Rifle 1 • Cartridges in large number The DGP disclosed Babu got one of his men to execute the Varanasi blast. Babu's name also figured in the Shramjeevi Express blasts. Babu has developed his links in almost every part of the country, , including Maharashtra and Gujarat. His main job was to supply explosive materials to terror module and select the target of the blast.

Date	*Killed / Injured*	*Details*
		Babu had received training at a camp in Pakistan and was associated with the HUJI since 2001. Sharma also said Babu was involved in the much-publicised kidnapping of Khadim Shoe owner Partho Burman Naushad's role in the HUJI was to provide safe places for keeping the RDX which was supplied to him by Babu. Besides this, Naushad was also tasked to motivate youths for training in Pakistan.
23 June, 2007	6/15	**6 killed in Assam explosion** Six persons including two children were killed and 15 others wounded in a powerful explosion near a mosque in Machkhowa area of Guwahati. The bomb was strapped to a bicycle and kept near a tea shop behind the mosque. Police suspects ULFA's hand behind the outrage but the outfit denied any involvement in it.
23 June, 2007		**ULFA asks Bangla migrants to leave** In what may have serious consequences for the law and order situation in the State, the outlawed "ULFA has set a deadline of 30 days for the illegal migrants, particularly from Bangladesh, to leave Assam. Commander of ULFA's 28 Battalion Prabal Neog called up local newspaper offices on the 22 June night to issue this threat. The outfit also warned the chief of Assam United Democratic Front (AUDF) Badruddin Ajmal against poblicising

Date	*Killed/Injured*	*Details*
		the atmosphere of the State on "communal" lines. Neog also asked the AUDF chief to leave Assam within 15 days, and "stop playing with the sentiment of Assamese people". The ULFA statement/threat has created sensation in the political circles of the State, as it is the first time that the ULFA has asked migrants to leave Assam. So far, ULFA's refrain was: "First, the "foreigners from India" must leave the State. The Bangladeshis can be dealt with later".
24 June, 2007	8/11	**8 militants killed in Jammu and Kashmir** Three militants were killed by Indian troops in a bid to foil cross-border infiltration near the LOC in Uri sector in Jammu and Kashmir's north-western Baramulla district. One soldier also laid down his life and another wounded in the clash. In a separate clash with the security forces in Keran area of the neighbouring Kupwara district, five militants were killed. Ten police men were wounded some of them seriously, in a landmine explosion at Maloora on the outskirts of Srinagar. These incidents occurred ahead of Union Home Minister Shivraj Patil's visit to Srinagar next week, primarily

Date	*Killed / Injured*	*Details*
		to oversee the arrangements made for the 2-month-long annual Amar Nath pilgrimage (= Yatra) beginning 30 June.
24 June, 2007		**Sainiks attack APHC leader** Shiv Sainiks assaulted a second-rung leader of the Mirwaiz-led APHC, Zaffar Akbar Butt who was addressing a press conference at Jammu Press Club. This was the sixth such incident in which a Kashmiri separatist leader was targeted in this fashion by Shiv Sena activists or other ultra nationalist forces is the State's winter capital, the first being People's Conference leader Abdul Gani Lone, who days after the assault was shot dead in cold blood by suspected separatist militants. Butt was injured when he was thrashed because his stubborn refusal to say "Hindustan, Zindabad" as demanded by the Sainiks. About 40 Sainiks led by their president Anand Sharma gate-crashed the moment Butt began to speak. Butt, a former HM commander, presently heads Jammu and Kashmir Salvation Movement JKSM, comprising mainly of former militants and a constituent of the moderate faction of the APHC.

Date	*Killed / Injured*	*Details*
31 July, 2007	4/Nil	**Militants kill Colonel in Uri sector, Jammu and Kashmir** Col V. Vasant and his radio operator L/LK Ganpat Shashikant fell victims to the militants' guns but not before killing two of the three infiltrating ultras in Khandanar area near LOC, in Uri Sector. Alerted by the intelligence, the Colonel and his troops had succeeded in pushing the militants back on the 30th evening. But his luck ran out on the 31st when the same group again made a foiled bid to infiltrate into the Valley. "More militants have taken refuge in a nearly forest", said Defence spokesperson Anil Mathur. The body of Col Vasant was sent to Bangalore on the 31st afternoon. Col Vasant is the second Commanding Officer (CO) to have been killed in an encounter in the last seven months. Col Gurbir Singh Sarna, CO 29 RR was killed in village Chak Behrampora in an encounter.
9 Sep., 2007	5/Nil	**5 NSCN (I-M) Cadre killed by Kuki rivals** Five separatists of the Isak-Muivah faction of the NSCN (I-M) were killed by the suspected members of rival group—the outlawed Kuki Liberation Army (KLA)—fighting for an independent homeland for the minority Kuki tribe in the adjoinng

Date	*killed / Injured*	*Details*
		state Mampur's Naga-majority northern areas, near Jotsoma, some 30 kms from Kohima. This is the latest in the violent gang war between two ethnic groups in the North-East. Specifically, both groups belong to southern Manipur: Tangkhul Nagas (to which tribe Muivah belongs) and Kukis. Five bullet-riddled bodies were found on 9 Sep 2007 by the side of a river close to Jotsoma. The dead included PK Stone, the priest of the NSCN-IM's Headquarters at camp Hebron, near Dimapur, and his wife Mariela. Probably, the KLA militants followed the vehicle carrying the five NSCN-IM members from Kohima and attacked them in an isolated area. The attack is seen as retaliation to the killing of 10 KLA cadre by the NSCN-IM on 3 Sep at village Tangkhul Hundung in northern Manipur's Ukhru district, some 70 kms north-east of Imphal. The NSCN-IM had claimed responsibility for the attack on the KLA cadre, dubbing them 'anti-socials'.
10 Sep., 2007	2/Nil	**ULFA kills 2 Hindi-speakers again** Two ultras of the outlawed ULFA, came riding a motorcycle and killed the owner of a hotel and his driver in Talap town of Tinsukia district on 10

Date	*Killed / Injured*	*Details*
		Sep 2007 at 7.15 PM. Both the victims—Tarun Kundu and his driver Rambilas Shah—were originally from Bihar but had been staying in Assam for quite a long time. The killing of the two Hindi-speaking people once again triggered fear and panic among non-Assamese migrant workers. The Karbi—Anglong district has had a string of brutal attacks in the run-up to Independence Day (2007) in which some 30 Hindi-speaking people were killed by ULFA in collaboration with the Karbi Longri National liberation Front (KL-NLF).
10 Sep., 2007	7/5	**Seven killed in Jammu and Kashmir** Six militants and a jawan were killed and five persons, including three members of CRPF's women contingent injured in separate acts of violence in Jammu and Kashmir. Sub-Inspector JR Yadav, Head Constable Neelam Sharma and Constable Jaswinder Kaur were injured when militants hurled a grenade on a CRPF vehicle in Rainawari area on the 10th morning, hours before UPA Chairperson Sonia Gandhi's arrival in Srinagar to attend a women's meet. Hizbul Mujahideen claimed responsibility for the attack. Pawan Kumar was killed and another jawan injured when ultras opened fire on a joint search party of police and army at Rajwar forest in Kupwar district.

Date	*Killed / Injured*	*Details*
		Troops guarding the LOC shot dead four militants who were trying to cross over from POK in Gulmarge sector of Baramulla district in the early hours. Four AK rifles and eight magazines were recovered from the slain militants. This was the second operation in quick succession which foiled a major infiltration bids. The last such foiled attempt was on 9 Sep when four foreign militants were killed in Machhal sector of Kupwara sector.

Notes

1. Devi Cherian, *Pioneer*, 3 Dec., 2006.
2. Seema Mustafa, *Asian Age,* 16 Feb., 2007.
3. Cited Shariq Majeed, *Tribune*, 28 May, 2007.
4. Bibhu Prasad Routray, Research Fellow, Institute for Conflict Management, *Indian Express*, 6 July, 2007.
5. Faizan Haider, *Pioneer*, 5 July, 2007
6. Rashid Ahmad, *Hindustan Times*, 30 July, 2007.
7. Aloke Tikku, *Hindustan Times*, 30 Oct., 2006.
8. Arun Joshi, *Hindustan Times*, 30 Oct., 2006.
9. Raghav Ohri, *Indian Express*, 1 Aug., 2007.
10. Indian *Express*, 12 Aug., 2007.
11. Riyaz Wani, *Indian Express*, 8 Aug., 2007.
12. Samudra Gupta Kashyap, *Indian Express*, 12 Aug., 2007.
13. Mohit Kandhari, *Pioneer*, 11 Sep., 2007.
14. Dhaval Kulkarni and Satyajit Joshi, *Hindustan Times*, 8 June, 2006.
15. Bhavna Vij—Aurora, *Outlook*, 24 July, 2006.
16. Rahul Mahajani, *Week*; 23 July, 2006.
17. Alok Sharma, presently an SSP, serving at Nainital, Uttarkhand.
18. *Indian Express*, 10 Oct., 2006.

19. Praveen Swami, "From an unknown name to an emerging nightmare", *Hindu*, 28 Oct., 2006.
20. Mohd Amir Rana, in his authoritative 2002 book, *A-Z of Jihadi Organisations*.
21. Praveen Swami, *Frontline*, 20 Oct., 2006.
22. *Ibid.*
23. Ghulam Yazdani, *Pioneer*, 2 Dec., 2006.
24. Mohd Safi Shamsi, *Indian Express*, 1 May, 2007.
25. Jyotsna Jalali, *Indian Express*, 6 May, 2007.

9

Terrorist Attacks in India Part 1

India has been the victim of secessionist and terrorist violence right since its independence: North-East, Jammu and Kashmir, Punjab and Naxalite Left-Wing Extremism.

But in the recent years, the country has the duleious distinction of the worst-affected victim of the terrorist scourge next only to Iraq—a war-torn country. It has been obvious for quite some time that the Jihadist terrorists have the capability to choose the place and timing of attack at will. And they have been doing so with frightening regularly.

This chapter discusses some of the major incidents to hit India since mid-1980s. Some of these have been subjected to in-depth analysis.

TRANSISTOR BOMB BLASTS IN DELHI: MAY 1985

This was arguably the first case of serial blasts in which Indians were involved in revenge killing follow Indians. It was frightening act of terrorism of its own kind. At the end, 69 people lay dead and 127 injured across northern India in May 1985.

The bombs were rigged into innocuous-looking transistors, placed on the equally harmless-looking bicycles. The unsuspecting victims were either killed on the spot, or seriously injured.

Next days newspapers carried some macalere pictures of mangled bodies, some headless and others sans limbs—and all blood-spattered. Delhi obviously took sometime to return to normal life and daily routine.

"Two decades of suspense have ended for five accused in the 1985 transistor bomb blasts that killed 69 people and injured 127 in Delhi, with a Delhi court deciding on 11 June, 2006 there was insufficient evidence to indict them for 'conspiring to over awe the centre'." (Tribune, 12 June 2006).

Additional Sessions Judge Vinod Kumar who is trying nine cases connected with the blasts at Delhi and neigh bouring cities in Haryana and UP, has discharged the five (Jagir Singh, Sukhjinder Singh, Paramjit Singh, Shahid Singh and Surjit Kaur) of all charges for insufficient evidence.

This stage arrived long last with the Delhi High Court's repeated directions to speed up the legal process in the case that has been dragging on for 21 years.

"Over the past few months, the court has framed charges of murder and attempted murder against half a dozen persons setting the stage for trial to begin. However, the remaining accused, of whom at least four have died while the rest are out on bail, continue to wait and watch.

The five accused who were discharged are among over 50 people named in the case registered in 1985 with Patel Nagar police station in west Delhi, according to which the main conspirator of the blasts was Delhi - based income tax lawyer Kartar Singh Narang, who died some years back.

The prosecution case is that Narang and his accomplices MS Oberio and MS Khalsa (also deceased) planted bombs disguised as transistors to avenge the killings of Sikhs in and around Delhi in the 1984 riots that erupted after the assassination of Prime Minister Indira Gandhi.

Acting on information that transistor bombs were being manufactured in Narang's house, the police conducted a raid on 12 May, 1985 and arrested him alongwith Oberoi and Khalsa for their "involvement in unlawful activities."

The police says the names of four of the five discharged (Jagir, Sukhjinder, Paramjit and Shahid) were allegedly written on slips of paper recovered by the investigators from Khalsa and Oberoi.

The police case against Jagir: "In his disclosure statement Khalsa has admitted to having given Jagir a transistor bomb to be planted in Banglore, besides Rs. 1,000 to purchase a gun". They also said Jagir was "instigated to take revenge against the Hindus.

But the court pointed out that apart from the disclosure statement, there was nothing to prove any overt participation by Jagir in the conspiracy.

Sukhjinder was allegedly absconding when the police reached his house, and when eventually caught, the investigators found literature suggesting that he had knowledge of and he had participated in the conspiracy to over awe the Centre.

Similarly, Paramjit and Shahid were charged with alleged conspiracy, with the former accused of attending a meeting where he was "asked to participate in the extremist activity."

Court shot down these allegations, observing that there was no concrete material to show participation in the offence, or overt knowledge of conspiracy.

The charges against Surjit Kaur were somewhat different, with the police relying on Oberoi's disclosure statement where he claimed to be on visiting terms with the accused. Oberoi says he had left six bombs at Kaur's house and told her to "keep them and wait for instructions". Apart from this disclosure, there was nothing in court records to suggest her participation in the crime.

It is rather difficult for a layman to comment on this case where having put in 21 years of exertion, the police faces mortification with the trial judge declaring four of the five accused as "Not guilty". What could be the reason for this rank inefficiency of the police? What are the insurmountable hurdles in the path of the police investigators? Or, is it that the judge is too fastidious? But what baffles the non-legal fraternity is a simple question: Why should it take 21 long years for a case of this nature to reach a trial stage? Is something wrong with our judicial system? This, in any case, is not the place to discuss this legal conundrum. It better be left to more qualified persons!

WHY IS MUMBAI TARGETED REPEATEDLY?

Why are the terrorists so focussed on attacking Mumbai? Why are they so intently determined to destroy it?

There are reasons and it is not difficult to see them. In one word, Mumbai is still the financial capital of India. It still is the leading centre of industrial, commercial and cultural activities. Some of these are mentioned in the succeeding parts.

Mumbai: The Repeated Target

The metropolis has been targetted several times in the recent years.

- 12 March 1993. A series of blasts ripped through 13 places in the city, killing 257 people and injuring 713. First case of RDX usage. Suspect plotter: Dawood Ibrahim.
- 2 December 2002. Powerful explosion kills two and injures 31 in a BEST bus outside Ghatkopar suburban railway station.
- 6 December 2002. Bomb explodes in a food plaza at Bombay Central railway station, injuring 2 people.
- 27 January 2003. Crude bomb planted in a bicycle explodes in a packed shopping complex outside Vile Parle railway station kills one and injures 30 people.
- 13 March 2003. 11 people were killed and 65 injured when a powerful bomb exploded in a "ladies special" train as it was entering Mulund station at peak hours.
- 25 August 2003. Two successive blasts at the Gateway of India and Gaveri Bazar killed 46 people and injured more than 160. RDX was planted in taxis parked at both these places.
- 11 July 2006. Seven Lethal bombs exploded in as many trains and as many minutes beginning at 6.24 PM on Tuesday killed 181 people and injured 733.

Why Mumbai?

Knowing its determination to destabilise, preferably dismember, India, Pakistan targeting Mumbai should not come as a surprise, rather, it should he expected. For India, Mumbai is too precious to burn. It is City of Gold, Maximum City, and City of Dreams. It is all this and much more. We admire its exuberance, its vitality, its resilience. But we also should not ignore its contradictions and paradoxes. So it is a city at once blessed and cursed.

It is a city of vast wealth. Among the four or five metropolises, it is the only one entitled to be proclaimed as micro cosmic India. It indeed is India's true multing pots—of people, of religions of tongues, of castes, of cultures, and ethnicities if you live.

People from all States of the Union, as also from large number of nations, have made it their home. Take the Muslims alone. One will find every variety in the Ummah. From the bacon–eating followers of MA Jinnah to the 5-times-a-day namaazis. Shia, Sunni, Bora, Khoja, Agakhani and Ahmedia rule shoulders in the city. They live, laugh, and flourish in the city. Same is true of the Hindus—of all castes and creeds from all corners of India. Like wise, the Buddhists, Jains, Sikhs, Parsis at all are well represented here.

Consider now its sweat-and-blood wealth. Compared to it, Bangalore is an arriviste, a new entrant. When we think of India as a 21st-century economic super - power, Mumbai springs into attention. Mumbai is the real business, financial, services and entertainment capital of India. "This is where the Tatas, Birlas, Ambanis and Singhanias conceive and execute projects that bedazzle *Forbes* and *Time*." Mumbai's contribution to the nation's corporate and personal tax revenues is enough to establish its primacy.

Against these blessings, the city is cursed by the presence of communal canker that troubles it occasionally. If some analysts ascribe the 1993 blasts to the Ayodhya incidents, others blame communalist elements for there troubles. If the fanatics belonging to the LET, JEM, SIMI and Al Qaeda succeed in their ulterior designs in destroying Mumbai's social and economic fabric, the city will go under. If Mumbai goes under, so does India. We all know it. Unfortunately, so do the terrorists. So not surprisingly, Mumbai remains the most targeted city.

MUMBAI IS THE FINANCIAL CAPITAL OF INDIA

In the recent years, Mumabi has been repeatedly targeted by the terrorist out fits. The reason is not far to see, as explained a little later. It is the financial capital of India. The simple way of paralysing a nation is to subvert its economy. This exactly is the aim of the anti-India ultras - both of home-grown and foreign varieties.

Of late, other towns may be coming up as industrial and commercial centers, but Mumbai still remains the hub of the nation's economy. Hence its fatal attraction for the terrorists.

MUMBAI SERIAL BLASTS : 1993

13 bomb blasts shook Mumbai on 12 March 1993. It was hell and complete may hem, and the city was under siege.

As some analysts averred, these serial blasts were to avenge the destruction of the Babari Masjid at Ayodhya in 1992. Islamist terrorists executed these blasts after a lot of planning and preparation.

The places attacked, north to south, are mentioned below :

Tuhu Centaur

Airport Centaur

Sea Rock Hotel

Worli

Parel

Nair Hospital

Masjid

Sachiralaya

VT

Bombay Stock Exchange (BSE)

Nariman Point

Colaba

Toll: 257 killed and 713 injured accused : 123

Judgement Day at the TADA Court 1993-94 Sep. Nov. 2006

12 Sep.	4 members of Memon family convicted, 3 acquitted
14 Sep.	Mohd Ghansar found guilty
18 Sep.	Asghar Mukadamm, Shahnamaz Qureshi Convicted
19 Sep.	AG Turk convicted
21 Sep.	Parvez Nasir Ahmed Sheikh Convicted
22 Sep.	Dawood Phanse, Sharif Parkar Convicted
25 Sep.	Iqbal Yusuf Sheikh, Nasim Barmare guilty
26 Sep.	5 Constables guilty, 3 other acquitted
27 Sep.	Mushtaq Tarani guilty

28 Sep.	Dawood Phanse guilty, 5 acquitted.
29 Sep.	Five Convicted
3 Oct.	Niyaz Ahmad Sheikh guilty, one acquitted
5 Oct.	Nasir Dhakla, Mohd Sheikh guilty, one acquitted
6 Oct.	Sheikh Umer, Shahid Qureshi, Zulfiqar Convicted
9 Oct.	Mohd Pawale guilty
10 Oct.	3 fishermen convicted, 2 others set free
11 Oct.	Suleman Mohd Kasam Ghante, Yusuf Khan, Rashid Umar Aluware, Abdul Aziz Gharatkar convicted.
12 Oct.	Ashfaq Kasam Hawaldar acquitted, 4 other convicted. The four convicted—Mohd Ethestam, Shahnamaz Khan, Sharif Khan Adhikari and Sajjad Alam alias Baba—were aides of 'Tiger' Memon. They had helped him in landing the arms and ammunition at Shekhadi in Rajad district and facilitating their transport to the city for the 1993 blasts.
16 Oct.	Muzamil Kadri, Khalil Nazir, Gulam Shaikh and Tusiram Surve convicted. Anant Bhoir acquitted.
17 Oct.	Sayyed Abdul Rehman Sheikh, Manoj Gupta, and Mohd Kasam Lajpuria convicted. Shakeel Shahabuddin Sheikh and Devdas Ghule acquitted.
18 Oct. 1993-94	The special TADA court convicted three Tiger Memon aides. Issaq Hajwani, 77, arrested on 1 April 1993 and released on bail in 1995, was found guilty of all charges—conspiracy, under going arms training at Sandheri and possessing 13 grenades and later throwing them in the sea near Gandharwari village. Hearing the verdict an agitated Issaq should at Judge Promod Kode, "I am innocent. You know it well, still you have held me guilty. I am suffering from heart ailment and you are aware of the fact."

His son, Sikander, found guilty, also shouted at the judge. The third accused to be found guilty was Shahnwaz Hajmani.

The TADA court has till date delivered its verdict on 72 accused, of which 53 have been convicted and 19 acquitted.

19 Oct.	Two guilty
2 Nov.	Three guilty
6 Nov.	Five guilty
9 Nov.	Four guilty
10 Nov.	Four guilty
14 Nov.	One convicted, one acquitted
15 Nov.	Four guilty
16 Nov.	Two guilty
20 Nov.	Two guilty
23 Nov.	Two guilty
24 Nov.	Two guilty
27 Nov.	One guilty, one acquitted
28 Nov.	Sanjay Dutt and four others guilty
4 Dec.	Six aides of Tiger Memon found guilty. Pronouncement of the judgement completed.

1993 Blasts: Prouncing the Judegment completed: 4 Dec. 2006

Special TADA count of Judge Promode Kode on 4 December 2006 completed pronouncing the judgement against all the 123 accused involved in the serial blasts case of 1993. On this last day, it convicted six aides of Tiger Memon who were involved in lobbing hand grenades on residents of fishermen colony in Mahim. Three people were killed in the attack and 55 injured. The convicted persons are named here:

1. Bashir Ahmed Usman Ghani Khairullah.
2. Zakir Hussain Moor Mohammad Shaikh.
3. Abdul Khan.
4. Feroze Amani Malik.
5. Moin Quireshi.
6. Salim Rahim Shaikh.

Of the total accused, 123, the court held 100 guilty, 23 were acquitted for lack of evidence or given the benefit of doulet.

List of men found guilty and their crimes

1.	Yakub Memon	:	Conspiracy
2.	Yusuf Memon	:	Same
3.	Essa Memon	:	Same
4.	Rubina Memon	:	Same
5.	MS Ghansar	:	Zaveri blast
6.	A Mukadam	:	Plaza blast
7.	S Quereshi	:	Same
8.	AG Turk	:	Century Bazaar blast
9.	PN Ahmed	:	Katha Sheikh Bazaar, Hotel Sea Rock blasts
10.	Dawood Phanse	:	Conspiracy
11.	SA Gafoor	:	Landing arms
12.	M Iqbal	:	Sahar airport blast
13.	N. Barmare	:	Airport blast
14.	Vijay Patil	:	Conspiracy
15.	A. Muleshwar	:	Transporting smuggled arms-RDX
16.	PM Mahadik	:	Same
17.	Ramesh Mali	:	Same
18.	SY Pashilkar	:	Same
19.	M. Tarani	:	Juhu Centaur blast
20.	Sarfaraz Phanse	:	RDX landing
21.	Gul Mohd Noor	:	Conspiracy
22.	Sheikh Ibrahim	:	Same
23.	Mohd Hanif	:	Same
24.	Sheikh Usman Khan	:	Same
25.	Mohd Sayyed	:	Same
26.	Niyaz Ahmed Sheikh	:	Same
27.	NA Kadar	:	Conspiracy

28.	Mohd Rafiq	:	Conspiracy, armstraining
29.	Mohd Shahid	:	RDX landing, arms training
30.	Parvez Mohd	:	Conspiracy
31.	SA Shaikh	:	RDX landing
32.	Mohd Farooq Pawle	:	Air India building, Sena Bhavan blasts
33.	Yeshwant Nagu Bhoinkar	:	Providing trawler for RDX
34.	AD Shaikhdare	:	Same
35.	Shahjahan Ibrahim	:	Same
36.	SM Kasam	:	Conspiracy
37.	Yusuf Khan Qayoom	:	Transporting arms, RDX
38.	R. Alware	:	Transporting RDX
39.	AA Gharatkar	:	Landing RDX
40.	Sajjad Alam	:	Same
41.	Sharif Khan Abbas	:	Same
42.	Shahnawaz Khan	:	Conspiracy
43.	Shaikh Mohd	:	Same
44.	M. Umar	:	Possessing weapons
45.	Khalil Ahmed	:	Same
46.	Gulam Hafiz	:	Same
47.	T. Dhondu	:	Sloring RDX
48.	Sayyed Abdul	:	RDX landing
49.	M. Bhanwarilal	:	Same
50.	Mohd Kasam	:	Same
51.	Irraq Hajwani	:	Armstraining
52.	Sikandar Hajwani	:	Same
53.	Shahnawaz Hajwani	:	Same
54.	U Potdar	:	Bribing Customs Officer
55.	SM Shaikh	:	RDX landing
56.	Jayant Garav	:	Same
57.	SS Talwadekar	:	Allowing RDX landing

58. A Qureshi : Possessing arms
59. A Rehman : Same
60. M. Yusuf : Same
61. SA Yusuf : Same
62. J Kadri : Same
63. FAF Ahmed : Same
64. J. Gambas : RDX landing
65. A. Surti : Possessing arms
66. SI Kadri : Transporting arms
67. RL Jain : Transporting RDX
68. A. Patel : Possessing grenades
69. F. Motorwala : Conspiracy
70. Mujib Podkar : RDX landing
71. EM Tufel : Possessing pistol
72. AS Mubarak : Possessing rifle
73. AA Ahmed : Possessing arms
74. MR Musa : RDX landing
75. Rubina Baya : Arranging conspiracy meeting
76. I Ghawte : Parking RDX-Laden Scooter
77. Mulchand Shah : Operating hawala account for Tiger Memon
78. Ejaz Pathan : Conspiracy
79. MD Khan : Possessing arms
80. NM Khan : Storage of RDX
81. LA Khan : Same
82. SS Khan : Conspiracy
83. AA Sayed : Possessing arms
84. MS Sayed : RDX landing
85. RK Singh : Taking bribe
86. M. Ahmed : Carrying weapons from Sanjay dutt's house
87. SN Thapa : Conspiracy

88.	Sanjay Dutt	:	Possessing arms
89.	Y. Nallwalla	:	Destroying proof
90.	Kerse Adjenia	;	Same
91.	Z. Kazi	:	Aiding terrorist acts
92.	Samir Hingora	;	Conspiracy
93.	Rusi Mulla	:	Keeping pistol given by Dutt's friend
94.	Ibrahim Musa Chouhan	:	Carrying arms to Dutt's house
95.	Bashir Ahmad Usman Ghani Khairullah	:	Grenade attack
96.	Zakir Hussain Noor Mohd	:	Same
97.	Abdul Khan	;	Same
98.	Firoze Amani Malik	:	Same
99.	Moin Quereshi	:	Same
100.	SR Shaikh	:	Conspiracy

Sentencing the accused: Some select cases

17 Jul 2007 — Resuming the sentencing in the 1993 Mumbai serial blasts case after a month, Special Judge PD Kode sentenced the following two to life imprisonment and slapped hefty fines on them:

1. Imtiaz Ghavte, sentenced to life and fined Rs. 2,27,000 for his involvement in hatching the conspiracy and executing it. He was found guilty under several sections of the IPC, the Terrorist and Dirruptive Activities (Prevention) Act (TADA) and the Explosive Substances Act.

   The prosecution case was that Ghavte participated in RDX landing at Shekhadı. He was present at the

Al Husseini building, where vehicle bombs were readied. He planted RDX in a scooter at Dhanji street in south Mumbai on 12 March but the bomb did not explode.

Hence he was found guilty for attempt to murder and damage to property.

The Judge noted that the prosecution did not press for death sentence, as there was no explosion and Ghavte was HIV positive and medically unfit.

2. Nasim Barmare too was found guilty of criminal conspiracy and committing Lerrorist act not resulting in death, among other offences. He was sentenced to life and imposed a five of Rs. 2,30,000.

   He was found guilty of acquring weapon training, participating in a conspiracy meetings, preparing vehicle bombs and hurling hand grenades at the Sahar Airport. However, no one was injured and there was no damage to property.

3. SN Thapa, the former Additional Customs Commissioner could not be present as the suffered from viral fever.

18 July, 2007 — The special TADA Court awarded death sentence to three men convicted in the 1993 serial blasts case for planting explosives. Abdul Ghani Ismael Turk, Mohd Mushtaq Musa Tarani and Pervez Ahmad Nasir Shaikh are the first among the 100 people convicted in the case to get capital punishment.

19 July, 2007 — The special TADA Court sentenced three more Tiger Memon aides to death in the

1993 serial blasts case. Two of them—Asghar Mukadam and Shahnawaz Qureshi—planted the bomb that killed 10 persons at Plaza Cinema in Dadar and the third, Shoal Ghansar, parked an RDX-laden scooter at Zaveri Bazaar where 17 person died in the explosion.

The death sentences are subject to confirmation by the Supreme Court.

Now follow brief details of the three accused.

Asghar Mukadam, 48

Special Judge PD Kode first called Mukadam to the dock. First accused arrested in the case, his statement to then Deputy Commissioner of Police Rakesh Maria, who cracked the case, led to many arrests. Mukadam worked for Tiger Memon as an accountant.

Mukadam not only parked on RDX–laden Maruti van, which exploded at 3.13 PM, at Plaza Cinema, he also drove three others—Convicts Mushtaq Tarane and Parvez Shaikh and absconding accused Anwar Theba—to Centaur Hotel in Juhu, Airport Centaur and Hotel Sea Rock in Bandra, where the three planted bombs. Mukadam was also present when RDX was being filled into the vehicles a day before the blasts at Al-Hussaini building in Mahim.

He had argued that since he was employed with Memon, he was "bound to do what his master said". Judge Kode said: "the principle of agency was not applicable. Tiger Memon was involved in smuggling and he (Mukadam) joined him knowingly."

The Judge sentenced Mukadam to death on three counts: conspiracy; commission of a terrorist act causing death; and murder.

Shahnawaz Qureshi, 44

He was convicted for accompanying Mukadam to Plaza Cinema and parking the Maruti van laden with RDX. He was also convicted for undergoing training in Pakistan and for participating in the landing of arms and ammunition at Shekhadi.

Judge Kode ruled: "He has been convicted for conspiracy. The training was effectively used. He took the van and gave courage to Asgar. He has been held liable for conspiracy in which innocent people were killed."

He was sentenced to death on three counts: Conspiracy; commission of a terrorist act causing death; and murder.

Shoaib Ghansar, 44

He was convicted for driving an RDX-laden scooter and parking it in front of Narayandas Jewellers in Zaveri Bazaar. The bomb went off at 3.05 PM and killed 17 people. The explosion created a crater in the road. The judge said: "His confession states that after parking the scooter in Zaveri Bazaar, he went to masjid and offered namaz begging forgiveness for his sins. This means he knew what he was doing."

The Judge sentensed him to death on two counts : Commission of a terrorist act resulting in death, and murder. Ghansar was in Maruti Van with Mukadam when the latter dropped off three co-accused at three hotels where bombs were placed. He was also present when RDX was being filled into vehicles.

20 July, 2007

Judge PD kode awarded death sentence to Mohd Iqbal Mohd Yusuf Shaikh for his role in the blast conspiracy, though a scooter bomb planted by him on 12 March, 1993 in central Bombay did not explode. He was also convicted for ferrying fellow convict Nasim Barmare, who has already been sentenced to life imprisonment by the court, to a flyover near the international airport where the latter threw a hand grenade.

With this the number of accused given death sentence in the case has risen to seven. Kode held that his case fell in the category of "rarest of rare", and he deserved maximum punishment due to the extent Shaikh was involved in two separate terrorists acts on the same day.

Beside the death sentence, Kode also awarded life imprisonment to two others. Former Additional Collector of Customs (Preventive) Somnath Thapa, convicted for allowing the landing of arms and explosives prior to the blasts, was shown leniency and awerded a life sentence since he is suffering from cancer.

Bashir Khairulla, who was part of a group that threw hand grenades at the Fishermen's Colony in central Mumbai to incite communal violence, was sentenced to life imprisonment.

So far, with these awards, to the court has awarded sentences to 87 of the 100 accused convicted for their role in the 1993 serial blasts. 13 persons, including actor Sanjay Dutt, convicted for illegal weapons possession, are still to receive their sentences.

24 July, 2007

The special TADA court sentenced to death three convicts—Zakir Hussain Shaikh (34), Feroz Amani Malik (37), Abdul Aketar Khan (49)— who had lobbed grenades at the Fishermen's colony in Mahim on 12 March, 1993, killing three persons and injuring six. An accomplice, Moin Qureshi (31), who was 17 at the time was spared the death sentence because of his tender age, and awarded life imprisonment,

25 July, 2007

One person, Farooq Pawle was sentenced to death for planting a vehide filled with explosives and fitted with timer device near the Air India building and Shiv Sena Head quarters, Sena Bhavan.

Pawle becomes the 11th convict to he awarded capital punishment for his involvement in carrying out 12 serial blasts on 12 March, 1193, that killed 257 people and injured over 700.

The resulting blast killed four persons and injured 38.

27 July, 2007

Mumbai. It was a black Friday for the Memons, India's first family of terror. Special TADA Court Judge PK Kode sentenced three Memons to life imprisonments and gave Yaqub Memon—the most educated among them—the death penalty for conspiring to cause the 12 March, 1993 serial blasts which ripped Mumbai —then Bombay —apart on a Friday leaving 257 people dead and over 700 injured.

The Judge made it clear that he was not passing the harsh order because of the "close relationship" there Memons shared with the absconding mastermind, Tiger Memon, but because there was evidence against them individually for their acts.

On hearing his death sentence—the 12th handed down in this case by the court—the 45 year-old Yaqub exclaimed loudly, "Oh Lord, for give him for he known not what he does." He was quoting from the Bible, not the Quran. He was the last of the Memons to be read out his sentence, but he must have known it was coming. Before him, his two brothers had been given the lighter life imprisonment on health grounds: Yusuf, 34, suffered from schizophrenia and Essa, 33, diagnosed with a brain tumour.

The Memon family was first to be declared guilty in the case on 12 September, 2006, when the judgement started to be handed down. Of the eight who stood trial, four were held guilty and three acquitted. Their father had died earlier while on bail. Ten months later, an alder-looking Yaqub brought the curtain down on the dozen death sentences handed down in the tortuous trial that had spanned over 14 years.

Of the 100 convicted till date, 96 have so far been sentenced, none of the four left has been convicted of any crime that could invite death punishment.

Some brief details about the four Memons held guilty by the court follow:

Yoqub Memon, 45

Conspired to caused the March 1993 Blasts ; arranged for finance and managed its disbursement among co-accused. Also arranged for air tickets to send men for arms training to Pakistan via Dubai; possessed arms in notified area.

Sentence: Death and a fine of Rs. 3.75 lakh.

Essa Memon, 33

Found guilty of criminal conspiracy to cause the blasts, allowed flat to be used for carrying out terrorist activities.

Sentence: Life in prison and a fine of Rs. 1.5 lakh.

Yusuf Memon, 34

Found guilty of criminal conspiracy to cause blasts. A schizophrenic, his sentence as also Essa's was reduced on health grounds.

Sentence: Life in prison and a fine of Rs. 1.5 lakh.

Rubine Memon, 39

Wife of the eldest Memon brothers, Suleiman Found guilty of conspiracy to cause blasts and of letting her car being used for carrying arms and ammunition. Hence found guilty of aiding the blasts.

31st July, 2007

Sentence: Life term and a fine of Rs. 1 lakh.

Special TADA Court judge PD Kode sentenced actor Sanjay Dutt to 6 years' rigorous imprisonment for the legal possession of arms and fined him Rs. 25,000 Dutt has already served 16 months in jail as an under trial.

Dutt's friend Rusi Mulla was let off under the Probation of offenders Act.

The other (last) two convicts Kersi Adjania and Yusuf Nalwalla, were sentenced to two years' rigorous imprisonment and five years respectively. But Adjania was granted bail for three months to enable him to appeal in a higher court.

Following the sentencing of Sanjay Dutt and his friends, the process of hearing and sentencing in the 1993 Mumbai serial blasts case by the TADA court is complete.

Khaki disgrace : TADA Court Convicts policemen: 1993 blasts

If some Coast Guard officers allegedly let of 8 LET militants for a consideration of Rs. 10 lakh, five policemen were found guilty in the Special TADA Court hearing the 1993 Bombay blasts case.

It was the first time in history that policemen brought ignominy to their organisation.

Sub-Inspector (SI) Vijay Patil, constables Pandarinath Mohadik, Ashok Muneshwar, Ramesh Mali and Shrikrishna Pashilkar of Shrivardhan police station in Raigad, were out on patrol on the night of 9 January, 1993, when they intercepted trucks laden with RDX AK- 56 guns, 9 MM Pistols and ammunition. But they chose to look the other may and allowed the trucks smooth passage. The explosives in the trucks were used in the (1993 Bombay) blasts.[2]

Patil was found guilty of being party to the conspiracy because, as head of the police team, he allowed the trucks to pass through", said Special Judge PD Kode . "The others were only following Patil's instructions, hence they were not held guilty on the court of conspiracy, but convicted for aiding and abetting terrorist act." Constables Krishna Mokal, Krishna Pingle and Manohar More, who were part of the patrol, were acquitted for want of sufficient evidence against them. Patil broke down in court soon after the verdict was announced.

"The consignment arrived at Shekhadi Coast by vessel from Pakistan and the policemen allowed its passage at the Ghondgar Phata after taking Rs. 7 lakh as bribe from main accused Tiger Memon's men", said a CBI officer. Interestingly, the men on trucks did not have cash on them but some silver bricks. "Patil took the silver bricks and told them they could have them back when they brought money", said the CBI officer.

Patil allowed the trucks to pass a he had received instructions through the co-accused Uttam Podar, a landing agent, and Jaywant Gurav, a customs official. " It was at the instructions of the customs official that the police cooperated with the men after accepting Rs. 7 lakh", said the officer. The consignment was taken to Tiger's Al-Hussein building at Mahim.

"As policeman, they should have acted responsibly. It would have saved innocent lives. It is a serious lapse. The blasts would not have taken place, had the Cops taken action that night", said Special Public Prosecutor Ujjwal Nikam

The policemen were taken into custody and their bail bonds were cancelled.

Film on 1993 Mumbai Blasts

Anurag Kashpyap had made a film - called *Black Friday* — on the 1993 Mumbai blasts. It was based on journalist Hussain Zaidi' book *Black Friday* . It had faced a lot of trouble with the Censor Board and the TADA court. Finally, the Board wanted the Director to remove the tag line: The True Story of the Bombay Blasts of 1993. It was complied with. Majid Memon filed a case against the Director of the *Black Friday* , accusing him of prejudice against the complainant. The film was cleared by the TADA court after a legal battle was won by Kashyap.

After the Director had worked his may through the Censor Board and TADA court, 27 January 2005 was fixed for the premiere of the film. Everything seemed to have fallen into place. And them, a day before the premiere, they got a stay order. So it was back to square one.

Verdict in 1993 RSS office attack in Chanai : 21 Jun 2007

A designated court, under the now defunct TADA Act, on 21 January 2007 sentenced three Islamists — Abubacker Siddique, Hyder Ali, [the late Imam Ali who was killed in a police encounter in Bangalore in 2002 after he escaped from prison] and Kaja Nizamuddin to life imprisonment for their role in a bomb blast at RSS Headquarters, Channai in 1993, in which 11 persons were killed and seven others injured.

The TADA court, how ever, acquitted four others, including Al-Umma founder SAB asha, of any involvement in the blast, that is significant in the sense that it marked the first instance of the use of the RDX by the Islamists in South India. The blast took place in central Channai at the Tamil Nadu Head Office of RSS on 8 August 1993, sending shock waves in the country.

Seven men were sentenced to five years' rigorous imprisonment for various subsidiary roles in the incident; six of them under Sec. 3(4) of TADA for harbouring principal suspects and abetting the offence.

In a 505 – page judgement, designated Judge T. Ramasami made an interesting observation, as he blamed lack of religious tolerance as the motivating factor behind the crime, equally blaming a section of the society for needless criticism and condemnation of the Holy Quran and the life of Prophet Mohammad that led to the "heinous and in human crime."

The court found four persons mentioned in the opening para guilty of procuring eight kg. of explosives, storing it in a godown, priparing bombs and planting them in the RSS office. The court sentenced Siddique, Hyder and Nizamuddin to life imprisonment on 11 courts, All three were found guilty of committing terrorist acts leading to death under Sec. 3(2) of TADA, conspiracy under Sec 120-B IPC and murder on 11 counts under Sec 302 of IPC. They were also convicted under various other provisions of IPC, Explosives Act, and Explosive substance Act. They were handed over a ten-year prison term for causing grievous injuries. All sentences are to sun concurrently

Rafique Ahmad was found guilty of possessing incriminating material that "showed he was promoting enemity between

Muslims and Hindus in a manner prejudicial to the maintenance of religious harmony", and was, therefore, sentenced to three year's rigorous imprisonment under sec 153 - A of IPC.

Shahabuddin, who had burnt two spirts belonging to Imam Ali, a principal conspirator, in a bid destroy evidence, was sentenced to a five-year term under Sec. 201 of IPC for destruction of evidence.

Six others—Abdul Rahim, Ahmed, Gnaniar, Syed Mohd Bukhari, SK Ahmed Ali, Mohd Zubair and Moosa Moinuddin—were found guilty of harbouring the main suspects under Sec. 3(4) of TADA.

Mukhtar Ahmed, SA Basha, Ameenuddin Sheriff and Mohd Abdul Aslam were acquitted of all charges.

Jihad Committee founder Palani Baba, an accused in the case, was murdered in the late 1990, while Mushtaq Ahmad, a key conspirator, is yet to be apprehended.

Many of them had undergone long years in prison before they obtained bail, and the judge said the jail terms would be set off against the time they had already served in jail.

The case was handed over to the CBI after it was found that RDX and PETN had been used in the explosion and that it had inter-State ramification.[3]

Coming within a few months of the Mumbai serial blasts of March, 1993, and in the year Immediately following the destruction of Babri Masjid (i.e. disputed structure in Ayodhya) the incident created panic and concern in Tamil Nadu.

As many as 18 persons were listed as accused in the case. Some more information, in specific terms, is appended below:

- Three of the accused were missing from the verdict today. One of them, Imam Ali, was gunned down by police in Bangalore on 29 September, 2002 after he escaped from custody in Madurai, Another, Jihad Committee Founder-President Palani Baba, was hacked to death by suspected RSS sympathisers. On 29 January, 1997. The third, Mushtaq Ahmad, is still absconding.
- The charge sheet in the case was filed on 8 June, 1994.

- Of the 431 persons cited as witnesses, 224 were examined during the Course of the trial which commenced on 7 August, 1995.

Coimbatore serial blasts : 14 February, 1998

Three were 19 bomb explosions in the textile town of Coimbatore on 14 February 1998, leaving 58 people dead and over 200 injured.

"More than nine years after the Coimbatore serial blasts, the Special Court trying the case will tomorrow (1 August 2007) pronouncement its judgement on whether the 220 crore charges against the 166 accused hold or not." This is the report in a daily datelined : Chennai, 31 July, 2007.

17,000-page charge sheet, prepared by a Special Investigation Term (SIT), said a seven-member suicide squad had been assigned the task of assassinating the then Union Home Minister LK Advani, who was in the town to address a public meeting.

The accused include people's Democratic Party (PDP) leader Abdul Nazar Mahdani (also spelt Maudhany), leaders of the banned Al Umma, and Syed Ahmed Basha and his deputy Mohd Ansari .

Sessions Judge K. Uthirapathy "is expected to pronounce the sentences after 6 August (2007), when he would start hearing the arguments by the defence"— this is the stage after he would have announced the judgement on 1 August on 166 accused as being 'guilty 'or 'not guilty'.

A day before the judgement day, " a tight security Cordon is in place to ward off any trouble in the town, known to be a communal hotbed".

The bomb blasts had gone off on the afternoon of 14 February 1998, just minutes before Advani was to deliver his speech. Apart from lives lost, Rs. 14 crore worth of property was damaged.

The SIT of the Crime Branch - CID (CB-CID), which probed the case along with the city police, arrested 168 people. While most of the arrests took place in Tamil Nadu, Kerala, Karnataka and Andhra Pradesh, one of the accused was held in Kolkata. Most of the accused belonged to the Al-Umma, founded by Basha and the Jihad Committee. Both the outfits were banned soon after the bombings.

While one of the accused subsequently turned on approver, another died in custody.

The Charge sheet says the Coimbatore bombing was code named 'Operation Alla-u-Akbar' and executed to avenge the killing of 18 Muslims in communal riots and police firing triggered by the murder of a traffic police constable in November, 1997.

A communally sensitive town since the early 1990s, Coimbatore has seen several incidents of violence and murder. The riots that followed the killing of police constable had virtually crippled the town for months.

In the White Paper he tabled in the Assembly, then Chief Minister M Karunanidhi blamed the Babri Masjid demolition in December, 1992 for the spread of religious fundamentalism in Tamil Nadu. He explained further:

> "The conspiracy to assassinate Advani when he visited Coimbatore had been hatched by Al Umma Chief Basha, his Deputy and General Secretary Mohd Ansari and PDP leader Mohdani in Kerala and Coimbatore."

Time line of the case

- 14 February, 1998: 19 bomb blasts across Coimbatore; 58 dead and over 200 injured.
- 7 April, 2000: Special Court constituted to try cases.
- 23 October, 2000. Charges framed.
- 7 March, 2002. Trial commences; 1,300 witnesses examined.
- June, 2006. Prosecution and defence arguments begin.
- 10 April, 2007. Arguments end.
- 13 June, 2007. The Judge rules that the verdict will be pronounced on 1 August, 2007.
- 1 August, 2007. The judgement is out.

The Prime Accused

Abdul Nazar Mahadani. He is the leader of the People's Democratic Party, and a prominent Islamic leader of Kerala. Top Keerala politicians, including Chief Minister VS

Achuthanandan, have been seeking his release. He is also said to enjoy support of Tamil Nadu Chief Minister M Karunanidhi. This 2007, in the White Paper mentioned above, the same Karunanidhi had said in the state assembly in 1998 that Mohdani was part of the conspiracy to assassinate Advani.

Syed Ahmed Basha. He is Al-Umma founder, who rose very fast to prominence. Basha is also named in the blast at an RSS office. His brother and son are also accused in the Coimbatoor Case.

Mohd Ansari. He is deputy and General Secretary of Al-Umma.

Serial blasts in Coimbatore: Some relevant question: June 2007

The serial blasts ripped Coimbator in February, 1998, killing 59 and leaving over 200 maimed or injured

As the judgements day nears (special court in Coimbatore trying the bomb blasts case, is scheduled to announce the date of the verdict on 13 Jun 2007) for this case, "a 47-minute documentary whipping up sympathy for Abdul Nasar Mohdani, a key accused in the case, has been quietly doing the rounds in Tamil Nadu, Kerala and Gulf countries", report a news story in a daily[4] dated, June, 2007.

Who is Abdul Nasar Mahdani?

He is the key accused in the case and one of the 156 accused in the case, most of whom are the members of the banned Al Umma outfit, facing trial for the past eight years. The prosecution and defence arguments in the case were completed a week back and the judgement was reserved.

Mahdani, Accused No. 14, had been charged under Sections 302 IPC (Murder), 3o7 IPC (Attempt to Murder), 153-A IPC (creating hatred among the communities), Section 5 of the Explosives Act and Section 25 of the Arms Act, for "collecting and transferring explosives to the town, ripped by a series of bomb blasts on 14 February, 1998."

The Kerala Government has been stepping up pressure on Tamil Nadu to release Mahdani on bail. The ruling DMK has been providing special treatment for him.

As recent as 18 May 2007, Kerala's CPI (M) State Secretary Pinarayi Vijayan called on Mahdani at the Coimbatore prison where he has been lodged since 1998, spending nearly an hour with the PDP leader.

Film makes a case for him

While all these exertion by Kerala to press Tamil Nadu to release Mahdani on bail are going on, the film titled Kaithijen Kathai (A Prisoner's Story) makes out a strong case for Mahdani's release among the Muslims.

The film, produced by Media Steps managed by Aloor Shanavas, 25, who claims to be a Human Rights activist, traces the "Impressive political growth" of Mahdani's Islamic Sevak Singh (ISS) and its transformation to the People's Democratic Party (PDP) after its ban, his incarceration, eight years of torture in Coimbatore prison, lamentation by his parents and strong condemnations by Muslim political outfits and PDP colleagues.

But the attempt at poignancy with visuals of Mahdani, "earlier weighing 116 kg. and now a more 46 kg", interviews and speeches of supporters, the background score and the underlying note of "injustice" hopes to whip up emotions even as the special Court in Coimbatore is scheduled to announce the date of the verdict on 13 June (2007).

The CD with Tamil Narration and interviews in both Tamil and Malyalam had seen brisk circulation, free of cost, in parts of Tamil Nadu, particularly Chanai and Coimbator Kerala besides Malayasia, Singapore, Dubai and a few more Gulf countries. The young director of the Mahdani documentary is now in the process of producing it in English.

The documentary is an outright effort aimed at proving that Mahadani and so many Muslims arrested in this case are innocent. The relatives, the politicians and the innuendo are weaved together in a web of possibilities all meant at a make-believe: "the police the system, judiciary at all have joined hands to malign the Muslim community and paint it in all the lurid colours. The producers must answer one simple question: "Is it possible in the first decade of the century, and that too in India?" It is, of course, important to note what the producers of this documentary say, and equally important to judge its credibility.

Shanavas says: "The documentary is about how Mahadani and several more innocent Muslims have been languishing in prisons. In fact, the DMK won Muslim votes on the assurance that the government order passed by the Jayalalethaa regime, restricting Mahadani's movement to the prison, would be revoked"

The documentary begins with visuals of Mahdani, as leader of the ISS, nearly a decade ago, addressing public meeting and goes on to show his arrest by the Tamil Nadu police in connection with the Coimbatore blasts case. The back ground narration in Tamil by Shanavas question the 'fairness' of Mahdani's arrest and trial.

At one point, the camera grabs bites of his parents, Abdus Samad and Asma Beevi, at their home town in Kollam, in Kerala, pans to public speeches by leaders of the Tamil Nadu Muslim Munnetra Kazhagam (TMMK) in Tamil Nadu, exhorting the state government to release Mahadani on bail. One TMMK leader is seen proudly declaring that 113 legislators and all the political parties, 'including the BJP', in Kerala, have demanded his release. This only proves Mahadani's greatness", says he.

The film also shows good work done by Mahadani for Muslims in the social fields. There are shots of orphans in the Kollam's Al Anwar Islamia University, established by Mahadani, appealing for his release. The film ends with visuals of wives of Muslim prisoners linked to the Coimbatore Case speaking in emotion-choked voice of their plight and that of their children.

It concludes with a challenge, as the narrator says: "Let those who have faith in the system reply to this (the agony of the prisoner's families)". The film raises some disturbing issues.

It is indeed interesting, nay surprising, that this daily - the doughty and intrepid Indian Express—has no uncomfortable questions to ask of the producers of this film, nor biting and sarcastic comments to accompany the controversial, biased, and essentially one-sides narration of this news story as is its wont in such cases. Some simple questions are added here:

- What is the motive behind the film? Is it to vilify the entire Indian judiciary and the political dispensation? Is it to prejudge the case before the court announce its verdict? Is it to influence the Court, come as the film has on the eve of the day of its verdict on the case —perhaps, a fortnight away.
- Is the film meant to bring disrepute to the Indian polity Indian judicial system, Indian police, and even Indian public and the intelligentsia for failing to rise to the defence of the innocent Muslims — a wronged minority.
- At a more sinister level, is it aimed at generating Hindu-Muslim disharmony, if not hostility. At the best of times, the Hindu-Muslim relationship remains generally strained. The attacks and killings of the RSS members periodically in various parts of Kerala is indicative of this malady. Why provide a spark to inflammable mixture?
- At another level, one can accuse the film and its producers of inciting anti-India sentiment among the Muslims not only within India but also in foreign lands, Viz the Gulf Countries.
- A more question is about funding : What is the source of money behind producing this film? Equally important, who are the people behind the Media Steps? What are the antecedents of Aloor Shanavas? In India, we have Human Rights activists and Human Rights activists whose motives often are anti government, anti-majority and at times even anti-national — all in the names of protecting minority — a enphemism for Indian Muslims — rights!

It is time the media and authorities look into the activities of people like Shanavas and motive of films like the one discussed above — where sole motive is to whip up sympathy for people like Mahdam, the key accused in the coimbatore blasts care.

The politicians and political parties will have their selfish motives to paint individuals like Mahdani as milky white because they need him to deliver the votes of his followers of 155/PDP en block.

If in Kerala, it is CPM-led Lift Democratic Front and the Congress (I)-led United democratic Front vying for Muslim votes, in Tamil Nadu, it is DMK and AI-ADMK doing the same. This is the importance of Muslim Community and their vote. Hindus divided among the political parties, Unmindful and often contemptuous of Hindu religious interests, are taken for granted. It is the Muslim votes that makes the wining balance. Hence the compulsion of every political party — bar the BJP _ to woo the Muslims, which is cause enough for the parties like the BJP and Shiv Sena to accuse them of appeasement'!

Judgement out: Criminal Justice system draws flake: 1 August, 2007

On 1 Aug 2007, punishment was handed down to 153 of the 166 accused brought to the trial. Under normal circumstances, the successful prosecution of almost all the accused in a major tourism case should be a cause of public satisfaction. But the investigation, prosecution and judgements in the 1998 Coimbatore bomb blasts case have left a lot to desire — raising some disturbing question about the criminal justice system of India.

Even though a Special Court was constituted to handle the care, nine long years separated the crime — in which 58 persons lost their lives — and the punishment. Because of this unconscionable interregnum of nine years, "the verdict will hold little meaning for the survivors of the blasts and the relatives of the victims. As the case dragged, public sympathy shifted to many of the accused who were held on minor charges, but could not get bail. A stand out example of an accused morphing into a victim is Abdul Nasser Maudhany, the founder of the Kerala-based PDP, who was acquitted of all charge after more than nine years in prison". This is a daily dated 2 August, 2007, voicing its criticism of India's judicial system, in an editorial appropriately titled "Making victims of the accused".[5]

So many analysts have no doubt found valid reasons to criticise our system where cases drag on and on. In this particular case, the prolonged trial gave the ailing Maudhani a martyr's halo as the trial drew to a close. The PDP leader appeared to have been denied bail because of the sensational nature of the case; and also because he being one of three leading accused was believed to have a role in the horrible acts of violence. All this may non look ridiculous since he has now been acquitted of all changes in the Coimbatore blasts case.

But denial of bail to the accused here need a fresh look. Surely justice requires that bail must he be the norm, and imprisonment through an inordinately long trial period the exception, especially when the accused are unlikely to run away from the reach of the law. People can't be blamed if they quote the contrast between the treatment meted out to Maudhuani in this case with Sanjay Dutt in 1993 Mumbai blast case. Dutt who was eventually handed down a long term in prison was granted the bail while Maudhani was denied liberty for nearly a decade before his acquittal.

There is another aspect related to such long running trials. Although 153 of the accused have been convicted, the verdict having been deferred in respect of five others, many of them face relatively minor charges. Indeed, there would be many convicted after the sentences are announced, who are likely to walk free, with the period they spent in jail being set off against their sentence. Barring two who were arrested a year later, all the 166 accused brought to trial were arrested in 1998, within a year of the blasts. They have thus spent close to nine years in jail. Only 69 among them have been found guilty of conspiracy; the other 83 have been convicted for less serious offences under the Indian Penal Code, and under the explosive substances Act, the Arms Act, and the Tamil Nadu properties (Prevention of Damages and Loss) Act.

Literally, in the case of many of the accused, the trial was the punishment. Crime and punishment in this case is yet another painful reminder that India's criminal justice system is in the need of major structural reforms.

It needs to the stated that the Coimbatore long-running trial was not an exception – in fact it is part of the norm. If this took nine years to reach the termination stage, the 1993 Mumbai blast case took 14 years for the same. And in the July, 2006 train blasts case, police took a year to file the charge sheet.

To end on a familiar theme, in the case of some accused in the 1993 Mumbai blasts case, the sentence awarded was less than the time they had already spent in prison. Consequently, they walked free.

PARLIAMENT UNDER ATTACK: 13 DECEMBER, 2001

India has suffered terrorism for decades but its worst nightmare of a terrorist attack came on 13 December, 2001. That was the day when the very heart of the Indian democracy came under attack. Three (or four, the police and intelligence agencies were unable to put an exact number on them) terrorists gained access to the premises through the main gated entrance manned by the security personal and reached the very doors of the circular building of India's Parliament in New Delhi.

The situation was saved for India and the world not only by the armed guards deployed around the building who immediately comforted the intruders by engaging them in fire fight but also by the civilians manning the door who shut them immediately on hearing the gun shots. Not only were the ultras shut out of the building, each each of the terrorists was killed by the security personnel who themselves suffered nine fatalities including a civilian.

One shudders to think of the catastrophy if even one of the terrorists had succeeded into entering the house, as the entire political leadership of the nation, including the Prime Minister AB Vajpayee, was inside.

India ordered total mobilisation of its defence forces. The military was on the borders for one year, waiting for the command "go"

It is a known fact that during this one year's active deployment, India twice 'almost' ordered the troops across its borders with Pakistan which, too, understandably had moved its forces to the borders. Anyway, the dangerous stand-off was over once India with drew its forces from the borders, with Pakistan following suit.

The active hostilities might be over after a year or so, but the consequent developments to the 13 December, 2001 attack are nowhere near its end.

A trial court in 2002 awarded death sentence to Mohd Afzal, Shaukat Hussain Guru and SAR Geelani, a Delhi University lecture. As India unduly delayed the execution, a member of Hum Rights activists started appealing for mercy for Afjal's and then there was a queue of such appellants. Even after the

Supreme Court on 12 January, 2007 dismissed Afzal's curative pleas seeking review of its order upholding his death sentence, the torrent of mercy pleas has not staunched.[6]

Mercy plea for Mohammad Afzal

- "All those who are supporting the demands for clemency for Afzal Guru are traitors. Ghulam Nabi Azad for Azad is a traitor"

  Rajnath Singh President, BJP

- " Terrorists like Afzal Guru should be shot at the time of arrest and time should not be wasted in long court proceedings if the government wants to finish terrorism in the Country."

Ms. Bitta, Chairman, Anti-Terrorist Front, at New Delhi, 27.10.06

Sequence of events since conviction:

- 2002 the trial court awarded Afzal, Shaukat and Geelani death sentence. Shaukat's wife, Afsan Guru, got five years' imprisonment for conspiracy.
- The Delhi High Court in October, 2003 upheld the death penality of Afzal and Shaukat while acquitting Geelani and Afsan.
- Two-judge bench of the Supreme Court in August, 2005 confirmed death to Afzal and granted reprieve to Shaukat
- In September, 2005, the apex court dismissed the review petition filed by Afzal following which the only available remedy was a curative petition.
- On 13 December, 2006, exact five years after the attack, Afzal filed the curative petition pinning hopes that the court will take cognisance of his plea that he was not given fair trial. He complained of being denied a counsel of his choice and alleged that *amicus curie*, who defended his case, was unacceptable to him, which resulted in a grave miscarriage of justice sufficient to discard his

conviction. Under Article 21 of the Constitution, no person could be deprived of his life or personal liberty except according to the procedure established by the law.

- According to Afzal's curative petition, settled by senior advocate Indira Jaising, the right to representation by a legal practioner of one's choice guaranteed under Article 22(1) is regarded as vital and fundamental for safeguarding personal liberty in all legal systems. On this ground, the impugned judgement ought to be set aside.
- Quoting rights contained in the International Convention on Civil and Political Rights that a person accused of a criminal offence had a right to be defended by an effective Counsel during detention, trial and appeal, Afzal demanded mercy. The European Court of Human Rights to the extent that the essences of legal aid not end with the nomination of a lawyer and extended to replacing him in case he was unable to fulfil his duties.
- 12 June 2007. The Supreme Court dismissed Afzal's curative pleas seeking review of its August, 2005 order upholding his death sentence. The court also turned down the plea of Shaukat Guru, who is sentenced to ten years.
- A bench of three senior most judges of the Supreme Court comprising Chief Justice YK Sabharwal, Chief Justice - designate KG Bala Krishnan and Justice BN Agarwal along with justice PP Naolekar disposed of the petitions on 12 June after a month -long in Camera hearing. Justice Neolikar was part of the two-judge Bench that uphild Afzal's conviction in Aug 2005.
- The court hold that there was no infirmity in its previous order thereby holding Afzal's contentions devoid of any merit. Afzal is facing death sentence for his role in plotting the attack on Parliament on 13 December, 2001.

With this decision of the highest court of the land, parliament attack convict Mohd Afzal facing the gallows, can now court on President mercy alone. The dismissal leaves no lagal remedy with Afzal to appose the death penality except for the mercy petition filed by his family before the President. The President is learnt to have called for the opinion of the Union Home Ministry (MHA) "whose reply is still awailed". This unconscionable delay on the part of this Ministry, obviously actuated by political motives of the ruling combine, the UPA, is the source of plethora of mercy pleas by all and sundry

This deliberate dilly-dallying by a nodal ministry on the life and death issue for a nation, does not speak well of a nation's will to fight the terrorism that has claimed over 80,000 lives on the last court, which continues to mount. It is no surprise that analysts assert that it is time India has a declaratory policy on terrorism. Any soft-pedalling on the issue and not carrying out Supreme Court's order on such an important threat to nation's security will only further encourage and embolden the terrorist to enhance the frequency and the fatal potential of their dastardly in human attacks.

In the attack on Parliament, nine security personnel lost their lives fighting the militants. The families of these martyrs have been demanding justice by awarding death to all the accused in the case. At the same time, Human Rights activitsts who are pleading mercy for Afzal are creating pressure on the government and some sections of Indian society against his execution.

Finding the government's silence on the issue too disturbing, these families returned the bravery medals (awerded to their deceased kin) to the Government, to protest its inaction on the issue, on the 5th anniversary of the terrorist attack on Parliament (13 December, 2006).

Queue for Mercy Plea: So many are pending before Afzal's

Nearly two dozen mercy petitions are pending with the Ministry of Home Affairs (MHA) as of 8 October 2006, the latest being the plea submitted on behalf of Mohd Afzal facing execution in the 2001 Parliament attack case.

The petitions include those of Nalini, Murugan, Santhan and Perarivalan, who were awarded death on 11 May 1999 by the Supreme Court in the Rajiv Gandhi assassination case. The earliest petitions dating back to 1992, are those of four Punjab convicts, who have been facing execution ever since.

The last hanging in India took place on 14 August 2004 in Kolkata, when 39-year-old Dhananjoy Chatterjee was executed after the rejection of his two petitions. The charge was that he hit a 14-year-old girl brutally in the head and raped her even as she was dying. The case triggered a debate on the capital punishment with the human rights activists keeping a vigil and taking out processions outside the Alipore Jail in Kolkata.

The MHA receives 15-20 mercy petitions every year. No time frame is fixed for dealing with them.

From April 2000 to February 2001, 28 petitions for commutation of death sentence under article 72 of the Constitution were death with. During this period, the Ministry received 10 other petitions for remission of sentence and pardon from persons sentenced under Central laws.

The President during this period granted remission of the balance sentence to five Latvian nationals, convicted in the Purulia arms drop case, and to a Norwegian convicted under the Narcotic Drugs and Psychotropic Substances Act, 1985.[7]

Pro - and anti-mercy battle goes on

Some more political heavy weights have jumped into the Pray.

- 10 Octber, 2006. All India Anti-Terrorist Front Chairman MS Bitta met the President along with relatives of the victims of Parliament attack and demanded in a memorandum that the death sentence to Mohd afzal be up held.
- 12 October, 2006. Tamil Nadu Chief Minister M. Karunanidhi has favoured the abolition of capital punishment. His article in the DMK party mouth piece Mursoli assume significance as the debate over mercy plea for Mohd Afzal Guru, awaiting the gallows, hots up in the Country.
- 12 October, 2006. A BJP delegation led by senior leader LK Advani called on President Kalam asking him to reject the appeal for clemency from Afzal's family. The delegation informed the President that such a move would send wrong signals to terrorists.
- JKLF Chairman Yasin Malik was also in New Delhi 13 October, 2006 to garner civil society support against the death sentence.

They are ranged against each other:

Against Mercy	For Mercy
1. BJP	1. Congress Party (J and K)
2. Shiv Sena	2. NC
3. Rajnath Singh, BJP	3. PDP
4. LK Advani, BJP	4. All separatist outfits
5. MS Bitta	5. Mufti Mohd and Mehbooba Sayeed
6. The Pioneer	6. Omer and Farooq Abdullah
7. Bal Thackeray	7. GN Azad, CM, J & K
8. Families of nine security personnel who fell while fighting those terrorists	8. CPM, J & K
	9. M Karunamdhi, CM Tamil Nadu
	10. Leftists
	11. The Asian Age
	12. The Hindu
	13. The Times of India
	14. A G Noorani
	15. Ram Jethmalani
	16. Arundhati Roy
	17. Some national and international entities

Farooq: Death penalty for Afzal too harsh

Former Jammu and Kashmir Chief Minister Farooq Abdullah on 14 October, 2006 said on Karan Thapar's 'Devil's advocate' programme on CNN-IBN channel that death sentence to Afzal was "too extreme" and he fears for the life of the judges who sentenced them.

The NC Leader initially told Thapar that Afzal was innocent but later changed it to "the sentence is too harsh."

As is his want, he spoke passionately:

> "You want to hang him? Go ahead and do so. But consequences of hanging him must also be remembered. One of the consequences will be ..... We have paid the price for Maqbool Bhatt's hanging by the judge (Neelkanth Ganju) who was shot dead in Kashmir. (This Sessons Judge had handed down the capital punishment to the co-founder of the JKLF in early 1980s). The judges in this case too must be protected."

Farooq warned that terrorists would do things that would destroy Hindu-Muslim relationship. Citing the 1993 Mumbai blasts following which "thousands (a clear and irresponsible exaggeration) of Muslims were put in jails to extract information from them. I don't want such things to happen in India..... because some crook, some badman will go and do something in a temple. Some body will do something in a mosque."

Some comments are called for here itself. We must note how careful he is to avoid use of the term 'terrorists' which is exactly what he is meaning all the while. The terrorist, for Forooq, is merely "a crook or a body man" without panning his statements in too deliberate a manner, let it be said simply that his arguments so far are too fecitious and so will be the ones that follow. Yet again, it is difficult to believe that its is same Farooq Abdullah giving such populist but asnine arguments against hanging a terrorist who, not many years back painted himself in national colours of a brave anti-terrorist politician when he publicly disclosed that he was firmly apposed to the 1991 release of the jailed terrorists from the State's prisons to secure the release of daughter of Mufti Syeed, then Home Minister of Prime Minister VP Singh. So much so that he insisted on getting the order for their release in writing from IK Gujaral. He obviously painted three of them - country's Prime Minister and his Home and External Affairs Ministers — as 'capitulationists'. He himself, of course, was a great anti-terrorist fighter in white shinning armour. Apart from the question of public propriety which he violated when he disclosed some details about a sensitive issue against the norms and rules of conduct expected of senior political functionaries, serving or retired, the important question to ask is : Where is that doubty and intrepid Farooq of 1991? In 2006, has he suddenly lost his nerve? Who is the real Fooq: 1991 vintage or his 2007 version? May be, like so many politicians, he was right then, and right now! Earlier he was in power, in 2007 he is out of it !

Reverting to his Karan Thapar interview for his further reasoning: "the peace process with Pakistan would suffer because President Musharraf would have tough time controlling his army chiefs of various regions. Some army chief might come up and throw him out, where will the peace process go, then? It will go back to zero." Now some observations he made during the course of this interview, including some mutually contradictory:

- "Afzal was innocent but the lower court turned down his request for appointment of a defence lawyer."
- Had Afzal got the right lawyer in the lower Court, it would have been proved that he was not directly involved."
- "The Supreme Court judges were also fallible and the evidence put forward by the police is not absolutely infallible."
- Later in the interview : "The evidence put forward before the honourable judges has been correctly said (analysed) by them but the sentence passed by them is too extreme. Too harsh."

No further comments are affered. But a simple question be added at the end: is he playing to the gallery/

"Commute his death sentence": Two forums: October, 2006

The Pakistan-India People's Forum for Peace and Democracy (PIPFED) and All-India Committee Against Death Penalty Committee have urged President APJ Abdul Kalam to consider sympathetically the mercy petition of Mohd Afzal, and commute his sentence. In separate statements on 14 October, 2006, they drew his attention to the growing consensus worldwide against the death penalty.

The Forum said a large section in Kashmir as well as Human Rights defenders, jurists, and members of the civil society in boath India and abroad believed that death sentenced pronounced on Afzal to be "unjust." While the actual perpetrators of the attack were killed, the four who were brought to trial were not directly involved in carrying it out.

"PIPFFD expresses its deep concern at the possible impact of the execution under the current circumstances of doubts regarding the case against Afzal and calls for clemency from many quarters. The hanging of Afzal Guru would undoubtedly be a set-back to the peace process and have negative impact on the gradual normalisation in the region."

The Committee said that on moral grounds also the sentence should be commuted." The causes of violence were inherent in the socio-economic and political system and without changing the system, violence and terrorist activities could not be stopped by hanging a few individuals."

The Committee said 120 countries had abolished the death penalty either in law or in practice. "It is an inherently unjust and arbitrary punishment. Global studies suggest that death penalties are being awarded mostly to poor, less educated and marginalised sections. In India, such punishments are being given to the landless, Dalits, backward classes and Muslims mainly."

E-Mail threatens PM and President

Senior Kerala officials, including the DGP and Home Secretary received threat on 26 October 2006 via e-mail that Prime Minister Manmohan Singh and President APJ Abdul Kalam would be assassinated during their forth coming visits to the state. The e-mail sent from the same mail ID contained reference to Afzal Guru, facing execution for the 2001 Parliament Attack, and radical Islamist (PDP leader) Abdul Nasser Madani under detention for the Comibatore blasts. This persuaded analysts to believe it was an attempt to pressure the government on Afzal's.

At the end of it, the eneprit turned out to be a foolish jilted lover.

Indian skies on high alert: 9 December, 2006

Security cover over the Indian skies was tightened after a renemed warning that an aircraft out of India might be hijacked and taken to Bangladesh to secure the release of Mohd Afzal Guru, sentenced to death by Supreme Court for plotting the attack on Parliament.

The alert was sounded after inelegence agencies warned that Pakistan-based militants might hijack an aircraft to demand release of Guru, for which a high-wattage campaign has already been launched by high-profile activists including some lift leaders, Luddite liberals and Arundhati Roy.

Two LET militants arrested at Palam (Delhi) with RDX: 11 December, 2006

Days ahead of the fifth anniversary of the Parliament attack, two LET militants - Gulzar Ahmad Ganai, 20, and Mohd Amin Nazam, 29 — have been arrested from Mohipalpur bus stop south Delhi, near Palam airport. Both belong to Kashmir Valley.

The police also recovered seized 1.5 kg. or RDX, six detonators and Rs. 6 lakh from them.

British MPs demand 'Justice' for Afzal Guru

Two British Labour MPs, Roger Godsiff and Jeremy Corbyn on 26 January, 2007 joined supporters of a rights groups, South Asia Solidarity Group (SASG), in holding protest demonstration in front of the India House in London, demanding "Justice" for Mohammed Afzal Guru, facing death sentence in the 2001 Indian Parliament attack case.

The demonstrators, numbering 20 to 30 and holding anti-India placards, urged President APJ Abdul Kalam to protect the human rights of Afzal. The protestors said that under international human rights standards people charged with crimes punishable by death are entitled to the observance of strictest fair trial guarantees in view of the irreversible and most extreme nature of the penality.

Godsiff's Burmingham constituency has a large Muslim population, with roots in Pakistan - Occupied Kashmir (POK), and that fact perhaps explains in part his presence among the protestors. However, the demonstration held on India's Republic Day was ignored by all of Britain's Asian - origin MPs and many other whose constituencies also have large number of Muslim and Kashmiri Voters, line Godsiff's Birmingham.

Afzal, 35, a resident of Sopore, in Jammu and Kashmir and arrested in December, 2001 in connection with the terrorist attack on Parliament on 13 December, was sentenced to death by the trial court. His appeal against this judgement has been rejected by the Supreme Court.

Afzal's mercy plea is pending with the Republic's President. The Congress-led UPA Government's inaction on the mercy plea is subject of apposition's criticism. The critics assert: (1) Government's decision is the line with its general policy of appeasement towards the Muslim Community. (2) it is delaying the execution because of vote-bank polities. Elections are due in Jan./Feb. 2007 in three States (Punjab, Manipur and UP) and his hanging before the polls would adversely affect its prospects at the hustings (3) not taking action even after the Supreme Court has confirmed about India's commitment to war on terrorism.

The Government says the time taken to decide on mercy plea to the President could range from 2 months to more than one year - depending upon the nature and complexities of cases in question.

Center against time limit on mercy petitions: March, 2007

Unfazed by protests against the delay in hanging the Parliament attack convict Mohd Afzal, Home Minister Shivraj Patil told Parliament on 14 March, 2007 that the Government has no plans to put a time frame for deciding on the clemency petition of terrorists on death row.

Answering a question from the Shiv Sena leader Manohar Joshi in Rajya Sabha, Patil said "it will be impractical to provide a time frame." He went to the extent of suggesting that sometimes even prosecution fails to file the charge sheet within the stipulated 90 days. (Relevance of citing this laxity on the part of the prosecution in the context of fixing a time frame on deciding on mercy plea by the convicts is difficult to appreciate).

Government's stance comes in the wake of the emotive campaign BJP and Shiv Sena unleashed in the local body polls in Maharashtra and UP as well as just-held Punjab and Uttarkhand elections wherein they cited the delay in Afzal's hanging to back up the charge that the UPA Government was not willing to get tough with terrorists for reasons of political expediency. The campaign is believed to have paid dividends to the two saffronites in the polls.

When BJP's Sushma Swaraj asked if the President applies his own mind on issues like mercy pelitions or goes by the decision of the cabinet, Patil said according to the Constitution "whereever the President is mentioned, it means the Executive, the Cabinet." So it is the Cabinet which takes the call on whether a convict gets a pardon.

On the clemency petition of Afzal, Patil said it was referred to the Delhi government for opinion, after which it has to come back to the Central government.

Afzal case for European Parliament: April, 2007

The UK-based South-Asia solidarity Group (SASG) announced on 14 April, 2007 that the case of Afzal awarded death sentence in the Parliament attack case "will be raised in the European Parliament during President Kalam's visit to Europe later this month (April, 2007)"

The decision to this effect was taken at a meeting of leading human rights and legal experts held in London of 12 April in support of Afzal Guru. The SASG said : "The meeting decided to urgently bring the details of Afzal case and miscarriage of justice before the European Parliament. British MPs Jeremy Corbyn, Roger Godsiff, John McDonell and George Galloway have already signed a letter to the Indian President Urgin him to show mercy to Afzal Guru"

A book by Nandita Haksar, *Framing Geelani, Hanging Afzal: Patriotism in the Time of Terror,* was released at the meeting. Moazzam Begg, one of the nine Britons detained at the Guantanamo Bay, called for an international campaign to get justice for Guru.

He spoke about his own experience and drew parallel to Guru's case.

Amrit Wilson from the Group said: "The forces of Hindutva and the so-called war on terror have led to an erosion of democratic values in India. In trying to bring (US President) Bush's version of 'democracy', India is becoming an authoritarian state."

Time to stop shouting about "Afzal is innocent" : November, 2006

Ever since the trial court awarded death sentence to Afzal

in 2002, there has been a vociferous, systematic campaign to depict him as an 'innocent' man done in by the vicious Indian police and judicial systems. There was no let-up in this campaign —one is forced to dub it as 'motivated'—even after the Delhi High Court upheld the death penalty of Afzal in October, 2003 and the Supreme Court confirmed it in August, 2005.

More out of desire to be part of the show, than any conviction perhapse, some British MPs and the European Parliament members also joined the chorus, made louder by the day by Indian Human Rights NGOs and the usual suspects like the liberal - Left combine. It must be acknowledged that jumping in the fray in such situations, where it is a question of protection the human rights of hardened criminals and inhuman maranders which the terrorists certainly are, is a fashionable practice there days, and more importantly, also politically correct.

Amidst this cacophony of loud appeals of mercy for 'innocent' Afzal, who faces gallows, come an investigative report telecast by the CNN- IBN on 26 November, 2006, which has Afzal's elder brother Aijiz admitting on camera that he (Afzal) was indeed a Jaish-e-Mohammed terrorist.[8] This fact must have come as a shattering blow not only to those sanctimonious warriors engaged in securing reprieve for Afzal but also to Delhi's, commentariat, or chattering classes if you wish.

Had the fact of Afzal being a JEM terrorist been asserted by the police or any other government agency, it would have been dismissed with disdain and contempt. After all, those campaigning for the condemned terrorist to be spared the noose have shown scant regard and lesser respect for nation's judiciary, including the Supreme Court, claiming that Afzal did not get a fair trial, which of course, is nothing but outright calumny disguised as freedom of expression.

But now that his elder brother has admitted that Afzal was not only a JEM terrorist but was also working for Ghazi Baba, who organised terror attacks within and outside and was put down by security forces in 2004, our Liberal-Left intelligentsia, which is stranger to the concept of 'nationalism', and abhors the very idea of national interest, will find it difficult to portray him as an "innocent victim" of a "demonic state" where, to quote writer-turned -activist promoting 'fashionable causes, Arundhati Roy, "democracy does not exist."

To say that Afzal's case was not explained to the court is gross misrepresentation of the truth by members of his fan club. He may not have been defended by a lawyer of his choice, possibly due to unavoidable reasons, but competent lawyers were made available far his defence in the court. And his defence lawyers were intelligent enough not to produce his younger, Hilal, in the court, since he had a different take on the events, as a witness. It would therefore be fair to suggest that the absurd demand for clemency is not only misplaced but also lacks credibility, and therefore deserves to be rejected out of hand,

Having dealt with the main issues concerning Afzal's culpability, and sprill, uncalled for mercy pleas by his fan club, there are certain other aspects of investigative report which bears scrutiny. For one, the report shows the intelligence and security agencies operating in Jammu and Kashmir in poor light and raised important question which needs to be answered by authority unless it prefers to remain indifferent about the need to plug loop holes in the existing system that enable terrorist like Afzal Guru to strike high-profile targets with amazing impunity. It has now emerged that security forces and intelligence agencies allowed Afzal Guru free play for all of 2000 and 2001 to plan and execute the attack on Parliament House. During this time, he was in regular touch with Ghazi Baba and there was enough evidence to retrain him from proceeding further with the crime for which he has now been sentenced to death. Those charged with conducting counter-terrorism operations, for some inexplicable reason, field to piece together enough intelligence input to nail Afzla before he and his fallow terrorists involved in the attack on Parliament House almost succeeded in their evil enterprise.

This obviously cannot be explained away as a mere over sight. Afzal's background and his associations demanded that his movements be tracked. But unfortunately, this simple principle of counter-terrorism was followed in breach. This disclosure raises three questions. First, whose decision was it not to track Afzal Guru. Second, had responsibility been fixed for this abysmal lapse? Third, what steps has been initiated to ensure that this does not happen again. The answers, if any, would be available with the Union Home Ministry. But tragically, as many analysts over, managing internal security is not any longer the core competence of this Ministry under its current political management.

Considering the facts mentioned above, may be it is time to revive the appointment of a Minister of State for Internal Security in the Home Ministry as it happened so many times in the past. Such a step may play some leakages in the all-important sphere of internal security when the nation is faced with a serious terrorism situation.

Afzal mercy plea: It is all politics : October, 2006 First a brief case file details

Case File

A brief summary follows.

Evidence

Recorded conversations prove Afzal provided the Ambassador car, case and shelter to the fidayeen.

Mercy plea : Process

After the Supreme Court uphold the death sentence of Afzal, the 13 December, 2001 Parliament attack accused, in 2005, he was set to be hanged on 20 October, 2006. The date was subsequently postponed indefinitely. After the highest court uphold his death sentence, his supporters prepared a plea for mercy which he reportedly refused to sign but it was put in on his behalf by his wife Tabassum

Now the clemency petition is with the President. All the issues / discussions that follow pertain to the period prior to 20 October, 2006.

As is the practice, mercy petition to the President, APJ Abdul Kalam, has been forwarded to the Home Ministry. President is bound by the advice of this Ministry.

Counter Petition

A delegation of relatives of the martyrs of the Parliament attack met the President to press for justice. They requested that the mercy petition be rejected out of hand.

Threat to return the medals

The family of the posthumous Ashok Chakra awardee, CRPF constable Kamlesh Kumari has threatened to return the medal if the Afzal plea is entertained. The families of other posthumous awardees too followed with similar public threat.

The snow balling controversy

The death sentence of Afzal has raised a serious controversy like never before for what so ever reasons. The opposition to his hanging is led by some well-known faces like Abdullah Azad the Mufti duo Nandita Haksar and Arudhati Roy. Ranged against them are the families of the martyrs mentioned, the well-know anti-terrorism fighter, the intrepid MS Bitta, and political heavy weights like LK Advani, Rajnath Singh and Arun Jaitley. Yes Congress is intent upon sitting on the fence.

Two 'famous' U-turns

Jammu and Kashmir Chief Minister Ghulam Nabi Azad does not own or deny it, but his letter to Prime Minister Manmohan Singh pleading clemency for Mohd Afzal Guru marks one of the most remarkable—or, is it 'dubious'–turnarounds in political posturing. After the December, 2001 attack on Parliament, Azad, then Congress General Secretary, had demanded "stringent punishment" for the conspurator. "However, as the beleagured Chief Minister of a State on the chief conspirator of the attack, he seen things differently."[9]

BJP, in no mood to relent on its uncompromising stand on the issue, in the current context has an opportunity to further heap the minority appearement allegation on the Congress which always finds itself in a dilemma when it comes to anything remotely concerned with the minorities.

If Afzal case too, congress is as indecisive. As a national party it has to sing in tune with national sentiments but also faces fringe voices calling for prendo-liberalism – a fashion in certain circles today. Some of its factions cite Sonia Gandhi's appeal for clemency to Nalini, then facing death sentence in the Rajiv Gandhi assassination case, though it was on the ground that Nalini had a doughter to look after. The Afzal case is different. But significantly, the Congress has not yet proclaimed its stance. Like a good lawyer, which he actually is, its spokesman Abhishik

Manu Singh vi, made a neither here nor there statement on the issue: "We neither support nor decry his (Azad's) stands". But a clear cut assertion come from AICC General Secretary Digvijay Singh even if it was deemed his personal view : "There should be no clemency for Afzal as he has conspired against the state." But congress' response assumes importance as the President is bound by the Home Ministry's advice. More on this later, but first the second instance of U-turn.

Only some months ago, Farooq Abdullah wanted to shine as a knight in shining armour in the role of a no-nonsense anti-terrorist politician. He stunned the nation by speaking out on issue which are best left un-commented upon. Certain sensitive issues are almost like state secrets. He said he as Chief Minister was dead-set against the release of terrorists in his prisons in exchange for relief of then Home Minister Mufti's doughter. He had to accede on orders of Prime Minister. And now the same Farooq wants clemency for Afzal. He has some strange reasoning : " If Afzal is hanged, there will be bloodshed in the Valley (He actually used more colourful if macalere language). Some one will shoot down the judge concerned."

The debate goes on: some other participants and issues

The debate on the issue has serious implications for the nation. The intensity and diversity of responses over Afzal's hanging have been so fierce that it threalens to test and determine nation's response to terrorism. "Suddenly there are a number of backers for Afzal's elemency petition emerging from the woodworks, from Azad to Arundhati Roy to Yasin Malik to Farooz Abdullah. Each one has a reason—Azad fears a back lash in Kashmir, Roy is from-life and anti-capital punishment while others have their own political constituencies to cater to Surprisingly, even co-accused SAR Geelani, who clearly benefited from the same judicial system which set him free after the special court had sentenced him to death, now finds fault with it. "I do'nt say he is innocent, but he has not got justice."

It is not only Azad, several other Kashmiri leaders, sensing a ripe issue and seeing opportunities due to competitive politics of the valley, have jumped into the fray. The essential reason could be the populist appeal of saving a Muslim coreligionist from the gallows, what even his crime. Any, but any, Muslim cause will be popular in the Valley. Malik landed in Delhi to meet leaders of various UPA allies to plead Afzal's cause. He met Left leaders like AB Bardhan and Prakash Karat even if he could extract no assurances from them. Karat may have said nothing so far but his stand on clemency is well documented. He had apposed the LTTE-backed stir in Tamil Nadu in 2000 on clemency for Nalini, then facing death in the Rajiv Gandhi assassination case. Though he was all for clemency to Nalini, he was opposed to the same for her husband Murugan and the two other accused.

Azad is also believed to have pointed out to the Prime Minister the delicate law and order situation that might arise in his state of the hanging is carried out on the date set, 20 October, 2006, which also happens to be the last Friday of Ramzan. He wanted the hanging, at least, to be deferred for this reason. PDP chief Mohbooba Mufti has declared that Kashmiris will appose the hanging of Afzal and his sentence should be commuted.

Incidentally, 20 October is also observed of Martyr's Day by the Security forces.

The BJP's stand is clear and its delegation called on the President to impress upon him the need to reject the petition. "Any mercy will only weaken our resolve against terrorists", asserts its General secretary Arun Jaitley. Its President Rajnath Singh is clear on the issue: "There is no need to grant pardon to Afzal. It will send wrong signals." That is the crux of the issue. Here is an accused who nearly brought India and Pakistan to war though an act of terrorism, and now suddenly there is ground swell of sympathy for this criminal! There is surely something wrong somewhere in this whole charade of the surrealist play acting!

LK Advani was the Union Home Minister at the time of attack and had taken it as a personal challenge to get to the bottom of the conspiracy. He has often accused the Manmohan-led UPA of being soft on terrorism and he would not want the Congress lot off the hook. And Congress' attitude is crucial on the issue of Afzal's mercy petition, because the President is bound by the advice of Home Ministry, Presently under a Congress man. Constitutional expert Diljit Titus says: "In this matter he has no discretion as he can only forward the petitions to the Ministry which in turn can seek the opinion from the concerned state governments and then submit a detailed report to him: if the report is negative, the President has to reject the plea."

And Congress may not be a free agent in this case, as it has its past conduct to haunt it if it is inclined to appease the Afzal supporters and friend. After having lambasted the NDA for its weak-kneed response to the Kanda has hijack an release of prisoners including the dreaded Massood Azhar, the Congress can not plead leniency for Afazal. Surely, there is a spectre of law and order situation in Jamu and Kashmir, but can that he made an excuse for soft pedalling on all such future cases? Will the clemency granted to Afzal not become a precedent'? Then, the Centre will have to take a long term view on the issue. Verdicts on so many incidents of terrorist violence are awaited, and the one on 1993 Mumbai blasts cases are awaited before the end of 2006. Any move by the Congress to lean towards a safter option for Afzal could open a Pandora's box.

It is not just a political issue. Human demotions too are inter woven with the case and decision on mercy petition. "It is heart-breaking to see some people demand capital punishment for the Jessica Lal murder accused but clemency for Afzal. If the President grants clemency to Afzal, my daughter's sacrifice would go in vain", says Rajaram, father of the CRPF constable Kamlesh Kumari who died in the attack on Parliament. Posted at the entrance to the main building, she had been the first tier of resistance. She was awareded the highest civilian honour, Ashok Chakra, posthumously for her bravery and dedication to duty. Now her family had threatened, as mentioned at the beginning, it will return the medal if Afzal's sentence is commuted. Others awarded similarly, too, have annouseed to fallow suit. The ripple effect of such an action and the perceptions of an indecisive government unable to take a principled stand on such a crucial threat that threaten's India's integrity and sovereignty are something the Congress can ill afford, particularly so when the general elections are less than two years away.

Meanwhile, Afzal has tried becoming an Islamic martyr. First there were reports of his refusal to sign mercy petition. It was an obvious attempt at putting up a brave front, literally, in the face of the gallows. Then during the period in which his trial was concluded and the two mandatory appeals were exhausted, Afzal transformed himself from a moustached and trousered urbanite to a bearded and scarved maulana which in some way augments his appeal with the extremists. But the courts have consistently found him guilty of the conspiracy.

His lawyers have argumented for him on some legal grounds. His advocate Nandita Haksar says: " The courts have relied heavily on his confessional statement and under our legal system that cannot be the sole ground". His supporters also cite article 20(3) of the Constitution which states," No person accused of any offence shall be compelled to be a witness against himself." Evidently, it is the view that has not been received by the apex court which up held the verdict of the lower court and the High Court.

What an irony that the person who helped terrorist attack the highest podium of democracy is now seeking to use that very system of democracy to seek clemency.

Mercy for Afzal will be surrender to terrorism

It is time to take a stand on the issue: will the mercy to Afzal meet the ends of justice or will it be a surrender before the mindless terrorists' murderous intent? In this part, something like a last word, various aspects of the problems consequent to Afzal being granted mercy will be looked at. Will it affect our future decisions in such situations? What kind of message will it convey to the terrorist bent upon "bending" and "breaking India, and to the international community at large?

One simply cannot understand all the noise, the song and dance being made over a hanging: that too of some one who was found guilty of a heinous crime, but is now, in some way, on his way to martyrdom even before he is dead. In a word what is the issue? Here is a man accused of mastermending the terrorist attack on India's Parliament; he is tried and finally awarded the death sentence. Now, in order to have the death sentence commuted, every trick in the book is being deployed — including Arundhati Ray, who is always to castigate India for any acts of commissionor omission.

Even more bizarre is the reason offered by Chief Minister Azad of Jammu and Kashmir in his petition to the Prime

Minister: "Either commute the sentence or postpone hanging or else there will ne law and order problem in his state." Does Azad imply that no terrorists can even be hanged for crimes they commit only because there will be a resultant law and order problem? This is another form of urbane or subtle giving-in.

What is the signal we are sending to the world? That we have Kangaroo Courts that can't even deliver basic justice. Because this is what Afzal's family have been saying: they waited for the verdict to tell the world that they did not get a fair trial. Nandita Haksar should have raised her voice all along. She did not.[10]

Even worse, we are telling the law enforcement agencies that terrorists in this country can get away: one is sitting in Karachi and the other will be in prison, become media celebrities, but never pay for their crime.

How will the children of those who died in that attack be feeling when they see criminals get away only because our media know no better? How will the current security personnel must be feeling when they see how justice has been subverted at the altar of clever spin doctoring.

In a country where a bomb blasts trial takes 13 years, we should be happy that in this case justice has been delivered and delivered pretty quickly. To now circumvent the process would be suicidal and a big blow to every institution we hold sacred.

An analyst is critical of then President Dr. Kalam, for having time to meet a convicted man's family. Did he have time to meet those children who lost their parents at the hands of the terrorists that December forenoon outside India's Parliament?

Like Dr. Kalam, we are slowly becoming a weak nation, more prone to the shrillness of the NGO noise than to the simple logic.

All kinds of arguments are being marshalled to spare Afzal's life. Some fear Afzal Guru would turn into a martyr and inspire more youths to become terrorists. They for get the other and more sinister possibility of him becoming another Massod Azhar. One regret that will always grow at India's collective conscience is why Azhar was not hanged while he was in custody. Today he is free to kill and maim.

Do we want two Masood Azhars?

Overactive NGOs are helping/encouraging Terrorism

Some NGOs are activists who have made a profession of running India down found a new cause celebre in the death convict. Having tasted blood with the exoneration of Afzal's co-conspirator SAR Geelani, the emboldened brigade of India bashers are now convinced they notch up another victory by getting the present pusillanimous Congress leadership, whom the opposition has often blamed of being saft on terrorism, to buckle under pressure . Its Jammu and Kashmir Chief Minister has already come out in support of the India bashers, even if his NO2 in the Cabinet (Mangat Ram Sharma) made bold to sound a note of public dissent. The Congress seems to be petrified at the thought of taking a decision either way. Expectedly, it is accused to playing vote -bank polities on the issue of hanging Afzal. If earlier in 2007 it postponed the hanging, concerned with its electoral fortunes in UP Assembly, the critics say the accused may earn reprieve again because India - US Nuclear deal—related crisis by the Communists is seen as pushing into mid-term elections in 2008. The only senior Congress leader to pick up courage and demand execution of Afzal is Digvjay Singh — former Chief Minister of Madhya Pradesh and one of its few mass leaders.

There hardly seems any justification for the mercy plea. Afzal was one of the terrorists who stormed Parliament on 13 December, 2001 and it was he who first opened fire on security personnel, apparently killing three of the six who died protecting the majesty of democracy and the nation's honour that fateful morning. He was tried, convicted and awarded death by a POTA Court — a verdict upheld by the Supreme Court. The same process of law, failing sufficient evidence against his co-hort SAR Geelani, acquitted him.

The Pro-Mercy brigade is now braying for the judiciary's blood, claiming that Afzal did not get a fair trial. This was reiterated by his wife Tabassum, who false asserted before TV cameras on 5 October, 2006 that her husband even did not get the services of a lawyer — something patently false. May be, he did not get advocate of his choice but the was certainly provided the services of a lawyer. This (false) charges she had apparently conveyed to the president also. "The duplicity of the *jholawalas*", and analyst wrote, "who have taken control of

Tabassum, in a way reminiscent of Teesta Setalvad's strangled hold over Zahira Shaikh prior to the latters somersault, is mind boggling." If SAR Geelani got a fair trial in the same case, how come Afzal Guru did not? The logic — perhaps, bottom line is better term — of the NGO brigade's contention is rather simple: It is justice only if it conforms to their likes and dislikes. If the Supreme Court refuses to stop construction of the Sardar Sarovar Dam, it shows the Indian judiciary to be contemptible. If it frees Geelani, it covers itself with glory. If it awards death to Afzal, it is back in the dog house.

The things have not stopped here. The habitual India bashers and professional agitators, unable to explain the logic behind such self-serving if contradictory assertions, have graduated to claiming that "most terrorsist outrages in India are suspect". One of them made bold to declare on a TV channel that the chutisinghpora massacre (on the eve of the visit of President Bill Clinton) was "staged", while the named bomb blasts were the handiwork of Bajrang Dal, the attack on the RSS handiwork of Bajrang Dal, the attack on the RSS Headquaters in Nagpur "suspect", and there were big question marks on the Malegaon incident.

All such utterances coming from overzealous activists are indicative of a diseased mind as far as a normal Indian citizen is concerned, May be such deprave outpourings earn their perpetrators brownic points from their foreign collaborators, especially the Pakistani and Bangladeshi ones.

There need be no doubt that such vicious anti-India assestions will be much quoted abroad. This obviously a blatant and outrageous misuse of freedom of expression that we all are so proud of in India.

All such assertions are inane and patently false. Then, even to not-so-obliquely suggest that the attack on Parliament was "staged" by Indian agency is reflecting of depravity of their mind. But what followed these contemptible initial irresponsibilities was even worse: A book titled "Strange Care of Terrorist Attack on the Indian Parliament" was published with contributions from the likes of Arundhati Roy. Majority of Indians might dismiss the book as a political tract aimed at tarnishing the image of Indian polity and nation, the *joholawala* brigade will take it as God's oven truth about India's wrong doings!

To paint India black, there NGOs can go to any limits. In fact, they heve descended to wringing out every drop of emotion, with the help of a section of an irresponsible media, especially television. They staged an impressive tearjerker on 5 October, 2006 on the four court of the Rashtrapati Bhavan — something an Indian film scriptwriter could be envious of. The leading light of the India-baiting joholawala brigade, one Nandita Haksar, was in full flow. "Caressing seven -year-old Ghalib, son of death merchant Afzal Guru, she claimed that the (tutored) child told President Kalam that his life's ambition to become a doctor would remain unfulfilled if his father's life was snatched away. The boy cutely stood , suitably melancholic, under Haksar's ample protection while his mother and grandmother recounted their interaction with a sympathetic President. Split TV cameras, meanwhile, kept zooming in of that blabbering classe's icon Arundhati Roy who can be guaranteed to cheerlead any gathering that aims to berate India's pride, rule of law or economic progress."[11]

There are some other aspects about the mercy petition that call for a closes look. To be entertained by the authorities, such a petition must inform whether a death row convict is remorseful of his action, or at least he regrets it. In the instant case the death peddler is not only unrepentant, but has actually refused to sign his mercy petition. At least he is an honest jihadi who carried out the Parliament attack in the belief, even if highly misplaced, that by attempting to destablise India he was responding to a higher call. Afzal was obviously driven by the same conviction that motivated several well-educated, sop histicated men to hijack planes and fly them into the WTC towers on 9/11 the same year.

Like them, Afzal was ready to embrace death in the process, just as his five Pakistani colleagues did that morning. Why should the activists be eager to save his life. Especially when we already have the sad experience of Masood Azhar who had to be freed in exchange for passengers on IC 814? "May be it is precisely in the hope that fellow jihadis will stage yet another successful hijäck and get Afzal released that the Hate - India agitators have mounted their tear-jerker campaign."[12]

It is no surprise that most Indians clearly see the aim of these NGOs and hyper active human rights activists pejoratively dubbed *jholawalas*: to destabilise, weaken and eventually the Indian state and subsequently the civilisation itself. In any other country, they would deservedly have been declared Fifth Columnists and prosecuted for treason. But in India they stand exalted as celebrities who hog large chunks of airtimes and column centimeters to spew anti-India fire.

If these NGO's agenda is transparently honest, it is not clear why the congress is seen to be going along with them? Its vote-bank politics has been mentioned above. Its action on the Sachar Committee report is again seen as a step towards the Muslim appeasement. Arjun Singh is adding his mite by systematic destruction of institutions of excellence to get OBC flocking to the Congress Party. The clemency for Afzal will do the same for the Muslims.

Is the Grand Old Party of India descending to the level of the self-serving brigade of anti-India NGOs and India-bashing individuals named above?

Is.SC rewriting criminal jurisprudence for the convicts?

Shaukat Hussain Guru is Parliament Attack Case convict. His appeal, review and curative petitions had already been dismissed. His curative petition, the last judicial remedy available to a convict, was dismissed in January, 2007. Shaukat is under going 10-years, sentence after his conviction attained finality in the case.

On 27 August, 2007, an unprecedented move, the Supreme Court (SC) decided to entertain a petition filed by Shaukat. A bench of Justice PP Naolekar and RV Ravendran issued notice to the Delhi Government seeking its response to Shaukat's petition challenging his conviction on the ground that he was not charged under the Section 123 of Indian Penal Code (omission to apprise magistrate/court about an act of waging war by accused persons despite having its knowledge) and not heard on this aspect. He has filed a writ of habeas corpus seeking a direction to the authorities to release him.

Appearing for Shaukat, senior counsel Shanti Bhushan submitted that his continued detention amounted to violation of his fundamental right to life and liberty guaranteed under Article 21 of Constitution.

Senior Counsel PN Lekhi said: "It has never happened in a criminal case. The SC is rewriting the criminal jurisprudence of the country. He could have raised this point in his appeal, review, or the curative petition. Who prevented him from doing so?"

Another senior counsel Rajeev Dhavan had a different view: "the question is whether there is fresh cause of action and whether his fundamental right was violated or not ...and it is the court's duty to examine any challenge made on this court."[13]

MULUND TRAIN BLAST : MUMBAI : 13 MARCH 2003

12 Persons were killed and 73 injured in an explosion in the ladies' compartment of the Karjat-bound local train as it arrived at Mulund station.

For more than two months, the police could make no headway. It was after another blast on a city bus at Chatkopar on 29 July the same year (2003) that the police identified the persons involved and the key perpetrators were revealed after Hanif's arrest in the Gateway of India blast.

The arrest of 17 persons brought out the involvement of educated people in terror activities for the first time.

Trial in the case is pending.

TWIN BLASTS MUMBAI: 25 AUGUST, 2003

Explosions in two taxis at the Gateway of India and the Zaveri Bazar killed 53 persons and injured 153

Investigations were immediately transferred to a team headed by Joint Commissioner of Police Rakesh Maria and a week later Sayed Mohd Hanif, his wife Fahimida and two others were arrested. Two others were arrested later. The trial continues (27 May 2007) and all the accused are in judicial custody.

The accused told the police that they had formed the "Gujarat Muslim Revenge Force" and were in Mumbai to seek revenge for the massacre of Muslims in Gujarat. After the arrests, police seized 25 kg. of explosives, timer devices and wires from Hanif's house.

Notes

1. Mustafa Plumber, *Hindustan Times*, 5 Dec., 2006
2. Raghu Mahajani, *Week*, 8 Oct., 2006.
3. K. Venkataramanan, *Pioneer*, 22 June, 2007.
4. *Hindu*, 2 Aug., 2007.
5. *Ibid.*
6. Abraham Thomas, *Pioneer*, 13 Jan 2007.
7. *Hindu*, 9 Oct., 2006..
8. Edit, "Socked in the eye", *Pioneer*, 29 Nov., 2006.
9. Neeraj Mishra, *India Today*, 23 Oct., 2006.
10. Suhel Seth, *Asian Age*, 9 Oct., 2006.
11. Chandan Mitra, *Pioneer*, 8 Oct., 2006.
12. *Ibid.*
13. Staya Prakash, *Hindustan Times*, 28 Aug., 2007.

10

Terrorist Attacks in India Part 2

DIWALI EVE BOMBINGS IN DELHI: 29 OCTOBER, 2005

As many as 67 people were killed and 207 injured in three powerful bomb blast in Delhi on 29 October, 2005. The high number of casualties made the bombings the deadliest terrorist attack in India of 2005. The bombings came only two days before the major Hindu and Sikh festival of Diwali, and less than a week before the major Islamic festival of Eid ul-Fitr.

The bombs were triggered in two crowded markets in Central (Paharganj market) and South (Sarojini Nagare Market) Delhi and in a bus in the Govindpuri area in the south of the city.

Though the Special Cell of Delhi Police has arrested five terrorists who funded and supervised the blasts, the real perpetrators are still at large (*Indian Express*, 27 May 2007). The Cell has filed four chargesheets against the five accused and in likely to frame charges at the next hearing on 26 May 2007. All the accused have applied for bail which will also be considered on 26 May. Names of the accused: Ghulam Ahmad Dar, Mohd Hussain Fazli, Mohd Rafiq Shah, Ghulam Ahmad Khan, and Farooq Ahmad Battoo,

While the Delhi police killed on Abu Huzefa in an encounter in Srinagar, the alleged conspirator Abu Al-Qama of LET is still on the run, as are the persons who planted the RDX. Later, officials admitted that there men could have fled the country.

A little-Known group claims responsibility: 30 October, 2005

A day after a synchronised string of bombs tore through packed holiday season markets in Delhi, a little known militant outfit in Kashmir took responsibility.

A man called the Kashmir News Service to say that his group , he identified as In Inquilabi (= Revolutionary) had carried out the bombings.

Joint Commissioner of Police, Delhi, Karnail Singh told the reporters that the lead was being investigated. He gave a little different name of the organisation: Islamic Inquilabi Mahaz (= Islamic Revolutionary Front). He said it was linked to the LET - or, possibly a front for it -, the Pakistan-based militant organisation, carrying out maximum number of terrorist activity in India.

Indian Institute of Science (11Sc) Bangalore attacked: 28 December, 2006

BANGALORE, India — A professor was killed and four others were wounded at a science conference in India on Wendesday (Dec. 28) by a gunman with possible ties to a terrorist group, according police.

Police said the gunman sprayed automatic gunfire during a conference at the Indian Institute of Science, based in the southern Indian city of Banglore. Professor M.C Puri from the Indian Institute of Technology Delhi, was killed in the attack, according to police.

Several others were seriously hurt, including Vijay Chandru, founder of the Indian-developed palm-computer, the Simputer, according to a report from the *BBC News* service.

The Indian Institute of Science is leading postgraduate college in India's technology hub of Bangalore.

The incident occurred *Wednesday* evening when delegates were leaving after a seminar at the institute, where among others, K. Kasturirangan, chairman of India's Space Research Organization, were present.

According to the *BBC,* the assailants approached the delegation in an ambassador car. One of them got out and fired randomly outside an auditorium door and than the car sped off, according to the report.

It is too early to be certain if terrorist's are behind the attack. But some suspect the attack was carried out by the Lashkar-e-Toiba group, reportedly one of the largest terrorist outfits operating in Pakistan. The group is also suspected of involvement in the attack on India's Parliament in New Delhi in 2001.

An update

No direct arrests have been made till date (27 May 2007). According to the Bangalore police, the attack was carried out by terrorists based in Bangladesh with links to HUJI an JEM and was funded and supported by the LET

The Bangalore police through IB inputs, interrogation reports of the terrorists arrested in Hyderabad, and investigations have surmised that Shahid, a Hyderabad native, currently linked to the Hyderabad Mecca Masjid blasts, based in Bangladesh and linked to the HUJI and JEM, played a key role in the IISc attack while seven people have been arrested, none of them have been linked to the attack. The arrested include Abdul Rehman, South India head of the LET, Chand Pasha, Mehboob Ibrahim Sab Chopdar, Ashr of Pasha, Mohd Irfan, Nazmuddin *alias* Munna and Noorullah Khan.

RSS HEADQUARTERS TARGETTED: 1 JUNE, 2006

RSS Headquarters (Hedgewar Bhavan) at Nagpur was attacked by the Islamic terrorist in the early hours of 1 June 2006. This was bound to happen one day. The RSS is the prime target of hate dinned into the ears of terror recruits by its leaders. The security establishment had expected such on attack to materialise one day — any day - and therefore adequate security had been provided at the Nagpur Headquarters of RSS.

Summary of Events

1. 3.50 AM. Car carrying three terrorists and fitted with beacon lights breaks though the first barricades on the street leading to the RSS Headquarters.
2. 4 AM. Police stop the car and there is exchange of fire between it and the ultras. Three of them killed.
3. Near escape. Had it been for their ability to locate the target, chances are that the terrorists would have succeeded in their plan. A police patrol grew suspicious when it noticed the militants' car making the rounds of the congested area.
4. Heavily armed. The ultras were carrying three automatic rifles, IEDs, nine magazines and thirteen hand grenades. Nagpur Police Commissioner SPS Yadav asserts the

quantity of explosives was enough to below up the building.

5. Who were they? While police identified the dead as "Islamic militants", no extremist outfit immediately claimed responsibility. Police thought there were no indications about the culprits belonging to Nagpur.
6. View from outside Nagpur:
   - security officials said the terrorist's plan—rising up towards the target in a beacon-fitted car—was inspired by various attacks since 20003. Following this trend seemed amateurish and a copy cot approach noticed during the last three years.
   - Hours after three men posing as policemen were shot dead 100 metres from RSS Headquarters, a group of Maharashtra's anti-terrorism investigators left Mumbai for Nagpur to find out if the three were linked to terror calls busted this year across the State and study their motivation.

Gujarat killings used to motivate terrorists

Since 2003 and especially this year (2006), diverse Islamic outfits — from little-known groups in Hyderabad to the LET in Kashmir —continue to use Gujarat's communal killing to motivate the cadres and create new terror cells to further their plans. There is no dearth of new adherents for this cult of violence promoted and mustered by the Islamist extremists, once the mullahs and maulvis brain wash the young faithfuls in the name of Islam, always misquoting and mis inter preting the injunctions from the noble Quran. For the new cells, division of duty is well thought through: educated youth as the brains and semi-literate ones as the bombers (Sarita Kaushak, Nagpur; Rathin Das, Ahmedabad; and Archis Mohan, New Delhi: *Hindustan Times*, 2 June, 2006).

There were the sentiments of officials interviewed by the journalists across the country.

With investigations pending, SPS Yadav simply called the slain men " Islamic militants". But later he told a daily: "I do not discount what has repeatedly been revealed during the unraveling of the terror cells across India as continuing motivation: the anti-Muslim Gujarat riots of 2002.

"The terrorists, particularly the ones from Hyderabad, Maharashtra and Gujarat, have during interrogations pointed out how the Gujarat riots led them to believe that there was an anti-Muslim atmosphere in India," said Delhi's DCP (Special Cell) Ajay Kumar. An IB officer only confirms the hate-promoting *mantra*: "In UP, demolition of the Babari Masjid is a fading motivation, but Gujarat remains a tonic. Last year's (2005) attack at Ayodhya and the Varanasi blasts this year (2006) were proof of it."

An intelligence official in Delhi said: "Gujarat under Modi is now closely matched by agencies in Pakistan and even in Bangladesh. Every development impacting minorities is matched there and used/exploited to incite disgruntted members in the community.... everything (I repeat), even the decision not to screen the Amir-Khan-starrer. Fanaa."

Modi: A victim of hate campaign

A M Biyabani, a 23 year-old B.Com. student and one of the eleven arrested from Aurangabad for smuggling in weapons, told interrogators in Mumbai on 22 May: "Gujarat Chief Minister Narendre Modi is our target No. 1."

This hate, said intelligence experts, is further fuelled by actions like the 1 June announcement by Modi of a Rs. 10 lakh reward to the police unit that shot dead the alleged terrorists in Nagpur: "This is an attack on our nation's culture and challenges our patriotism."

Interestingly, of late being pointed by the press as the next Hindutva icon, Modi is known for his roots in the RSS. When it comes to populist inclinations in the politicians, the congress is no less guilty than the rest of them. Modi's munificence was quickly matched by the Congress-led Maharashtra Government.

Bangalore Police Commissioner Ajai Kumar Singh Akhilesh said: " Several Muslim organisations are propagating anti-Modi campaigns across the country."

India must Match out : It is Under Attack

India must watch watch out. It is target of the Islamists and a 'Satan' as declared by their patron saint Osama bin Laden. If like the Babari Masjid, Gujarat too becomes a faded memory, new reasons and excuses, genuine or cooked-up, can always be manufacture. As the empirical experience shows, Muslim street can always be inflamed into a frenzied lot by an extremist leaders who are never in short supply in that community. We may not have too many Javed Akhtars, Shabana Azamis or Maulana Waheed uddins, but we can have any number of rabble rousers among the Muslims.

There have been any number of terrorist attacks in the country, particularly, during the last three decades. If there have not been more of these, it is not for want of trying on their part. Some attacks fail become of human errors on their part, and others averted/foiled by the intelligence agencies.

In Karnataka, plots to attack the Almatti Dam, a power grid and the Kaiga Nuclear Plant were busted and 13 arrested "in the last six months" (Nov. 2005-May 2006). Yer again, in late 2005, terrorists has struck at the Indian Institute of Science (IISc)in Bangalore, killing a professor from the IIT, Delhi.

So it is mouse and cat game, in a manner of speaking, and the latter had to be alert all the time. In the given scenario in India, intelligence agencies just cannot afford to be off guard against the terrorists. They are first sung of battle, headed by the political authority in the final analysis, intervened by the security establishment. Any dissonance among these three songs will create circumstances, for the success of the terrorists at the cost of the nation. There simply is no place for clash of petty egoe's in this grim situation. Nation demands the very best from each one of us, whatever our station in life.

Mumbai Serial Blasts : 11 July 2006

As an analyst put it, "Want to bring Mumbai to a stand-still?", just halt its suburban rail services. The mastermind of the 11 July terror attacks knew it as well. As seven bombs went off in seven trains in as many minutes, it virtually derailed life in the city.

7 Train Blasts in Mumbai

Table 1

Ser	*Time PM*	*Location*
1.	6.24	Khar
2.	6.24	Mahim
3.	6.25	Jogeshwari
4.	6.26	Borivili
5.	6.30	Matunga
6.	6.30	Bandra
7.	6.31	Bhayandar

Source: The Oullok, 24.7.06

Table 2

- 6.20 PM: Khar - Santa Cruz (sub-way); train departed Churchgate for Borivli at 5.48 PM.
- 6.23 PM: Bandra station; train departed Churchgate for Borivili at 5.50 PM.
- 6.23 PM: Mira Road; train departed Churchgate far Virar at 5.19 PM.
- 6.24 PM: Jogeshwari; train departed Churchgate for Borivili at 5.36 PM.
- 6.21 PM: Matunga Road; train departed Churchgate for Virar at 5.57 PM.
- 6.28 PM: Borivili; train departed Churchgate for Virar at 5.37 PM.
- 6.33 PM: Mohim Station; train departed Churchgate for Borivili at 5.54 PM

(*Source:* The week, 23.7.06)

Rail Networks in Question

Mumbai's rail network is divided between the Western Railway (WR) and Central Railway (CR). While WR runs between Churchagate and Virar; CR has two services: Main Lime and Harbow line. The total number of daily commuters is close to seven million, analysts calculate. This is half the load of the entire Indian railways. The WR, which was targeted by the bombers, runs 65 km. from Churchgate towards Virar, carrying 45 per cent of the seven million commuters. Each compartment is designed to carry about zoo commuters . Thus a nine-coach train has capacity of about 1,800 while a twelve - coach train can ferry 2,400 commuters. But at peak hours, the load is between 4,000 and 5,000 commuters to a train. The average time gap between two local trains at termmals points is around 4-5 minutes.

Thus day's blasts happened in first class compartments of trains on the WR, after they had crossed Dadar on the way to Virar from Churchagate.

Intelligence Failure?

A week or two is not adequate to fix responsibility of determine the efficiency of the intelligence agencies. But politicians cannot wait. Deputy Chief Minister RR Patil, who is also the Home Minister, blamed (the next day) railway's security for the blasts and added that the Central intelligence input was weak. But the RDX suspectedly used in the blasts apparently reached Mumbai from the interiors of Maharashtra, policing of which was very much a responsibility of his department, the analysts asserted. Later in the might, Chief Minister Vilasrao Deshmukh decided to hand over the investigation to the Anti-Terrorist squad (ATS) headed by Special Inspector-General KP Raghuvanshi.

Security of the Network and Passengers

In hind right, it can be said that there has not been great concern or any committed effort towards building or maintaining security on Mumbai's suburban network. As a cynic remarked, those who planted the bombs on 11 July did not have to penetrate any security cordon and systems, for the simple reasons because thus were no systems to breach. People blamed the railway authorities for the lapse. Surely deployment of uniformed policemen on the platforms and in the trains could gave had some salutary effect. But this is only true in part.

A look at the statistics will be of help. From the figures quoted earlier, certain facts stares in the eyes. The high density of commuters and ultra-quick turn around time means that there would be around 20,000 people at, say Churchgate station every 4-5 minutes. Asks an exasperated senior WR official: "How on can we put any security system and make work? It would take ten times the time to clear a single train out of platform. This is not your airport or even a regular railway network, we need specially - devised systems."[1]

A beginning was made in this direction when two days after the blasts, the railways began installing the closed-circuit television at strategic locations. Experts advise the installment of gadgets like x-ray devices at the entry points to detect explosives. Sniffer dogs can also be of help. An analyst has a final word: "Tuesday was a wake-up call like no other to address the commuter security."[2]

Intelligence : A Scapegoat or culprit?

It is a sensitive issues and various experts have their views on the subject. But it needs to be emphasised that there can never be definitive answers to contentious questions concerning success or failure of intelligence when incidents like serial train blasts occur as no intelligence agency functions in public glare. Then there are inter-agency tug of war — or, war of words — shifting the blame to each other. Whatever the truth, a detailed discussion on the wider aspects of intelligence functioning will be of interst, and this obviously would go beyond the events of 11 July in Bombay.

First about the serial train blasts. Experts feel it is really no surprise that India's intelligence apparatus was taken unawares yet again by the Mumbai's rail blasts not to speak of specific inputs, even the Government's technical intelligence-gathering arms saw no warnings coming. The local subsidiary intelligence Burean (SIB) was no better, failing to translate any inputs into hard intelligence that could have pre-empted the terrorist strike.

Definite clues apart, the intelligence agencies did not have broad leads on a possible attack, sources told a weekly.[16] Rumours about the J&K police forwarding some inputs based on the interrogation of a LET militant on 30 June 2006 were denied by the union Home Ministry. Said a senior intelligence officer wryly: "If we had specific intelligence inputs, wouldn't we have done something about it"?

So is it yet again a case of "intelligence failure", a phrase routinely rather habitually, bandied about by the authorities to conveniently explain away systemic failures that have long dogged India's intelligence apparatus. The fault lines were yet again exposed by the 11 July strikes. The lack of coordination was obvious not only between external and internal intelligence agencies but coordination even between the SIBs and the State police has also been strained.

Coorduation is an important factor that impinges upon the efficiency or otherwise of the intelligence agencies. In spite of a Joint Intelligence Committee in place at the centre, the coordination at the lower or middle level is minimum, even abysmal. One-up manship is the major reason. There is hardly any mechanism to mark or trail resident agents who build up shipper cells for terrist outfits in a city like Mumbai where population is in a state of constant flex. It a tough challenge but that is where the assistance of local police comes handy and proves of immense importance. It is almost like a foundation stone.

But adding to our cup of woes is the mismatch between the global sophisticated terrorist and an ill–equipped intelligence operative, working within a cumbrous bureaucratic set-up.

There are other problem areas also. It is appalling that a large number of sleuths in the IB are from Stare of Central forces or from other Centrad services. No doubt they are imparted basic training on induction but all important question begs an answer: How effective would they be in thwarting the improvised tactics of the modern terrorist? "A case in point was an officer from the Army Vetermary Corps who got inducted into the IB as incharge of technical communications in the highly volatile Jammu region."[3]

The problem with India's intelligence, feel observers, starts at the very top. Presently (October 2006) both IB and RAW are headed by officers who are externally competent but have little exposure of PKH Tharakan, Secretary (R), heading RAW was brought inform the Kerala police' months before he was to retire, ESL Narasimhan reportedly never headed an independent SIB, was still made director IB. He was staff officer to NSA MK Narayanan when he headed the Agency. Must we smell cronyism or a Keral connection? Insiders asserts that 2-year fixed tenure granted to both intelligence chiefs barely months before they were to retire sent out wrong signals.[18] Besides affecting morale, it has led to the exodus of several senior officers experienced in dealing with terrorism. A back of accountability at the top has ensured that India's security apparatus is open to infiltration as was demonstrated by the espionage ring functioning within the NSC secretariat.

A day after the Mumbai blasts the Prime Minister convened a high-level meeting to discuss the issue. It was also attended by three service chiefs and Tharakan besides the NSA. It was reported that none of the participants, when asked by the Prime Minister, came up with the options on how to deal, with terrorism.

India's reluctance, rather refusal, to look at any "tough options", say IB sources can only mean that it will continue to bleed."

Is it confusion, back of coordination, or one-up manship? While state DGP PS Pasricha emphatically said there was prior intelligence on the terrorist strike and understandably his Home Minister stood by that assertion The Chief Minister, Mumbai Police Commissioner AN Roy and ATF Chief Raghuvanshi denied this out right. They denied being privy to any such intelligence reports and asserted that intelligence did not go beyond a general regular alert that Mumbai could be the target of terrorists. Roy honestly admitted that the blasts caught him and his force "off-guard", that the terrorists had "taken them by surprise." and that they would have taken steps to prevent it had there been specific intelligence reports.

Former top cops in Mumbai posit that local intelligence is not as strong and definite as it used to be in the 1990s. If that be so then how come that the team investigating the March 1993 blasts did not have any clue about the involvement of the underground, specifically of the D-Company, in the incidents for a good 48 hours after. The initial probe trailed Khalistani militants and then Kashmir terrorists until a chance clue led them on the Dawood trail.

To an extant, initial investigation has been hampered and a day was lost due to confusion between the investigating agencies themselves. In the initial hours, the Mumbai police insisted that the Railway police force conduct the investigation since the blasts had taken place under their jurisdiction. Within a day, however, with a change of mind at the top-most levels, the blasts probe was back with the ATS. But even as the ATF settled down to conduct the investigation and packed off special teams to sensitive town across the State, it was announced that a Special Task Force (STF) would be constituted under top cap Rakesh Maria to handle investigation. Maria along with AS Samra and MN Singh — who were then police commissioner and joint commissioner respectively — had cracked the March 1993 blasts case.

Line of Investigation

Two days after the 11 July blasts, the line of investigation reported by hit a dead end. This May or may not be true, based as these are on press reports. Some sources say the police see the LET as the mastermind behind the attacks, assisted by the SIMI, now functioning under the sobriquet of Tehbaz-e-Fasche Islam (TEFI), which provided the logistical and resource support for the dialolical plan.

Pursuing the LET-SIMI trail, intelligence is examining the possible link between the massive arms and ammunition haul form the record tire cities like Aurangabad, Manmad, Malegaon etc. across Maharashtras in early may and Mumbai rail blasts Tuesday. It may be too early to link the two, but the possibility is preponderant. The recovery made from these second-rung towns including the three mentioned above stunned even the police: 30-45 kilos of RDX; 16 × AK 56s; and over 60 grenades and other ammunition. The May haul remains the definitive pointer to major underground activity. Acting on the information gleaned from their operatives, the Mumbai police ATS had made arrests as early as January 2006. It then began combing operations in April-May. Besides the said recoveries, the ATS also made 20 arrests then. When an early morning 1 June 2006 attack on the RSS Headquarters at Nagpur was foiled and 3.5 kg of RDX along with 3 × AK 56s were recovered, the Mumabi police believed they were on the right track—and the trail.

It was easy to surmise that there must have been more caches of RDX and arms that remained undiscovered either in the Aurangabad. Malegaon raids or in Nagpur. Sources say that blast investigation is now trying to see if, and how, some of the non-recovered RDX might have some how found its way into Mumbai. As one analyst put it, " If the recoveries of RDX made in May 2006 was the tip of the iceberg, the 11 July blasts were the iceberg."

Menwhile, the Gujarat police are looking for links between the Ahmedabad railway station blast of 19 February 2006 and 11-7 blasts. The RDX used in Ahmedabad was brought by the Karnavati Express from Mumabi.

In the early stages, there were a number of theories — or conjectures flying about in the air. A source disclosed that in the first hour after the blast, two calls were made to Karachi and one to Dubai from Mumbai Central. Police believe Rahil, a LET operative who masterminded the New Delhi blasts of October 2005, and his associates Imtiyaz and Zabiuddin Ansari, who has contacts with the banned SIMI in Aurangabad are behind the blasts.

This source also espoused another theory. The fact that all the blasts had taken place in the first class compartments and that many victims were Gujaratis indicated that the intention was to avenge the Gujarat riots. "It was a confecture." More than 12 Gujaratis lost their lives and 75 were injured in the blasts.

As for the explosives used, RDX was the prime suspect. This along with another device is discussed below.

RDX Explained

Cyclotrimethyl enetrinitramine, also known as RDX, cyclonite, hexogen or T4, is an explosive nitromine widely used by the military. I am its pure state, RDX is a white, crystalline solid. As an explosive, it is usually used in mixtures with other explosives. It is stable in storage and is considered the most powerful of the military high explosives (HE). RDX is also used as a major component of plastic bonded explosives used in nuclear weapons.

The discovery of RDX dates from the 1890s when a German, Hans Henning, offered it as a medicine. Its explosive properties were not discovered until 1920. It was widely used during World War II, often in explosive mixtures with TNT.[4]

The acronym RDX is expanded /interpreted in the following ways:

- Royal Demolition explosive.
- Research Department (composition) X.
- Research Department explosive.

Its two properties are mentioned here:

- Explosive Velocity 8,750 metres per second.
- Melting point 205.5 degrees C.

Pencil Detonators

A pencil detonator of a time pencil, believed to have been used in the blasts, is a chemically activated time fuse to be connected to detonator. It has the same dimensions as a pencil. One type, the British 'Switch N. 10, Delay, is made of aluminium (or brass), apart from a copper section at one end which contains a glass vial of cupric chloside or sulphuric acid. Underneath the vial is a spring-loaded striker, held back by a thin steel wire. When the copper tube is crushed, the liquid eats through the wire holding back the striker. The striker hits the percussion cap on the detonator and sets it off.

Pencil detonators are colour coded to indicate the nominal time delay, which can range from 10 minutes to 24 hours. The time delay varies according to the concentration of the corrosive liquid in the vial. Pencil detonators are immune to detection or jamming via electronic counter measures because they use a chemical time fuse.

The Unholy Trio

It was the worst week for the UPA government — and for the country. On Sunday, 9 July, the IBM Agni-3 test flopped. The next day, the prestigious geosynchronic satellite launch vehicle, which was to announce India's entry into an elite space chub, Misfired. On Tuesday, the 11th, the terrorists created havoc and may him Mumbai by serial-blasting densely-packed passenger coaches of its commuter trains and lobbed grenades at tourists at five places in Srinagar.

If it was the ISI hand in 1993, there is less talk of the ISI today and more about the Pak-based LET and the local SIMI.

NOT that the ISI has turned into bay-scouts. To avoid international gaze, it has outsourced most of its operations to groups like LET.

The LET, which used to train an arm infiltrators, has transformed into an amorphous body that raises funds and coordinates the activities of smaller groups —something which was earlier done by the ISI.

But worries the intelligence agencies is the possibility of an Al Qaeda connection, beyond the astensible SIMI and LET links. The terrorism expert Braman feels "the blasts inspired and guided by Qaeda but carried out by the LET and SIMI."

Kasuri ups the ante

Even when the opposition blamed it for its soft approach towards Dawood-shielding Pakistan, the government acted with caution in the immediate aftumath of 11 July blasts. "Competitive Pakistan-bashing thought air waves could have led to a communal carnage in Mumbai, as its happened in 1993", said a Home Ministry Official.[5]

But India's tack changed by what Pak Foreign Minister Khurshid Mohmud Kasuri told the *Reuters* in Washington: "I think the Mumbai incident —however tragic it may be, and it is undoubtedly very tragic — underlines the need for the two countries to work together to control this environment, but they can do so if they resolve their disputes". The purported link between terrorism and a "root cause" naturally touched Delhi's raw nerves. The Pak Foreign Office tried the damage control by denying Kasuri ever made such a statement: "It was an interview with *Reuters* in which too issues were lumped together. At no stage did the Minister linked the Mumbai blasts with the issue of solving Kashmir Problem." But the damage has been done.

If a Pak journalist wrote," In a slight shift from a predictable script of blaming Pakistan for India's woes, New Delhi latched on to a statement of ..... Kasuri to trigger a blast of the diplomatic kind" his Indian counterpart[6] wrote, "ulltimalely it was the remark by..... Kasuri that gave India the handle to remind Pakistan of its written commitment to fight terrorism." Till Kasuri's statement, India had avoided pointing a finger at

Pakistan, as mentioned above. Kasuri forced its hands, providing MEA spokesman Navtej Sarna to term it as "appalling " the Linking of the terrorist attack "to the so-called lack of resolution of disputes between India and Pakistan" Sarna added: "It appears.... Pakistan will cooperate with India against the courge of cross-border terrorism and the terrorist violence only if such so-called disputes are resolved." He did not stop here, further declaring, "We would hope that the government of Pakistan rejects any such linkages", thereby giving Pakistan enough wriggling space to distance itself. Pakistan indeed did so, as described above. Sarna also called upon Pakistan to "take urgent steps to dismantle infrastructure of terrorism on territory under its control, act resolutely against ups and individuals who are responsible for terrorist violence and fulfil its solid commitments enshrined in the India Pakistanis joint Press statement of 6 January 2004.[7]

It is ironic that kasuri burnt his fingers with an irresponsible remake on Kashmir issue because he is criticised as an inveterate 'dove' on India, and is not among those whom you expect to issue insensitive statements against a nation reeling under a trgedy.

Is it tit for tat between India and Pakistan

At least one Pakistani journalist thinks so. When Mumbai was racked by multiple bomb blasts that Tuesday evening, Pakistani TV channels promptly switched from their live coverage of elections in Muzaffarabld to ghastay images of mutilated bodies and wrecked train bogies. Voices of condemnation poured in from all quarters. But Hamid Mir, the popular GEO TV host who in famous for his interview with Osama bin Laden, thought Tuesday's terror attack in Mumbai was only to be expected.

Mir told an Indian Weekly:[8] "Mumbai was waiting to happen. After the massive terrorist act in Nishtar Park in Karachi (around 50 people were killed there in April), it was only a matter of time that something similar happened in Mumbai. This is part of the tit-for-tat process between India and Pakistan. A glance at the pattern of the last two years, reveals that if something happens in New Delhi, you can expect a similar act in Lahore. Some goes for Mumbai and Karachi. The media in both countries fail to criticise their respective intelligences agencies — ISI and RAW."

No body holding any responsible position can obviously, vouch for the veracity of such assertions. But it is also equally true that some elements in Pakistan hold this perception, placing the ISI and the RAW on equal footing. Through a clever juxtaposition of happenings in one country against those in the other, some Pakistanis might be doing their duty as Pakistani nationalists and patriots, but they are serving neither the truth and accuracy nor the facts of the ground situation. There is simply no such neat balance as Mir would like Indians to believe. It is a mere play to palm off sectarian killings in Pakistan as doings of the RAW, an much-undeserved credit for the Indian intelligence agency. Yet again, the post-Afghanistan and post-9/11 terrorism in Pakistan is of home-grown variety. It is the monster turning on the keeper. If some Pakistanis want to believe that the ghastly and murderous terrorism in India is mere pay-back for the equally ghastly acts of Indians on their soil, there would be few objective takers of this preposterous postulation. It may be misplaced patriotism but certainly not balanced journalism.

"11-7 mastermind had plotted Modi's assassination also."

Faisal Sheikh, 31-year-old engineering drop-out, said to be a senior LET operative, told his interrogators on 8 Oct. 2006: "From 2001, when 1 returned from Bahawalpur in Pakistan after being personally recruited and trained by LET,s 'India Commander' Azam Cheema, I did every thing Babaji (as 53-year-old Cheema is called by his recruits) wanted." The Plan was foiled by Ahmadabad police which shot dead the four potential assassins — including Ishat Jahan a 19-year-old BSc. student from Mumbra, Mumbai — on 16 June 2004.

"After four of our members were killed, I sent some money to Jahan's family through Ehtesham Siddiqui", confessed Faisal. Siddiqui", too has been arrested for the 11-7 blasts.

Faisal was arrested by senior police inspector JK Hargude on 27 July 2006, with a lead from his own cousin Noman Sheikh, who too has been arrested. Faisal revealed to Hargude that he spent 6 months at Bhavalpur in 2004, undergoing intensive training in arms and explosives, and interacting extensively with Cheema and his ISI bosses.

7 Accused retract: 9 October 2006

Seven of the 16 accused in the 11-7 serial blasts case retracted their confessions before a special court saying that their statements had been taken under duress. It is seen as set back to the prosecution in the case as the stand of the accused to resile their statements comes 10 days after the Mumabi police claimed to have cracked the case.

These seven accused are Faizal Shaikh Muzammil Shaikh, Tanvir Ahmad Ansari, Mohd Kamal Absari, Ehtesham Siddiqui, Sohail Sheikh and Zamir Ahmad Ansari.

Appearing before the special judge MR Bhatkar, the accused said that the police had obtained their signatures on blank sheets and that they were also not produced before a magistrate or deputy commissioner of police for recording of their confessions. Under the provisions of the Maharashtra Control of Organised Crime Act (MCOCA), it is mandatory for the police to produced an accused person before a competent authority and record his confession.

What is surprising is that they retracted their confessions while still under police custody. The retraction normally comes when the accused is placed under judicial custody. Defence lawyer Shaheed Azmi said the disclosure of the accused about their "forced" confession was considered significant because they have told the court about the police "pressurising" them to sign blank sheets at the first available opportunity.

After their retraction, the court remanded the accused to judicial custody for the first time. They shall be produced again on 20 October. Of the 16 accused, 12 have been arrested under the MCOCA. Of these 7 retracted their statement (on 9.10.06), while 5 others will be produced on 13 October for extension of remand.

Coming as they do ten days after the police cracked the case, the retractions — aimed at diluting the allegations against them and derailing the investigations — may hamper the ATS in building a foolproof case against them. Among the retractions, the one made by Faizal Sheikh is a big blow for the prosecution, considering that he played a key role in the conspiracy and actually perpetrated the terror acts.

Faizal and other accused had told the Mumbai police the way the conspiracy had been hatched and how the blasts were actually executed.

The details:

- Their training under LET; Bahawalpur Commander Azam Cheema in Pakistan.
- How 11 Pakistanis made it into India in the run-up to the blasts, and the nature of roles played by them.
- They also explained how the explosives were prepared, placed inside pressure cookers, and later planted in the first class compartment of Mumbai trains.
- How funds came to the raised for the blasts.

Incidentally, Defence Lawyer said: "In a legal conference with me, Faizal told me senior police officers had begged before him with folded hands to give a confusion."

It is worth a re-emphasis that it is unusual that the accused retracted their statements even before they were remanded to judicial custody. All such unusual tactics, if they can be termed so, will be discussed in some detail when it is time to examine if the accused, ably guide by their defence lawyers are acting on the guidelines as laid down in the Al Qaeda Manual, discussed in this book.

As for Faizal, he had gone far beyond the scope of 11-7 investigations —reportedly "confessing" to the police that he was also part of the LET plot to assassinate Gujarat CM Narendra Modiin 2004. Ahmedambad police had succeeded in foiling this plot.

Eight Muslim MPs meet the Chief Minister: Alleged Torture

Families of 11-7 accused filed sworn affidavits with the offices of the Prime Minister and Chief Minister Vilasrao Deshmukh in September 2006, alleging torture and brutality by the Mumbai police in the 7-11 investigation. Maharashtra DGP PS Pasricha said on 100 October 2006 that was looking into the allegations after receiving the affidavits in the last week of September.

After the families filed the affidavits in september, a debgation of eight Muslim MPs had met the Chief Minister. "The police was then instructed not to harass the Muslim Community in general and the city police chief, AN Roy, circulated a letter to the Muslim leaders in Urdu, asking them to contact him in case of any complaints."

The relatives, including those of the alleged kingpins Faisal and Muzammil Shikh, alleged that police used "fourth degree" methods, holding women and old relatives hostage to extract confessions from the accused or ensure the arrest of suspects. Human rights activist advocate Maharukh Adenwalla said: "such methods were used during the investigation of 1993 blasts as well..... These people have been brave to come forward and file affidavits. These affidavits will obviously hold,"

All the affidavits say that they were threatened not to contact any lawyers.

Meanwhile, the seven accused retracted their so-called confessions statements in the specially designated MCOCA court on 9 October.

Cracking 11-7 case: A Pak on the Back (October, 2006)

"London Cops to take lessons on 11-7," reads a headline in a daily[25] of 10.10.06. The Mumbai police was reported to be gearing for the proposed visit of the Landon police for studying the strategy undertaken by them in investigating and cracking the 11 July serial train blast case. A happy, if not elated, Police Commissioner AN Roy told the daily: "They are intersted in knowing how we went about investigating the case. It would be an academic exercise whereby they will learn in detail about the case, the evidence collected by us, and the manner in which we proceeded to solve the case".

The London police had asked for the date convenient for their visit. It was not till then known whether the London police team would be formed by members of the Scotland Yard or the specialised Counter Terrorism Command of the Metropolitan Police.

If the London police team comes down to Mumabi, it would be second instance where the 11-7 case would be discussed at an international level. On 6 October 2006, the US Ambassador

David Mulford disclosed that the US and India had discussions over evidence and other aspects of the 11/7 case.

IMPORTANT POSTSCRIPTS: ATS DISCLOSURES

Mumbai Police Commissioner charged the Anti-Terrorist Squad (ATS) under KP Raghuvanshi to investigeter the 11 July terrorist attack on Mumbai's suburban trains. Some of their select findings are recorded in the succeeding para graphs.

ATS gets more details: 8 October, 2006

One of the 11 Pakistanis involved in the 11-7 had come to Mumbai to offer his expertise for making those seven deadly bombs, and fled soon after the blasts. He assembled the bombs using RDX (2-2.5 kg), ammonium natrate (4-5 kg) and a detonator comprising a quartz timer in a pressure cooker at the residence of the accused Mohd Ali in Shivaji Nagar slum in north-east Mumbai between 8 and 10 July a transported to the house of the mastermind of the blasts, Faisal Sheikh in Subarban Bandra. Sheikh was an expert in radio sensitive, remote sensitive and light sensitive detonators. In a light sensitive device, the detonation is triggered due to fluctuations in the intensity of light and the blast occurs in 19 minutes.

RDX used in the blasts was brought from Pakistan by one Ehsamullah while the ammonium nitrate and cookers were procured locally.

Some other points gleaned from the press briefing by Mumbai Police Commssioner AN Roy on the ATS investigations in 11-7:

1. Pressure cookers were used strategically in the blasts as they cause high intensity explosions and are compact in size.
2. The core of each cooker comprised a lump of RDX (2 kg) placed in the centre, surrounded by aluminium nitrate (4 kg). A detonator comprising a quartz timer was placed over the explosives to trigger the explosion.
3. Of the 11 Pak suspects two have died after the blasts. Abu Osama was killed in an encounter in Mumbai on 22 August and Salim, a planter, died in the blast.

ATS draws wanted list on 11-7: 26 October, 2006

The Anti-Terrorism squad (ATS) of Mumbai police claimed 26 October 2006 that four of the six accused in the 11-7 blasts confessed to exact roles played by them in the incidents. The confessions of the four accused — *Mohd Ali*, Naved, Sajid and Majid — have been recorded. ATS Chief KP Raghuvanshi gave details:

- The bombs were assembled at Mohd Ali's residence at Govandi by a specialist team of Pakistani and Indian nationals.
- Majid facilitated the movement of six Pakistanis who crossed over India from Bangladesh.
- Junaid, arrested from Belgaum on 3 October handled the entire support system and logistics and was among the masterminds.

The recorded confessions of these four had come in handy to establish Pakistan's hand in the 11-7 blast. Now follow more details.

Thus on the 26th, Mumbai police not only named a majority of Pakistani nationals walked in the 11-7 blasts but also came out with telling details of the roles played by some of them in planning and executing the explosions. Three of these are briefly described above.

The ATS revealed the "wanted list" of Pakistani nationals on the 11-7 blasts two days after the Prime Minister declared that India had "credible evidence" of Pakistan's involvement in the blasts.

Ten of the accused in this case are Pakistani nationals : Azam Cheema, Aslam, Hafizullah, Saabir, Abu Baker, Kasam Ali, Ammujan, Ehsan Ehsan Ehsanullah, Abdul Razak and Sohail Shaikh.

Others named in the remand application filed before the special MCOCA court judge Mrudula Bhatkar on 26 October are Pune - born Rizwan Daware, Rahil Shaikh (the UK-based brother of Faisal and Muzammil), Nepal-based Hafiz Zubair and Abdul Rehman

Giving further details, Raghuvanshi said that one of the accused, Majid (Full name Mohd Majid Mohd Shafi and briefly discussed above) who was remanded to judicial custody till 9 November on 26 October, had facilitated six of the Pakistanis' entry into India across the 24 Paragans district bordering Bangladesh. "They brought RDX into India. They also helped local people assemble the bombs and plant them into the trains", ATS sources said.

Of the four who made confessions, Sajid was the one who helped the Pakistanis in assembling the electronic cercuits used in the bombs and Naved served as the local guide. Junaid played a key role in executing the blasts.

The ATS emphasised the role of Bahawalpur - based LET commander and ISI operative Azam Cheema, who trained several of the 11-7 blast perpetrators.

Two Pakistanis, who were, part of these blasts, are no more: Salim from Lahore, killed at the blast site at Khar and Abu Umid alias Abu Osame, killed in a police encounter at Antop Hill in north-central Mumbai.

The ATS repeatedly it was Asif Khan Bashir Khan alias Junaid alias Abdullah, arrested at Bolgaum on 3 October, who headed the "organised crime syndicate" that engineered the serial blasts.

10,000-page police file and some unanswered questions

The Mumbai police's ATF has charge sheeted the accused and has a thick 10,000-page file on the case. In this voluminous effort, the analysts and journalists have found some holes — unanswered questions. There are mentioned below.

RDX Trail

The ATS hasn't been able to provide conclusive evidence on how RDX was brought into Mumbai. According to the charge sheet, the RDX used in the blasts was procured from across the border and brought to the city by alleged Pakistani national and LET operative Ehsanullah. In May 2006, he was escorted to the city by Kolkata - based operative Mohd Majid. He was brought from the Bangladesh border alongwith three other Pakistanis.

But Ehsanullah remains a mystery. All that the police knows is that for sometime he lived in Mumbai with Asif Khan Bashir Khan, alias Junaid in Thane.

Pakistan Connection

The ATS claims that the blasts were sponsored and supported by perpetrators from Pakistan. But according to the charge sheet, at least two of the alleged Pakistanini bombers are unidentified. While the ATS claims to have identified those involved in the blasts at Matunga, Bandra, Jogeshwari, Borivli and Mira Road, it has failed to identify the Pakistani or local bombs accompanying them in Nahim and Bandra.

First Timers

The ATS chargesheet claims a reconnaissance of trains was carried out two months before the blasts by six accused. However, according to the list of planters submitted to the court, only two were among those six accused. The rest were first-time bombers, including Bihar-based Kamal Ansari and the nine Pakistani nationals who accompanied Faisal Sheikh. While Faisal was first detained on 22 July (2006) and questioned by the Mumbai Police Crime Branch, his involvement in the blasts came to the fore only after he was handed over to the ATS and arrested five days after his detention.

Pressure Cookers

On 30 September, 2006, then Commissioner of Police AN Roy said at a press conference that the IEDs planted in the trains were concealed in Kanchan Pressure Cookers. National Security Advisor MK Narayan and also subsequently mentioned pressure cookers. However, there is no mention of the pressure cookers in the charge sheet.

Hawala transfers

The ATS claims Dubai-based accused Rizwan Mohd Dawrey and prime accused Faizal Sheikh sent 40,000 Sandi Riyals through hawala to Khalid Iqbal Sheikh in April, 2004. But *hawala* transfers are received in a country in local currency. So, how come the ATS seized Saudi Riyals if they were sent through hawala ?

Police's "Unassailable" Case and Findings under microscope

Mumbai Police Commssioner AN Roy told a stunned, television audience early Oct. 2006 that "it was an Oct. of war carried out on behalf of the ISI through the Lashkar-e-Taiba" Thus in little less than three months after the 11 July serial train bombings, that killed 187 and injured 890, Mumbai Police claimed to have a full account of just who carried out the attacks, and how. "While their is little doubt that the Mumbai Police is headed in the right direction, it is unclear if the details of the story will survive the rigorous international scrutiny that it will be subjected to in the coming months.[9]

Main Culprits and execution of the attacks

Interrogation of 13 men arrested so far show that 11 Pakistani nationals and seven Indians executed the terror strikes. Roy says Pakistani nationals entered India through Nepal or Bengladesh in March to plan the bombings. One , a Lahore resident, called Salim, died in the explosion he helped set off. Another, Mohd Ali was shot dead in an encounter in Antop Hill area in Mumabi soon after the Bombings.

A separate cell of seven Indians facilitated the Pakistanis to carry out the attacks. Each bomb was planted by a joint team comprising an Indian and a Pakistani. This system might have been put in place because the Pakistanis would not have known the working of city's train system and needed help to leave crowded compartments.

Forensic experts established that the explosives — a core of between 2 and 2.5 kg of RDX, combined with some 3.5 to 4 kg of ammonium nitrate — were packed inside five-litre pressure cookers , which were than concealed inside cloth bags and camouflaged with newspapers and umbrellas.

Police learnt from questioning shopkeeper that eight pressure cookers were purchased. But "it remains unclear what the devices were used for."

The seven team of bombers hired taxis to reach Churchgate station in south Mumabi about 6 PM on 11 July. The teams boarded local trains? Placed the bombs in overhead luggage racks in first class coaches and apparently got off a few stations later. The first bomb went off at 6.24 PM at Khar. A minute later the next bomb exploded at Mahim. By 6.30 PM all seven bombs had exploded on local trains running on the Western line.

Breaking the Case

The break through came when call records showed that several phone calls had been made from Navi Mumbai to a village on the Nepal border in the days before and after the blasts. The calls had been made to a Lashkar operative, Kamal Ansari, who had served time in jail after he was held in the course of a 2002 IB Counter-terrorism operation. Since then, he had been thought to be making a living selling toys.

Ansari was brought to Mumbai and subjected to narcoanalysis tests, which involve placing suspects in a hypnotic state using barbiturates. These helped the police to gain some insights into the identities of some other suspects. For example, police learned that SIMI's Maharashtra General Secretary Etesham Siddiqui had played a key role in the operation. Among those interrogated was Faisal Sheikh who handled funds for the operation. Police recovered some 26,000 Saudi Riyals from his house, which was believed to be just a small part of far larger *hawala* payments routed to Mumbai from the Lashkar's Pakistan-based bosses. Rizwan Dawre, an Indian national based in Riyadh, has, now been named as the person who handled the hawala transactions on behalf of the Lashkar.

Meanwhile, interrogation of Lashkar operatives arrested in the course of a separate operation that led to the recovery of arms and explosives from the Aurangabad area produced separate leads. Men told the Mumbai Police that they had been instructed to contact Feroz Deshmukh, a librarian at the Islamic Research Foundation (IRF) for orders on what to do with their weapons cache. Interestingly, the IRF is listed among a handful of approved religious information centres of the official website of the Lashkar's parent organisation, Jamaat-ud-Dawa (JUD).

Deshmukh was then asked to chat on the Internet with Rahil Abdul Rehman Sheikh, a top Lashkar organiser, who had sent at least a dozen men for training at its Bahawalput facility. From his safe-house in Dhaka, Mumbai police says, Rahil gave Deshmukh the number for a Kolkata - based Lashkar organiser, Mohd Majid Sheikh, who in turn provided the Mumbai police with details of just how the Pak national involved in the bombings transited through the India-Bangladesh border. ATS Chief Raghuvanshi says *the police are searching for three or four* suspects, including some who planted bombs.

India has shared much of the evidence from the investigation with the US in an effort to build pressure on Pakistan to act against the Lashkar's Core commanders. Prime Minister Man Mohan Singh has also said that the "evidence will shared with Pakistan when the Foreign Secretaries of the two countries meet later this year (2006)."

Forensic coulroversy

Although both the Government of India and the Mumabi police appear convinced that an unassailable case has been built up, serious questions remain on the integrity and the content of the evidence available so far. Most important, the scientific literature suggests that the foundation of the case, narcoanalysis of the key suspects, may be flawed.

Narcoanalysis is a controversial procedure. *In 1989, the Supreme Court* of New Jersey, USA, disallowed the use of evidence obtained from sodium-amytal-induced interviews, after finding that it was not a valid scientific technique. Among other things, the court heard evidence that drug-induced interrogations could cause hypermanesia, a state where subjects fill in gaps in their stories with imaginary or false material; hypnotic recall, where non-existent thoughts or feelings become embedded in the original memory; and a memory hardening, a process by which subjects come to confidently believe that imaginary events were in fact true.[10]

In a recent paper prepared on the subject for the Andhra Pradesh Police's Criminal Investigation Department, Superintendent of Police M. Sivananda Reddy pointed to the "baffling mixture of truth and fantasy in drug-induced output." By disrupting the suspect's defences, Reddy noted, barbiturates "may sometime be helpful in interrogation, but even under the best conditions they will elicit an output which is partially contaminated by deception [and] fantasy." In general, they "provide rapid access to information that is psychiatrically useful but of doubtful validity as empirical truth,"

Sivananda Reddy observed that the comprehensive examination of the issues by the US, 9th Circuit Court of Appeals in the case of US vs Solamon had concluded that "narcoanalysis does not produce reasonably reliable statements." "The almost total absence of controlled experimental studies of 'truth drugs' and the spotty and anecdotal nature of psychiatric and police evidence", he concluded, "require that extrapolations to intelligence operations be made with care." Indeed, the real use of test appears to be as a form of deception. "A major vulner ability they produce in the subject", Sivananda Reddy observed, "is a tendency to believe he has revealed more than he has and this can be used by the interrogator for subsequent interrogation of the subject under normal circumstances."

Psychiatrists involved in narcoanalysis have long been clear about the limitations of the science. As early as 1954, the American pshychiatrist John McDonald noted that suspects subjected to narcoanalysis sometimes confessed to crimes they could be demonstrated not to have committed or continued to practise deceipt. "It is clear from these accounts", McDonald observed, "that narcoanalys is often unsuccessful in eliciting the truth," while defending the utility of narcoanalysis he flatly noted that it could neither be used to "determine the truthfulness of a statement made to the police", nor to "obtain confessions from suspects." In McDonald's view, psychiatrists called on to participate in such exercises "should on ethical grounds refuse to perform narcoanalysis."

Why, then, has the Mumbai police built its case around drug-induced statements? "It is far pleasanter to sit conferrable in the shade," wrote the British colonial administrator James Stephen in 1883, "rubbing red pepper in a poor devil's eyes, than to go about in the sun hunting up evidence". In the century and a quarter since, police forces have often turned to technical variants on the same practice—with little success. While high-technology processes such as P-300 brain-wave mapping can detect whether certain kinds of visual information is stored in the brain, for example, knowledge of a murder weapon; science is yet to arrive at a means to sender painstaking investigation redun.

A good deal of investigation remains, not withstanding the Mumbai Police's progress. Explanations are needed, for example, as to why the Lashkar took the unprecedented decision to commit large number of Pakistani nabonals for the Mumabi bombings, risking detection of the operation and international exposure, when it had trained Mumbai-based cadre to execute the operation. Just why Mohd Ali chose to stay on after the bombings, when all his counterparts left will need to be explained. Again why did police at first claim he was a Jaish operitive? Most important of all, there is so far no evidence on just when, where and why the decision to bomb Mumbai was made, and who made it.

All these are important questions — a big ask. Top Western India Lashkar operatives Rahel Sheikh, Zahiduddin Ansari and Fayyas Kagdi, all succeeded in escaping from the country, and now seemed solely outside the reach on Indian law - enforcement organisations. Pakistan has already made it clear that it will not turn over Lashkar operatives to India, even if evidence is provided of their involvement in terrorist crimes. It most certainly will not make ISI officers available to Indian interrogators. The ISI is, after all, part of the Pakistan Army and its Director General, Lt. Gen. Mohd Zaki, reports directly to Gen. Musharraf, in his capacity as the Chief of the Army Staff.

If a coherent and full account of the serial bombings is to emerge, the Mumbai Police must heed James Stephen's admonition, and "go about in the sun." India, Foreign Secretary Shiv Shankar Menon said recently, wants Pakistan to "not only talk but take action against terrorism on the ground." Pakistan, though, will only be compelled to do so if India arrives at its door step armed with hard facts—facts robust enough to survive the most sceptical scrutiny.

Some analysts rightly consider it a futile effort: no hard facts — however hard —will survive that sceptical scrutiny. Pakistan has no intention of cooperating with India against its own people — be they LET operatives or the ISI officers. It has already made a declaratory policy announcement to this effect. India should simply expect no help from Islamabad in counter-terrorism field. It is time some Indians stopped days dreaming!

Will the police and the system succumb to motivated pressure: October, 2006

There were reports in early Octobeer, 2006 from Mumbai that relatives of those accused of carrying out the horrific train blasts on 11 Jul 2006 petitioned the Prime Minister's office and Chief Minister Vilas Rao Deshmukh of Maharashtra, alleging police atrocities. Such reports are extremely disturbing.[11]

Police was the target of these petitions. The affidavits sworn by the relatives — and facilitated by Muslims organesations, community lawyers and the usual gaggle of human rights activists — charge the police with extracting forcible confessions, and using relatives of those under interrogation as hostages. "To cement the religious connotations the entire episode has acquired, a team of Muslim MPS met the Chief Minister and expressed its anguish at the supposed "forced" confessions."

It is obvious that an attempt is being made to brow beat and demotivate the investigating authorities in Mumbai even before the case reaches the courts. Their case is being sought to be discredited in advance of judicial secrutiny.

They obviously are following a precedent. Earlier this year (2006), after Afzal's death sentence was confirmed (in Parliament attack case), the supporters of the mastermind behind the 13 December 2001 outrage began a campaign saying "his story has not been heard", and that he had been convicted on the basis of fraudulent confessions. What Affzal's friends sought to do after the judgement, the Mumabi train blasts suspects are seeking to do at the initial stage itself; they are simply attempting to pre-empt the criminal justice system. Backed up by political class, this clever but alarming move puts the Mumabi police under enormous pressure. The "Afzal flue" has jumped cities.

Two inferences flow from this campaign of some sections of the Indian society to mount motivated pressure on the system affecting its functional impartiality and ability to deliver justice. One, the potential unraveling of the Mumbai police's diligent detective work on the 11 July 2006 terrorist attacks, and this indeed is a real danger now, under religio-political pressure tactics, which translate to naked bullying, and this only strengthens the case for an effective, specific anti-terror law. It is generally acknowledged by analysts that UPA Government's decision to repeal POTA on assuming power in 2004 was hasty. It seriously handicapped India's terrorism fighting capacity, particularly so in the absence of any alternative legislation. And among other aspects, a POTA-type law immunises the police against terrorists and witnesses who may want to change their testimony as per their convenience. Two, Maharashtra Chief Minister Deshmukh played a passive, dutiful postman 'forwarding' petitions to the Mumbai Police Commissioner. Mumabi Police is part of his administration and motivated complaints should not be allowed to create a wedge between it and rest of the administrative structure. "In the last week, the Mumbai Police Commissioner has been blamed for many things: oppressing City's Muslims and, by implicating the ISI in the train bombings, endangering the so-called India-Pakistan anti-terrorism initiative. This enqustion must stop. The Congress-led state Government (and at a much wider level, congress-led UPA Government at the Centre) can not throw law enforcement agencies to the wolves. It must stand by its men. That means Chief Minister Deshmukh must support his police force.

To start with, Chief Minister will do well to issue a statement affirming his complete and absolute faith in the integrity of Mumbai Police and its leading officers, who have an overuse responsibility to deal with waranding war ending terrorists. This is one way to shield his police force against the motivated and partisan criticism, and to bolster its rank. A demotivated and demoralised police will be no asset to the Chief Minister. It, of course, needs no emphasis that all credible complaints must be inquired into.

All Chief Ministers must resist the temptation of adopting populist measures that comes in the way an efficient system.

An update

Between 6.23 PM and 6.28 PM, seven explosions rocked the first class coaches of subarban trains, killing 187 and injuring 817.

A charge-sheet has been filed against 113 arrested persons and 15 who are still at large, 10 of whom are Pakistani nationals.

The 13 accused are in judicial custody and have been looked under the stringent Maharashtra Control of Organised Crime Act (MCOCA).

The state Anti-Terrorist Squad (ATS) claims in its 10,000 page charge-sheet filed on 29 Nov 2006 that the conspiracy was hatched in Pakistan by the LET 'Commander', Azam Chima alias Babaji and city-based Faizal Ata-ur-Rehman Sheikh and executed through a module of operatives involving locals and Pakistani nationals. The ATs claims that the RDX for this purpose was smuggled in by a Pakistani national, Ehsanullah, via the Bangladesh border and that he brought with him five Pakistanis.

These claims are unsubstantiated as none of the accused Pakistani Nationals have as yet (27 May 2007) been arrested. The ATS, which had earlier claimed that the explosive devices were hidden inside pressure cookers and planted in the bogies, has failed to find any evidence.

The trial to start on 20 June 2007

- On 11 July 2006, seven bombs ripped across suburban trains during evening rush hour, killing 187 and injuring 890.
- The trial of the 13 accused, suspected to belong to the LET or SIMI, will begin on 20 June 2007 at a special Maharashtra Control of Organised Crime Act (MCOCA) court in Mazgaon (*Hindustan Times*, 20 June 20007).
- The accused include the two alleged masterminds: LET 'commander' Faisal Sheikh and former SIMI President Asif khan alias Junaid.

HOW THE CASE WAS CRACKED: A PAINSTAKING ENDEAVOUR

"It was blinder of a case with no leads. The Mumbai Police, however, pieced together phone calls, money trails and pressure cooker handles to unravel the conspiracy behind the meticulously planned mayhem that killed 187."

Some of the details have already been given in the earlier pages here. What follows is a little more coherent account of this guresome perpetration. But first of all, some statistical details.

Prime numbers

- 20 Kg RDX was transported from across the Pakistan border via the Kandla port.
- 40 policemen and four IPS officers worked with the ATS on solving the case.
- 50 policemen and five dogs worked at the blast sites to sniffout evidence.
- 200 phone calls were made by Faisal to his girl friend Manisha, a bar girl.

TIMELINE : PLANNING STAGE TO 'BOOM"BOOM'.

Mar 2006

Conspiracy is hatched. LET India commander Azam Cheema masterminds blasts in his sprawling mansion at Bahawalpur with two modules of LET and SIMI, with their leaders.

May 2006

50 persons from India and Pakisatan are sent to the training camp at Bahawalpur. They are trained to make bombs, fire guns and resist interrogation.

25 Jun 2006

LET infiltrates bombers: *Kamal Ansari transports* two Pakistanis via Nepal boarder; Abdul Majid transports five via Bangladesh border; and unknown man escorts four via kutch.

27 June 2006

The elven man are lodged at four different places in Mumbai suburbs —two in Malad, four in Bandra, two in Borivli and three in Mumbra.

8-10 July 2006

Ehsan ullah transports 15 to 20 Kg RDX from Pakistan via Kandla port. Ammoniumnitrate bought in Mumbai. Eight cookers purchased from two different shops in Santa Cruz.

9-10 July 2006

Bombs made in Mohd Ali's one-room flat in Govandi. Each cooker filled with 2-2.5 RDX and 3.5-4Kg ammonium nitrate. Tharsported to Shikh's Bandra home.

11 July 2006

Terrorists divide themselves in seven groups, two Indians and one Pakistani in each. Each group carries one pressure cooker in black Rexine bag, covered with newspapers. Planters get off at Churchgate station and use the sub-way that connects platforms to board trains.

Why did they choose pressure cookers?

Packed with explosives, the humble cooker becomes a deadly force multiplier. The bomb is triggered by an alarm clock completing a circuit. The blast wave from an RDX explosion travels at over 8,000 mtrs per second, and from the confines of a cooker the wave has thrie the force. Nepal's Maoists first used cooker in a wave of attacks, which led India to ban their export in 2003. They were first used in India in the Varanasi blasts of 7 March 2006 killing 21.

(*Source*: India Today, 16 Oct 2006)

INVESTIGATIONS: PUTTING THE PIECES TOGETHER

A mamoth task

Police started from scratch as there were no clues on the sites. All they had were seven charred train compartments and the knowledge that ammonium nitrate was used.

The first steps

ATS Chief Krish Pal Singh Raguvanshi split officers into steven teams for the seven blasts. He sought RAW and IB inputs. Police detained over 400 people from Navi Mumbai, Mahim, Mira Road, Bhyander, Malegaon and Aurangabad, but without any success.

The Cooker handles

Police sift through blast sites and find pressure cooker handles and parts of aluminium lids in each of the seven apartments. Shops in Santa Cruz, which sold cooker traced.

Break through

First success came on 18 July when police intercept phone calls from Mumtaz Choudhary to his brother-in-law Kamal Ahmid Ansari, who was trained in Pakistan, at Basupatti, Bihar.

Tracing the RDX

Cotton swab method reveals Faisal Sheikh's house in Bandra was used to store bombs.

The names is

Kamal Ansari and Ehtesham module was unearthed by the ATS, the Crime Branch unveiled the module led by Faisal Shiekh. Mastermind Raheel Sheikh still mising.

Planning starts at Cheema's Bahawalpur house

March, 2006, it is LET India Commander Azam Cheema's palatial house in Bahawalpur, Pakistan. He is playing host to a congregation of faithful, the new converts and pilgrims to the world of terror. Jihadis all, these like-minded or rather mindless fanatics, from various parts of the world had assembled for the sermon

The air was thick with religious fervour and idealism. One cue from this high priest (Cheema) could kick start another round of bloody " freedom struggle" or signify grue some killing of the innocent any where in India. These killing machines are 'manufactured' in the jungles near Bahawalpur. "LET training camps at Bahawalpur were now swarming with 50 men waiting to become juhadis." Situated right in the middle of a jungle, this camp is the school for teaching terror. It trains men in identifying, handling, firing, and dismantling weapons. A major part of curricula is devoted to education in making, planting and finally testing explosives in special water tanks. The trainees are also taught the use of modern communications tools—form Internet satellite phones—to effectively and efficiently carry out their mission

This describes normal activities in the training camps run by the LET and at the Cheema house in a major town of Pakistan

Sitting in a regal room of this palatial house day in March 2006 were some Indian visitors awaiting audience with the Presiding Deity! They had reached there via Bangladesh, Nepal and Iran. That fateful raing night, says the police, the blueprint of a plan designed by the ISI and to be executed by the LET, was drawn. The joint task force was all set to orchestrate one of the biggest carnages that Mumbai was to witness in days to come — the serial bomb blasts that killed 187 people.

Task force converges to Mumbai

Two man from Pakistan stepped across the Nepal-India border to enter Bihar in June 2006. On the 25th, a tall hefty Kamal Ahmed Ansari escoted these two inconspicuous passengers to a Mumbai - bound train at Patna. The dark night of 25 June provided the perfect setting, camonflaging the motive of these three men. They melted into the populated suburbs as soon as they arrived Mumbai.

Ansari and his wards, of course, were only a part of the big team. By the time the trio reached Mumbai, the entire team of 11 Pakistanis - who had sneaked through horous border from Nepal, Bangladesh and Pakistan — was in place. So was the Indian conbugent. As already explained above, seven two-member teams, a Pakistani and an Indian in each, were fromed for the operation.

Terror had arrived in Mumbai, literally. It had taken the group three months — from that rainy night in Bahawalpur in March 2006, to plan and excute an attack that shook the commercial capital and shocked the country one more time.

The Count-down begins

By 27 June, 11 Pakistanis had reached Mumbai. By 8 July, they had already settled in the new environment in middle and lower class Muslim localities in the suburbs and Mumbra. The RDX was on its way to Mumbai.

Smuggled through the Kandla port in Gujarat, it was transported by road to Mumbai, Ehsan Ullah, the dark and well-built man accompanying the most deadly contraband from Kandla port, had procured 20 kg. of RDX, roughly the amount that caused the maximum casualty at Century Bazaar in 1993. Since beginning of 2006 (till September) the Maharashtra police had seized over 400 Kg of RDX, but this was one shipment that slipped the dragnet. What is worse, the police fear some other consignments too may have reached their destination and may be 'safe' with the sleeper cells for future use.

Unlike the 1993 blasts, this time RDX was not the only substance used for sabotage and destruction. Dr. Tanvir Ansari, a Unani medicine practitioner at the Saboo Siddique hospital at Byculla, procured 20 Kg of ammonium nitrate, which when mixed with RDX, increased the explosive force by a facture of three. Ammonium nitrate was procured from the quarries in Thane where chemical is available for the well-connected. Money was no problem. Hawala payments from Saudi Arabia via a Techie, Rizwan Ahmed Davre, were sent to Faizal (Faisal) Sheikh, who is suspected to be the LET chief of Mumbai. The ATS which recovered 26,000 riyals (Rs. 316,956) from Sheikh's house, estimates that over Rs. 60 lakh had been sent to Faisal via hawala in the past two years.

Here is an interesting coincidence. On the Morning of 9 July, some where in distant Orissa, India was preparing to test its longest surface-to surface nuclear - capable ballistic missile Agni III which could cover 3,000 Km to strike as far as China. India was obviously catering against external threats to its national security. But an internal threat of even graver proportions was going unnoticed. In reality, the real enemy was right under her nose, on her own soil, all set to target the soft core, Mumbai. In a dingy one-room flat owned by Mohd Ali, an alleged LET operative, at Shivaji Nager, Govandi, locally made Knachan pressure cookers were filled with 2 Kg of RDX and 3.5 Kg of ammonium nitrate to create a lethal mix. Once ready, the 'bombs' were transported to Sheikh's one-room tenement in up market Perry Cross lane in Bandra.

It is usual Tuesday evening on 11 July. The pressure cooker bombs suitably concealed, are carried by designated bombers from Bandra by 4 PM in taxis to reach Churchgate by 5.15 PM. Taxix were abandoned at Charchgate and the groups headed for the subway. The groups emerged separately on the fast-train platform numbers 3 and 4, slipping into the first class compartment of the crowded 6 O,clock trains. The bags were strategically placed on baggage over heads under wet umbrellas use on rainy monsoon days. As the moment of insanity drew closer, the groups got off the respective trains at different stations. Seven bombs exploded between 6.24 PM and 6.35 PM on Matunga, Mahim, Bandara, Khar Road, Jogeshwari, Bhyander and Borivli. Barring the one bomber killed at Khar, the operation was a success.

The First Clue

The magnitude of the attack was stunning, leaving the police groping for clues. The first one emerged from the tests at the forensic laboratory at Kalina when the substance used in the blasts was identified as RDX mixed with ammonium nitrate. It was clear to the sleuths, who worked through the night, that this was no rogue attack but a well-planned terror onslaught. Mumbai Police Commissioner AN Roy was to remark a few hours after the attacks: "Blasts were planned with great precision and there was no spot evidence."

There was no dought that piecing together the jigsaw would be tough. Minutes following the seven blasts ripping as many first class apartments, panic-stricken passengers and rains played deterrent in collecting evidence. Strewn between the remains of the train's compartments and Charred bodies were going to be pieces of evidence, key to the trail that would later lead to people and places across the border. But in those initial hours, the situation was nearly a blinder for us, as Roy put it starkly.

The night that followed saw the otherwise ignored Bomb Detection and Disposal Squad (BDDS) swing into action. Its 20 officers, 50 constables and 5 dogs worked round the clock searching for clinching evidence on the spot. Split across the different blast spots and wearing gloves and carrying umbrellas, its sleuths had a big break at the Jogeshwari site where they found pressure cooker handles. They also traced charred pieces of alumnium lids of the cookers.

Having got the first leads, ATS Chief Raghuvanshi put together a team of four IPS officers and over 40 policemen, who were split into seven teams for seven teams, assisted by two technical support teams. Raghuvanshi set a punishing pace for his men, not sparing himself. An ATS official put it well: "we were humbled by our chief who himself slept for less than four hours everyday for the first month."

Some early arrests

But early clues, including some 400 arrests on suspicion, did not lead the investigators to the real culprits.

On 18 July, ATS intercepted telephone calls of a certain Mumtaz Choudhary of Navi Mumabi to Kamal Ansari in Basupatti in Bihar, near the infamous Nepal border. Large number of calls and location of Ansari raised suspicions. While Mumtaz's records seemed clean, IB told ATS that Ansari had been trained in Pakistan.

A team of ATS flew to Bihar to arrests Ansari. But Mumtaz was arrested from his house at Navi Mumbai. So dramatic was Ansari arrest and so urgent the need to laring him to Mumbai that an IAF aircraft was drafted for the latter. The other arrest was of a shoe shop owner Khalid Aziz Sheikh at Madhubani in Bihar. Ansari and other LET operatives alleged by used the shop premises as a meeting ground.

In Mumbai, another team of ATS was designated to investigate the alleged LET leader Rakeel Shekh's involvement in the blasts. He was wanted in the Oct. 2005 blasts in Delhi. Raheel, atthough cornered in Mumbai, managed to escape. But a Crime Branch team cracked the connection while interrogating Pune-based ex-SIMI activist Feroz Deshmukh. He revealed that Raheel had taken a loan of Rs. 15,000 in May 2006 and promised him that a certain Noman would return it to him. The trail led to Noman who confirmed that he was supposed to collect the same amount from Faisal Sheikh. While the police could not get Raheel, it managed to nab Faisal Sheikh, alleged to be closely associated with Azam Cheema, on 27 July from Mumbai.

Faisal, it turned out, is alleged to be the Western India commander for LET and one of the key players in the conspiracy. The loan loop only confirmed ATS' allegation of Raheel's links. Faisal's brother Muzzammil was also arrested. Simibarly Ehtesham Siddiqui, Maharashtra General Secretary of SIMI, was arrested from Navi Mumbai after another accused Tanvir Anasari revealed that he was asked to pick up explosive substance by siddiqui. Interestingly, investigators discovered a series of calls from a phone booth to Faisal's phone. The calls were by 25-year-old bar girl Manisha Chavan, who had been in a relationship with Faisal for 18 months. Manisha, who knew Faisal as Sameer, helped the police to identify him and corroborate their findings.

In a sense, the core had been cracked, but the police was careful to collect subestantive evidence, which came from narcoanalysis tests of Faisal, Kamal Ansari and Siddiqui at the Forensic Sciences Laboratory at Bangalore. Although the tests could not be used as evidence against the accused, they helped the police in putting together pieces on how the blasts were carried out. The tests also confirmed that an unclaimed body from the blasts lying at the Sion hospital was that of Salim, a terrorist from Lahore who had planted one of the bombs.

In a self-congratulatory vein, Roy said: "It has been a beautiful piece of highly professional investigation by our team." Indeed scientific tests such as narco-analysis, telephone analysis, and the cotton swab method to determine the presence of RDX gave the police quite a few clues. Tanvir Anasari also revealed during narco-analysis that he had guests from across the border. *"Kuch memhan Pakistan seaaye the"*, he revealed.

A number of Missing links

The case may have been cracked as the police claims, but all this can be called "preliminary sucesses". Some vital questions are yet to get answers.

The circumstantial evidence of ISI involvement through proxies and terror groups is clear, but the police will need conclusive evidence to make the charge of Pakistani involvement stick. Unlike the earlier bomb blast case, there have been no confressional statements as of early 2007.

The question, how the RDX came in through the Kandla Port, is not clear. Meanwhile, there have been allegations of some Coast Guard officials betting off some LET militants for a consideration of Rs. 10 lakh.

Similarly, the police have claimed that Abu Osama, the Pakistani national killed in an encounter at the Antop Hill a few days after the blasts, was also one of the accused in the 7-11 blasts case. But that begs a question: If nine of the Pakistani accused fled the country, it is rather curious that osama stayed back for a good 10 days before beeing killed in an encounter!

Obvious by, more work needs to be done by the police. But it is hopeful of following the missing links through further interrogation of those now in custody under the MCOCA. Among the question the police must be anxiously seeking answers to are:

1. How many groups have filtred through?

2. How many modules are active in Maharashtra and beyond?
3. What is the extent and depth of sleeper network in Maharashtra?

What is important is that the evidence has to be credible. But patching the missing links is vital not only to prove a point to Pakistan, it also has an implication for India's internal security paradigm. Tying up the loose ends and the success of the investigations will be the first step towards preventing the next attack. Alternatively, these very loose ends could become the beginning of the next terror aggression.

Undoubtedly, the initial successes not withstanding, the police still have a job to do—and fast.

VILLAINS OF THE PEACE: BRIEF SKETCHES

This section should end with brief sketches of 11 culprits.

Kamal Ahmed Mohd Vakil Ansari

The LET operative and one of the three module heads: He transported two Pakistanis into India via the Nepal border and planted the bomb that exploded of Matunga. He was arrested on 21 July from Basupati village (near Nepal border) in Madhubani, Bihar.

Tanvir Mohd Ansari

The Unani medicine practitioner, who is also a SIMI member, was arrested from his residence at Nagpada on 24 July. He learnt to rig explosives in Pakistan. On being asked by Ehtesham Siddiqui, he got 20 Kg of amonium nitrate to make bombs. He had concealed the bottles in a locker at Saboo Siddque Hospital in Agripada.

Zamir Ahmed Latif Chabiwala

Arrested from Worli on 26 July. He is a member of the LET module based in Mumbai. He provided logistical support to Pakistani planters

Sohail Mehmood Sheikh

He was arrested from Pune on 26 July, and is a LET operative based in Mumbai. Accused of providing logistical support to the planters, he is a faith healer by profession.

Faisal Ataur Rehman sheikh

The Western India commander of LET was arrested on 27 July. He led the LET module from Mumbai and planted the bomb that exploded at Jogeshwari station. He lodged Pakistani militants in his house at Bandara. Faisal also arranged for budding jihadis from India to be sent for training to Bahawalpur via Iran. He also handled the money received from Cheema.

About 26,ooo riyals were recovered from him and police estimate that he received Rs 60 lakh in two years.

Muzzammil Ataur Rehman Sheikh

A software engineer in Bangalore, he was arrested on 26 July. He helped his cousin Faisal with money and other logistical functions.

Ehtesham Siddiqui

The SIMI's Maharashtra General Secretary was arrested on 28 July. He is a accused of transporting RDX and making the bombs. He also planted the bomb that exploded in Mira Roiad. He was heading the third module that implemented the blasts.

Majid Mohd Shafi

He was arrested on 28 September from Kolkata. Accused of transporting Pakistanis into Mumbai via the Bangladesh border and Kolkata, he is believed to be an LET an Harkat-ul-jhadi-Islam operative. He also has close links with zabiuddin Ansari who is the prime accused in the Aurangabad arms haul of May 2006.

Asif Khan Bashir Khan Abas Junaid

Arrested on 3 October from Belgaum, Karnataka, the alleged SIMI activist is accused of planting one of the seven bombs. The bombmaker hails from Jalgaon district.

Abdul Wahid Din

He was arrested on 28 September from his residence at Mumbra. Accused of providing lodging to Pakistani terrorists, he is an ex-SIMI and LET operative.

Naved Hussain Khan

He was arrested on 30 Septenber from Hyderbad. A call centre employee, he is accused of planting the bomb that exploded between Khar and Bandra stations. He is suspected to be a LET operative from the Hyderabad module.

A year later, charges framed : 7 August 2007

A year after a series of blasts on Mumbai's local trains (on 11 July 2006) killed 187 people and injured over 800, charges were framed on 7 August 2007 against 13 arrested accused, including key conspirators Faisal Shaikh, the City Chief of the LET and Asif Khan Bashir Khan. But the trial will begin only after 21 August—the time given to the accused to get an order from the sessions court, on their petition seeking a transfer of the case from the special MCOCS court of Judge Mrudula Bhatkar.

Alongwith the 13 accused, 15 absconding accused, including LET-in-C (Training) Azam Cheema and two deceased accused — Salim died in the blasts an Abu Osama died in a police encounter —have also been charged for hatching the conspiracy.

The charge sheet names Cheema, Shaikh and Bashir Khan as key conspirators who hatched the plot in 1999. The prosecution's case is that between Feburary, 2006 and 11 July 2006, the accused held several strategy sessions, choosing local trains as the target for the blasts. Pakistanis arrived in Mumbai to help them execute the blasts. The bombs assembled in the house of accused Mohd Ali, were taken to Shaikh's house. These were then taken in rexine bags to Churchgate station and planted in seven trains. The series of blasts in seven train lasted some 10 minutes.

The day (7 August 2007) began with Judge Bhatkar calling accused No. 5 Mohd Majid, who had claimed on 6 August that he needed an Urdu translator to grasp the charges against him as he did not understand Himdi. The Judge asked him "how he has been filing applications so far." To this, Majid replied — in Himdi. He was consulting a lawyer from Kolkata, Mohd Hashmi.

She (the Judge) said: "Throughout the proceeding, accused No. 5 never informed the court that he does not understand Hindi. Now he informs the court in Hindi that he has submitted applications after consulting Hashmi. The court observes that accused No. 5 understands Hindi", and concluded that their is no need for an for Urdu translator.

On the plea of the accused to transfer the case, Bhatkar said: All accused have been detained for the last 8-9 months in prison. This court understands their emotional plight and expresses sympathy. Therefore, considering the situation, the court 15 days, that is till 21 August, to seek necessary orders from the competent court. (Before the principal judge)."

THE MEN WHO SPREAD TERROR ON THE TRACKS

Faisal Shaikh, LET Mumbai Chief

Worked for Azam Cheema, LET Commander-in-Chief (Training) in Pakistan; received arms training in Pakistan: sent his brother Mazammil, Dr. Tanvir Ansari, Sohail Shaikh, and Zameer Shaikh to Pakistan via Tehran; helped get the Hawala money for executing the 7/11 blasts; key conspirator along with Asif Khan Bashir Khan, housed and harboured Pakistani terrorists at his sentence; hosted 7/11 conspiracy meetings at his residence; helped assemble bombs; planted a bomb which exploded at Jogeshwari.

Asaf Khan Bashir Khan alias Junaid

Harboured Pakistani terrorists at his house; procured rexine bags, utensils, ammonium nitrate, detonators; helped assemble bombs; planted a bomb which exploded at Borivali station.

Mohd Ali, SIMI activist

Received arms training in Pakistan; his home was used to assemble bombs; attended 7/11 conspiracy meetings.

Majid Mohd Shafi, Kolkata resident

Helped Pakistani terrorists cross into India through the Indo-Bangla border, including Ehsanullah who brought the RDX.

Sajid Margub Ansari, SIMI activist

Procured timer electric circuitry and other devices; harboured Pakistani terrorists; helped assemble bombs; attended conspiracy meetings.

Kamal Ansari, Madhubani resident

Received arms training in Pakistan; helped Pakistani terrorists cross into India through the Indo-Nepal border

Ehteshaam Siddiqui, Mumbai Seeretary, SIMI

Harboured Pakistani terrorists; surveyed local trains to plan the blasts; helped assemble bombs; attended conspiracy meetings; planted the bomb that exploded at Mira Road station.

Zameer Shaikh, SIMI activists

Received arms training in Pakistan; surveyed local trains to plan the blasts; attended conspiracy meetings.

Sohail Shaikh, SIMI activist

Received arms and ammunition training in Pakistan; surveyed local trains to plan the blasts; attended conspiracy meetings.

Muzammil Shaikh, Faisal's brother

A computer engineer, he received arms training in Pakistan; surveyed local trains to plan the blasts; helpedin procuring hawala money to execute the conspiracy; attended conspiracy meetings.

Dr. Tanvir Ansari, SIMI activists

Received arms training in Pakistan; surveyed local trains to plan the blasts; helped assemble bombs ; attend conspiracy meetings.

Naveed Hussain, Call Centre employee from Hyderabad

Faisal's friend, he helped assemble bombs; attended 7/11 conspiracy meetings; planted the bomb that exploded at Bandra station.

Abdul wahid Din Shaikh, SIMI activist

Rented a Mumbai house where Pakistani terrorists Ammu Jan, Sabir Abu Bakr, KAsam Ali , Ehsanullah and Abu Hasan lived.

Notes

1. *Outlook*, 24 July, 2006.
2. *Week*, 23 July, 2006.
3. Saikat Dutta, *Outlook*, 24 July, 2006.
4. S. Anandan, *Week*, 23 July, 2006.
5. This criticism is certainly misplaced, at least in part. The two-year tenure man not given to them on a sebjective basis. It was

a result of the government decision to give minimum fixed tenures to certain appointments under the Central Government. These two, among so many others, became the first beneficiaries of this decision. To see motives behind it is being unfair.

6. *Week*, 23 July, 2006.
7. R. Prasannan, Week, 23 July, 2006.
8. Mariana Babar in Islamabad, Outlook, 24 July, 2006.
9. V. Sudarshan, *Ibid.*
10. Incidentally, Kasuri often regrets, of course, in private, India not having a Foreign Minister, with whom he could just pick up phone and sort out many issues routinely. He asks rhetorically: "Who do I call up for that purpose in New Delhi? There are protocal problems in calling up India's Prime Minster, who is holding additional charge of foreign ministry". Sympathising with his predicament, a cynical journalist wrote: "But Musharraf must be regretting having a valuble Foreign Minister like Kasuri". What he left unsaid is that if there are problems in not having a *Foreign Minister*, the same is true in having one—like kasuri.
11. Mariana Babar, *Outlook*, 24 July, 2006.
12. *Indian Express*, 10 Oct., 2006.
13. Praveen Swami and Anupama Kalakam, *Frontline*, 20 Oct., 2006.
14. *Ibid.*
15. Editorial, *Pioneer*, 12 Oct., 2006.
16. Prerana Thakur desai, *India Today*, 16 Oct., 2006.
17. Stavan Desai, *Indian Express*, 2 April, 2006.

11

Terrorist Attacks in India Part 3

Malegaon (Maharashtra) Blasts: 8 Sep., 2006

31 people died and 312 were injured in four blasts, of which three took place in the Hamidiya Masjid and Bara Kabrastan area and the fourth at the Mushawart Chowk.

The chargesheet filed by the state Anti-Terrorist Squad (ATS) on 22 Dec. 2005 is clear about the motive but fails to establish the identities of two Pakistanis involved. The pro be has also failed to establish the identities of two men who bought the bicycles used to plant the bombs though the charge-sheet says the prime conspirators and the planters have been arrested.

The chargesheet does not say how the explosives used in the blasts reached Malegaon from Mumbai. It says the explosives were brought to Mumbai in the third week of July by SIMI activists Mohd Ali Sheikh and Asif Khan and were handed over to prime accused Shabbir Ahmed Masiullah. But it does not explain where Sheikh and Khan got the explosive from, or why the police did not know about the involvement of Masiullah, who had been arrested by the Mumbai Police Crime Branch on 11 Aug, till three months after his arrest. All the 9 arrested accused, booked under MCOCA, are in judicial custody.

Two Unani Doctors Held

Two Unani doctors—Salman Farsi Aaimi (35) and Farogh Iqbal Makhdomi (33)—held in overnight raids at Malegaon and Govandi, in connection with the Malegaon blasts case, were produced before special judge MR Bhatkar in MCOCA court on 7 Nov 2006, which sent them to police custody till 21 Nov.

Seeking custody of the accused, the ATS, of Mumbai police said a search of Aaimi's clinic in Govindi had led to the seizures of large quantities of seditious literature, note books containing cuttings of newspaper articles and code numbers. ATS sleuths had also conducted cotton swab tests in the clinic to ascertain if it had been used to store RDX "The forensic results are expected".

The ATS claimed the duo was part of a conspiracy hatched in Feb 2006 to "commit insurgency by spreading hatred among communities and thus disturbing the even tempo of life in the society." With the arrest of the duo, the total number of arrests in the Malegaon blasts—in which 37 people were killed and 105 others injured—has gone up to five.

Both Farsi and Iqbal are SIMI activists. Significantly, Farsi was neighbour of Mohd Ali in whose Govandi residence explosives used in 7-11 Mumbai blasts, which ripped seven first class compartments of north suburban - bound locals, were assembled. Confirming that Farsi was neighbour of Ali, ATS Chief Raghuvanshi declined to rule out the links between Mumbai and Malegaon blasts.

Two Booked Afresh for Malegaon Blasts by ATS

On 14 Nov 2006, two persons—Sheikh Mohd Ali Alam Sheikh, 37 and Asif Khan Bashir Khan alias Junaid, 30—who were earlier accused in the 11 July Mumbai train blasts were booked afresh for their collaboration in the Malegaon blasts by the ATS.

Following the arrest of these two, the ATS claimed they have "clearly established beyond doubt" that 11/7 train bombing in Mumbai and 8 Sep Malegaon bomb blasts, are inter-related: "The two arrested persons had prior knowledge about both the bomb blasts. Junaid and Ali had provided RDX to some persons in Malegaon for making the bombs. The duo participated in various discussions held in Malegaon for planting the bomb. We received information about their involvement from Shabbir Batterywala, the prime conspirator in the Malegaon bomb blasts case".

8 Oct., 2006

The investigation into the 8 Sep 2006 Malegaon bomb blasts is in its final stages and going in proper direction, Deputy CM RR Patil, who is also the Home Minister, told the press.

Dec 2006 take over of Case by CBI and New Developments

CBI took over the 8 Sep 2006 Malegaon blasts case on 21 Dec 2006, the same day as the ATS filed chargesheet against

9 persons in the case. CBI was reported in first week of Apr 2007 to be wanting to question again Azim, surfacing to be an important element in this case of late.

Taseem Azim alias Larib Khan Gulab, a 28-year-old Pakistani national was arrested by Lucknow police Special Task Force (STF) five days after the serial blasts at Malegaon, in an operation backed by the Subsidiary Intelligence Bureau (SIB). During his questioning, it was revealed that Azim had been staying in Lucknow for the past two years and had been trained by ISI in Karachi. He had been operating on behalf of the ISI while running a placement agency 'Precyze Recruitment agency'.

Azim, termed by the STF as "young and intelligent" and by the ATS (of Maharashtra police) as a "goldmine" of information, also told his interrogators that in the span of two years of working for the ISI, he had visited Malegaon several times and established contacts with local persons. It was also revealed that Azim had contacts in the ranks of PoK-based HUJI (Harkat-ul-Jihadi-e-Islami).

SSP, STF, Vijay Bhushan said: "We shared this information with the Maharashtra ATS which immediately sent a team for detailed questioning of the accused in connection with the Malegoan serial blasts."

Then in the first week of Apr 2007 came the news about the CBI wanting to question Azim. "We want to question him to cross-check his revelations about his Malegaon links. And as he has admitted to having links with a terrorist organization, we are hopeful of getting more information." This was stated by an officer of the Special Investigation Team (SIT) of the CBI entrusted with the investigations in the case.

One is simply amazed at the amateurish and lackadaisical ways of police, including the CBI here, handling investigations of the important cases like Sep 2006 Malegaon terrorism. CBI had taken over the case from the State's ATS in Dec 2006, and Azim has been arrested by UP (Lucknow) police on 11 Sep 2006 and it is around 1 Apr 2007 that a daily[30] reports the CBI wanting to question Azim 'again'!

Azim's links with the Malegaon-based SIMI activists was revealed during his questioning by the Maharashtra ATF. During his visits to Malegoan, last of which was four months before the blasts, he had established these contacts to further his job of espionage and providing logistics information to HUJI. Though he had named local SIMI activists like Noor-ul-Huda Samshudoha, Shabbir Ahmed Masiullah, Mohd Zahid, Abdul Majid Ansari and some others, he denied any knowledge of the blasts. Later, Samshudoha, Masiullah, and Ansari were arrested by the ATS for their alleged involvement in the blasts and charged as being the prime accused who conspired and got the blasts executed.

Bhushan further added: "His questioning gave a lot of information to the ATF about the local SIMI activists and those who needed to be inquired further because of his links. We also found that he had well-established contacts with HUJI. We also found some documents and a diary containing telephone numbers of his contacts in Malegaon and across the border from his possession."

But the ATS never found Azim's involvement in the Blasts though it got its first leads about the incident from him. "He had links with the accused but we did not arrest him as we did not find his involvement", said the ATS chief, JCP KP Raghuvanshi.

The State had transferred investigations to the CBI after protests from the residents of Malegaon on the arrests made by the ATS. The ATS had contended that the nine arrested accused, alleged active SIMI members, had hatched and executed the conspiracy with the help of two Pakistanis in the textile town to "infuriate the entire Muslim community and trigger communal riots."

31 people had died and 312 injured in four blasts, of which three were inside the Hamidiya Masjid and Bara Kabrastan. The fourth was at Mushawart Chowk.

Over to CBI once again!

MARAD (KERALA BEACH) MASSACRE: A MIX OF POLITICS AND TERRORISM

8 Hindu fishermen killed in a gruesome manner on 2 May 2003 at Marad beach near Kozhikode, Kerala. "It may be years before the gory scene at Marad fades from the minds of the many

families who lived at the beach near Kozhikode," wrote a weekly dated 8 Oct 2006.[1]

Summary of the Events

This horrendous act of barbarity "has now come to haunt the states political brigade. The Thomas P. Joseph judicial inquiry commission report on the communal massacre, tabled in the Assembly recently, came down heavily on political parties, mainly the Congress and the Indian Union Muslim League (IUML), senior police officers and some extremist organizations".

The Marad massacre was in retaliation to the murder of four Muslim fishermen on 4 Jan 2002. The AK Antony government of the day dismissed it as a local feud, with no involvement of political parties or extremist outfits. The Joseph Commission, however, has a different story with different characters. It holds major political parties like the CPM, BJP and IUML and communal outfits like the RSS and National Democratic Front (NDF) responsible for flaring up a minor incident on 31 Dec 2001, into a major communal carnage.

The report exposes the direct link of the IUML with the NDF in this gruesome act. Antony came under the scanner for not ordering a CBI inquiry. He had said the decision was based on the advice of the Advocate General, which the report refutes.

The report reveals that the funds for the operations came from a person in the Gulf who had close contacts with two ministers in the Antony Cabinet. Is it this link that forced PK Kunhalikutty of the IUML to pressure the government against the CBI probe?

The subsequent government headed by Antony's colleague Oomen Chandy, has been held guilty for delay in tabling the report. The report had been submitted to the government on 20 Feb (2006).

With as many as 80 of its workers figuring in the accused list, the IUML has a lot to explain. Its local leader PP Moideen is named and MC Mayin Haji, Party State Committee member and Confidante of Kunhalikutty, apparently know about the conspiracy.

There have been repeated allegations that NDF cadres were masquerading as IUML workers, and Kunhalikutty was protecting them. Said a leader in the rival camp of the IUML: "There is every possibility that the NDF has been exploiting its covert links with the IUML to unleash communal conflict in Marad."

The report indicted senior officers listed here:

1. Ko Sooraj, then district collector of Kozhikode, ignored an intelligence report hinting at communal attack at Marad.
2. Sanjeev Patjoshi, then city Police Commissioner, neglected safety measures despite a warning of danger.
3. IG Mahesh Kumar Singhla, who headed the probe, ignored the likely involvement of external forces.

VS Achuthandandan government, all set to capitalize on the opportunity, has ordered a CBI inquiry in the Marad carnage. While in the opposition, his party, the CPI(M), had vehemently opposed a CBI probe, while the BJP had pressed for it. "This reveals the double standards of the CPI (M) on this issue," asserted Chandy.

These political games force the public to question the 'moral commitment' of parties. Though Marad beach has stayed calm for the past three years, the communal wounds are yet to heal. The politician though, seem to have a different agenda.

Terrorism-politics mix: A deadly potion

Terrorism and politics make for an explosive mix and if not checked effectively, the inter-party politics in Kerala, with all its ideological contradictions and religious rivalries could turn the state into a dangerous cauldron of interanee and violence. In view of this uneasy situation indicated by the communal killings of Jan 2002 and May 2003, a little more discussion of the relevant issues impinging upon the States stability and communal peace in the context of the two Marad tragedies is called for than a brief summary of events given above.

Findings of the Joseph Commission

The whole truth behind the revenge killings at the coastal village of Marad in May 2003, the worst communal incident in the recent history in Kerala, "is unlikely to be revealed soon, if at all," feels an analyst of a fortnightly dated 20 Oct 2006.[32]

More than three years after fundamentalist assailants hacked to death eight Hindu fishermen (and a Mushlim fellow attacker by mistake) there on 3 May 2003, the report of a judicial commission of inquiry has concluded, among other things, that the incident was a sequel to the largely politically motivated murder of five persons in the village in Jan 2002 and a fall—out of the then Congress-led United Democratic Front (UDF) government's "unjustified delay" in the prosecution of those accused of the crime.

According to the Joseph Commission report:

- Charge-sheets were filed against 393 persons in 115 cases relating to the Jan 2002 incident.
- Of these 393, 213 were activists of the RSS/BJP.
- 86 were of the Muslim League
- 78 of the CPI (M)
- The remaining 16 were the members of the Indian National League (INL) and the National Democratic Front (NDF), the post-1993 Muslim Fundamentalist Organization which claims to have its members in all major political parties.

The UDF, especially the Muslim League, had, forged an alliance with the RSS/BJP at that time to try and checkmate the dominant influence of the CPI (M) in the coastal regions of Kozhikode district.

Much to the discomfiture of major political parties in the State, the Commission, which was set up to inquire into the circumstances that led to the second Marad killings, has in a way, turned the spotlight on the facts and circumstances of the 2002 killings.

The report emphasizes what political Kerala already know but has tried to ignore: that the Jan 2002 incident was the result of "political interests and other vested interests" that developed following a minor altercation between too men belonging to the two different communites, which flared up into a major communal incident resulting in the death of five people, injury to several others and damage to several houses.

It says that delay in filing charge-sheets in the case was subsequently utilized by "Muslim fundamentalists, terrorists and other forces" to capitalize on the grievances of relatives of three Muslims killed and use it as a cause for vengeance against Hindus of Marad as a whole. It also says that inquiry by the State Crime Branch CID (CBCID) into the May 2003 incident had failed to unravel the "Larger conspiracy" and the sources of the large cache of arms and arms and ammunition unearthed subsequently in the area and of the sizeable funds used in the planning and execution of the murders.

The Commission's main recommendation, therefore, is a further inquiry, involving the Intelligence Bureau (IB), the CBI and the Directorate of Revenue Intelligence (DRI), into the "larger conspiracy" involving fundamentalist and other forces, and into the source of the explosives and funds that the CBCID "failed or refused" to investigate—an act that the commission described as "quite suspicious and disturbing".

The report is also critical of the role of the civil administration, the State police and the Crime Branch. "Despite the clear evidence that there was a long-drawn conspiracy and that the objective of the assailants was not merely to kill certain persons but to create bigger havoc and ignite large-scale riot, the CBCID team stuck to its simple theory of revenge killings. The question as to whether other forces were involved in the massacre was not even an issue for CBCID team". The Commission is scathing in its criticism of the Crime Branch.

The civil administration "continued to be lethargic in taking...remedial action after the 2002 incident even though intelligence reports had indicated that there was the possibility of violence again at Marad and that stock piling of weapons was taking place, mostly in Muslim–dominated areas. The intelligence report had suggested that the efforts of government-initiated peace committees were not yielding the desired results, that fundamentalist elements were active in the area and that the people feared an imminent bout of communal revenge attacks.

It was also known that the original plan for an attack one month before 3 May 2003 was dropped as the news had leaked and that the stockpiling of weapons had started three months after the first (Jan 2002) incident. There were also clear intelligence warnings about a "wordy altercation" between two groups in the Muslim Community inside the compound of the local mosque regarding "retaliation for the killing of Muslims in 2002".

And despite early intelligence warnings of possibility of police wireless information being leaked out by residents, curiously, the only police picket post with a wireless set operating at Marad was located in one of the residences, until well after the massacre.

Even when such information was available, the commission says there was only a token presence of the police on Marad beach on the day of the massacre and several days before that. There were only 13 policemen on duty at Marad, in a total of nine pickets on the beach, and there was not a single gun at the Marad police control room or picket posts. There were a few teargas shells and lathis and "even that the policemen could not effectively use as they did not have the mental make-up to do that in a charged situation."

The commission holds three key officials responsible for the situation : KO Sooraj, SK Patjoshi (the two have been mentioned above) and M Abdul Rahim, then Assistant Commissioner. Rahim has been criticized severally for the way he tried to shield one of the prime accused in the case. Sooraj was held responsible, being the District Collector and District Magistrate, for the failure of the civil administration to take timely remedial action to prevent the recurrence of violence at the Marad beach. It asks the government to inquire into the wide-spread allegation of the communal bias made against Sooraj "that cannot be ignored as baseless and could have had a bearing on the failure of the civil administration," including his action of allowing Muslim League leader (at present Minister of State for External Affairs) E. Ahimed to enter the controversial mosque on Marad beach defying prohibitory orders when the communal tension was high immediately after the massacre.

The commission criticizes the lack of rapport between Sooraj and Patjoshi that contributed to the lack of coordination between civil and police administrations, which ultimately affected "the effectiveness of the actions that had to be taken by both the departments in the riot-prone area".

The failure of police under Patjoshi is also criticized for its failure to prevent the 2003 massacre. "There was lack of coherence, trust and Coordinated action between the various branches of the police".

Individual Officers and Politicians Blamed

Besides Sooraj and Patjoshi, Abdul Rahim also came under commission's critical gaze. It has accepted several allegations that were raised against Rahim, including the one that despite intelligence reports about the activities of Bijli (son of Abobecker, an NDF activist killed in the first Marad incident), Rahim deliberately failed to question him properly or keep him under surveillance. The reports about Bijli ultimately proved true. He became the prime accused in the 2003 Marad massacre case and it was found by the CBCID that he, along with paternal uncle Mohd Ali, played a leading role in the conspiracy and the planning and execution of the murders. The commission says that Bijli was never kept under watch and was simply "let loose" and both Rahim and Patjoshi were responsible for it.

The commission also found that following the 2003 incidents, Rahim had tried to shield Bijli after his arrest by trying to convince fellow officers that "one of the accused was not really involved in the incident". Rahim had also tried to remain in Kozhikode even after he was transferred on the request of the then DGP KJ Josheph to the government, in the "public interest". "Rahim's appointment Kozhikode South Sub-division itself was 'shrouded in suspicious circumstances' and the allegation about his connection with the forces behind the conspiracy for the massacre cannot be ignored as baseless."

The DGP also had deposed before the commission that Rahim was posted at Kozhikode (South) without his knowledge and after the massacre he found the posting was done "to oblige a Muslim leader", whose identity he did not know. But significantly, the then Chief Minister Antony had filed an affidavit before the commission that the posting was a "routine one", and "there was nothing unusual in it".

The commission holds that the facts behind the mysterious appointment of Rahim at Kozhikode (South) Sub-division, which includes the communally sensitive Marad, could have "dissuaded the (then) government from ordering the CBI investigation". "There is the need for a deeper probe into who was interested in his posting and what the interest behind it was". The commission further found that (paraphrased):

> "Several activists of the Muslim League and the NDF were actively involved in the planning and execution of the [second] massacre and that it was unlikely that their activists were involved thus without the blessings of their respective leaderships, at least at the local level.
>
> "(The commission) did not come across any direct evidence on whether the NDF as an organization was behind the massacre but it is difficult to get such direct evidence for the involvement of the (secretive) organization, even though it did find that some of the local leaders of the NDF were indeed involved.
>
> "The local leader of the Muslim League PP Moideen Koya and other members of the local Mahal committee who were involved in the conspiracy for the May 2003 massacre or had prior information about it and the impending violence at Marad.
>
> "MC Mayin Haji, the Chairman of the Calicut Development Authority and a prominent leader of the Muslim League, too had prior intimation of the conspiracy.
>
> "Mayin Haji admitted (before the commission) that during Apr-May 200 Maoideenkoya had met him along with Mohd Ali. Though Ali had informed a leader of the stature of Mayin Haji about his desire to avenge the killing of his brother, he (Haji) failed to intimate the authorities about it, in spite of being well aware of the tense, sensitive situation in Marad after the Jan 2002 murder of three Muslim and two Hindu fishermen".

It is quite unlikely that such a large number of Muslim League workers, including a few local leaders, were involved in the conspiracy without the blessings of their leadership at least at the local level. That is the reason for the Muslim League General Secretary and the then Industry Minister PK Kunhalikutty opposing a CBI investigation and expressing his own apprehension that if such an investigation was allowed when the BJP was in power at the Centre, there was no guarantee that all Muslim League leaders, including himself, or his party leader Panakkad Shihab Thangal would not be put behind bars. But the report says there is no evidence to substantiate allegations that Kunhalikutty was in any way connected with the May 2003 massacre. Mayin Haji was given the UDF ticket—and lost in the May 2006 Assembly elections, significantly, when the commission report was already with the UDF).

But Kunhalikutty told the commission that neither he nor his party had stated that a CBI investigation was not required, but that "it was the cabinet" that decided that a CBI investigation was not necessary in view of the legal opinion given by the then Advocate-General.

Antony too had said that the advice of the Advocate-General was that since the CBCID, Kozhikode unit had already investigated the matter and filed charge-sheets in the case, it was not permissible under law to entrust the investigation to another agency. Antony as Chief Minister had also said in reply to specific questions that the government did not order a CBI inquiry, at the initial stage since, following the Muthanga incident (and police action against tribal people there in which one tribal person and a police-man were killed) into which the government had ordered a CBI investigation, there was a clamour for a judicial inquiry. Hence, "to avoid such a demand", a judicial commission was appointed "to inquire into all aspects of the massacre, investing it with wide powers"

The commission has come to the conclusion that this was only a "lame excuse" and drawn attention to the report of one of the officers of the State Special Branch that "a person nicknamed 'FM' (finance minister) who camee to Kozhikode from the Gulf Countries on 2 May 2003 was the source of money behind massacre", that two Cabinet Ministers of the State had "unimaginable connection" with the "FM" and that the government might be in trouble if the CBI investigated the case at a time when the BJP was in power at the Centre.

The commission has now accepted a plea by a well-connected Gulf-based business VB Mohammedkutty alias "Hilal Mohammed", that it should order the CBCID to inquire further into media reports that he was the "FM" mentioned in the report. CPI (M) State Secretary Pinarayi Vijayan subsequently alleged that Hilal Mohd, portrayed as "FM" in media reports, was the man behind AK Antony's election campaign at

Tirurangadi in the early 1990s when the latter, then facing power struggle within the Congress, sought to be elected with the support of the Muslim League from the North Kerala constituency. One of the candidates whom Antony defeated at Tirurangadi was the People's Democratic Party (PDP) leader Abdul Nasser Mahdani, now in a Coimbatore jail for his alleged role in the Coimbatore blast.

When the Special Branch report was shown to Antony when he was in the witness box, he "pleaded ignorance about it", the commission says. It further said: "It was quite unlikely that Antony, who was also holding charge of the Home Ministry, was unaware of such a serious report concerning two of his colleagues in the Cabinet." Or, it may be that the senior police officer in the Intelligence Headquarters (by inference, Inspector General Mahesh Kumar Singla) had not shown the report to Antony (in spite of regular intelligence briefings. The commission says that it appeared that the state government wanted to avoid an investigation by the CBI into the involvement of other forces behind the massacre, "without sufficient justification" and ostensilaly under cover of an opinion from the Advocate-General that "further inveestigation" (on which the CBCID had already filed the charge-sheet) was "not factually or legally permissible" as it opened up the possibility that the accused mentioned in the charge-sheet of the CBCID are not the real accused".

It further says that the legal hurdle (Section 73(8) the GPC) was only concerning "further investigation" into the same issue and not in the present case, on a matter outside the matters investigated by the CBCID "on the issue of larger conspiracy, involvement of other forces, the funding and collection of weapons."

It also says that the role played by Mahesh Kumar Singla on the issue of investigation (by the CBCID) into the involvement of "other forces" behind the massacre is quite suspicious and that his claim that he had not seen the intelligence reports is "simply false".

The commission says it was necessary for the State government or other appropriate authorities to investigate the alleged connection of Singla with KM Aboobackar, a Thrissur-based businessman with alleged links with the NDF (although commission found no evidence for this), and with whom Singla's father Bhagvan Das had a business partnership.

The commission says an inquiry is also required why the CBCID under the supervision of Singla failed or even refused to investigate into the involvement of other forces behind the massacre and the larger conspiracy. "Singla, who refused to give any direction to the CBCID team to investigate the matter, had proclaimed that the investigation did not reveal the involvement of other forces in the incident". Why did he do it, without having any facts to prove his assertion?

The Justice Thomas P. Joseph Commission of Inquiry, appointed on 23 Aug 2003 (soon after the CBCID completed its inquiry and filed charge-sheets against 115 people involved in Marad II) submitted its report on 20 Feb 2006 to the UDF governments. But, perhaps because of the remarks against it, and importantly against the Muslim League, a prominent constituent of the government, the UDF administration did not table the report in the Assembly, especially as the Assembly polls were only a few months away.

The new left Democratic Front (LDF) government tabled the report on 27 Sep 2006, along with the Action Taken Report, and announced that, among other things, it had requested the Centre to conduct a CBI inquiry as suggested by the commission.

The terms of reference of the CBI inquiry were to be announced later. But the trial of those charge by the CBCID was nearing completion towards the end of the 2006, "and the judgment was expected by Jan 2007."

Home Minister Kodiyeri Balkrishnan said "the government will ask the CBI to conduct the inquiry in a manner that does not affect the ongoing trial". But that is showing magnanimity to a political rival which is essentially a put-on—a political game. Even a political novice will know, given the findings and wordings of the commission at a number of places in its report, the new inquiry by the CBI will certainly put the UDF in a tight corner—a very uncomfortable situation. And it will remain in the dog house, as a result of this inquiry, for a long time to come. As in rest of India, politics plays a past in most of the decisions taken by its practitioners.

For the CPI (M) will be happy that the gift handed down by Justice Joseph will take the media and public gaze away from the theatre of the absurd being enacted by the two heavy weights of the CPM and consequent unbearable political embarrassment for the party in the state, and more so for its central leadership.

The opposition has blamed the LDF for practicing double standards in its public conduct. After all, while it was in opposition, the LDF had staunchly opposed a CBI inquiry into the case, under the cover of its principled stand on such issues. But now, under the fig-leaf of the commission's recommendations, it has reversed its "principled" stand. The counter-demand by the Opposition for inclusion of the facts and circumstances of the Jan 2002 incident in the terms of reference of the CBI inquiry is meant to rattle the ruling CPI (M)—to pay it back in the same coin.

The political chess-game over Marad has indeed reached a crucial juncture—even if its resolution and final results are in the womb of the future.

The issues involved in the case of the two Marad incidents have deliberately been discussed in great detail, even if it does not concern a terrorist incident involving the usual killings. This arguably is the first case in India where the game of politics was played employing terrorist methods. It the model is replicated thoughtlessly, it can prove costly for the nation. It is also important because a pioneering attempt at forging Hindu-Muslim political understanding against the CPI (M) was made. That it failed is not important. The fact of its being made is indeed important.

Malegaon: Yet Another Reminder of India's Vulnerability

With the disclosure by the DGP, Maharashtra, PS Pasricha in the last week of Nov 2006 that the Malegaon bomb blasts case "has been 'solved', there is certain clarity with regard to one of the most intriguing terrorist incidents in recent times."

At least 38 people, including many women and children, died and 297 sustained injuries in the serial bomb explosions at Malegaon in the Nashik district on 8 Sep. On 27 Nov, Pasricha disclosed that two Pakistani nationals, including one

Muzzammil, manufactured the IEDs and assembled the four bombs. He informed the media of some additional details:[33]

> "The conspiracy was hatched in Malegaon on 8 May on the occasion of the wedding of Noor-ul-Huda, one of the accused. All eight persons arrested in this case are former SIMI members. The RDX was transported from Mumbai to Malegaon in the third week of July (after the 11 July 2006 train bombings), and the bombs were made there. While eight SIMI activists have been arrested in connection with the blasts, an equal number are still at large. Both the Pakistani nationals are yet to be arrested. While one of those arrested, Zahid Ali, planted the bomb at Mushawarat Chowk, Huda and his accomplice Races Rajjab Ali planted bombs in the cemetery."

In the early stages of investigation, the police expectedly had not ruled out the possibility of involvement of some extremist Hindu groups like the Bajrang Dal in the dastardly terrorist attack because it had essentially targeted the Muslims. But at the later stages it was getting clear that they do not have the wherewithal's to carry out operations of this magnitude. Subsequently, the Maharashtra police reportedly ruled out the involvement of groups like the Bajrang Dal on two counts: "RDX is only available to Islamist terrorist outfits. Second, Bajrang activists have so far used only crude bombs, as seen in the blasts at Parbani and Nanded."

The modus operandi of 7-11 and Malegaon now look similar. Police said explosives used in Malegaon were a mixture of RDX, ammonium nitrate and fuel oil—the assortment used in 7-11.

Muslims, most of whom are reported to be migrant weavers from Uttar Pradesh, constitute the majority of Malegaon population. Will the Muslims kill Muslims? "To kill their own" is intrinsic to any terrorist strategy. Across the globe, Islamist terrorists are currently targeting innocent Muslim civilians; Iraq, Afghanistan, Pakistan, Palestine, Lebanon et al being some main instances. There may not be clear linkages, but a definite pattern of association among the various theatres of jihad across the globe is discernible. The spread of disorder and mindless violence are currently being orchestrated by the same forces whose ideological world view supplements the essential logic and dynamic of their operations.

It is significant to note in this context that Pakistan-based *jihadis* in Jammu and Kashmir have killed scores of their own "Muslim brothers and sisters", whose "rights" they claim to be fighting to protect. In fact, nearly 90 per cent of civilian fatalities inflicted by 'Islamist' terrorists in Jammu and Kashmir are fellow Muslims. Yet again, an apt parallel can be found in the Punjab of the days of Khalistan movement. 65 per cent of the civilian victims of the "Khalistani" terrorists, who claimed to have been fighting for the "Sikh rights", were themselves Sikhs.

Same is the case in India's neighbourhood. Sectarian violence between the majority Sunni and minority Shia communities, both part of the Muslim brotherhood, has claimed at least 2,435 lives between 1989 and 2006. A recent illustration of the same genre was the suicide attack in Karachi on 11 Apr 2006, when 57 people were killed and over 200 injured. Virtually the entire leadership of the Sunni Tehreek, which is of Barelvi orientation, was killed by extremists suspected to be belonging to Deobandi School. Ironically, the blast occurred at a stage erected in a Park where religious leaders and scores of the faithful were offering prayers at a meeting to mark the birth anniversary of Prophet Mohammed.

The syndrome goes beyond the world of Muslim terrorists The Liberation Tigers of Tamil Eelam (LTTE), arguably, the most lethal terrorist group in the world, has killed far more Tamils than the Sinhalese.

In the last two years, since July 2005 to be more specific, there have been at least six Islamist terrorist attacks outside Jammu and Kashmir apparently aimed at threatening communal amity in India, if not rendering it asunder. These attacks are mentioned, in brief:

1. Two of the six targeted Hindu places of worship; Varanasi on 7 Mar 2006 and the earlier failed attacks on Ayodhya on 5 July 2005.
2. One was in a Muslim place of worship—Jama Masjid in Delhi on 14 Apr 2006.

3. Another targeted Muslims near a mosque in Malegaon on 8 Sep 2006.
4. The one of the remaining two came on the eve of the Hindu festival of Dewali in Delhi. Targeting the shoppers in crowded markets on 29 Oct 2005 and sixth attacked the upper middle and elite (Gujaratis and other) passengers in the first class compartments of the seven suburban Mumbai trains on 11 July 2006.

In sum, more than 300 civilians lost their lives in these terrorist attacks, obviously meant for destabilization of India engineered through the consequent communal conflagrations.

The SIMI is a were India-based instrument, among so many other Pakistan-based and-sponsored terrorist outfits, which collectively aim to serve Pakistan's stratagem of weakening India by striking at its perceived "fault lines" and bleeding it through the continuing "policy of thousand cuts" Their intent and strategy is "increasingly apparent in a wide range of activities intended to provoke communal confrontations, to engineer terrorist attacks, and to recruit soldiers for a pan-Islamist jihad in pockets of Muslim populations across India".

Indians, out of complacency or a force of habit, tend to forget what chief of the Markaz-ud-Da' awa-wal-Irshad and the Amir of its military wing, the Lashkar-e-Tayyeba, declared at the huge congregation of the members of the former, on 6 Feb 2002: "Kashmir is a gateway to capture India and it is the aim of the Markaz and the LET to engineer India's disintegrations."

Such declarations are expressions of pan-Islamist ambitions shared fervently by all Islamist extremist groups operating in the region, and a forceful reiteration of Pakistan's larger strategy of destabilization beyond the "core issue" of Kashmir. Acts of terrorism, especially like the one at Malegaon, represent the culmination of years of preparation that are reflected in motivation and organizational development of Islamist extremism.

That Kashmir is only the penultimate agenda of Pakistan was made clear by no less a Pakistani than Zulfizar Ali Bhutto. He had publicly declared: "Assam is another unfinished business of the 1947 Partition of India." Bangladesh, Pakistan's successor state, is pursing the latter agenda even more passionately through continuous illegal migration of its nationals into India's North-East, particularly into Assam and West Bengal, and policy statements on *lebensaraum*—space in sparsely—populated Assam for its burgeoning population. The logic is simple: Assam's density of population is one-tenth of Bangladesh's! There is more to come, forceed by natural causes. In not-too-distant a future, as a result of global warming, thousands of square kilometers of Bangladesh's coastal areas are going to be submerged under water. Where will the fleeing millions go ? Huge majority of these refugees will obviously head for India's North-East, and the rest for Myanmar's South-West. The consequences for India especially will be too serious even to be imagined.

All such potential dangers to India's national security bears repetition, lest Indians complain that they were not warned!

Malegaon: 8 Ex-SIMI Cadres held: Nov. 2006

Maharashtra DGP Dr. PS Pasricha on 27 Nov 2006 claimed that the Anti-Terrorist Squad (ATS) of the Mumbai police "has cracked the Malegaon blasts case with the arrest of eight former activists of the Students Islamic Movement of India (SIMI).

The four blasts on 8 Sep 2006 killed 36 persons and injured over 100 others. The DGP told the press in Mumbai that the ex-SIMI members wanted to foment communal tensions between Hindus and Muslims by creating mayhem.

Dr Pasricha, however, said there was no direct evidence to suggest the involvement of Pakistan's ISI in these blasts although two Pakistanis were involved in the wider conspiracy. "They are still at large. One of the terrorists was trained in Pakistan. He said it was plotted by locals. The ATS team, headed by Joint Commissioner Police (JCP) Krishan Pal Singh Raghuvanshi, has appreciated the help extended by Malegaon's religious leaders. The police have an eye witness who was present when the cycle bombs were being assembled. One of the key persons involved is named Muzzamil", the DGP said.

The devices were a mixture of ammonium nitrate and RDX wrapped in plastic. The ATS has acquired records of bicycle purchases. It also managed to unravel how bicycles were parked at strategic points outside the mosque, Maliwara Chowk and Bada Kabrastan to provoke communal tension by killing worshippers on Friday's Shab-e-Baraat.

He disclosed the ATS has conducted brain mapping of eight SIMI suspects to piece together the larger conspiracy.

Although the case is claimed to have been solved, the DGP declined to divulge additional details as it may hamper further investigations focusing on a larger conspiracy.

MYSORE ARRESTS: SERIOUS SECURITY IMPLICATIONS

Two Al-Badr Militants Arrested from Mysore: Oct 2006

In a major break-through on the night 27/28 Oct 2006, the Mysore police in Karnataka captured two suspected Pakistani militants belonging to the Al-Badr outfit and uncovered a plot to blow up some vital installations in the state, including the Vidhan Soudha (Legislative Assembly building).

The arrests followed intelligence reports that Pakistan-based terrorist outfits were planning to target southern Indian states, including Bangalore, the IT hub of the country.

Less than a year after the Pak terrorists targeted the Indian Institute of Science, Bangalore, killing a Delhi-based professor, the Pak-duo arrested at Mysore had plans to attack the Central Institute of Indian Languages at Mysore, frequented by distinguished foreigners.

Karnataka DGP BS Sial said the Pak duo were captured after a shoot-out on Outer Ring Road in the Vijayanagar police limits.

Mohd Ali Hussain, alias Qassim and Mohd Fahad, both in their mid-twenties, were intercepted while they were riding a motorbike and captured after a shoot-out in which a militant suffered minor injuries.

- Fahad, hailing from Manshera in Pakistan, is a post-graduate in 'analytical chemistry', trained in making explosives.
- Ali Hussain from Karachi, a school drop-out, was involved in terrorist activities in Jammu and Kashmir before moving to Mysore three months ago.

The 'terror instruments' seized from them were some chemicals used for making IEDs, detonators' a laptop and a satellite phone with numbers linked to entities in Jammu and Kashmir; and some sketches of the intended targets like Vidhan Soudha and its newly constructed annexe.

The police would down load the date from the laptop, analyse telephone numbers and get in touch with the central intelligence.

Other items recovered from them include an AK-47 rifle, a pistol, a cell phone, a digital camera and passports. Sial disclosed the two men had received Rs. 12 lakh during the last eight months.

Fahad, familiar with computers and related software, had an Indian visa, was staying at Mysore for the past six months and running a shop, 'Royal Fancy Stores', as a cover for his activities.

Al-Badr is a banned outfit under the Unlawful Activities (Prevention) Act, 2004.

Fahad used Malayalli Roots to get Visa

Fahad, the Al-Badr militant, had come to India on a 45-day visa under the pretext of visiting his Malayalee grand perents. Fahad father Abdulla Koya was from Kappad, near Kozhikode, and had reportedly migrated to Pakistan in early 1970s. Fahad was born in Karachi.

The militant had come to Kappad in Feb 2006 and had overstayed his 45-day visa—with no one from local administration any the wiser for it. Abdulla's first wife still lives at Kappad. Informed by the Karnataka's police on the Kozhikode links of Fahad, the local police team was soon in Kappad.

After joining the militant ranks, Fahad had been used by the ISI in its operations in South India, said the officials. He came into the net of security agencies after he was spoted at Lal Chowk in Srinagar, after which was under surveillance. He has a four knowledge of Malyalam and after arrival at Mumbai airport in February 2006. He got his visa stamped for Karnataka and Kolkata.

His role in terrorist activities was confirmed by an Al-Badr member Samir Ahmed Bhat who was arrested in Pulwama district. Fahad had handed over Rs. 3 Lakh to that. During his stay in India, Fahad had applied for an Indian passport, ration card and other documents to back his claim of being an Indian. And surprisingly, he got all the documents.

Hussain alias Qassim had entered India through Leepa Valley in North Kashmir and had been staying in Nishat area of Kasmir before moving to Mysore for his assignment. He is wanted by Jammu and Kashmir police for several cases.

The two were planning attacks in Bangalore, India's IT hub. Aged around 24, both were traveling on a two-wheeler when challenged by the police. Two constables were also injured in their ensuring gun battle with police.

As this is an important arrest incident, with wider security implications, some additional aspects of it are discussed in the succeeding paragraphs.

Police search Al-Badr man's house in Kerala: Oct 2006.

The police on 28 Oct 2006 raided and searched the house of Mariam, step-mother of Al-Badr terrorist Mohd Fahad, who was arrested by Mysore police on the night 26/27 Oct after a shoot out.

The joint operation by Kerala and Karnataka police led to the seizure of 14 letters, one CD and some magazines from Mariam's house in Kappad. Kozhikode SP TM Aboobacker told the press that initial scrutiny found nothing incriminating in the seized material.

Fahad is the son of Abdulla Koya, a Malayali, who went to Karachi soon after the 1971 war. There he married a Pak women and took the citizenship of that country, taking on the name Abdulla Hay. Fahad was in India on a 45-day visa to "visit his grand parents" in Kappad.

Mariam is the first wife of Abdulla Koya. The two have a son and a daughter, settled in Mysore. Mariam, 62, is a cancer patient.

Fahad, Mariam told the police, overstayed his visa and has tried to get an Indian citizenship through some political influence but did not succeed so far.

As to why Fahad was not arrested and deposited after he was found to have overstayed is the question that stands unanswered. It is known fact that many Pakistani nationals come to Kozhikode on the pretext of visiting their roots—many Malayalis had migrated to Pakistan—and managed to overstay with political patronage. "Not long ago, the Kerala Assembly had passed a resolution that a few hundred such persons now living in Malabar are too old and be given Indian citizenship on compassionate grounds".

Fahad, a postgraduate in analytical chemistry, is adept at making bombs. No wonder, his expertise was being courted by a number of extremist groups in Pakistan and India. He has been traveling in India for the past one-and-a-half years.

Sources say he has friends in Chennai, several places in Kerala, and Mumbai. Karnataka police in coordination with Kozhikode police has made a possible list of his contacts in Kerala. Unconfirmed reports suggest Fahad had sexual and marital relations with some women in Kerala. Police are making inquiries with the relatives of Koya in Pala, Kottayam and Thiruvananthpuram.

It is a Pak Terror Network (Unearthed) in South India: Oct. 2006

A day after two Pakistani terrorists landed in the Mysore police net (late on 26 Oct 2006 night), the network they established in south India is beginning to surface. Fahad, the mastermind behind the plans, had obtained a birth certificate from Mysore city corporation and had procured a driving licence from Chennai. He was now in the process of procuring a passport in Kerala.

He told interrogators that he was asked to pay money for the passport. "A Mysore police team is now in Calicut to verify the claims. They are investigating under what name and address Fahad had procured licence from Chennai and passport from Kerala.

As the plot thickens, police from Kerala, Tamil Nadu and Andhra Pradesh are converging to Mysore city. A team of Anti-Terrorism Squad (ATS) from Bangalore police also met senior police officers in the city.

Mysore city police constituted four teams to probe their activities and have stepped their investigation, building the case against the two.

A team seized the file that pertained to the issuance of the birth certificate to Fahad. ACP Devaraja, heading the investigations, visited the Mysore City Corporation and interrogated its commissioner KN Chandrashekar. The city police also attached the file pertaining to issuance of driving licence to Mohd Ali Hussain, the second terrorist. The Regional Transportation Officer (RTO) met senior cops and clarified the position.

Karnataka Plans New Law for Tenants

Karnataka government, in wake of the arrest of two Pakistani nationals, is considering a law under which tenants will be required to register their particulars with the nearest police station. "The model will be New Delhi law on the subject", said Home Minister MP Prakash on 28 Oct 2006.

The police department had mooted the idea following the II Sc shoot out in Dec 2005 in Bangalore when a scientist was killed by the terrorists. The arrest of the two Pakistani terrorists in Mysore has added some urgency to the plan. "Rules on the law are ready, very shortly a draft notification will be issued," Prakash said.

Besides the tenants, the proposed law will also include registration of details of domestic servants.

How did Terrorists Obtain Maps and Photos of Rooms Inside Assembly?

A Special Karnataka Anti-Terrorist Cell (ATC) team arrived in Mysore 28 Oct 2006 to probe how the two Pak terrorists managed a reconnaissance of Vikas Soudha (State Secretariat) and Vidhana Soudha (Legislative Assembly), and even obtained maps and photographs of rooms inside.

Bangalore Police Commissioner N Achuta Rao on 28 Oct said the "team will primarily look into militant's plans to strike these two buildings—a serious security lapse". It would find out how they got access to the buildings.

"If they have photographs of the place, besides maps, they would have definitely reconnoitered the locations. It is a serious security lapse. Their terror map is wide-spread, and it is important now to find out other places the terrorists could have planned to strike," said an intelligence officer. The terror network runs wide receiving/gaining support not only from active cadres of Al Badr, LET and JEM among other terror outfits but also among many persons with fundamentalist leanings.

The officer, however, admitted that while intelligence networking itself needs to be made more effective, they will also have to look at counter-intelligence measures. The state police is also exchanging information with their counterparts in Jammu and Kashmir, Delhi, Hyderabad, and Mumbai, among other places, where the terror network has spread. Another officer added: “We (state police) are gathering more information *and then exchanging it* with other police agencies who have more experience in handling terrorism—related activities.”

Policeman among 2 held in Fake Passport Case

Head Constable Alvi, posted at Kondotty police station in Malappuram, neighbouring district of Kozhikode, and Mohd Afzal, a travel agent in Malappuram, were arrested on 6 Nov 2006 for allegedly helping Fahad secure a fake passport. The arrests were made by the Special Investigating Team (SIT) probing the case in which Pak national and Al Badr terrorist Mohd Fahad had secured a fake passport.

Fahad and another Pak national Mohad Ali Hussain were arrested in Mysore on 27 Oct 2006.

With this, the total number of arrests in the case has gone up to four. Mohd Ali, an Assistant Sub-Inspector at Vazhakkad police station in Malappuram and Abdul Latheef, a postman at Kavanthur Post Office, also in Malappuram were remanded in judicial custody till 20 Nov by Kunnamangalam First Class Judicial Magistrate Court at Kozhikode on 6 November.

There are reports of Fahad previously visiting the trouble-torn Marad with a person who was accused of murder. Fahad had reportedly gone to Nadapuram and Vellamunda in an autorikshaw. The three places visited by Fahad are deemed sensitive.

The SIT is investigating as to why Fahad had visited Vellamunda, the place people accused of the murder of CPI (M) worker Binu belonged to. “Some investigating reporters have got information on the people whom Fahad visited, while in Nadapuram”.

Mysore Arrest of Two Pakistanis: Success of Intelligence

The arrest of two Pakistani terrorists after a gun-battle in Mysore on 27 Oct 2006 has an important lesson for Indians. Had the police not been able to intercept the highly trained militants, they could have caused in calculable loss to the country. They had come to Karnataka with a devastating strike plan for Mysore and Bangalore, India's IT capital.

Last year (2005), terrorists succeeded in attacking the Indian Institute of Science Campus, Bangalore while an international conference was on. This time they failed to implement the designs of their masters not only because of the alertness of police personnel but also due to intelligence inputs made available to them. A timely actionable intelligence is sine non quo to fight terrorism, which continues to pose serious threat to India's communal piece and economic growth.

No place in India seems to be safe from this hydra-headed monster. The Karnataka plan was believed to be hatched by the Al Badr, which has its roots in Pakistan as also in Jammu and Kashmir in India.[34] Al Badr is only one of the terrorist outfits operating against India with Pakistan's help. This despite public disavowal by Gen Musharraf of any help to anti-India terrorist outfits. Notwithstanding all this, "Al Badr alone received lakhs of rupees from the ISI till very recently."

Pakistan will have to dismantle terror infrastructure still intact inspite of the public assurances to the contrary. There is also need for awareness drive within the country about the modules the terrorist outfits have created on its soil. Then there are sleeper cells in various parts which can be activated by the relevant outfit at any given time.

So far, Pakistan has not delivered on its umpteen promises to stop aiding and sponsoring cross-border terrorism against India. Will Islamabad deliver under the "recently concluded truce at Havana"? Yes, and only, if it is serious about it. The commonsense says there is no harm in testing Pakistan's sincerity one more time. After all, India is not at war with Pakistan, as Prime Minster Man Mohan Singh told journalists the other day. But conversely, Pakistan has always deemed India an 'enemy', and has waged a low-intensity war against it for decades, without a let up, its sanctimonious declarations notwithstanding. Hence, the urgent need to be on guard and maintain a strict vigil against the terrorists, including the ones lurking within our borders as parts of so many modules and sleeper cells, who remain capable of springing a costly surprise anywhere, anytime—as they have demonstrated in the recent years.

All this only goes to show that India cannot rest on Islamabad's bland assurances: voluminous verbiage and pompous promises! In India's case, 'the eternal vigilance is the cost of national security' is not a mere cliché!

SAMJHAUTA EXPRESS BLAST KILL 68: 19 FEB. 2007

The bombing of the Samjhauta Express that killed 68 and injured another 15 is only the latest in a series of the terrorist attacks on public transport transit systems around the world. Public transit systems across the world have for decades have served as a principal venue for terrorist depredations.

While attacks such as the Sarin gas attack in Tokyo or the bombing of the Paris Metro invited worldwide attention and consequent media/expert discussion as did the Madrid and London train bombings, similar outraged in the third world countries, somehow, do not attract attention on the same level and scale. May be, as cynics posit, life in the poorer countries is 'cheaper' and therefore its loss in these countries does not deserve that much comment and analysis. Yet again, compared to underground railway systems, the vulnerability of open, accessible public transit systems and their passengers to terrorist acts has been cast in sharpest possible relief.

The diversity of assets, immoveable and moveable, present a choice of options/threats available to the terrorists. Some assets may be targeted to inflict human casualties to spread panic and demoralization among the civilian populace; others might be aimed at providing misinformation/disinformation to the public; yet others for crippling mobility or economic activity within a city or metropolitan area; or even for obtaining sensitive information about the system. In short, the terrorist outfits and their sponsors aim to target communications, operations and/ or maintenance capabilities of the 'adversarial' state; or as the Pak jihadi groups would prefer to put it vis-à-vis India, 'enemy' state.

Some Analysts' Comments

A number of reasons and explanations have been offered by the analysts and scholars vi-a-vis the terrorist attack on the Samjhauta. Some have made an attempt to analyse the aims and intentions of the perpetrators of this ghastly monstrosity. All this is briefly discussed here. Militants usually carry out blasts where large number of people are affected. They look out for places where security is less and from where they can flee easily after planting the bomb. Besides the fairs and political gathering, the trains and passengers travelling in them are ideal targets.

Analysis of a former diplomat, G Parthasarathy, says: "Terrorists to disturb communal harmony when they attack Akshardham temple in Gujarat, a temple in Varanasi or Ayodhya and a mosque in Malegaon. Blasts in two coaches of the Delhi-Attari (Samjhauta Express) special train at Diwana near Panipat in Haryana were carried out to disturb the peace process between India and Pakistan. Timing is also one factor. This time blast accused a few days before the visit of Pakistan Foreign Minister Khurshid Mehmood Kasuri. Terrorists are sending a message: 'Carry on with peace process but remember we are also here'[35]." Larger the gathering, better it is for the terror maniacs. Publicity is the oxygen for the terror merchants, and it is one thing they hanker after—and desperately. That explains the reason for the then British Prime Minister Margaret Thatcher banning the media from publishing the photographs and airing the voices of the Irish insurgents. There are various places/occasions when the people gather in large numbers, presenting an easy but attractive targets for the terrorists. These are temples, markets, fairs and trains. In the history of terrorism, there are the very places where most terrorist acts like explosions, shootings etc. have occurred.

Security, rather lack of it, is another reason that explains terrorists choosing to attack the middle and lower middle-class. Places where upper-class goes is full of security whether it is airports or shopping malls.

The target is also shifted from larger cities to smaller cities and towns to introduce an element of surprise and unpredictabili. Blasts at Malegaon, Madiaon, Panipat etc can be cited examples of this trend. In the recent years, the militants have co-opted local people for logistics support and to carry out the end jobs but without disclosing their own identity too them.

Delhi police officials say the militants target general compartments of trains because they can gain entry without any cheque, and then they are also more crowded compared to the reserved compartments. Between the markets and trains, the terrorists seem to have preference for the latter for two simple reasons: one, the victims cannot easily escape the inferno and second, the perpenators can easily get away after planting their 'ammunition' at the desired spot.

Trains: The New Targets

It is obvious that form markets the terrorists have shifted to the trains, and they have been doing that for many years as the chronology here shows.

In India

1996, 30 Dec. : A bomb blast on the Brahmaputra mail between Kokrajhar and Fakirgram stations in lower Assam killed 33 people.

1996, 8 July : A bomb ripped through a passenger train at Lehra Khanna railway station in Punjab's Bathinda district, killing 33 people.

1999, 22 June : A powerful explosion rocked the New Jalpaiguri railway station, killing nine passengers and injuring 85 others, including 10 soldiers.

2000, 14 Aug. : Explosion in Sabarmati Express at Rauzabad, 30 km from Fáizabad, Uttar Pradesh.

Killed—9

Injured—36

2003

13 March : A bomb attack in a local (commuter) train at Mulund station in Mumbai killed 11, including four women, and injured 71.

2 April : Two bombs explode inside Lucknow-bound Century Express at Madiaon in UP. No fatalities reported.

2005, 29 July : Explosion on the Patna-Delhi Shramjeevi Express near Harpalganj, 60 km from Jaunpur in UP.

Killed—12

Injured—52

2006

7 March	:	One bomb each exploded at Varanasi's famous Sankatmochan Temple and the cantonment railway station, killing 13 people and injuring 32.
11 July	:	Seven bomb blasts targeting the railway network (rail stations and commuter trains) in the city of Mumbai killed 187 people and injured 625. It is to be noted that first class compartments of trains at Mira-Bayandhar, Jogeshwari, Mahim, Santacruz, Khar, Matunga and Borivli stations on the Western Railway were targeted, possibly as a past of a deliberate plan. Some theorists averred selecting the first class compartments was to avenge the killing of Muslims in the post-Godhra Gujarat riots as mostly the rich Gujaratis traveled in these compartments.
20 November	:	A bomb Blast inside a compartment of the Haldibari-Siliguri passenger train at Belakoba station in West Bengal's Jalpaiguri district killed 10 and injured 65 others.
2007, 19 Feb.	:	Two powerful blasts near Diwana, 10 km from Panipat in Haryana turned the Indo-Pak train, Samjhauta Express (Delhi-Lahore) into a moving inferno, killing 68 people—mostly Pakistani nationals—and injuring 15 others.

International

1995

17 Aug.	:	Paris, France; nail-filled bomb at sub-way station. 17 injured.
21 Aug.	:	Paris, France; time bomb on a commuter rail killed seven people and injured 61.
2000, 30 Jan.	:	Muridke, Pakistan; coordinated bomb blasts at bus stop and rail station, killing one and injuring three.
2001, 27 March	:	Manila, Philippines; bomb blast at light rail station. Nine killed and 63 injured.

2003, 24 April	:	Kfar Sava station, Israel; self-detonated explosives. One killed and 13 injured.
2004, 11 Mar	:	Madrid, Spain; multiple bombing of several trains Killed—119 Injured—1509
2005, 7 July	:	London, UK, series of coordinated bomb blasts involving London underground (tube) trains and a bus. Killed—52 Injured—713

Timers used on Samjhauta same as those in Malegaon: 23 Feb. 2007

Investigators probing the Samjhauta Express blasts said on 23 Feb 2007 that timers used to detonate bombs on this train that killed 68 people were of the same kind found in Malegaon.

Malegaon blasts had claimed 38 lives and left 100 Muslims injured when they were emerging from the graveyard after praying during the *Shab-e-Baraat*—a ceremony to commemorate the dead—in Oct 2006. Police blamed Pok-based LET and the banned SIMI.

The similarity between the timer devices was pointed out by Gujarat police officers "who have been camping in Panipat for the last two days (21—22 Feb 2007)".

Napalm-like Bombs: New Terror Weapons

While the identity of the culprits of the Delhi-Attari Express blasts was yet to be established, sources in the intelligence claimed that there were inputs on terrorist outfits being trained in the assembly and use of napalm-like bombs.[36]

Napalm is a mixture of inflammable liquids used in warfare. Its military version, the kind used by US forces in Vietnam, is jellied gasoline. The make-shift devices being used by terror groups, may be a far-degraded form of napalm but they are potent enough to cause wide-spread public damage and panic as witness in these blasts. Also referred to as 'kitchen bombs', these are easy to assemble.

Three suit cases containing inflammable liquids, explosives and timers had been planted in three coaches of the train, two of which ment off.

The perfection behind the preparation of this attack and the finesse with which it was executed point fingers at highly professional terror groups, with the LET topping the list.

Banned by Pakistan in 2002, it has been business as usual by it under a new name: Jamaat-u-Dawa (JUD), meaning Party of the Calling. Sources are linking the blasts to a conference organized by JUD Chief Hafiz Mohd Saeed on 4 Feb 2007 in Fatehpur near Lahore, where the call for jihad was reiterated. It was held at Al Saud marriage hall, and attended by some 2000 persons strictly on the basis of an invitation.

It is no secret that Saeed is the most vocal of Gen. Musharraf's policies on terrorism and Kashmir issues, and travels freely throughout Pakistan collecting funds for terrorism-related activities and organizing conferences for the same purpose—the ban notwithstanding.

Despite its professed ideology of waging jihad against India/ South Asia, Russia and China, JUD has not been banned by Pakistan. The US had tried to put JUD on the list of Al Qaeda affiliates when Pakistan was holding the UN Security Council presidency. The US was stopped in its tracks by joint machinations of Pakistan and China.

It is well known that JUD, first to arrive on the scene for relief and rehabilitation measures after the 2005 earthquake in PoK, gained a lot of public support and popularity due to its prompt help to the local population devastated by the tragedy. The fact that it was first to arrive on the scene and help the locals promptly can be ascribed to Pak Army's reported decision to prioritise the rescue of its own personnel.

Security on Trains: Not an Easy Task

If terrorists have shifted their gaze to the trains, as detailed earlier, they have reasoned it out fairly carefully. Here are some statistics to prove the problems faced by the intelligence and security agencies.

- Of the 7,130 railway stations in the country, only 702 have the Railway Protection Force (RPF) executing access control duties, for which a total of 3,464 (RPF) personnel are made available.

- At these 702 stations, RPF has 1,200 units of hand-held metal detectors and 14,00 door-frame metal detectors.
- RPF has close circuit TV cameras at only 41 stations.
- Only 2 bomb detection and disposal squads are available, and one of these is not even a full squad.
- Dogs available 190, including 90 sniffers.
- 1457 trains only are escorted by 4,135 RPF personnel daily.

No Breakthrough Yet but Certain Related Information

A week after the 18 Feb 2007 Samjhauta Express blasts, the agencies were not able to make any breakthrough about the identity of the perpetrators of the crimes. Yes, as tenuous a lead as a mark on a suitcase is all that the police had to unravel the conspiracy. Here are all available facts, assumptions and postulations put together by a daily.[37]

- **Timing.** It is a poor man's vehicle across the border, its unreserved ticket just costing Rs. 108. It can get you from Delhi to Attari on the border, and then to Lahore across it. The midnight tragedy on the Attari Special on 18 Feb.—68 died and for the first time on Indian soil most of the victims were Pakistanis—was well-timed: Just a day before the visit of Pakistan Foreign Minister Kasuri and a few weeks before the meeting of—ironically—Indo-Pak joint terror mechanism.
- **Terrorists took advantage of the lax security.** Some say the tragedy was waiting to happen. Security checks on the sensitive train and on the Delhi Railway Station were rare, and inadequate. Luggage was hardly screened, tickets for the unreserved bogies could be bought even a few hours before the train left, often without even proffering the passports. Guests were also allowed to sit in the coaches till the train left. There were no CCTVs at Platform No. 18 of the Heritage Railway Station from where the ill-fated train left. Nor were any sniffer dogs deployed. The perpetrators know all this, as also the fact that tighter checks would start only at Attari whence the train rolled on to Pak side. Police now says the perpetrators even did a recce of the train, and

the plan to plant the bombs at Delhi was a cake walk. They chose a Sunday night, "catching a sleeping security mechanism off guard."

- **Contents of 'deadly' suitcases.** Four bombs seemed to have been planted on the train, all believed packed in similar suitcases, each one weighing some 20 kg. of the four, two exploded, one burst later when the police tried to defuse it, and the fourth was successfully detonated. "The bombs were unique and never seen in India before", said Home Minster Shivraj Patil.

  The contents of each of the suitcase bombs were: 14 plastic bottles filled with petrol/kerosene; a home-made electric circuit; two metal pipes filled with potassium nitrate, sulphur, carbon and magnesium wires; and an Orpat digital timer. Each suitcase bore a mark "Kodak TM" and a tailor mark on its cover saying "Apollo 600". These were the marks the police found on the suitcase bomb they detonated. It was a crude bomb, but obviously the handiwork of an expert, who had thought through the entire operation.

  Head of the Special Investigative Team (SIT), Sharad Kumar, IG (Rohtak Range), supplies interesting, important information: "The aim was clear: To ignite a fire from the low-intensity explosion (a cloth had been placed inside the sealed petrol/kerosene bottles to inflame the incendiary). The fire spread rapidly after the blasts. If all four bombs had gone off, the police might have been deceived into thinking that the incident was the result of a fire and not a bomb blasts, which perhaps was the aim of the evil planners". The officials feared that the resultant debate over the (reasons behind the) arson, like Godhra's, with majority of the passengers/ victims being Pakistanis would have had implications not only for Hindu-Muslim relations within India but also for Indo-Pak peace process and joint anti-terrorism understanding.

- **4-5 bombers, possibly helped by local elements**

  Eye witness Yoursuf Mohd of Pakistan says he caught a glimpse of two-three people getting off the train as it was pulling out of Old Delhi station leaving behind "two suspicious suitcases". Another eye witness in the coach where a bomb went off, Rana Shaukat Ali of Pakistan, who lost his five children in the blasts, told the police that he saw two men, "both speaking Hindi well", and carrying suspicious luggage, arguing with ASI Kashmir Singh of RPF. Ali says they said they wanted to go to Ahmedabad and would get off the train when it slowed down.

The probe shows the two suspects were on the train without valid documents and tickets. At 11.30 pm, Ali saw them getting down from the train and 15 minutes later, a blast rocked the adjoining compartment near Diwana railway station. Another blast went off in the adjoining coach. "The suspects knew that the train slowed down at a certain point before Panipat", says IG Sharad Kumar.

- *The leads: telephone calls, suitcase, and identikit*

1. Thousands of telephone calls from old Delhi to Jammu and Kashmir and Pakistan are being probed on the presumption that bombers stayed in the area around the Delhi railway station. Police are hoping for a breakthrough, as in the Delhi serial blasts case where the intercept of a call by Tariq Ahmed Dar to PoK led to his arrest.
2. The markings on the suitcase holding the bomb detonated by the police are being chased—especially in Delhi's Walled City—to zero in on the supplier. Over a dozen suppliers have been questioned, but there is as yet no break-through. The timers used are similar to the ones used in the Malegaon, Varanasi and Shramjeevi Express blasts and the police are ascertaining if there are links in these attacks.
3. Sketches made by the police on the basis of eye witness statements are the other rather bleak lead. Two persons in Bikaner, Rajasthan, one in UP and another in Delhi, have been detained. But the investigators see a long, arduous journey ahead of them. "Both the Haryana and Delhi police need to work in close tandem to crack the case", says IG Kumar. Both India and Pakistan are counting on that.

An Update

As many as 68 people died, 13 were injured and 19 victims remained unidentified in these blasts.

Haryana police identified Abhinandan Bag Centre in Indore as the shop from where six suitcases, used in the blasts, were bought on 14 Feb. Shop-owner Huzaifa Halim Ali was arrested as were tailors Faqruddin and Iqbal Hussain who had stitched the bags. The three were brought to Panipat, but later released and the case against them dismissed.

Bangladesh-based HUJI and SIMI remain the prime suspects, but Haryana police seem to have failed to make any headway. "Till date, there have been no arrests and exact sequence of events is also a mystery".[38]

"UPA has only Itself to Blame" : Critics

There is a section of analysts who are convinced that the UPA has deliberately chosen to soft pedal the issue of terrorism in India for reasons of vote-bank politics. Its reasoning runs as follows :

> "It is astonishing that security arrangements for the Lahore—bound Samjhauta Express should have been so lax as to allow terrorists to plant explosive devices and inflammable material in two bogeys of the train that is meant to promote friendship between people of India and Pakistan with disastrous consequences. Catching people unaware at the dead of night, 68 people, mostly Pakistanis, were killed in the explosions and the resultant fire in the two bogeys.
>
> "It would be an understatement to describe the latest terror strike as a dastardly attack on innocent people; it is a grim reminder that precious little has been done by the UPA government to achieve any tangible game in the war against terror within India's territory. On the contrary, by repealing the POTA and subsequently refusing to crack down on terrorism despite several horrendous attacks in the mistaken belief that inaction will win the Congress Muslim votes, this Government has inflicted immeasurable harm on the country and made internal security a negotiable instrument to mollycoddle killers and their supporters/ patrons."[39]

For all his bluster about jihadis gaining ground and the need to be watchful, the NSA has failed to walk the talk, and it must be remembered that he happens to be the sole repository of all intelligence inputs. Prime Minister must accept equal blame for becoming a captive of his own rhetoric and believing vacuous grandstanding to be a substitute for effective counter-terrorism policy. "No one wants to comment on the Home Minister who was never considered to be equal to his job."

In the absence of any outfit claiming responsibility, and intelligence unable to determine the identity of the killers, it is anyone's guess as to who or which outfit is responsible for this outrage. It is entirely possible that bombers are of Pakistani origin and their mission was to derail the peace process between the two countries by triggering a domestic backlash against Gen Musharraf. At the same time, one cannot rule out the possibility of home-grown *jihadis* doing their masters' bidding. Whatever the identity of the mass killers, there is no gainsaying the basic fact that ensuring safety of the Samjhauta Express while it is on the Indian soil is the responsibility of Government of India. To that extent, the Pakistan Government cannot be faulted for its mocking comments.

The perpetrator of the cross-border terror has not missed the opportunity to paint the victim in bleak colours. And "We have only UPA Government to blame for this bizarre turn of events".

Had there been no security lapse and had the UPA Government been truly committed to fighting terrorism, whether of foreign or domestic origin, then Pakistan would not have had the vicarious pleasure of putting India on the defensive. While Prime Minister Man Mohan Singh on 19 Feb "meekly fumbled for an explanation, Gen Musharraf magnanimously suggested that the bombings should not be allowed to derail the bilateral peace process." The boot is truly on the other foot !

In any democratic polity, Prime Minster is primarily held responsible for any lapse—be it is political, economic or social spheres of national life—because he is the head of the government. But in the context of terror attacks/outrages in India, the Prime Minister heading the UPA coalition has been held more blame worthy by some analysts and critics, for it is his Congress party led by Sonia Gandhi that had removed a specific anti-terror law, the POTA, from the statute book—thus sending out wrong signals to the terrorists and the wider world beyond.

The above discussion is essentially focused around this 'cardinal sin' as some would put it. But what follows is a discussion of the wider range of issues involved in the context of the Samjhauta outrage, even if the central issue is the grave breach in country's security systems.

Were we Asking to be Worsted?

May be it is a harsh judgment, but some analysts have dubbed the latest terrorist outrage as "an avoidable tragedy." This may have been actuated by the near, unfailing regularity of terrorist's ability to inflict barbaric cruelties in any region of India.

Unfortunately, the story of the tragic Samjhauta blasts was not focused on "the central issue of gravest breaches ever of the (internal) security system of in the country."[40]

Exercised perhaps by the diplomatic spin-offs from the explosions, and the suffering of the luckless passengers under treatment at the Burns and Trauma wards of the Safdarjung Hospital, both the media and most of Indian think-tanks made only passing references to the cracks in the security system that led to what was really an avoidable visitation.

It needs to be said that no terrorist strike is totally avoidable. Had that been so, India would not have faced the brunt of this hideous technique of religio-political conflict adopted by crazed zealots in almost every of its wide-spread regions. Even a highly security conscious society like Israel has not been able to craft a fail-safe method of preventing determined terrorists from committing their evil acts.

Who or what, after all, can stop a militant, who is primed and convinced by a mullah/maulvi that his murderous act has sanction of his religion and it will help him enter the gates of heaven (= *bahisht*) for a life of luxury he could only dream on earth, from hurling himself as a (human) bomb in a crowded market place or driving a car laden with explosives on a busy street?

Leaving the human bombs aside, it is time to refer to a remark once made by the then US Defence Secretary Donald Rumsfeld. It was an eminently apt remark that had invited predictable derision from an anti-US media everywhere. That remark undoubtedly signified one of the more astute observations on the challenges confronting the international community in the shape of terrorism.

Rumsfeld had said—and he is being paraphrased here—in the war against terror, there are "known unknowns" and "unknown unknowns". To unravel the remarks, the former signifies sort of attacks that can be pre-empted because of a history of such attacks and the latter belongs to the category of terror attacks/strikes that cannot be prevented simply because these have never occurred earlier. In this light 9/11 was an "unknown unknowns," While the London, Madrid or Mumbai train blasts were "known unknowns". Our capabilities to win the war against terrorists—the invisible, insidious enemy—hinge crucially on the extent to which they can be *prevented* from carrying out their gruesome acts. But if that be the yardstick to measure success against terrorism, the Indian state has been embarrassingly—"Shamefully" may be more appropriate and fashionable term here but is not employed as it lacks grace and is outrightly indecent—unequal to the task. Given its lackadaisical approach to the counter-terror responsibility, the analysts have no hesitation in asserting that "it is asking to be clobbered by the terrorists."

A terrorist striking a crowded market place or driving into a mall or some public place with a car bomb is, by definition, not entirely preventable. However, the possibility of terrorists striking high security zones like, say Parliament House, or the Prime Minster's residence, or even hijacking a plane is preventable on the basis of their being "known" targets of terrorists. The Mumbai suburban train was for this reason different from the Samjhauta Express: The latter was "known" target of such an assault. After all, there are thousands of regular trains and a breach in the security of any of them can hardly be discounted. But there was and still is only one Samjhauta Express.

But what is most bewildering is the ease with which terrorists planted explosives on the Samjhauta Express. After all, it was not a train running between Begusarai and Mokama, it was making transnational journey; by extension, it should have been provided with security arrangements of international standards of transportation. Every passenger getting on board should have been screened, every piece of luggage in the compartments sniffed by police dogs and exposed to X-ray machines. This obviously did not happen; on the other hand, there was a newspaper report, not refuted by the Government, that as many as 50 tickets were issued for Samjhauta Express without passport verifications—a mandatory provision !

The safety of the passengers on this train, in particular, should have been seriously considered and planned diligently by the authorities concerned because it should have been on the "hit list" of the terrests since the day it began making its cross-border journey. The apparent failure of the Government to ensure it—all the rationalisations, notwithstanding—should have caused some heads to roll in the highest offices of the Rail Bhavan and the Home Ministry. This is because more than any other terror attack, the government owed for greater moral responsibility for the Deewana tragedy. Such serious errors of judgment and omission must be dealt with severely, lest the contagion spreads and the officials concerned become even more smug.

There is one more disturbing aspect of this 'avoidable' tragedy that needs to be highlighted. The fact that only two of the maximum five containers (in fact the suitcase bombs) blew up/went off and three did not shows that it was a lunch of amateurs who effected/executed the strike. If such greenhorn terrorists can achieve success in case of such sensitive/high value targets, it exposes our preventive mechanisms as hollow and totally ridden with horrendous infractions.

It is such perforations in the security apparatus that makes us sitting ducks for terrorists, and this promiscuousness reduced us to the laughing stock of the world—and a toast of the terrorists. In the days to come, success against terrorism will be measured not against the number of places that are bombed in Afghanistan, Somalia or in some such distant place but the extent to which the local police and intelligence system detects and thwart terror attacks.

It may sound strange to suggest that India learn some lessons on counter-terrorism from countries like the US and the UK who fell victim to terrorism only less than a decade ago while we have suffered over the long decades. The logic behind the suggestion is elementary: Their preventive and counter-terrorism measures have achieved eminent success in detecting the terrorist plans/strikes than their counterparts in India. The detection at Heathrow in London in the 2006 summer which prevented a terror plot of horrendous proportions was a case of an eminent success. Likewise, the US has made periodic arrests to cripple the terrorist plans. It is not that India has not made some success in this field here or there, but unfortunate fact is that terrorists have succeeded in inflicting costly terror strikes in various parts of the country at will.

So successes scored by some countries are in stark contrast to India failure in the preventive field. One may put it harshly—if not cynically—that the Samjhauta terror strike by a bunch of fumbling terrorists, blowing up compartments of a "high-security" train on Indian soil that was going to Pakistan, proved for India how not to wage war against terror!

Samjhauta Express Blasts: An Analystical Comment

Two intractable problem stand highlighted by the Samjhauta Express tragedy:

1. Appalling inadequacies of India's instruments for dealing with the challenges thrown by this tragic incident.
2. The even more frightening inadequacies of Pakistan for dealing with the Frankenstein of terrorism created (and nurtured) by it.[41]

Let us assume that this horror was inflicted despite Islamabad's sincerity as of now being an ardent fighter against terrorism and its inveterate enemy. This leaves us facing an evil force of huge potential, without any identifiable control on it. This has consequences for India. New Delhi must ignore the fact that Pakistan had created this whole vast network of terror and used it deliberately as an instrument of state policy against India. What is of urgent importance for New Delhi is to see how best to cope with the consequences mentioned above.

In the changed circumstances, Pakistan's intentions remain crucial. It is for the first time that the terrorists have struck both sides simultaneously, indicating how Pakistan itself is exposed to the vicious Frankenstein it had nurtured to be used against India at its will. Will this realization of its own vulnerability to the self-created monster, persuade it to mount its unilateral efforts and genuine cooperation with India to fight a common enemy.

Is the civil society in Pakistan ready for this responsibility? Pakistan used to have an "extremely sophisticated elite, whose doubtlessly honest commitment to Islam by no means excluded modern liberal thinking and preferences virtually indistinguishable from enlightened equivalents anywhere". As in India, such elites have been transformed or displaced by newly empowered elements of society. But there is an important differentiation in the orientations of the newly-emerged elements replacing the old elites in the two countries. While in India, these new forces have, so far, learned to function within a democratic system, in Pakistan the rise has been of the more traditional and religiously committed elements. The important question is : Do the groups, which provide modern, liberal pressures within Pakistan, have the sense to realize, and the strength to suppress, the threat they themselves face?

So many have left, and so many conform, the answer, as this analyst suggests, must surely be no-not without State support. We are told the regime faces so many challenges, and would face so many more if it tried harder to suppress its former henchmen; so we (India and Indians) have to be patient. This, in fact, is the start of India's problems in dealing with Pakistan and cross-border terrorism viz, this need and advice to be patient. This, as of now, is doubtless true ; while they created the mess, we all have to clear it together. This may be acceptable to India. This may even be incumbent upon it having set up a Joint Mechanism under Havana truce. May be, India had envisaged this unpleasant task. May be, knowing it all coming and discerning its own interest in clearing the sub-continent of this curse of terrorism, India had enticed Pakistan into this Joint Mechanism. In that case, it should come as no surprise because some analysts had written from Havana that India had persuaded Islamabad into partnership to fight terrorism. (It is altogether a different issue though that we are also aware of some Pakistani journalists asserting from Havana at that very time that it was master stroke of Pakistani diplomacy that pushed a reluctant India into the Havana truce). So far so good. But this 'do-gooding' (if one is allowed to coin this phrase) act should not be stretched into, as Pakistan and its friends are wont to do, "India must make concessions on its differences with its neighbours, especially on Jammu and Kashmir." India must be wary of such 'logic'.

"Remove the root cause of terrorism and you will remove terrorism", is a specious plea—by now, an over-used but 'reasonable sounding' cliché, a favourite slogan so-often brandished by supporters of 'freedom fighters' all over, and rejected out-of-hand all over the globe as a totally unacceptable rationalization of unmitigated evil. In fact, things should not be left with this unimbiguous rejection.

No causes, whatsoever, including the indisputably noble, can justify the horrors inflicted on innocents; and the motives of the terrorists, and their manipulators, who have harassed, nay bled India through 'thousand cuts' for decades, are far from noble. Accepted, the terrorists created, trained and nurtured by Islamabad may be turning against it for not presently going any further, particularly since the 9-11 and attack on Parliament. Accepted again, they may be out of Islamabad's control. Handling them with kid gloves may be Islamabad's compulsion. But this handling must be seen as a lot more convincing than it actually has been.

Even in this handling, kid-gloves variety, or otherwise, certain contradictions have been discernible over the years. Empirical evidence over past several years show that Pakistan has, as a result of policy decision, differentiated its cooperation on counter-terrorism issue with the US from the one with India on the same subject. While it has delivered hundreds, if not thousands, of terrorists to the US as demanded by the latter in post-Nine-Eleven period, it has not delivered a single one even for the original list of 20 over the last decade. Islamabad might have taken a U-turn in its Afghan police post 9-11 for reasons well-understood, but it made no such changes in its policy on handling anti-India terrorism, flourishing as hithertofore on its soil. Thus it is no secret that while cooperating (up to a point) with the US to catch anti-US and anti-Western terrorists, Pakistan exempted India-focused terrorists from this main campaign, retaining them as instruments of State policy against India—as, if and when required. And that is what (instruments of State policy) they remain, statistics of reduced incidence only proving at best that they can be controlled.

If we allow for Islamabad's limitations, it too must allow for both our mistrustfulness born of its past and the difficulty of reconciliating its peaceable professions with several of its continuing policies, notably its increasingly blatant efforts to revive the Taliban in Afghanistan.

Even accepting unreservedly that Islamabad had nothing to do with Samjhauta blasts at Panipat, where mainly Pakistani nationals were killed, we need to see whether the tragedy has shocked it enough to push it into genuine cooperation with India against the abominable creatures who are as dangerous to the kind of Pakistan its leaders claim to want, as to India. Will Pakistan join India in identifying the culprits in a meaningful may? Will the ISI tip off Indian covert agencies about the modules and sleeper cells located in India? Needless to mention, there are numerous ways Pakistan can help India without an unduly loud publicity. But the real question is : Will Islamabad be inclined that way?

The second lesson from the Panipat blasts concerns our own myriad domestic inefficiencies, neglects and failures. Indians cannot afford a day longer to let their country suffer from these inefficiencies, and from the machinery and instruments of State action, which have manifestly rusted into unbelievable worthlessness. It is not that there is no action, but most of it seems to be misplaced or misdirected: (1) doing the wrong things, (2) not doing anything, and (3) doing the right thing wrong (way). There are so many instances in each category that any observant Indian can compile his own fairly long list. The truth is that sloppiness, neglect of basic duties, misuse of authority at various levels, and all-pervading corruption have all become so much the norm of our public life that cleaning the Augean stables was a simpler task compared to extricating ourselves from this cesspool of the uncaring. Worst, the agencies entrusted with the responsibility of serving people's basic needs seem either unable or unwilling to perform, and often engage themselves in passing the buck.

But there are some disturbing questions and troubling facts. Some relate to the absence of an effective counter-terrorism policy. It may sound a harsh question : Do we have in place even the elementary precautions? Do we have a system to check and ensure that those entrusted with specific tasks are carrying them out? Authorities have not given full facts about the blasts, perhaps for valid reasons. But bits and pieces in public domain leave one staggered in amazement. It is bad enough that there were no security arrangements at Delhi railway station, the starting point of the Samjhauta, to check and anticipate such dangers; here we have our Home Ministry telling us it had advance information on the threat and yet nothing seemed to have been done. To add shame to our dismay, some passengers told the press that all the security personnel at Delhi Junction were interested was making money off the passengers. And what do we make of our railway security forces actually helping the possible perpetrator jump off the moving train—wrong in itself—just because they claimed another destination.

It is obvious that there have been failures of thinking things out in advance, of doing even what can be done within limitations of resources, of attending to the routine of one's duty. "The utter stupidity of the guards on the train raises the further issue of the kind of people our system now forces us to suffer in various positions of authority, high and low alike." Can a nation go on like this? But then the ultimate stumbling block : Will our politics permit reforms? The answer, as of today, is clear 'No'. The coalition at the Centre is riven with problems of reform in some other security-related issues. This is not the appropriate place to discuss any further details.

The world presently reckons us among the leading players in the international arena—an economic and military super power by 2040s. If we, indeed, are to reach there, can we continue with our lackadaisical ways?

Finally, and once again it can bear repetition: India must devise and put in place an effective counter-terrorism policy in place-earlier the better. Unless we do that, we are playing with our national security imperatives.

Target : Mecca Masjid, Hyderabad : 18 May, 2007

10 people were killed and 30 injured on 18 May 2007 when a bomb exploded in the historic Mecca Masjid adjacent to the Charminar, in Hyderabad, in the course of the Friday afternoon prayers.

Four more were killed at Shah Ali Banda, a short distance from Charminar, in police firing when a groups was attempting to attack a police inspector. The Home and Minorities Ministers were gheraoed when they visited Old City.

The Majlis Ittehad Musilmeen (MIM) called for a bandh on 19 May.

The JEM is suspected to be behind the blast. Police source said that the person who masterminded the attack was one Shahid.

The police defused two more live bombs after the incidents. These were placed to the left of the mosques *Wazukhana*, a rectangular water tank where the faithful wash their hands and feet before preceding for their prayers.

This is the first time that the bombs were found in the mosques premises. The 313-year-old mosque, built by Mughal Emperor Aurangzeb, is among the biggest and the largest in India. The bomb exploded at 1.20 pm, minutes before the prayers were to be wound up. It was an IED with a timer, which was activated by a mobile phone. The bomb was planted in a bag, and placed next to a steel tiffin box.

The incident rattled Old City. Enraged youth poured into the streets as the news spread. Some of them attacked shops while others forced shutters to be put up. Several Muslim youth assembled outside the mosque and indulged in heavy stone-throwing. Police bore the brunt of this attack. Such was the intensity of their anger that police could not manage to enter the mosque till after 3 pm. Police fired in the air to disperse the crowd.

Home Minister K Jana Reddy ordered additional troops (?), including the state's elite anti-Naxalite Greyhounds, to patrol

Old City. Reddy said later in the day, after a meeting with police top brass, that the culprits would be identified within 24 hours.

In most part of the walled aty, home to over 10 lakh Muslims, the situation remained tense. Hyderabad city police Commissioner Balwinder Singh said large number of policemen and the RAF men were deployed in the sensitive areas.

- The blast was similar to the last year's ones in the packed mosques targeted on Fridays in Malegaon and Delhi (Jama Masjid). They had triggered clashes and tension.
- Groups from outside Andhra Pradesh involved in the blasts says state DGP MA Basith. The sophisticated timer bombs are new to Hyderabad. LET and JEM use such bombs, says on anti-terror expert in Mumbai.
- The blast could have triggered communal riots in the city, possibly also the aim of terrorists.
- Were the Mosque authorities non-cooperative? The custodians of Mecca Masjid, target of a Malegaon-type attack involving Pakistan-backed jehadi outfits, had spurned the moves of Hyderabad police to tighten security in spite of intelligence inputs warning of an attack. The police found the Mosque anthorities non-cooperative.

  The warning came true on Friday when Juma namaz was on. To the central agencies, "the attack carried resemblance to the attack on a Borelvi mosque by on ISI-trained module drawn from among the Deobandis.[42]
- The suspicion at this point of time is on, as in the Malegaon case, the outlawed SIMI. Deendar Anjuman, another banned outfit which was found involved in similar atrocities in the past and has been quite active around Hyderabad, may have played the auxiliary.
- A senior MHA sought to reinforce the theory of 'the terrorists wanting to disturb the communal harmony of this large city: "It showed the desperation of the outside terrorist elements to foment trouble after they failed to

do so subsequent to attacks on Sankat Mochan temple in Varanasi, Jama Masjid in Delhi and a mosque in Malegaon. Even the days of attack were chosen to accrue maximum benefit in terms of arousing religious sentiments of the communities targeted: Tuesday for the Hindu temple of Sankat Mochan and Friday for the mosques."

- An alarmed Centre sent advisories to all states asking them to be on the alert in the wake of the incident.
- The locality housing the mosque has lately seen the clashes between the entrenched MIM and a determined effort by the CPM to gain a foothold in the area, with the Urdu newspapers also jumping into the fray.
- The Mecca Masjid has been associated with trouble and quickly turned into a flashpoint when community passions ran high, with unruly elements gathered inside raining stones and bricks on cops. Exasperated by the routine, the police insisted on getting the ground inside the mosque cemented to ensure that trouble-makers do not easily get stones to hurl at policemen.
- The initial investigation into the blasts reveals use of a mixture of ammonium nitrate with fuel oil, the same ingredients that were found from the blast sites in Malegaon on 5 Sep 2006—a finding that confirms that the ISI continued with its efforts to over come its reliance on RDX, a factor which would easily give its hand.
- Hyderabad has lately emerged as a home to many sleeper cells of ISI, with the trial of investigation into many terror incidents leading to the city. One RDX consignment headed for Malegaon, which was intercepted near Pune, had originated in the city.
- The analysts who know the highly—polarized Hyderabad city well said that this was the first time that the rampaging crowds did not make any distinction between Hindus and Muslims while targeting their victims. "They were plain angry and targeted people in power". Among those at the receiving end of the crowds were local MIM MLA Akbar Owaisi, fire brigade chiefs AK Khan and city Congress chief Shiv Prasad.

On the eve of Tableegi Jamaat congregation

The blasts took place just a day before the massive congregation of the Tableegi Jamaat began in Hyderabad on 19 May. It was attended by 200,000 Muslims. The observers remarked the Tableegi sessions in the earlier years too were preceded by similar incidents of violence.

Why was RAF missing from Mecca Masjid?

Local (read Muslims) in the Charminar area say they stay alert every Friday. In case they do forget this day of the week, they are soon reminded of it by the presence of the RAF in the area. However, the last few weeks "the RAF has been conspicuously lesent", the locals told the pressman. "This Friday, when their presence could have saved some lives, or perhaps even prevented the terror attack, this elite force in blue fatigues was nowhere to be seen. They came after the bomb went off". This, in a manner of speaking, could be a riposte to authorities' assertion that even after cautioning the Mosque management about the intelligence inputs indicating likelihood of an attack on it, the latter refused to cooperate against the possibility.

The RAF officials, who rushed to the blast site on Friday, said "they are deployed in the area based on the requisition made by the city police...We have not been deputed in this area in the last couple of weeks."

But the officials at the RAF headquarters in Hakimpet were more specific: "Our services have not been sought in the Mecca Masjid area after 19 March 2007 when an accident had occurred there. Their deployment there had ended on 20 March." An official gave another, more realistic reason on the issue: "Apart from not being requisitioned by the city police, the RAF too was, as a matter of policy, discouraging frequent deployments policy, as its regular presence may hamper its efficacy. Its deployment in Mecca Masjid was frequent but never routine."

'Blast suspect was trained at JEM camp'

Police sources in Delhi disclosed on 20 May that Shahid Bilal, the HUJI militant, believed to be involved in this blast, had undergone training at a JEM camp. Though he is now believed to be in Pakistan, modules operating under him are based in Bangladesh.[43]

Operating under several aliases such as Akbar and Shahbez, Bilal's real name is Abdul Rehman and he is cousin of Mohd Abdul Rauf, arrested by CBI in 2003 on charges of involvement in the assassination of senior BJP leader Hiren Pandya in Gujarat. Rauf was also allegedly involved in the murder of a local Hyderabad politician way back in 1999.

Police believe Rauf initiated Bilal into terrorism and sent him to Pakistan where he met Mufti Sufian Pantyangia and Rasool Khan, both from Gujarat, who are allegedly involved in the Hiren Pandya murder case. The duo sent Bilal for training to a Jaish camp, following which Bilal went to Bangladesh via Saudi Arabia in 2005. There he met Dr. Saeed of HUJI who introduced him to Ghulam Yajdani, another terrorist from Hyderabad who headed the LET unit in Bangladesh.

Two alleged Bangladeshi militants, Anishul Murshlin and Muhibbul Muttakin, who were arrested in 2006 by the Special Cell of the Delhi police, and purportedly disclosed that Bilal was involved in the conspiracy to carry out a suicide attack at the Special Task Force office in Hyderabad in 2005. He was also in close contact with those who masterminded explosions on board the Shramjeevi Express the same year.

Intelligence revealed that in mid-2005, Bilal's focus shifted to the southern states. Sneaking in, he stayed there for three months conducting reconnaissance of prominent IT companies in Bangalore and of vital installations in Hyderabad. While Yajdani and a top HUJI militant were gunned down in an encounter with the Special Cell of the Delhi police in 2006, Bilal began supervising HUJI operations in India, particularly in the southern states. That is why intelligence agencies are suspecting his involvement in the Mecca Masjid blast. At present, over half a dozen militants hailing from Hyderabad are operating under him. Some of them operate under code names such as Ejaz, Wazid, Aaghar Ali, Zuber, Aslam and Sayyad Noor.

"In Bangladesh, JEM, LET and HUJI seem to be working in-tandem to carry out terrorist activities in India. On several occasions, they have been found conducting joint operations at various levels," said a senior police officer.

MIM besieges DGP; Asks tough but expected questions

The situation in Hyderabad, scene of a deadly blasts on a historic mosque on 18 May remained fluid and tense on the 20th as its Muslim community continued demanding for a CBI inquiry into the blasts as also the subsequent police firing. 16 people died in both the incidents that touched of a state wide protest against the Government and the police.

MIM, a strong political entity in the State is leading the protest. It called for a bandh on 19 May, and on the 20th laid a siege on the DGP in Saifabad area in the heart of the city, demanding that the case be handed over to the CBI. It also demanded a judicial inquiry into the police firing and suspension of officers responsible for it.

More than a thousand demonstrators led by the party MP Asaduddin Owaisi, sat on a dharna on the road in front of the police headquarters, shouting slogans against Chief Minister Y.S. Rajsekhara Reddy and the police. Sudden demonstrations tool the police by surprise and blocked the traffic for a time. The protest was brought to a peaceful end. MIM threatened more such sudden demonstrations at a place and time of its choosing unless its demand was accepted.

Owaisi laid out his cards honestly, if on expected lines: "We do not have any faith in the local police, and the head of the SIT is the same person who has always been laying all the responsibility on the Muslims. CBI should investigate the case." As long as Additional Commissioner Rajeev Tiwari headed the SIT, no impartial inquiry could be expected.

Tiwari was also among the officials whose names did the rounds among suspects helping the Gujarat police in Sohrabuddin killing case.[44] The MP strongly objected to Tiwari making selective leaks to the media within a couple of hours of the blast suggesting that organizations with links to Bangladesh or Pakistan were involved in the blast.

Describing the police investigation as "Muslim stereo typing", owaisi regretted that the Congress Govérnment of the State had not shown any seriousness about the investigation: "We have been telling the government from the beginning that serious investigation should be conducted with an open mind and the real culprits arrested.

He said the Andhra Government was making the same mistakes in the investigations in Mecca Masjid blasts which the Maharashtra Government had committee in the Malegaon and Nanded blasts. He further added "The entire country is shocked and surprised by the brutality of the police under the congress Government of the state. If there is any difference between the Gujarat Government and this Government, then they should take immediate steps and order a CBI inquire."

Asked about the police claim that a wanted extremist Shahed Bilal was involved in the blast, he said if that be so he should be brought to book. "We are saying why are you blaming Muslims for everything? Whether attack is on a mosque or a temple or a public place, only Muslims are blamed. Why do you not work with an open mind?", he asked.

The MMA leader urged UPA chairperson Sonia Gandhi to intervene in the matter and direct the State government in the matter.

Is not MIM/Owaisi Protesting too much?

Here is brief history of Mecca Masjit blast's chief brain Shahid. But what was Behind Mecca Masjid blast/attack? A well-known analyst[45] of the subject put it rather well: "Communal violence, organized crime, and the global jihad intersect in Andhra Pradesh capital."

House 16-11-240, Moosaram Bagh, reads the address on the police dossier of the man the Hyderabad police believe planned and executed the Mecca Masjid bombing. This is the house where Abdul Rehman, alias Bilal and Shahid grew up.

Starting in Sep 2002, at least 14 youngmen from Hyderabad set out on secret trips to terror training camps in Pakistan. A decade earlier, the demolition of the Babri Masjid by Hindu fundamentalists had led several recruits from Hyderabad into the lap of the LET.

Rehman was one of those 14 men 26 now, he dropped out of college less than a year after his graduation from the Asafiya High School in Hyderabad. It is unclear if he developed links with Hyderabad based Islamist groups during this period, for Rehman's name only began figuring in intelligence records from Jan 2004. what is probable, though, is that he had at leas some knowledge of the not works that sustained the lashkar's presence in the city. Rehmand was related by marriage, through his brother Khaliq Rehman, to one of India's most wanted men—Gujarat Mafioso Yakub Khan Pathan.

Better known by the alias Rasool Khan 'Party', Pathan had long-standing links with the Karachi-based mafia Dawood Ibrahim Kaskar. In the wake of the Gujarat riots, Pathan took responsibility for transporting the new wave of jihadi recruits for training. According to the testimony of the mafia operative Javed Hamidullah Siddiqui, who was arrested in 2004, Dawood lieutenant Shakeel Ahmad Babu arranged the new recruits' passage on flights through Bangkok and Dhaka. Pathan, who has been wanted by Interpol ever since 1993, was waiting for them on their arrival at Karachi. While some recruits trained with the LET, others were routed on to the JEM.

Within months of their departure, the new recruits executed their first successful strikes. Asad Yazdani, a resident of Hyderabad's Toli Chowki area, helped execute the assassination of the former Gujarat Home Minister Hiren Pandya. He was killed for his role in the communal pogrom, as per the CBI inquiry. Pathan helped put together much of the infrastructure for the assassination.

Although new recruits had trained with LET and JEM, they turned to the Bangladesh-based HUJI for operational support. Founded by the Bangladeshi veterans of the anti-Soviet Union jihad in Afghanistan, the HUJI operates at least six camps where several hundred Pakistani, Indian, Thai and Myanmar nationals (obviously all Muslims) are known to have trained. Its founder, Mufti Abul Hannan, spent several years studying at the Dar-ul-Uloom seminary at Deoband, UP, and developed a large network of contacts among Islamists in India. He also built links with key figures of organized crime. Among the group's most high profile actions in India was the Jan 2002 terror attack near the American centre in Kolkata, executed in collaboration with Dawood-linked mafioso Aftab Ansari.

In 2006, the Delhi police arrested two of Yazdani's Bangladesh recruits, the twin brothers: Anishul Murshlin and Muhibbul Muttakin. Both confirmed speculation that Yazdani had executed several major strikes in India—one of these being the June 2005 bombing of the Delhi Patna Shramijeevi Express at Jaunpur. Yazdani, it turned, was also responsible for the Oct 2005 suicide bombing of the headquarters of the Andhra Pradesh police's counter-terrorism Special Task Force (STF). A Bangladeshi national Mohtasin Bilal had carried out the bombing—the first HUJI operation of its kind. From the twins, Indian intelligence also heard the name of the man Yazdani reported to—a man they know by the aliases Shahid and Bilal.

Investigation established that between Apr and June 2005, Rehman had been based in Bidar, Karnataka, organizing the safe-houses, communications infrastructure, and escape routes that allowed HUJI's Bangladesh-based cells to strike with such efficiency and ease. Yazdani was shot dead in Mar 2006, just hours after the bombing of the Sankat Mochan temple in Varanasi—another lethal attack that was traced to HUJI's Bangladesh-based cells. Rehman's brother, Zahid Rehman, was arrested on charges of aiding this operation, and is still in jail awaiting conclusion of his trial.

As of Rehman himself, there was but no trace/news. Indian intelligence informants have reported sightings in Karachi and Dhaka. But his family insists Rehman is in undeclared custody of Hyderabad police. Whatever the truth, the analysts are convinced of the fact that Rehman is just a minor part of a far larger story: the Islamist campaign against Hyderabad.

Global Jihad's Designs on Hyderabad

Hyderabad, like so many former Indian princely states has its history. The Islamists who dream of converting the wide world into a vast Ummah must have been mulling over this history for years. They publicly declared their plans in Feb 2002 with this announcement by LET's top ideologue Abdul Rehman Makki at a Lashkar rally: "The LET has set in place a new campaign to liberate Hyderabad from Hindu rule. It had been seized by force and would be won back through the sword".

Such language is not new. In 1948, over half a century before Makki's announcement of a new liberation campaign for

Hyderabad, Islamist guerrilla leader Qasim Rizwi had promised to fly the Nizam of Hyderabad's flag "on the Red Fort in Delhi". Rizwi's was not an empty threat, or a rhetorical flourish. Memoirs of the former C-in-C of Pakistan's armed forces, Lt Gen Gul Hassan Khan, speaks of an unnamed "elder statesman" helping funnel covert military aid to Rizvi's groups.[46]

For years before Makki's 2000 speech, the Lashkar has been attempting to build a network using local Islamists. Perhaps the most successful of the Lashkar's agents was Mohd Ishtiaq, the son of a shopkeeper from Kala Gujran in Pakistan's Jhelum district. Operating under the alias Salim Junaid, Ishtiaq obtained an Indian passport and even married a local resident, Momina Khatoon.

Ishtiaq, however, was arrested before he could do any real harm. In 1998, responding to pleas from Lashkar leadership, Hyderabad resident Mohd Azam Ghauri returned to India to help rebuild its networks. One of the three cofounders of the Lashkar's Indian networks, Ghauri had fled in the wake of serial bombings of 43 trains in Dec 1993, "an operation executed to avenge the demolition of the Babri Masjid.

Ghauri turned to friends in Hyderabad's organized crime cartels for help. In 1999, his long-standing friend, Dawood-linked hitman Abdul Aziz Sheikh, attempted to assassinate Shiv Sena leader, Milind Vaidya. Help was also sought, and received, from remnants of the mafia of Mohd Fasiuddin, which had executed local Hindu fundamentalist leaders Rapiah Goud and Nanda Raj Goud as retaliation for the 1992 anti-Muslim pogrom in Hyderabad. Soon after Makkki's speech, the new network set off bombs at cinema theatres in Karimnagar and Nanded.

Eight weeks after these bombings, Ghauri was shot dead in a police encounter. Islamists continued however, to attempt to build new networks in Hyderabad. In Aug 2001, the Hyderabad police arrested one of the most intriguing figures in this effort, an unassuming electrician named Abdul Aziz. While working in Saudi Arabia, Aziz had come into contact with an Islamist recruiter looking for volunteers to join the global jihad. Aziz served in Bosnia in 1994, and then fought alonside Shamil

Basayev's Chechin Islamists in 1996. In 1999, Aziz again flew to Tbilisi, in search of a second tour of duty. He was however, deported. With the help of funds from a Saudi Arabia-based Lashkar financier, Aziz returned home to try and initiate a jihad of his won.

Aziz, investigators found, hoped to draw on the resources of the Darsgah Jihad-e-Shahadat (or, Institute for Holy War and Martyrdom), an Islamist vigilante group set up in the mid-1980s. Although its website claims that the organisation's purpose is "protecting the life and properties of [the] Muslim community", and "preserving the honour and chastity of women", the organization also candidly states that "Islamic supremacy is our goal." Such groups may not have large-scale legitimacy among Muslims in Hyderabad, "their hard-line polemic is attractive to young people infuriated by communal violence".

What the Mecca Masjid bombing makes clear is that the Islamist threat to India's cities remains in place, notwithstanding the decline in violence since the Mumbai serial bombings. Under intense pressure from the US and EU since the 9/11, Pakistan may have been compelled to rein in the Lashkar zealots. Attacks on mosques, Islamist terrorist groups appear to hope and reason, will be blamed on Hindu fundamentalist organizations—and thus provide the pretext they so eagerly and fervently awaiting to throw off the shackles.

When the police does not fall into this well thought out trap, and put the blame for the Mecca Masjid blast on the Islamists, not only the LET and other such terrorist outfits feel 'cheated', even the Owaisis of India cry foul—"police always blaming the Muslims for all attacks, be they on temples or mosques". It is not only the LET and its kin and the Owaisis' but also the Praful Bidwais and the AG Nooranis of India who will be literally jumping with joy if some Hindu 'terrorist'—an oxymoron, if ever there is one—is blamed for a Friday mosque bombing even if prematurely, mistakenly or falsely! This, of course, is unlikely because Hindus are individually cowards, and particularly if it is a question of killing innocent persons including women and children, it is unthinkable! (That a collectivity of Hindus can act irrationally under grave provocation is, of course, a different issue).

Owaisi, of course, is young and new to India's political realities. He may never have read the Feb 2002 Makki speech. Even if he has, even then he will like to speak the way he did about the Hyderbad police, Mecca Masjit blast and subsequent police firing on the furious, uncontrollable Muslim crowds. Political Islam has certain compulsions in India, and the Owaisis can't escape its demands. Hence his rhetoric about "Muslims being always blamed for all types of acts of terrorism".

Finally, a word on realities of life in Pakistan vis-à-vis the issue under focus. There is no doubt that President Musharraf of Pakistan is under intense pressure to roll back his policy of being a front-line ally of Bush's US in its 'war on terror'. It is uncertain how long could he resist this pressure. Not only for his coalition partner MMA, an average Pakistani detests, no doubt inflamed and incensed by the persistent den made by the mullahs and maulvis, the American *satan*. He has been further weakened by the popular, public support the 'suspended' Chief Justice of Pakistan has been amassing against Gen Musharraf.

The only saving grace for the mankind is that the international community is well aware of the dangers of Islamist extremism, and particularly after the 9/11. Certain effort is afoot to confront and defeat—or at least, to thwart—the Islamist terrorism.

Jalna Man Carried Explosives

Even as the CBI on 18 June 2007 started fresh investigations into the 18 May blasts at Mecca Masjid, the Special Investigation Cell (SIC) of Hyderabad police, set up to probe the blasts, made a major breakthrough when one of the arrested accused, Shoeb Jagirdar, 38, "confessed" that he had brought the explosives used in the blast.

Jagirdar, a resident of Jalna in Maharashtra, told the SIC he delivered the explosives in February to a man in Hyderabad who he had never met earlier. A senior SIC member said Jagirdar, a former member of the SIMI in Jalna, got involved in the conspiracy more than ideological reasons for sake of money.

Jagirdar, first person to be arrested in connection with this case by the SIC, has since been remanded in judicial custody, and the CBI will now have to procure his custody from the court to question him further for as to how did he come in possession of the explosives.

A SIC team had arrested him on 25 May from Jalna where he owned a meat shop. Subsequent investigations revealed that he had not only delivered explosives but had also tried to procure a passport from Nayeem by getting false documents prepared. He was subsequently booked for criminal conspiracy and under the Passport Act.

The SIC had zeroed in on Jagirdar on the basis of the details revealed by a SIM card of the cell phone which was used in the blasts. The SIM card was found to have been sold by one Mohd Sayeed of Jorasanko area of Kolkata to an unidentified person on the basis of a driving licence of one Babulal Yadav who was later found to be non-existent. West Bengal police traced Sayeed to Jamtara district in Jharkhand on the instructions of Hyderabad police.

Sectarian Rivalry Behind Blast: FIR: 8 June 2007

The First Information Report (FIR) registered by the police in connection with the blasts in Mecca Masjid on 18 May 2007 has said that its motive was to kill Sunnat-ul-Jamat people (Sunni Muslims) by Ahl-e-Hadees militant groups.

The FIR, copies of which were released to the media by Hyderabad MP Asasuddin Owaisi on 8 June, has described the unnamed Ahl-e-Hadees militant groups as the main accused in the case, but added that the role of the LET and HUM will have to be checked.

The FIR spoke of the ongoing rivalry between the Sunnat-ul-Jamat people and Ahl-e-Hadees.

The FIR assumes significance because it links the terrorist outrage to an internecine war within the Sunni Muslim community. The Ahl-e-Hadees groups has drawn most of its adherents from the breakaway elements of the Tabligh-i-Jamaat. In Hyderabad, and earlier in Malegaon, the blasts coincided with scheduled meetings of the Tabligh.

Strongly denouncing the FIR, the MP challenged the police to show even a single incident of any rivalry among any Muslim sects in Hyderabad. He alleged the police were attempting to divide the Muslims on sectarian lines for its sinister designs and divert the investigations of the Mecca blasts case into a wrong direction.

Owaisi also released a copy of the other FIR in the police firing case soon after the blast in which five persons were killed. He now spoke like a Muslim politician, spitting fire on the police during his press conference:

> "Both the reports show the hatred of the police towards the Muslim community. These reports are nothing but cock and bull stories, fabricated to mislead the government and people and give a bad name to the Muslim community.
>
> "I reiterate my allegations that extremist Hindu organizations like the Bajrang Dal could be behind the blast."

Police report says nine persons were killed and 58 injured in the blast in the courtyard of the mosque.

19 policemen, including a Deputy Commissioner and an Assistant Commissioner, were injured in the subsequent stone pelting.

The detailed report on the police firing at Moghalpura and Shah Ali Banda areas, prepared by the Moghalpura police station, said 81 rounds were fired from six self-loading rifles and two .303 rifles, 20 of which were fired towards the mob.

Justifying the firing, the report said a mob of 500-600 people' had gathered and tried to kill the police personnel and workers at a petrol bunk.

MECCA MASJID BLAST: AN ANALYTICAL REVIEW

At the end of it all, hw does one see this terrorist outrage? One thing seems fairly clear: It is a sectarian war. But obviously, a detailed look is called for.

Is Sectarian War First step to Terrorism?

At one level, 18 May Mecca Masjid blasts in Hyderabad is validation of the assertion that Muslims themselves are the biggest victims of the currents driving contemporary jihad.[47] "By all accounts, this act of terrorism was not aimed at Hindus or any other groups of 'infidels' but was the direct result of a sectarian crisis, a civil war almost, within the city's Muslims.

The growing presence and influence of "outsider" Tableeghi Jamaat preachers was objected to by the entrenched religio-political establishment and, somewhere along the way, led to an explosive clash. It would be easy here to point the Tableeghis as the villains, the puritanical Wahaabis out to shatter the city's supposed multicultural character. After all, Tableeghi Jamaat is not new to such vitiation. It was seen as responsible for the aggressive proselytisation in Gujarat, changing the character of Islam in parts of the State and leading to, ultimately, the tragedy at Godhra. In Pakistan, the Tableeghis are at the forefront of Islamisation of everything from the civil society to the cricket team; a Tableeghi *fatwa* is suspected to have prompted the murder of Bob Woolmer.

But Hyderabad does not lend itself to such simplistic and black and white explanations. If the old city is fertile ground for a Tableeghi-style hate campaign, it is because the incumbent groups—their political expression being the Majlis-e-Ittehad-ul Muslimeen (MIM)—have encouraged a ghettoisation of the city's Muslims and actively promoted an exclusivist agenda. As such the arrival of newer sects and votaries of Islamisation has not followed the route of arcane theological debate, but deteriorated to the level of a political battle, street violence and, finally, terrorism during (18 May) Friday prayers.

It was fortunate that death toll from the blasts did not cross the double digit mark and the police managed to defuse two other bombs found inside the mosque complex Given this situation, the crowds should have been grateful to the police. But what did they actually do? How did they conduct themselves. They began to riot and attack the police, leading to firing and killing of four protesters. If the purpose of the terrorists who masterminded that Friday's blasts was to provoke an extreme response from the residents of the area they succeeded eminently.

It is obvious that the local Muslims led by the MIM acted irresponsibly, forcing police to open fire. But the MIM had the reason to act the way they did: By asking for CBI inquiry, aim was to paint the state police as partisan and anti-Muslim. After all, even when the mosque had been attacked and the Muslims had been the targets, surely the Muslims could not have been the perpetrators of the heinous crime. How could Muslims kill Muslims? Not that they did not know that exactly that is what was happening in so many areas of the world: Iraq, Afghanistan, Palestine and Lebanon—just to mention four major trouble-spots of the world. The aim of the MIM was to exploit this god send opportunity: If a mosque has been attacked, sure certain non-Muslims are behind it and why the police is not arresting any Hindu terrorists. If some Hindus had been arrested, that would have been an occasion they all—Muslims, Secularist Congress and Left, and the journalist of their ilk-have been waiting for to shout from the house tops for all who cared to listen: "Muslims are not the only terrorists in India!"

Among the journalists, one must be named who has constantly raised his voice against the communalists in India. Belonging to the daily Hindu school of ideology, he, of course, rails against the Hindu communalists led by the BJP, and Bajrang Dal, day in and day out. As for he is concerned, communalism in India has only hue and that is saffron. He too was besides himself with joy when the Mecca Mosque came under terrorist attack. Obviously, the Hindu terrorists were the culprits and he wrote in triumphant strain: "Now that the identity of the culprits is no secret, all those who usually blame the Muslims at the drop of a hat are maintaining silence in this case for obvious reasons. Once the facts started surfacing, he went into silence. Honesty demanded that he write a second piece correcting his initial error of perception. He never did that. The name of this worthy? Praful Bid wai!

Two Lessons

Two lessons can be drawn from the bloodletting in Hyderabad. One, the idea of a sectarian war within Islam turning into catastrophic terrorism is no longer a remote West Asian nightmare, limited to Shia-Sunni clashes in Iraq. After Hyderabad, it is natural to see Malegaon blasts of Sep 2006 in similar light, despite the Union Home Minister's strange insistence that two are unrelated. The upshot of this will be a more challenging internal security environment. Two, the unilateral attack on the police (one aspect of which has been discussed above) is symptomatic of a growing tendency among the community's mobs to resort to "direct action". A year ago, the protests against the Danish cartoons led to agitated Muslims attack Hindu-owned shops in Hyderabad and Lucknow. The hapless shop-owners were as non-plussed as the police in Hyderabad that 18 May Friday. "These dual manifestations of Islamist instincts are made worse by a political leadership in denial. Instead of defending his police force, the Andhra Pradesh Chief Minister apologized for the firing and offered a CBI inquiry. His desire to quench the immediate fire is understandable. But did he really have to go this far? Some recent terrorist attacks are summarised hereafter

Holy Places Under Attack

Date	*Killed / Injured*	*Details*
30 March, 2002	10/29	*Raghunath Temple in Jammu* Two Kashmiri militants attacked the temple in the center of the main bazaar. 10 killed, including 4 security men and 2 militants *Status of the case probe still on*
24 Sep., 2002	40/95	*Akshardham Temple, Gujarat* Two terrorists enter Askhadham Temple in Gandhinagar, Gujarat firing indiscriminately and hurling grenades. 40 killed included 2 NSG men and two terrorists *Status of the case* Two accused were killed in the encounter.
5 July, 2005	5/0	*Ayodhya's Ram temple attacked*

Date	*Killed / Injured*	*Details*
		Six terrorists storm makeshift Ram Temple at Ayodhya, UP. Police gun down 5, while the sixth terrorist blows himself up. *Status of the case* Militants' driver Rehan Alam and eight more held. Probe still on.
7 Mar., 2006	28/101	*Sankat Mochan Temple, Varanasi attacked* Blasts at this Hanuman Temple, near the Banaras Hindu University, Varanasi. Subsequently more blasts at Varanasi Cantonment railway station. *Status of the case* A charge sheet filed against 6 accused, including the mastermind Mohd Waliullah on 18 Feb 2007.
14 Apr., 2006	0/10	*Explosions inside Jama Masjid, Delhi* It was after the Friday evening prayers. 14 people were injured *Status of the case* Some locals were picked up probe still on.
8 Sep., 2006	40/312	*Mosque at Malegaon hit* Two bomb blasts during Friday special prayers on the

Date	Killed / Injured	Details
		occasion of Shab-e-Barat hit Bada Kabristan (main graveyard) and Mushaira Chowk in Malegaon, Maharasthra. Suspects: LET, SIMI *Status of the case* CBI probe still on, the investigative agency still does not have "substantive leads".
18 May, 2007	10+4/52	Mecca Jasjid Friday prayers attacked at Hyderabad. Suspects: HUJI of Bangladesh.

Some Other Recent Terrorist Attacks

Date	Killed / Injured	Details
25 Aug., 2005	46/162	*Twin blasts, Mumbai* Two powerful car bomb explosions in South Mumbai
29 Oct., 2005	71/198	*Blasts in New Delhi* Two blasts at Paharganj and Sarojini Nagar/Lajpat Nagar markets and one in a DTC bus kill 71 pre-Deevali shoppers.
28 Dec., 2005	1/6	*Attack on IISc, Bangalore* Grenade lobbed at Indian Institute of Science, Bangalore. Assailants also opened fire. One scientist killed and six others injured.
7 Mar., 2006	21/65	*Serial blasts, Varanasi* Blast at Sankat Mochan Hanuman Temple, followed by two explosions at Varanasi Contonment railway station

Date	*Killed / Injured*	*Details*
11 July, 2006	209/714	*Mumbai serial train blasts* Seven blasts in first class compartments of trains at Mira-Bayandhar Jogeshwari, Mahim, Santacruz, Khar, Mathunga and Borivli.
8 Sep., 2006	38/153	*Malegaon blasts* Twin blasts in Malegaon in Maharashtra on auspicious day Friday prayers
18 Feb., 2007	68/17	*Samjauta India—Pak Express attacked* Two powerful explosions rip through two coaches of the Lahore bound train near Panipat—Bombs had been placed in suitcases. *Stutus:* Unresolved.
May, 2007	0/14	*Gorakhpur: Golghar locality* Unidentified terrorists planted three bombs in tiffin boxes which were then tied to children's bicycles. *Status*: Under investigation.

Terror kills 43: Hyderabad-II: 25 Aug 2007

At least 43 people were killed and over 70 injured after two explosions, barely minutes and five km of each other on the 25 Aug 2007.

Explosion rocked Lumbini Park a popular amusement spot, hosting Asia's largest Laser show—abutting the Hussainsagar Lake and in front of the state secretariat main gate and at Gokul Chat a popular eatery in the busy Koti area in central Hyderabad, hours after the city police arrested four persons, including a Dubai national, and seized counterfeit currency of Rs. 2.36 crore in the old city.

Tension escalated in the capital as the injured were rushed to hospitals in ambulances, cars and city buses. The 10,000 strong city police were ordered out on the streets to check any violent backlash.

At Koti, one of the busiest junctions of the capital, there was a large gathering at Gokul Chat when the blast took place consequently, casualties here were more—29 a dead and scores injured—as the blast took place inside the building.

A red alert has been sounded across the twin cities of Hyderabad and Secunderabad, nighbouring Karnataka and New Delhi.

The first blast was around 8 pm inside an open air ampitheatre at Lumbini Park. It tore through the middle rows, 8-11, during laser show, leaving ten killed. Late evening rains ensured that the entertainment Park, at least, was less crowded—the usual weekend count here is around 1500 visitors.

Such was the intensity of the blasts that many bodies were blown to bits, while others were mangled beyond recognition.

40 Engineering students from Amruthavahini Engineering College in Sangamner in Maharashtra, some 50 km from Pune, who had come to the city on an industrial tour, were among the most affected victims.

Though no terrorist groups has claimed responsibility for the blasts, suspicion centred on the Harkat-ul Jihadi Islami (HUJI). Chief Minister YSR Reddy said it was a terrorist act. The Centre rushed a team of senior officers to Hyderabad, including Special Secretary (Internal Security) ML Kumawat. "It appears to be the handiwork of terrorists", Union Home Secretary Madhukar Gupta said.

One reporter said: "Preliminary police investigations have revealed that the blasts might have been caused by IEDs loaded with RDX". A police officer said the explosives used in the twin blasts were similar to the one used by terrorists in the 18 May Mecca Masjid blasts. This led some to allege involvement of Bangladesh-based HUJI.

Police later recovered two unexploded bombs from a cinema hall in the busy Dilsukhnagar area and another from Narayanaguda. A bomb threat was received by an IMAX hall near Lumbini Park.

Forensic experts who visited the site said slurry explosive with metal balls was packed in containers and detonated with a timer.

Just about three months ago, a powerful explosion (18 May) ripped through a massive congregation at the Mecca Masjid near Charminar, killing nine persons. In the violence that followed, five persons were killed in police firing.

"The 18 May blasts as well the 25 Aug explosions did not lead to a communal conflagration, as the perpetrator would have hoped for".

Hyderabad: A Trail of Terror

Why Hyderabad is in attractive target for the terrorists has been discussed earlier. So, it should come as a no surprise that the city has a history of terrorist strikes allegedly masterminded by Islamic groups/ISI. Here is a police roster of the most lethal ones.

- 26 Feb 2001: Bomb explodes outside state secretariat, no loss of life.
- 21 Nov 2002: Scooter bomb kills one person at Sai Baba temple, Dilkush Nagar.
- 28 Oct 2004: Main water pipeline to the city blasted at Patancheru.
- 4 Nov 2004: Blast outside police control room. No casualties.
- 12 Oct 2005: Special Task Force office suicide-bombed. Two killed.
- 7 May 2006: Three injured in Odeon theatre blast.
- 18 May 2007: Mecca Masjid blast. Death toll 14.
- 25 Aug 2007: Twin blasts in the city kill 43.

Hyderabad Blasts Strikingly Similar to 2005 Delhi's

As the toll in the Hyderabad blasts rose to 42 on 26 Aug, intelligence sources detected striking similarities between the twin explosions and the 2005 pre-Diwali blasts in Delhi that killed 59 people. Apart from the fact that both took place on a Saturday evening, the choice of targets and manner of execution have a lot in common.

While the Andhra Police were looking for similarities between the Mecca Masjid blast and 25 Aug explosions, the latest intelligence inputs could end up giving a new twist to this act of terror. "The day, the timing, the venues, the precision and the modus operandi—all reveal remarkable similarities and make the Hyderabad explosions seem a replica of the serial blasts that struck three areas in Delhi on 29 Oct 2005", an intelligence source told a daily.[48]

As the Delhi 2005 terror was timed for Diwali festival of Hindus, so was the 25 Aug one timed for their Vinayaka Chavithi festival, a fortnight away. The idea obviously is to disturb the atmosphere of gaiety just before major festival—and also to sabotage communal harmony.

Striking Hyderabad also has an additional reason: to hit India's economy. After all, the city is one of the rising stars of the Indian economy.

Some relevant facts about 29 Oct 2005 serial blasts:

1. The first blast took place in the main bazaar of Paharganj near the Delhi Railway Station around 5.30 pm. The area is popular with large number of backpackers and tourists. Again, the blasts site was a medical store near a *chaat* shop.
2. The second explosion took place inside a bus in Govindpuri area about 6 pm. It is an over crowded down town colony of Delhi.
3. The third explosion rocked the bustling upmarket area of Sarojini Nagar in Sough Delhi at 6.10 pm. This too was near a *Chaat* and juice corner.

So in Hyderabad, terrorist selected a tourist spot, Lumbini Park for the first blast and then Gokul Chaat shop in a busy market in Koti area quite similar to the busy Sarojini Nagar in Delhi. The third blast was averted after the police retrieved a bomb with a tier form Dilsukhnagar, a locality akin to Delhi's Govindpuri, the intelligence source told the Delhi.

So, are these two deadly serial blasts the handiwork of the same group of terrorists? The Sarojini Nagar blast mastermind is an LET 'commander', believed to have fled to Pakistan. Another suspect has been shot dead in an encounter while three have been arrested. Four suspects are still at large. But where are they?

Police Suspect Foreign Sleeper Cells

After confirming that the twin explosions were carried out by cross-border terrorists, the police is suspecting the role of sleeper cells of the HUJI and JEM combine based in Bangladesh. These two terror outfits were suspected of triggering the 18 May Mecca Masjid blast in the same city.

Police said they were examining the role of Shahed, alias Bilal, a main accused in the 18 May explosions.

The experts assert the twin explosions are clear cases of intelligence failure. Though the Mecca Masjid blasts was a clear indication of terror group activity and the presence of sleeper cells, the officials did not sustain their efforts to arrest the terrorists. A senior police official said: "The counter-Intelligence Department that is tasked to keep a tab on ISI-sponsored terror activities failed miserably. There was an attempt to divert the police attention with bomb hoaxes."

The IEDs made of the slurry and detonated mechanically were earlier known to have been made by modules belonging to the JEM.

"Huge amounts of fake currency were found in the city. A Dubai and Pakistani angle is being suspected in this", said an intelligence official.

Meanwhile the police said that high explosive slurry (ammonium nitrate plus emulsifier) was used in all the bombs (the ones that exploded at Lumbini Park and Gokul Chat and the unexploded one at Malakpet) were connected to mechanical timers for detonation.

Two important points need to be added to the above text:

- Intra-police bickering is normal and quite understandable in such major acts of terrorism, and its name is 'blame game'. But what is more urgent is to stress the political interference impelled by the minority vote-bank considerations (discussed in detail earlier). After the arrest of a Bangladeshi, the police wanted to investigate certain aspects of Mecca Masjid blast, but it was denied permission lest the Muslims feel offended. Then came the 25 Aug blasts. Both the cases were handed over to the CBI that enabled the state political leadership to wash its hands clean of the related problems!

- TV channels quoting Pakistani media, beamed the news that Hyderabad blasts mastermind, Shahid alias Bilal was killed in a shoot-out in Karachi, on 12 September.

Hyderabad-I blast: 18 May 2007: Probe going nowhere

On 18 May 2007, a bomb explodes in the open-air courtyard at the historical Mecca Masjid as Friday prayers are concluding. Bomb squad defuses a second bomb. Cops rewind to that blast three months backs, but that probe is going nowhere.

Main Accused

Fingers point to Shahid Bilal alias Abdul Rehman, 24, a former Hyderabad resident linked to terror groups like the JEM, LET, and HUJI, an explosives expert with a history in Hyderabad.

The Status of Investigations

21 May: NSG reports similarities with the Malegaon blasts on 8 Sep 2006.

22 May: SIM card in failed bomb's mobile phone timer traced to a shop in Jharkhand, bought using the ID of Babulal Yadav. But Yadav is unaware of purchase.

23 May: Police turn to narcoanalysis of Sameer Sheikh, an alleged LET operative, who claims to have transported men from Bangladesh to Hyderabad.

25 May: Hyderabad police arrest Shoaib Jagirdar, a 52-year-old butcher from Jalna in Maharashtra. Police say he visited Hyderabad with Sheikh.

7 June: Sheikh taken into custody by the Hyderabad police, the only one formally arrested for the blasts.

15 June: Abdul Sattar, 27, a mechanic is arrested by the Hyderabad police.

26 July: CBI issues look out for two persons believed to have bought the SIM cards; a NOIDA yoga teacher claims his photo used.

Bangladeshi Student Questioned at Vellore

Shahi Rafsan Jani, a Bangladeshi women student suspected to be linked to the 25 August blasts was on 10 Sep 2007 was brought by the police for investigation to Vellore town, where she has been studying at a local college and staying in a rented house.

Jani, 23, whose brother Ridwan Gazi and three others are prime suspects in the blasts case, was arrested on 1 Sep in Hyderabad for possessing invalid Visa documents. But it was later found that she had left the valid papers in Vellore. She has a valid passport and a student visa valid till 2008. She is a second year undergraduate student of English literature in Auxilium College, Katpadi, near Vellore.

She was picked up in a place where Ghazi was residing in Hyderabad on the suspicion that she might have been a carrier of the RDX explosives used in the blasts.

Ridwan and Irfan, who is just 12, are said to Jani's brothers. Investigators in Hyderabad on 9 Sep released the sketches of the two, along with those of two other: Hussain, 18 and Mashiluddin, 24. All four are Bangla nationals suspected of involvement in the blasts.

Ever since reports surfaced that the Hyderabad police had picked up a girl student of Auxilium college, the Tamil Nadu police had begun its own informal investigation without any request from their counterparts in Andhra Pradesh. They found her name in the foreigners' registery maintained in the office of the Vellore district Superintendent of Police. On 10 September, a police official said the Vellore police was engaged in marking the days on which she had obtained leave of absence between May and August, the period related to the blasts at the Mecca Masjid on 18 May and the 25 August explosions.

The college principal had disclosed to the police that Jani had gone home to Bangladesh during the summer vacation in

May, taken two days' leave in July, and sought five days' leave from 28 August. She had left Vellore for Hyderabad only after the blasts.

Hitting Hyderabad Important for Islamists

Jan 2005 witnessed considerable consternation in old quaters of Hyderabad. A section of Muslim population in that area was agitated because the king of Sandi Arabia was visiting Delhi but not Hyderabad. Their agitation was covered rather extensively by the Urdu press. The aggrieved ones were bitter that in the good old days, when oil had not been struck in Arabia, and it was the rich and mighty Nizam who used to be the benefactor of Saudi kings. An analyst explains: "The rest of the city found this behaviour strange. But modernity and economic development have bypassed these sections. They hark back to the past in search of the golden era when Nizam's was the biggest and richest Muslim Kingdom in the world".

But these are not the only reasons for some sections feeling 'ignored'. During Nizam's days, 10 per cent of the Muslim in the largely Hindu population occupied 90 per cent of the Government jobs. They had perceived themselves as the 'ruling class'. No wonder they flocked to Qasim Rizwi when he vowed to plant Nizam's flag on the Red Fort in Delhi and enacted the worst massacres of the innocent till the Indian Army marched in Sep 1947 and put an end to his insurrection. Some of them still remember him as a great Muslim and hark back to days of his brave anti-India fight. Even more important, the city was known to be communally sensitive and first serious Hindu-Muslim riots took place in 1937. During the first three decades after Independence, there were riots fairly frequently. As for the Muslims of the Old City are concerned, the are in the grip of one family Owaisi, which heads the MIM. Presently, the MIM is under the control of the third generation of that family.

In the circumstances delineated above, it should come as no surprise that Pakistan's ISI and Bangladesh's HUJI find the old city of Hyderabad a fertile ground for recruiting jihadis. This is especially so in the aftermath of the 9/11, which gave an impetus to the process of radicalization of the old city population.

Moazzam Khan, a retired professor speaks sincerely, even if in anguish: "Our religion does not teach killing. But with these activities not only are they shaming Islam but also making us vulnerable. But then, enemies across the border are least concerned with peace in India. They want to incite one community against the other. It should be noted that at least 10 of those killed in the two blasts are Muslims."

But liberal voices like Moazzam's represent a largely ineffectual Muslim middle class in Hyderabad. This is especially so in the context of politics practiced in Old City where the MIM lords own one Lok Sabha seat and five Assembly constituencies.[49]

City's troubles can be traced back to the mid-1990s when the ISI began picking up recruits from Hyderabad. When Indian intelligence got wise to it, the ISI outfits changed track—and their identities. Pakistani operators realized that Indo-Bangla border was more hospitable, being more porous.

Sources disclosed another interesting link between Hyderabad and Bangladesh—economic. This economic connection is of recent years. Over these years, many technicians—mostly fitters, tradesmen and artisans—have found part time employment in Bangladesh. "Small companies have taken up contracts in Dhaka for six months and have been sending men there. This have rendered infiltration and indoctrination easier."

The process received a jolt only when there was a blast on Dussehra (2006) day in the office of the Special Task Force (STF) of the Hyderabad Police Commissioner. The perpetrated died but the police identified him as a Bangladeshi. The incident brought the Bangladeshi angle into prominence. It was there even earlier but had been ignored by the authorities.

Hyderabad is a major IT center today in the country. The IT era truly began there in 1999 when US President Bill Clinton brought Microsoft along with him. In the years since Clinton's trip, investment in the software buttressed the BPO boom. So when Clinto's successor George W Bush too decided to drop by in Hyderabad in March 2006 (five months after the Saudi King decided to skip the city, he thought is fit to order the opening of a full-fledged Consulate in Hyderabad.

This was a significant decision as there was a US Consulate already in Chennai. By choosing Hyderabad, the US had ignored the claims of Bangalore. “All this means that from the point of view of jihadis, Hyderabad becomes an attractive target. Hitting it can give massive mileage to the jihadists’ cause,” says a police officer.

Occupied by its anti-Naxalite campaign, the Andhra Police has obviously not been focusing on Islamist terror. This lopsided priority has handed down one success after another to the jihadis.

HUJI FAQS: A RISING TERRORIST STAR

For some time now, the HUJI has been vying for attention with the LET and JEM on the terrorism charts. What follows in relevant information on the outfits under different heads.

What is HUJI?

The Harkat-ul Jihadi al-Islami (HUJI) was set up in Pakistan in 1980 as an organized militia to fight the Soviet troops in Afghanistan. Once the Soviets pulled out, many militia members turned their attention elsewhere. And some began looking at Bangladesh as a safe base. Over the years, the original HUJI declined in power and influence. 1992 saw the birth of HUJI (Bangladesh), reportedly on the instructions of Osama bin Laden. With its slogan, *Amra Sobai Hobo Taliban, Bangla Hobe Afghanistan,* the outfit’s primary aim was to establish Islamic rule in Bangladesh. Later, HUJI Bangladesh become part of the International Islamic Front (IIF) set up by bin Laden in 1998.

Where is it Based?

It operates out of Bangladesh and Pakistan. Over the years, operatives have developed a network across India as well. Several alleged HUJI members and sympathizers have been arrested from West Bengal and Uttar Pradesh in the last few years. In Bangladesh, it has bases and camps in areas around Chittagong and Cox’s Bazaar, stretching all the way to Myanmar in a belt known for smuggling and arms running.

Who are its Leaders?

In Bangladesh, the group came up under the leadership of Shaukat Osman alias Sheikh Farid. Another senior leader Mufti Abdul Hannan is currently in jail, facing charges under the Arms Act.

In India, the outfit has three dreaded faces. Abdul Sahil Mohd alias Shahid Bilal, who is believed to have built the organization in the south and is suspected to have masterminded three terror attacks in Hyderabad in the past two years: 25 August twin blasts, Mecca Masjid attack and the strike on the STF. He is believed to be in Pakistan presently.

Jalaluddin Mullah alias Babu Bhai, the second leader, is known to be the commander for north India. He was arrested in June 2007 by the STF of the UP Police. He confessed to having delivered explosives including RDX across the country since 2004, including a consignment to Delhi before the Sarojini Nagar blasts. Babu Bhai is also an accused in the abduction of Khadim Shoe Chief Partha Roy Burman from Kolkata in 2001.

The third member of the leadership trio is Rasool Khan "Party" from Gujarat. He is said to be the head of the outfit's Maharashtra operations. He had recruited Bilal into the HUJI.

Where do the Cadres come from?

The group has trained large number of Muslim Rohingya refugees from Myanmar. When Harkat-ul-Ansar was outlawed, the Bangladeshi remnants returned home and became part of HUJI. After 9/11, more militants left Pakistan and moved to 'safer' Bangladesh. "It is said that there were three groups within the Taliban—Arabic speakers, Urdu speakers and Bengali speakers", says EN Rammohan, former DG, BSF, who has followed the HUJI and other militant outfits over the years.

In Bangladesh, the outfit is believed to have some 15,000 men and many sympathizers.

Is it Linked to Other Groups?

"HUJI is the cat's paw of ISI and DGFI", says Ajai Sahni of the institute of Conflict Management, referring to the military intelligence wings of Pakistan and Bangladesh. LET and JEM chip in with help from Pakistan and cadres of the outlawed SIMI provided local support. The recent strikes should not be seen as pure HUJI operations but "multi-group affairs", Sahni maintains. A significant change over the past few years is the nature of operations. Earlier, militant outfits operated in cells. Now, points out Sahni, there is "operational discontinuity". Individuals work without knowing the other operatives.

Anonymous contacts and PCO to PCO calls at fixed times mean that even if one persons is nabbed, the link ends and the conspiracy cannot be cracked.

What has HUJI achieved

Security agencies believe HUJI (Bangladesh) has been involved in Sankat Mochan Temple attack, in Varanasi, the Mumbai blasts, the Malegaon blasts in Sep 2006, the Mecca Masjid blasts in May 2007 and the 25 Aug 2007 twin blasts. The outfits' name also figured in the attack on the US Consulate in Kolkata in Jan 2002. However, the LET and JEM are also suspected to be involved in these attacks.

In Bangladesh, it was allegedly involved in two unsuccessful attempts to assassinate Sheikh Hasina in 2000 and a plot to finish off progressive intellectuals, including writers.

Its Funding Sources

HUJI is believed to have received direct funding from al-Qaeda. It receives money from charities, mainly based in Saudi Arabia and Pakistan. In India, the outfit has enough funds. Intelligence agencies believe its operations are funded through fake currency notes, narcotics and cattle smuggling.

Incidentally, a fake currency racket was busted in Hyderabad shortly before the twin blasts. As for cattle, these are illegally transported from Rajasthan, Punjab, Haryana, Delhi and MP to Bangladesh through Bihar, West Bengal and Assam. The magnitude ranges from a conservative 15-20 lakh animals per year to a more alarming figure of 50-60 lakh. The trucks return with arms and ammunition.

HUJI Role in Focus Again

As the Prime Minister Man Mohan Singh on reviewed the security situation and the probe into the Hyderabad-II gathered momentum, the focus of the intelligence is believed to be firmly on the Bangladesh-based HUJI, whore footprints had also been found on the 18 May Mecca Masjid blast.

The meeting chaired by the Prime Minister was attended by Home Minister Shivraj Patil, NSA MK Narayanan, Cabinet Secretary, Home Secretary and Director, IB. Patil, who had visited Hyderabad with a high level delegation, also briefed the gathering about the developments.

The initial suspicions of the involvement of Mohd Abdul Sahil, alias Bilal, the HUJI's India operations chief, seemed to be turning into strong belief with the similarities of the twin blasts with the Mecca Masjid blast in May. (Intelligence agencies obviously seem to be working on all possibilities while solving the 25 August blasts. We have already seen an intelligence 'source' finding so many convincing similarities between the 25 Aug 2006 blasts in Hyderabad and those in Delhi on 29 Oct 2005.)

Sahil, also known by aliases Shahid and Bilal, operates through his second-in-command Amjad and foot soldiers Imran and Sattar living in the walled city. Bilal, a Hyderabad resident, is now based in Karachi and had masterminded the 18 May Mecca Masjid blasts.

The involvement of HUJI became apparent as the investigators pieced together the contents of the devices used in the twin blasts on 25 August. The core of the explosives, RDX, remained the same both on 25 August and on 18 May, only the packing differed. While in May blasts, RDX was used with TNT, in August blasts, it was used with ammonium nitrate.

"Sleuths are seething with regret as they had repeatedly warned state authorities of the possibility of such strikes following the arrests of Aurangabad resident Sheikh Naeem and three others in March (2007) with RDX at Petrapol on the Bangladesh border. Interrogation of the suspects had revealed that 8 kg. (?) of RDX had already reached Hyderabad, enough to blow up the entire city." (The paragraph from a daily of 27 Aug 2007 is decidedly quoted in original to show that the daily is not forthright in coming out with the whole truth. It says "sleuths are seething..." but fights shy of giving reason for this "seething". The same daily had earlier—a few days ago—written clearly that the intelligence/state police had requested permission to probe the case further based upon Naeems arrest and subsequent disclosures but the political leadership had refused permission. The probe was bound to lead some arrests in the old city and it was something the state Government was not prepared to countenance. It is all for political considerations—or reasons of vote-bank politics as it critics would say. Any arrests would have generated immediate protests, including the violent demonstrations, from 'a' particular community and the Government simply can't afford to anger/ displease/antagonise this community. Hence the denial of the permission. Will the crities be wrong if they say the Mecca Masjid happened because police was disallowed to investigate into Naeem's disclosure? Again half-hearted probe into Mecca Masjid led to 25 August. As to the tactics of extremists ensconced in the Old City to hinder inquiry into the terrorist strikes, one instance should do. While six or seven lives were lost in the Mecca Masjid blast, four were lost in the police firing when it was trying to control the crowds which went violently berserk while protesting the blast. While it may be inappropriate to suggest that this daily is being economical with the truth in this case when it is claiming to be offering 'full coverage' of the issues involved, the legitimate question remains: what are its reasons or compulsions for shying away from telling the entire truth as it certainly knows?)

The intelligence has even uncovered the reason behind this horrendous massacre on 25 August: Bilal wanted to show that he is alive and kicking and no one should doubt his capabilities on terror front! This is how the top investigators put it: The Lumbini Park blasts was organized to counter the raging buzz on the Internet that Bilal had been rendered ineffective and in-operational. This buzz was something that haunted HUJI's anti-India terror chief and this blasts was his way of stepping up his visibility in the chatrooms. Conversations of Bilal with Amjad, his deputy and Imran and Sattar, his foot soldiers, and they had cautioned authorities in Hyderabad accordingly.

Notes

1. Vinu Abraham, *Week*, 8 Oct., 2006.
2. Krishna Kumar, *Frontline*, 20 Oct., 2006.
3. Cited Kanchan Lakshman, *Pioneer*, 2 Dec., 2006.
4. Editorial, *Tribune*, 30 Oct., 2006.
5. G. Parthasarathi, *Pioneer*, 22 Feb., 2007.
6. Vijay Mohan, *Tribune*, 21 Feb., 2007.
7. Aman Sharma, *Indian Express*, 25 Feb., 2007.
8. *Indian Express*, 27 May, 2007.

9. Editorial, *Pioneer*, 20 Feb., 2007.
10. Gautam Siddharth, *Pioneer*, 25 Feb., 2007.
11. K. Shankar Bajpai, *Hindustan Times*, 26 Feb., 2007.
12. Vishwa Mohan and Pradeep Thakur, *Times of India*, 19 May, 2007.
13. Devesh K. Pandey, *Hindu*, 21 May, 2007.
14. *Pioneer*, 21 May, 2007.
15. Praveen Swami, *Hindu*, 23 May, 2007.
16. Quoted Praveen Swami, *ibid.*
17. Editional, *Pioneer*, 21 May, 2007.
18. Jinka Nagaraju, *Times of India*, 27 August, 2007.
19. Kingshuk Nag, *ibid.*

12

Fighting Terror Bilaterally

INDIA : COOPERATION WITH OTHER COUNTRIES

There has been a sea change in the attitude of the international community in fighting the scourge of terrorism since the 9/11.

Before that date nations like India were fighting terrorism almost single-handedly. There indeed were 'condolences' conveyed ritually by the US and others after major terror strikes on this country's soil, but nothing beyond that. But after 9/11, things are changed. Each nation is signing agreement with others to fight joint anti-terrorism battles. Cooperation and jointness are the watch words today to defeat the evil.

Combating Terrorism Jointly

India already has entered into anti-terrorism agreement and understanding with several friendly nations in the recent past. This is bound to pay dividends in our fight against terrorism.

Prime Minister Man Mohan Singh said on a Oct 2006 before embarking on his official visit to Britain and Finland (the current chair of the EU): "Given the common threats we face, cooperation in the area of combating terrorism has become particularly significant." He also reiterated that our dialogue with the EU, our largest trading partner, has expanded to issues like counter-terrorism.

Counter-terrorism : India's Joint Groups with Other Countries

1995	Egypt
1997	Canada
1998	Germany
2000	UK and US
2001	France and the EU
2002	China, Israel, Kazakhstan, Russia and Croatia

2003	Uzbekistan, Thailand, Turkey, Singapore, Australia and Tajikistan
2004	BIMSTEC, Mauritius, Indonesia, Myanmar and Poland
2005	Japan and Canada
2006	Pakistan

INDIA AND BANGLADESH

Illegal Immigrants Remain a Serious Threat in Assam/ North-East

The immigration from Bangladesh, (earlier, East Pakistan, and still earlier East Bengal) mostly illegal, has host, a serious threat to India's security, integrity and security over the decades. Some aspects of the issue of recent times and some related developments are discussed in the succeeding pages.

Supreme Court strikes down Foreigners (Tribunals for Assam) Order

On 5 Dec. 2006, the Supreme Court of India struck down the Foreigners (Tribunals for Assam) Order, 2006 which protected illegal Bangladeshi migrants in the name of protecting minorities from harassment. The Bench consisting of Justice SB. Singh and Justice PK Balasubramanyam ruled that the notification was void because it put the onus of proving that some one is an illegal migrant solely on the complainant.

The Assam Gana Parishad (AGP), whose general secretary Sarbananda Sonowal, was one of the five persons to challenge the validity of the Order, described it as a slap on the face of the Congress. The BJP, which has always taken a stand against the large—'huge' will be more appropriate term—number of illegal migrants in Assam in particular and in the entire North-East in general, hailed the supreme court as the institution that knows the right from wrong.

The issue must be looked in its perspective. Only the Assamese can understand the motivated, and self-serving, approach of the Congress party to the issue. Let is be said right here that the nation's interest are subservient to this Party's own political gains. The Congress-led UPA Government had brought in the Foreigners (Tribunals in Assam) Order in Feb 2007, after the Congress and its allies suffered a loss of face when the apex court scrapped the controvertial Illegal Migrants (Determination by Tribunals) Act (IMDTA) of 1983 on 12 July

2005. The order itself was violative of the basic tenets of justice, as it provided for two sets of rules or laws to deal with the same issues. There was even more essential reason for Supreme Court frowning on the 2006 Order—and scrapping it. The Order had deviously brought back an obnoxious provision of the impugned IMDTA. So the Supreme Court had no hesitation in scrapping the Order of 2006.

The original IMDTA, 1983 was the cause of the whole trouble. To put it simply, the mischievous legislation was cleverly drafted to favour the illegal immigrants in Assam, as also their continuous influx. This Act provided flawed arguments that the Congress and other parties used to favour and ingratiate the illegal migrants from Bangladesh and gave them precedence over the rights of the indigenous Assamese—nay Indians. The Congress has always demonstrated an enthusiasm to 'protect' minorities from harassment while showing little or concern for the indigenous people of Assam,[1] who are being reduced to a minority by the migrants from Bangladesh and their predecessors, the people who came in illegally from East Pakistan.

When the Supreme Court struck down the IMDT Act in July 2005, it clearly said the Act was ultra vires to the Constitution and that it served more to protect the Bangladeshi than to detect and deport him. That was a severe indictment of the drafters of that 'ill-intentioned legislation but also the oldest party of the nation which misused it to perpetuate its rule in the state with the help of the illegal migrants from a neighboring nation.

The Supreme Court had in 2005 also unanimously directed the Assam Government to set up tribunals under the provisions of the Foreigners Order of 1964. But the Congress-led regime at the Centre, instead of acting in accordance with the directive of the apex Court, amended the very provisions of the Foreigners Order of 1964 and introduced the Foreigners (Tribunals for Assam) Order 2006, under which the essential idea that the whole country is governed by the same single law in dealing with the same illegal migrants in any part of the country was thrown to the winds. So, in a manner of speaking, the defiant Centre restored the very obnoxious provision to the statute book the Supreme Court had struck down while throwing out the IMDT Act 1983 in 2005.

That is why the apex court on 15 Dec 2006 felt compelled to restate the point it had earlier made on the IMDT Act. It found the notification making the 1964 Order inapplicable to the state of Assam by amending its Clause 2 "unreasonable and arbitrary, and violating Article 14 of the Constitution of India."

The Supreme Court also pointed out that the order of 2006 did not serve the purpose sought to be achieved by the 1964 Act or the Citizenship Act or by the obligation cast upon the Central Government to protect the nation under Article 355 of the Constitution.

But what is of even concern is that the Central Government is either ignorant or willfully ignoring the consequences of threat of illegal migrants in North-East, especially in Assam and West Bengal. If some critics accuse New Delhi of playing with national security interests by not bestirring itself about dangers posed by the illegal migrants, they are not wide of the mark. The threat has assumed alarming proportions, especially in Assam. Of its 23, seven have already become Muslim-majority districts, and there is no denying the fact that the root cause of this demographic change is the influx from Bangladesh. It was not long years back that India's Chief Election Commissioner had expressed serious apprehensions that foreigners taking part in the electoral process at state and national levels were actually compromising India's sovereignty. That warning seems to have little meaning for powers that be! Indeed, "Muslims of East Bengal/East Pakistan or Bangladesh origin today decide the fate of elections in at least 50 of Assam's 126 Assembly constituencies."[2]

What is even more dangerous, the things do not stop at the illegal occupation of political space by the foreigners. The state's economy itself is gradually slipping into the hands of the migrant.

The ecology of the state is also being adversely affected with large tracts of the natural course of action of the Brahmaputra and other rivers being illegally occupied by people of migrant origin. What was Congress Governments reaction? Instead of stemming and removing the encroachment, the Congress Government of Assam only issued land settlement documents to the encroachers! Some way to defend a nation's sovereignty and security, this!

Successive Union Home Ministry reports speak of an increase in the clout of Islamic fundamentalist and militant groups in Assam and the North-East who receive support from Pakistan in cahoots with Bangladesh. While intelligence reports detail how Islamic fundamentalist and militant groups patronized by Pakistan have been active in Assam, there are also reports about the recruitment and regular despatch of large numbers of youths belonging to areas dominated by suspected illegal migrants to Bangladesh and Pakistan for arms and other training provided by the Directorate General Forces Intelligence, the ISI, LET and other outfits.

There have been other warnings as well. In mid-2006, a militant from Assam, who had under government training in arms and subversive activities in Bangladesh and Pakistan and had also allegedly worked with Omar Rasheed Sheikh's gang, managed to escape from custody in Guwahati.

Here is the latest reported by a daily of 3 Sep 2007. Bangladesh police reportedly arrested terrorist Abu Hamza on the Indo-Bangladesh border on a tip-off from Hyderabad (South India) police. The latter believe Hamza, once a resident of Santosh Nagar area of Hyderabad, was behind the blasts at the Task Force office in Oct 2005 and at Mecca Masjid on 18 May 2007. His arrest may provide a lead to link the series of recent blasts.

Police believe Hamza is responsible for smuggling RDX into the country on the orders of Harkat-ul-Jihadi Islamia (HUJI) militant Mohd Shaheed alias Bilal... sources said it might take sometime to have him extradited to India.

Then, there is the 1988 report of Lt. Gen. (Retd.) SK Sinha, then Governor of Assam and presently of Jammu and Kashmir, which unambiguously stated that the day was not far when the illegal Bangladeshi migrant, who already dominates Assam's districts bordering Bangladesh, would demand merger of those districts with the neighboring country. That will be the beginning of Pakistan's much-talked about "unfinished agenda of the Partition": taking over Assam from India. In the changed political scenario, Assam will go to Bangladesh!

A journalist who specialize on the issue says about the Congress instance on the illegal migrants: "Yet the Congress continues to invent newer legal provisions to protect illegal migrants. That the government did not bother to honour the Supreme Court's directive of 12 July 2005 to constitute tribunals in Assam under the Foreigners Order of 1964 was more proof, if more proof was needed, of the party's insensitivity to the interests and concerns of the indigenous Assamese."[3]

Deadline for Border Fencing Put off yet Again: Jul 2007

The completion of Indo-Bangladesh border fencing despite several deadlines being revised so often still hangs in the balance. It has become an issue of serious contention between the AASU and the governments at the Centre and State levels.

The Centre had in Jan. 2006 fixed Dec 2006 as the target for completing the border fence which was later rescheduled for Mar 2007.

This dead line again was not met. There months after the expiry of the revised deadline—of Mar 2007—for sealing the Indo-Bangladesh international boundary, "the centre has now fixed Mar 2008 as the new target for completing the project". The AASU was informed about the new deadline by the Centre at a tripartite meeting that reviewed the implementation of the Assam Accord signed in Aug 1985. Officials who attended the meeting included Border Management Secretary UN Panjiara, Joint Secretary: Home (North-East) Naveen Verma and Assam Chief Secretary PC Sharma, among others.

The AASU has been protesting the delay and are doubting the very sincerity of the Government in stopping the influx. AASU adviser Samujjal Bhattacharyya puts it rather plainly: "That the Indo-Bangla border fence is still incomplete that itself was refixed several times by the Government, speaks volumes about the insincerity of New Delhi in tackling infiltration from Bangladesh."

As a last word, the adviser said: "It is now more than clear that the Government, whether in Delhi or in Dispur, is not interested in securing country's border with Bangladesh."

Now for some statistical information relevant to the issue of illegal infiltration:

- India shares over 4,096 km of total boundary line with Bangladesh.

- Of that total, 263 km border is with Assam.
- The total length of Indo-Bangladesh border to be fenced is 3,286.87 km.
- The Government has fenced only 2,455.80 km till Dec 2006.
- In Assam, of the total border of 263 km only some 190 km was fenced till Dec 2006.

Even if one takes the risk of being dubbed a born pessimist, one must make a dark prognosis: Being painfully aware of the Government's past record of repeatedly fixing and refixing the deadlines only to he revised yet again as a regular regimen, it is doubtful if the balance of the planned fencing project – 831.07 km in total, that includes some 73 km in Assam—will be completed by Mar 2008, the last re-refixed deadline, hopefully.

AASU General Tapan Gogoi was frustrated enough to describe ground realities as they are:

> "Influx from Bangladesh has already changed the demography of Assam. The entire process of detecting and deporting Bangladeshi infiltrators has become a farce"

Even the officials were honest enough to admit that the Foreigners Tribunals could detect no more than 54 Bangladeshi emigrants.

In Assam destined to be doomed? Or, to put it differently: Is it already too late to retrieve Assam?

Indian security minders must ponder over such dark clouds over India's North-Eastern horizon and prescribe the correctives to avoid the doomsday—the career-conscious with the political ukase, and the India-loyalist without it.

"Merge West Bengal with East Pakistan": Pak Minister in 1957 (A page from history)

The news story from the *Deccan Chronicle* of 5 Apr 1957 is reproduced below:

> "Karachi : Pakistan's Interior Minister, Mir Ghulam Ali Khan described the unanimous passage yesterday in the East Pakistan Assembly resolution demanding full autonomy for East Pakistan as a 'move the ultimate consequences of which will be secession of East Pakistan and its merger with West Bengal'."[4]

Security Endangered by Immigrants from Bangladesh: Jun 2007

The subject has been discussed in fair detail in the opening chapters of this book. A certain overview of the issue, concerning this threat to India's security from immigrants—legal, and large number of them, illegal—from Bangladesh, in the context of India-Bangladesh cooperation in joint fight against terrorism is considered necessary, particularly in the light of some developments that surfaced of late.[5]

Here is the 12 June 2007 report in a daily under the heading, 'Bangladeshi worked for RAW for six years':

> "Delhi police is looking for a Bangladeshi who has been on the run for the past two years after it was found that he had concealed his nationality to get a job in the Research and Analysis Wing, the nation's external intelligence agency."

The report quoted a senior police officer as saying: "We believe that he may have run away with some vital documents pertaining to the Agency. We tried to trace him but all our efforts failed...He was holding an extremely sensitive post and this is definitely dangerous as our national interest is involved."

As a senior journalist read this report, he remembered going through a paper by Naresh Chandra, a distinguished former member of the IAS, 'Illegal migrants from Bangladesh', in the anthology *Illegal Migration from Bangladesh,* edited by B.B Kumar and published by Astha Bharati. Chandra, who had been Union Home Secretary, Cabinet Secretary and India's Ambassador to the United States, wrote:

> "I remember some work was going on in my house at 1, Jan path and people were digging a trench for laying down some cable for lighting and so on. And I found that all of them were from Bangladesh. They could not speak a word of Urdu or Hindustani. When I tried to talk to them, it was very clear. That was the house of the Home Secretary! Illegal migrants were working in that house! So, I called a meeting of the Chief Secretaries of West Bengal, Bihar, Assam, Tripura, Manipur, etc. At least one Chief Secretary said that his Government was not willing to do anything. He frankly admitted that before me...I would not name the State.[6] But he said, 'Look: it is very difficult to persuade the State Government to take effective measures."

Reading this account, one shudder's to think what might have happened if one of the Bangladeshis was an agent of his country's Directorate General of Forces Intelligence (DGFI), and grabbing an opportune moment, had sneaked into the house and planted some electronic device which could transmit all conversation taking place inside and all phone calls made by Home Secretary Chandra. Dhaka would have been a privy to every move planned by India to bolster its national security, particularly in its internal sphere.

Since the DGFI had close functioning links with Pakistan's ISI Directorate, Islamabad too would have been privy to all that sensitive information. What implications the compromised security situation would have had for our counter-terrorism battle against Pakistan-sponsored cross-border terrorism needs hardly be laboured.

Chandra adds in the paper, "We have come a long way since then." But what he wrote thereafter made it very clear that he was by no means satisfied by distance travelled, which should not come as a profound surprise, given our lackdiasical attitudes to the issues concerning our national security. Infiltration from Bangladesh continues and some of the border districts of West Bengal and Assam—one analyst puts the number at 4 and 7 in the two states respectively—have witnessed a vast demographic change. [Worst fears are that these 11 districts in the not too distant a future can demand a separate political entity for themselves under a barrage of "accusation's" real or mostly imagined: their minority status not being duly respected, their minority rights in social, economic and political fields being ignored and as a final weapon, interference by the state in their religious affairs. With religious extremism on the rise in both Bangladesh and Pakistan, it is not difficult for these two countries to induct a dozen or so foreign-trained terrorists including a couple of suicide bombers in each of these district. And the resulting mayhem is not difficult to imagine. That would have laid the foundation of another Pakistan in India's East (and North-East), as predicted years back by so many geo-strategic thinkers and security analysts including the wise Henry Kissinger].

That is not all. Things have gone far beyond this stage. Islamist terrorism outfits active in Bangladesh such as the Jama'at-ul-Mujahideen Bangladesh (JMB), Jagrata Muslim Janata Bangladesh (JMJB), Ahle-e-Hadith Andolan Bangladesh

(AHAB), and Harkat-ul-Jihad-al-Islami Bangladesh (HUJIB) had—and still have still cells in India's border districts. Mohd Asadullah al-Ghalib, Ameer of AHAB, used to cross over into West Bengal without any travel documents and hold meetings with his supporters at will; and so did Siddiqui Islam, better known as Bangla Bhai, Operations Commander of the JMJB.

This was one-time Union Home Secretary and Cabinet Secretary painting a serious picture years back. Things have only becomes worse with time. Bangladesh has almost replaced Pakistan as the main spring board of Islamist terrorist strikes in India, while continuing to harbour on its soil secessionist insurgent terrorist outfits active in India's North-East. All this, analysts assert, underlines the fact that the continuing mass influx from Bangladesh cannot be just treated as a mass movement of hungry men and women in search of livelihood. It is supported not only by Bangladesh's governments, but also a section of its intelligentsia.

What must be most jarring to the Indian ears must be the Bangladesh claim and annoying made publicly and officially by its top political functionaries, including its Prime Minister, that there is not a single—not a single—illegal migrant from Bangladesh in India. And what must go down as the most arrogant, tongue-in-cheek statement till date is the reasoning: "our per capita income is higher than India's, why would our citizens go across to India?"

DN Bezbaruah, the highly respected former editor of *The Sentinel*, a well known English daily published from Guwahati, Assam, in his essay 'our land, their living space' in *Bangladesh: Treading the Taliban Trail*, edited by Jaideep Saikia and published by Vision Books, refers to an article by Sadeq Khan, a former diplomat and a well-known member of Bangladesh's intelligentsia. The article, published in Holiday of 18 Oct 1991, begins thus: The question of lebensraum (= living space for the people of Bangladesh), has not yet been raised as a moot issue. All projections, however, clearly indicate that by the next decade of the 21st century, Bangladesh will face a serious crisis of *lebensraum*. No possible performance of population planning, actual or hypothetical, significantly alter this prediction."

Khan then advocates a borderless world and migration of work force, adding: "There is no reason why regional and international cooperation could not be worked out to plan and execute population movements and settlements to avoid critical demographic pressures in pockets of high concentration." He leaves no one in doubt about what he means when he further says: "The natural trend of population overflow from Bangladesh is towards the sparsely population lands of the South-East of the Arakan side and of the North-East in the Seven Sisters side of the Indian sub-continent."

The use of the expression "Indian sub-continent and not India, of which the seven North-Eastern States referred to as Seven Sisters are a part is clearly intentional and designed to imply that they are part of the sub-continent and not India! There is clear attempt here by the ISI and DGFI to work jointly to set up an independent Islamist state comprising parts of North-Eastern India, Bangladesh and Myanmar, has to be seen in this context and cannot be dismissed as a paranoid psyche as most of Indian analysts and scholars are wont to do, either because they are too lazy to see through the *stratagem*, or lager to be politically correst when the *secularism* reign supreme in India. It is an unfortunate fact that no eminent Indian jouralists like Kuldip Nayar, Inder Malhotra, Khushwant Singh, S. Nihal Singh, N. Ram, M.J. Akbar, Shekhar Gupta, Saeed Naqvi et al have ever written a single article on this serious issue that endangers country's integrity and sovereignty, drawing country's attention to the sinister designs of our eastern and western neighbours.

May be they are mindful of the influence the Muslim community exercise in Indian polity and they all want to be part of the mainstream phenomenon where any issue that adversely impinges upon the Islam and Muslims in India is generally not criticized or touched upon/commented in negative term. The lead of course comes from the politicians who always work keeping their party and individual interests in mind. Unlike Hindus, who are generally divided among various political parties and have no religious agenda or common driving motive and seldom vote as a monolithic political block, the Muslims generally vote as advised by their political leaders and/or commanded by their religious leaders—the imams, maulvis and mullahs. Hence the need for all political parties—bar one or two exceptions—not only not to antagonize them ever but also create their vote-banks among them.

On the other hand the same eminence grise named above will go on condemning Hindus, in the name of their anti-Hindutva fervour on an issue where Muslim community has been wronged for reasons right or wrong e.g. Gujarat's anti-Muslim riots following the Godhra train tragedy where a coach full of Hindus was torched and all its occupants were burnt alive. The latter was simply forgotten which was the cause of the former. As a result Mody, the Chief Minister of Gujarat, has been demonized and it is a sign of Indian secularism and a badge of liberal credentials for journalists—and of course by politicians of the Congress, Left and all other non-BJP formations—to keep condemning anti-Muslim Gujarat riots day in and day out, for years on end. But there was no demonization of any individual or party after the anti-Sikh riots of Delhi in 1984.

It is time India, particularly the political class and the cognescenti, takes this threat to its security and integrity more seriously than it has done so for. Tomorrow may be too late. The threat has been clearly outlined by the papers included in the two books mentioned above. Particularly significant are contributions by K.P.S. Gill and Prakash Singh (DGs of police in Punjab and UP respectively) in the book edited by Kumar and by Bertil Linter in the book edited by Saikia.

Let this brief discussion end with a warning by a senior journalist : "Unless we are careful, our 'Look East' policy may well end up as a lost North-East."

Arunachal Expels Bangladeshi Infiltrators: July 2007

The determined drive against the suspected Bangladeshi infiltrators in Arunachal Pradesh has raised an alarm in Assam. It has created a piquant situation for the Assam government as the All Assam Students' Union (AASU) has accused the Tarun Gogoi-led Congress Government of not taking any action against those who, after being expelled from the neighbouring state, are taking shelter in Assam.

The drive was launched on 5 Aug 2007, and the All-Arunachal Pradesh Students' Union (AAPSU) too subsequently joined the campaign, organizing meetings and urging the local people to inform the authorities about the presence of any suspected person.

Reports from Arunachal Pradesh said Bangladeshi infiltrators had entered the state to take up manual work in view of a number of construction projects coming up there. A large number of them were also working as daily-wage labourers and vendors.

The AASU has complained that while Arunachal Pradesh was pushing them out, the Assam Government was doing nothing. Tapan Gogoi, General Secretary of the AASU (which had conducted a sustained and occasionally violent agitation in the 1980s against the foreigners in Assam—essentially meaning illegal Bangladeshi infiltralors—and subsequently reuled Assam for two 5-year terms) said: "Bangladeshi infiltrators who had entered Arunachal Pradesh are being thrown out. They are taking shelter in Assam. But our Government is doing nothing".

The AASU also demanded that the Bangladeshi nationals ousted from Arunachal be kept in detention camps and then deported. "You cannot allow Assam to become a dumping ground. But the Assam Government is just sitting idle."

It is obvious that the AASU leader is simply repeating himself. And there are reasons for it: Their over record was dismal on the subject during their ten years' rule in Assam. More on it later.

The Bharatiya Janata Yuva Morcha (BJYM) the youth wing of the BJP, on its part has sought the Governor's intervention into the matter. The state unit president of the BJYM, Dilip Saikia, put it as straight as it could be: "The Congress-led Government seems happy that more Bangladeshis have arrived. For the Congress, every Bangladeshi is just a vote, nothing else matters!"

Meanwhile, Arunachal Pradesh Chief Minister Dorjee Khandu has denied that his government had dumped any foreign national into Assam, adding: "We are only pushing out those who were staying in our state without any valied document."[7]

Now to end up on a note about AASU's performance during its ten years of rule in Assam on the question of illegal infiltrators staying in the state. It bears repetition that AASU had carried out a 6-year-long anti-foreigners agitation in Assam and consequently ascended to power in 1985, as Asom Gan

Parishad (AGP), the political arm of the AASU. During these ten years, it is widely known that they could not deport more than 1000 illegal infiltrators. Some critics assert the number did not touch three figures. Chief Minister Praful Mahanta spent first term learning the ropes and quarrelling with his No 2 (Bhrigu Phukan) in the cabinet. During his second stint (1996-2001), Mahanta ruled with the help of a pro-Bangladeshi-infiltrators party. In one word, AASU/AGP has no moral right to criticize congress on the issue.

Anti-Bangladeshi Infiltrators Sentiment on the Rise: Aug 2007

The issue of hundreds of Bangladeshi migrants who entered Assam after being driven out of Arunachal Pradesh and Nagaland is hotting up, with several organizations including the student groups demanding their identification and expulsion before they disappear.

Leading the move is the All Assam Students Union (AASU), which has despatched a delegation to New Delhi to meet Union Home Minister Shivraj Patil and apprise him of the situation. AASU President Sankar Prasad Roy asserted: "Assam cannot be a dumping ground for Bangladeshi migrants." A daily reported this on 25 July (2007).

The All Bodo Student's Union (ABSU) on its part has warned Bangladeshi *migrants* to quit the four Bodoland Territorial Council (BTC), districts as early as possible. The ABSU, which is politically opposed to the Bodo People's Progress Front (BPPF-H) a partner of the ruling Congress-led Alliance, has got its support for keeping Bangladeshi migrants out of the four Bodoland districts.[8]

In Lakhimpur and Sonitpur, districts bordering Arunachal Pradesh, the district units of AASU have already launched agitation movement to press the Government to take action against the Bangladeshi migrants. A similar demand has come from Jorhat where suspected migrants' families arrived "after they were pushed out from Nagaland last week."

In Kokrajhar, the arrival of 16 families of Bangladeshi migrants created a lot of tension, with the ABSU and BPPF-H saying these families were trying to acquire government land by claiming to be victims of ethnic violence that occurred in Barpeta in 1993-94. The ABSU on 23 July set a deadline of one week for these 16 families to quit the district.

"Some groups are trying to settle Bangladeshi families ousted from Arunachal Pradesh and Nagaland by claiming they were victims of 1993-94 violence. But even if that be true, there is no question of settling them in Kokrajhar because the riots did not take place here", ABSU President Rwngwra Narzary said.

The BPPF (H) has also made it clear that Bangladeshis would not be allowed to settle in the Bodo autonomous districts. "We cannot allow these suspected Bangladeshi migrants to settle in the Bodo districts" said Khampha Borgoyari, Deputy Chief Executive Member (DYCEM) of the Bodoland Territorial Area Districts (BTAD) Council.

Chief Minister Tarun Gogoi, however, says those pushed out from Arunachal Pradesh were not Bangladeshis but Labourers from Assam who did not have valid entry documents to work in the other states. This statement has further agitated the students and opposition parties, with AGP President Brindban Goswami asking on what basis did the Chief Minister defend the suspected Bangladeshis.

The BJP planned to despatch a team comprising six MPs to study the migrant issue.

AASU activists adopted a variety of mean to express their strong feelings against the Bangladeshi migrants in Assam. On 24 Aug 2007, they detained a goods train in Jorhat district, demanding a permanent solution to land encroachment by oustees from Nagaland in Assam.

Assam Admits Bangladeshi Presence: Aug 2007

The Congress-led Government in Assam on 7 Aug 2007 admitted the presence of over 40,000 Bangladeshi infiltrations in the state.

The revelation—rather acknowledgement—came in the form of an answer to a written question in the state Assembly on the issue which Assam Accord Implementation Minister Bhumidhar Barman said as many as 42,449 Bangladeshi infiltrators have been identified in the state since the signing of the Accord in 1985.[9]

The Minister also admitted that of these 42, 449 Bangladeshi infiltrators, only 2,221 have been expelled from the state till date. The question was asked by opposition Asom Gana Parished (AGP) legislator Ramendra Narayan Kalita. Barman however did not clarify what the government had done about the remaining 40,228 infiltrators in the state.

Interestingly, on 6 Aug the state government has informed the Assembly that 12,914 persons were identified as illegal Bangladeshi infiltrators "under the prevailing laws" till 30 June 2007. Then the government was not sure exactly how many of them had be expelled. "The process of expulsion is going on", was all that Foreign and Environment Minister Rockybul Hussain (replying on behalf of Chief Minister Tarun Gogoi) said while replying to a question raised by Independent legislator Pranab Kalita.

Meanwhile, in another document laid in the Assembly also on 6 Aug, the Government had said 32 Foreigners' functioning in the state had declared 29,539 persons as 'foreigners' (obviously, Bangladeshi infiltrators) till May 2007. This information was contained in the annual administrative report of the department of Assam Accord Implementation.

Barman, on the other hand claimed that the open influx from across the Indo-Bangladesh border had indeed stopped, "but I cannot deny that people are trickling in stealthily from the other side. He was replying to a question by legislator Drupad Borgohain (CPI).

Replying to another question by AGP's Girindra Kumar Barua, Barman said of the 2221 expelled Bangladeshis, 405 were expelled between 2004 and 30 June 2007. The Minister also admitted that barbed wire fencing along the Indo-Bangladesh border in Assam was yet to be completed, despite expiry of 31 Mar 2007 deadline. Barman blamed the "lengthy and cumbersone land acquisition process, irregular fund flow, adverse weather conditions in remote and low-lying areas and tension in the Surma sector between June and September 2006, as the reasons behind the delay in completion of fencing.

Joint Indo-Bangladesh Fight against Terrorism: 19 Feb 2007

"India and Bangladesh today agreed to jointly combat terrorism and put bilateral ties on an irreversible higher trajectory". This was reported by a news agency after visiting

EAM of India, Pranab Mukherjee, held takes with the leaders of the host country at Dhaka on 19 Feb 2007.

Mr. Mukherjee said both sides agreed to jointly combat terrorism, which today poses "the most grave challenge to our society and threatens the rapid economic development of our nations." His Bangladesh Counterpart, Iftekhar Ahmed Chowdhury, said his talks with Mr. Mukherjee largely covered cross-border security issues when he categorically told the latter that no external terrorist group would be allowed to use the Bangladesh soil.

There is simply no way to know if such solemn commitments are meant to be taken seriously. Or, even if they are made with a serious intent. It is known for a fact that the ULFA leaders are ensconced in palatial residences in Dhaka/Bangladesh and their fighters are lodged/trained in camps on that country's territory. It is for certain that Dhaka will never do a Bhutan on Indian insurgents sojourning there. As an analyst says: "Statements/commitments, like the one made by Chowdhury, are far form, a formality, more correctly and honestly—a diplomatic inanity."

India and Belarus sign Extradition Treaty: Apr 2007

India and Belarus on 16 Apr 2007 discussed various issues, including the ones related to security and terrorism, and expressed the desire to further strengthen bilateral relations.[10]

Union Home Minister Shivraj Patil and Belarus Interior Minister Vladimir Naumov expressed satisfaction at the current level of understanding between their countries during their 45-minute interaction at New Delhi 16 Apr.

Patil informed his visitor that "India has suffered a lot due to terrorism but has been able to contain the menace." He expressed satisfaction over the fact that there was growing realization in the international community about the need (and urgency) to contain terrorism.

The two countries signed an Extradition Treaty which will provide for extradition of fugitives, including economic offenders.

The salient features of the Treaty include the following:

- Provisional arrest and obligation to extradite.
- Extradition procedures.

- Grounds for refusal to extradite.
- Rule of speciality.

Both sides declared that "terrorism, in all its manifestations, poses a serious threat to global pace and stability", and agreed to further strengthen cooperation bilaterally as well as in the multilateral context to combat this phenomenon.

In the sphere of terrorism, the two countries asked all the member states to step up efforts for expeditious conclusion of the Comprehensive Convention or International Terrorism at the United Nations.

Belarus backed India's claim for permanent membership of the UN Security Council as both sides stressed the need for greater efforts by all countries to accelerate the process of UN reform, including expansion of the Security Council, in both permanent and non-permanent categories.

INDIA AND BRAZIL

Brazil General visit Anti-Terrorism School: 8 Dec 2006

Brazilian Chief of Army Staff Gen Francisco Roberto De Albuquerque visited the Counter-Insurgency and Jungle Warfare School (CIJWS) at Vairengte, on the Mizoram-Assam border. He was shown around the training infrastructure and facilities by the commandant of the school, Brig R.M. Painuli and apprised about counter-insurgency and anti-terror training, PRO of CIJWS, Col US Bhawa told the PTI on the phone.

Gen Albuquerque said Brazil would send troops to undergo training at the institute next year.

EU-Anti-Terror Czar in India: 9-10 Oct 2006

As if to prove the point made by the Indian Prime Minister on 9 Oct 2006, EU counter-terrorism coordinator Gijs de Vries arrived New Delhi same day at the invitation of the Indian security establishment. He held talks with the concerned Indian interlocutors for designing ways to build up "operational capacity" and to establish "new channels of communication" to reinforce the strategic partnership and security dialogue between EU and India.

Analysts believe the 2-day visit by the EU's "anti-terror czar" is the result of the first ever security dialogue between India and EU in May 2006 and adoption of joint action plan at the 6th EU- India summit at New Delhi in Sep 2006.[11]

The joint action plan lays down that India and EU will "work together to reduce terrorists" access to financing and to fight money-laundering and explore the link between drug trafficking and terrorism." The sources said the joint action plan provides the necessary framework and roadmap for identifying pathways to future cooperation. New Delhi has already made it known that it intends to share evidence of Pakistan's complicity in the 11-7 Mumbai train blasts with the governments of Britain and Finland and sensitise the EU on India's concerns about cross-border terrorism.

The EU has indicated that it desires India to sign up for the Paris-based Financial Action Task force (PATF) and harmonise its laws with that of 25-member EU, to bolster the efforts being made by the Europeans to prevent the financing of terrorism. India had affirmed its commitment to seek the PATF membership when its President visited India in Apr 2006.

A former politician from the Netherland, Mr. De Vries became EU's first counter-terrorism coordinator in March 2004. He functions under EU Foreign and Security Policy Chief Javier Solana.

INDIA AND ISRAEL

Israeli Advisory on Terror Attack in Goa: 14 Dec 2006

The Goa police has tightened security in the run up to the year-end tourists season after warnings of terror attacks by Israeli anti-Terror unit. Israel intelligence has warned that Al-Qaeda would carry out the Bali-style serial bombings in Goa beaches, targeting tourists.

Israel's National Security Council Counter Terrorism HQ "recommends that Israeli citizens avoid as much as possible staying at (these threatened) sites." The warnings from Israel came following reports that Al-Qaeda operatives had carried out dry-run attack's in a number of places in Goa.

The warning was bound to be taken seriously since it came from the Israeli Prime Minister's Office and its Anti-Terror unit, the Elkana Har Nof.

Israel warns of al-Qaeda: Centre down-plays it: Dec 2006

On 13 Dec 2006, Israel issued a travel advisory to its citizens warning of a possible Bali-type attack on the tourist heaven of Goa to coincide with Christmas and New Year Eve. It needs to be noted that while the advisory spoke of a "concrete" and "specific threat", both the Union Home Ministry and the Goa Police down played it the very next day.

The reports say the Israeli themselves did not seem to be deterred at all and were seen cavorting on the legendary beach of Goa. Figures show that 1,664 Israeli tourists visited the state this year, with 336 making it in Dec (2006) alone (till the 10th). The figures are only expected to go up as the 2006 draws to a close. Though most of them are on tourist Visas, there are 19 who are on long-term visas. In 2005 also, maximum tourists from Israel visited Goa in December.

Israelis, who are to serve mandatory stints with their national Army, have been visiting India in large numbers to celebrate the end of the rigorous regimen.

Besides Goa, Himachal Pradesh, Uttarkhand (earlier Uttaranchal) and Rajasthan have also been a big draw with the Israeli youth, some of whom visit even Jammu and Kashmir ignoring their Government's advisories to the contrary.

Now to the reaction of Indian authorities to the 13 Dec 2006 advisory issued by Tel Aviv. While asserting that they were prepared for any eventuality and that a general alert was already in place to deal with the terror threat, Goa police cautioned against panic. Even the Centre did not seem excessively concerned even though it, just a few weeks earlier, had braced for a terrorist attack to coincide with the just-held International Film Festival (of India-IFFI, for short).

Pratap Singh Rane, as expected of a Chief Minister of a state where tourists contribute handsomely to its economy, also sought to down play the warning: "The state was safe for the tourists and stringent security measures are in place to protect them. We have taken all possible steps to ensure security in the state. There is no reason to fear. We are always prepared to tackle anything".

"There is no such specific threat but yes, the state because of its popular international appeal, is on a general alert," said local SP, Sharad Agarwal. He painstakingly elaborated on the arrangements, bringing out state government's anxiety over a possible exodus of tourists because of terror threat. He disclosed that "the state's 4000-strong police force has been bolstered by two companies of CISF, and has a solid intelligence backing."

In fact, the senior officer went on to even reveal that the state has developed a good network of informers among shack owners on the beach and employees of hotels and restaurants. "Special vigil was being maintained on coastal belts like Calangute, Chapora and Arambol—all favorites with tourists", he concluded.

What ever be the reaction of the Israeli advisory among the Goan political rulers and the police, India's leading expert on terrorism feels the Jihadi threat in Goa is real. Before going into such details, first the text of the advisory.

In a travel advisory on its Hebrew language website, posted on 13 Dec 2006, Israel's Foreign Ministry said:

> "Within the framework of Al-Qaeda's terror threats in India, there is now a concrete threat focusing on the Goa region where multitudes of visitors, including Israelis, gather in late December. Israel's Counter-Terrorism Authority has recommended that Israeli citizens stay away from sites in Goa, popular with Westerners and Israelis, over the next few weeks."

On 15 Dec 2006, DEBKA, a well-known Israeli think-tank, which disseminates information and analyses relating to terrorism, posted the following comments on its website (www.debka.com):

> "Information has reached Jerusalem that al-Qaeda is in an advanced stage of preparing coordinated attacks on the big, end-of-year seasonal parties held by Westerner and Israeli tourists in the Indian province. Israeli travellers are advised to cancel their trips to Goa, or at least stay away from the big parties. Some 4,000 Israelis have booked flights to India for the winter season. They will be joining the thousands living there. A standing terror warning is still in force for Egyptian Sinai and Turkey."

Before the Christmas and other holiday seasons, Israel issues a general terrorism threat advisory for the benefit of Israeli tourists travelling abroad. In the past, such advisories used to cover places such as Turkey and Egypt. The pre-Christmas advisory issued this year has covered Goa too. The advisory has received more than the normal attention because it has characterized the threat as "Concrete" and identified Al-Qaeda as a possible source of the threat.

Ever since the terrorist strikes by the pro-All Qaeda Jemmoh Islamiya (JI) in the Indonesian tourist resort of Bali in Oct 2002, and again in Oct 2005, the Indian security agencies in their plans for strengthening physical security have taken into account the vulnerability of the Indian tourism infrastructure and particularly in places such as Goa.

Arrests of Terrorists from Goa

On 11 Mar 2006, Tehreek-ul-Mujahideen cadre, Tarique Jalal alias Tarique Batlo, was arrested from Margao railway station. It was reported that one kg of RDX, two Russian-made hand-grenades, two electronic detonators, two cameras, and a mobile phone were seized from him. There was a greater alert in Goa after this arrest. Then there was one more related arrest in the some month.

Shamim Ahmad, a suspected activist of Lashkar-e-Tayyaba (LET), reportedly a resident of Goa, was arrested on 30 Mar (2002) at Jelenabad (Jehenabad?) in Gulbarga, Karnataka. The seizures from him included an AK-47, two hand-grenades, a mobile phone, maps of dams and power grid installations in Andhra Pradesh, some audio video cassettes, and printed material in Urdu.[12]

These arrests obviously should indicate the possibility of the presence of sleeper cells of Pakistani and Kashmiri *Jihadi* terrorist outfits in Goa not necessarily for organizing terror strikes in Goa itself, but for providing back-up support to *jihadi* terrorist strikes in other parts of India.

The possibility of terrorist strike in Goa by pro-al-Qaeda elements from Pakistan and India "has been receiving greater attention this year (2006) than in the past in the wake of the two arrests mentioned above and the Mumbai blasts of July 2006, in which some 187 suburban train commuters were killed. Investigation till date has indicated that the blasts were organized by LET, with the help of some Indian Muslims belonging to the SIMI.

While Goa has thus come to be viewed by the Indian security agencies since Oct 2002, and more particularly, the Goa authorities have reassured intending tourists as well as those already in Goa that there is no reason for any undue fear. This as also assurances from Goa Chief Minister Rane in the wake of the Israeli travel advisory have been detailed above.

It is not clear on what basis the Israeli authorities have issued their alert to their citizens. In 1992, terrorists suspected to be belonging to the Jammu and Kashmir Liberation Front (JKLF) attacked a group of young Israeli tourists in Jammu and Kashmir, killed one of them and took another hostage.

The hostage was released following a large of telephone calls received by the JKLF leaders from Kashmiris living in Europe, US and Canada, that the attack might cost the Kashmiri organizations the political and moral support the US. Pak ISI had instigated the attack by disseminating false reports that the Israeli tourists actually belonged to the Mossad, the Israeli intelligence agency, and that they had come to Jammu and Kashmir to assist the Indian security agencies in their counter-terrorism operations.

While there has been no other targeted attacks on Israelis since then, in Apr 2006, after the visit of US President George Bush to India in Mar 2006, Osama bin Laden had disseminated on audio message describing his global jihad as directed against the alleged anti-Islam conspiracy of Christians, Jews, and Hindus.

All said and done, this expert on terrorism feels there is need to be on guard in Goa after the arrest's of terrorists in Goa.

India and Pakistan

Pakistan has directly been responsible for almost all terrorist violence on the Indian soil, including the terrorism perpetrated by the terror modules and sleeper cells created by it in India.

As a cheaper option, terrorism became an instrument of its foreign policy to 'snatch' Jammu and Kashmir from India through the strategy of a thousand cuts. Post-1971 war, Pakistan also aims through terrorism to avenge its humiliation and loss of East Pakistan by striking at India's integrity and sovereignty.

Pak Offers help to Probe Terror Groups in India

India wants Pakistan to sign extradition treaty and Mutual Legal Assistance Treaty (MLAT), say a Pakistani daily of 21 Jan 2006.[13]

Amidst spats on terrorism and Balochistan at the recently concluded foreign secretary-level talks, Pakistan has offered India help in investigations if India provides "concrete evidence" of the involvement of any group based in Pakistan in terrorist activities in India.

India, on the other hand, wants Pakistan to sign an extradition treaty and Mutual Legal Assistance Treaty (MLAT) to ensure that action is taken against criminals and dug smugglers.

The Pakistani offer came against the backdrop of Indian concerns over unabated cross-border terrorism during the two-day talks between Indian Foreign Secretary Shyam Saran and his Pakistani counterpart Riaz Muhammad Khan, which ended on 18 Jan 2006.

When India specifically referred to the recent terror attacks in New Delhi and Bangalore, Pakistan said it would provide assistance in investigations if given details of the investigations. India said the investigations had established the role of Pakistan-based elements of Lasher-e-Taiba in the terror attacks. The Indians also told Islamabad that if such incidents continued, it could have a negative impact on the ongoing peace process.

Officials said on 20 Jan 2006 Pakistan was told that if it were serious in fighting terrorism and cooperating with India, it should enter into an extradition treaty and MLAT with New Delhi. The Pakistanis did not respond to the Indian suggestion, they added.

India said it had given a list of 20 fugitives, including that of Dawood Ibrahim, to Pakistan about two years ago, seeking their deportation. Pakistan has been claiming that they were not in the country. Officials said Pakistan's response to Indian concerns over terrorism was 'negative', though they were positive on other areas.

The issue has been figuring in talks at various evils between both countries and will come up during the coming home secretary-level meeting in Islamabad expected in March.

"Indian in Afghanistan Killed on Pak order": Taliban: 14 May 2006

In a surprising development in the killing of Indian Engineer K. Surya Narayan in Afghanistan on 30 Apr 2006, a Taliban commander, wishing to remain anonymous, claimed that Pakistan's ISI had a hand in his killing in southern Afghanistan.

The commander told the Kabul-based private Tolu Television that Amir Khan Haqqani, the military commander of Taliban fighters in Zabul province, had opposed the killing of Suryanarayan. He claimed that the engineer was eventually killed by Mullah Latif, a militiaman under the command of Mawlawi Mohd Alam Andar, allegedly on orders from, Pakistan's ISI; a little known website afgha.com quoted the television channel report as saying.

Expectedly, Pakistan dismissed the charge as "nonsense" Refuting the allegation, Pakistan's Information Minister Sheikh Rashid Ahmad told an Indian TV Channel on the 14 May afternoon that "ISI was not involved in the killing" and that Islamabad was ready "to clarify the matter with New Delhi." Pakistan's Foreign Office spokes woman told the press: "We have been condemning the killing of civilians where ever they occurred as acts of terrorism. It is not the government's policy to sponsor the killing of civilians. Tolu TV had made such accusations against Pakistan in the past also, attributing the comments to some Afghan officials, which were later denied."

Following the accusation, Afghan President Hamid Karzai's Chief of Staff Jawed Ludin said administration expects Islamabad to clarify its position on the accusation. "The reports on Pakistani ISI involvement in the incident are very important to Afghanistan", Ludin said.

Suryanarayan, who was working for a Bahraini company, Al Moayed, on a telecom project in Afghanistan, was abducted on 28 Apr in Zabul province on the main highway linking the capital Kabul to the southern city of Kandahar, birth place of the Taliban movement, and his body was found on 30 April. Following his killing, Afghanistan's rebel Taliban outfit had said Suryanarayan was killed while he was trying to escape.

This assertion by a Taliban commander about Pakistan's hand in the killing of this Hyderabad-based engineer, only strengthens the assessment of the MEA that the ISI, anxious to deter India from expanding its presence in Afghanistan, was behind the killing.

According to the reports on the Tolo Channel based on extensive interviews, the Taliban gangsters who abducted Suryanarayan on 28 April got split in two camps. While one group wanted to release him in exchange of ransom and had set a 24-hour deadline for the purpose, the other, working under the influence of the ISI, wanted to do away with him to send a signal, and succeeded in having its way.

The killing of Suryanarayan was the third incident in the past four months wherein an Indian has been targeted in Afghanistan. The Taliban abducted Maniappan R. Kutty, a Border Road Organisation jawan and engaged in building of the Zarang-Delaram Highway, four months ago. Three days after Kutty's kidnapping, his body was found at Kandahar province.

In February this year (2006), Indian engineer Bharath Kumar, working with a Turkish firm, was killed in a bomb blast in Farah province.

Indian doctors working in various hospitals in Afghanistan have also received threats from the Taliban, ousted from power in 2002.

New Delhi has taken up the issue of security of all Indians, working in Afghanistan, with Kabul at the highest level. The issue was also discussed when Afghan President Karzai visited New Delhi this (May 2006) month.

India and Pakistan at it Again: Jun 2006

Pakistan on 5 June 2006 described as "baseless" the accusation by National Security Adviser M.K. Narayanan that it was not doing enough to prevent terrorist attacks in India. Foreign Office spokeswoman Tasneem Aslam told a private TV

Station that Pakistan had repeatedly asked India to provide evidence to back its accusations, but it had failed to do so.

Newspapers in Islamabad Narayanan as telling Times Now television that terrorist attacks had increased in India and terrorist networks had expanded their reach beyond Jammu and Kashmir. He said Pakistan could do more to curb these attacks.[14]

He said it was unlikely that Prime Minister Man Mohan Singh would visit Pakistan this summer. There was speculation that Singh, "who has been invited by President Musharrar, would make the trip this June or July."

Asked to react to Indian charge, Aslam said accusing Pakistan was not a correct approach.

Indian High Commissioner Shiv Shankar Menon made a similar accusation at a public meeting at Islamabad on 3 June. "The India-Pakistan peace process has covered a lot of ground but Pakistan has to do more to prevent terrorist attacks in India", Menon said, addressing a meeting on conflict resolution organized jointly by the Rotary Clubs of India, Pakistan and Afghanistan.

"Terrorism is an enemy of civilized societies everywhere, and this is increasingly more remains to be done to curb the menace of cross-border terrorism", he said.

The Indian Envoy drew attention to the "public rehabilitation of terrorist organizations" in Pakistan since the Oct 2005 earthquake and said: "Terrorist training, communications, and support continue" with some variations in pattern.

Giving terrorists a veto over the process by making their satisfaction a prior condition carried a real risk. Some other observations by Menon:

- While Pakistan has often expressed impatience with the CBMs which are a hallmark of this peace process, and asked India to move ahead on the "core" issue of Kashmir, he made a strong pitch for such measures, asserting that it was these that had provided impetus to the process.
- "Our experience over the last few years proves that the people of India and Pakistan are actually ahead of their

establishments, and have provided the arriving force to the peace process. People-to-people contacts and C.B.Ms should continue unconditionally and wholeheartedly if the harder issues are to be successfully addressed".

- It was "illogical" to link normalisation of relations to a solution on the hardest problem.
- "Doing so only postpones the benefits available to both countries from normalizations, making them hostage to the most difficult issue that we face."

Dawood Ibrahim Kaksar: An India-Pak Crime Sheet and Biographical: Sep 2006

That India's 'most wanted' is safely ensconced in Pakistan is not in doubt – it never was. A fortnightly in late Sep 2006 pieced together his life and times in Pakistan. It is a useful biographic which must be known not only to the investigative agencies but also to the public.

Mastermind Behind 1993 Bombay Serial Bombing

How the mastermind functioned in India and wrought havoc in Bombay in 1993 can easily be illustrated by the evidence of Shahnawaz Qureshi in that serial blasts case.

Oureshi told a Mumbai court after he was convicted in the last quarter of 2006 for his role in the serial bombings that ripped apart the city in Mar 1993: "My house was set ablaze during the riots, and then I was misled. I was taken to Dubai, on the pretext of finding an alternative job. From Dubai, I was taken to Pakistan and then sent back to India via Dubai."

During his evidence, Qureshi was struggling to explain his motives for parking a van filled with high explosives outside Mumbai's Plaza cinema in Mar 1993. But after his conviction, he faces a life in prison, or even death.

But the man who misled Qureshi—and organized, funded and executed the Mumbai serial bombings—is not likely to see the inside of a prison any time soon. He simply is beyond the reach of Indian law. "If Dawood is still alive, his life most likely resembles those of the make-belief mafia lords who litter the scripts of the many pop films he financed."

The Ratnagiri-born son of a police constable Dawood prefers to rise after noon. After a game of tennis, he sets off to one of the several highly secured safe houses (in Karachi) from which he conducts his business. This evenings are built around large doses of Black Label whisky, 'teen—patta' gambling and *mujra cabaret* performance. "Carousing through the night", recorded the well-known Karachi-based journalist Ghulam Hasnain, the last Pakistani journalist unwise enough to expose official denials that the terrorist was in that country, "Dawood and his companions quit only at dawn and then collectively offer prayers."[15]

India formally demanded Dawood's extradition from Pakistan during the 2001-02 military crises. But there has been little hard evidence about his whereabouts in Pakistan, till June 2006 when the Karachi-based newspaper *The News* reported that Dawood had shifted his base to the Pak-Afghan border, after undergoing extensive plastic surgery. In a tongue-in-cheek assertion, the daily wrote: "The tribal areas bordering Afghanistan and Pakistan, which were being searched for Osama bin Laden and his lieutenants, are now being combed for the man accused of the Mumbai blasts." As early as 2002, Indian intelligence reported that Dawood and his second-in-command Shakeel Ahmad Babu were hidden in an ISI-run safe house near Peshawar.

Here is an interesting interlude on the Don affair. For the first time, obviously as a result of the Indian exertions, Dawood was a subject of an Interpol Special Notice, with two Karachi addresses as likely hideouts of the outlaw, in Apr 2006. Feeling uncomfortable with this official recognition of Pakistan as safe haven for an international terrorist, by then designated as such by the US and UN, Islamabad pulled all stopes mid-2006 and started lobbying with the UN panel—committee 1267—to have these two addresses deleted from the special notice. It succeeded and both the Karachi addresses indeed were deleted. In early 2007, under counter-moves, the UN committee 1267 had second thoughts on the deletion. Damage was partly undone when one of the two addresses was restored and added to the special notice in question once again.

Pakistani support for Dawood has long been evident. Indian intelligence had found out that shortly after the Mafiosa left Dubai for Karachi in the wake of the Mumbai serial bombing, he was issued a passport back dated to 12 Aug 1991, bearing the number G-866537. Soon thereafter, the three of the 1993 bombing accused were accommodated in the posh areas of Karachi:

1. Dawood moved into a 6,000-sq. mtrs plot in the up market Clifton area of Karachi that had amenities such as a swimming pool, a gymnasium and a tennis court.
2. Shakeel was gifted with a similar premises in the Defence Housing Authority enclave.
3. Abdul Razzak 'Tiger' Memon, the third author of the Mumbai blasts, purchased several properties, including the multistory Kashif Crown Plaza situated on the Shara-e-Faisal boulevard.

When a Karachi residents, association protested the encroachment of public space by the Memon family, it was told to mind its oven business. A member of the association told Hasnain: "The ISI told us it is a Dawood Ibrahim building. This is the man who has done a lot for Pakistan. So we should not raise our voices."

Soon after taking over in 1999, Gen Musharraf's regime threw its weight behind Dawood. The General had told L.K. Advani in July 2001 with a straight face: "Dawood Ibrahim is not in Pakistan." May be, in a technical sense he was right. With the help of two business associates of the mafia, Rakesh Tulshiyan and Shahid Sohail, Dawood indeed had been moved to a safe house in Malaysia for a fortnight. Indian intelligence says Dawood was housed in a property owned by Bukhari Syed Abu Tahir, a Sri Lankan national who is believed to have played a role in the smuggling of centrifuges used for enriching uranium.

If nothing else this web of links shows just how much protection Dawood's wealth has bought him. By mid-2002, he had made considerable investment in Singapore, Malaysia, Kenya and Tanzania, routed through a network of front companies. Hasnain writes: "Dawood and his men have made heavy investments in prime properties in Karachi and Islamabad and are major players in Karachi bourse and in the parallel credit system, or *hundi.* His businesses include gold and drug smuggling. The gang is also allegedly heavily involved in (cricket) match fixing."

Wealth obviously has purchased respectability. Don's daughter Mahrukh was married to former Pakistan cricket captain Javed Miandad's son. Though the young couple was never suspected of involvement in any mafia activity, Javed's financial links with Dawood have often been commented upon. Dawood is believed to have made substantial investments in businesses controlled by a prominent Karachi business family to whom Miandad is also related by marriage.

The huge wealth, though, came at price to him, but ironically, with inimical implications for India: At the insistence of Pak covert services, a percentage of the profits from his mafia operations had to be routed to the Islamist terror groups the ISI patronized. Evidence showed these links were forged soon after 1993. Late that year, the Jammu and Kashmir Islamic Front (JKIF) issued photographs of Tiger Memon along with its top commanders, taken at its safe house in Srinagar, as it 'claimed'. This was an obvious attempt to disprove Indian claims that the terrorist was in Pakistan. But unfortunately for the JKIF, and unknown to its leadership, one of its commanders, Usman Majid, was soon to defect to the Indian side. Majid, now (2006) an MLA from Bandipora, brought with him evidence that the photographs were taken at an ISI safe house in Muzaffarabad and provided the first account that mafia money was helping to pay for terror operations in Jammu and Kashmir.

In Oct 2003, a decade after the Mumbai blasts, the US Department of Treasury finally designated Dawood Ibrahim a terrorist. It recorded in details: "The Mafia lord is involved in large scale shipments of narcotics in the UK and Western Europe. Ty syndicate's smuggling routes from South Asia, the Middle East (West Asia) and Africa are shared with Osama bin Laden and his terrorist network. Successful rouges established over recent years by Dawood Ibrahim's syndicate have been subsequently utilized by bin Laden. A financial arrangements was reportedly brokered to facilitate the latter's use of these routes. In the late 1990s, Dawood Ibrahim traveled in Afghanistan under the protection of the Taliban. The US also charged him with funding "groups working against India, such as Lashkar-e-Taiba".

In a sense, Dawood Ibrahim is in a prison: the prison all covert agents make for themselves, and from which they can exit only through death. Put simply, he knowns too much about Pakistan's covert services to be allowed to ever stand trial anywhere in the world.

Taj Mahal Hotel: Site for Planning 1993 Hell

The tinkle of ice cubes hitting the crystal and wafts of exclusive, costly perfume greet patrons of Harbour Bar at the Taj Mahal Hotel: the sounds and smells of Mumbai's ultra rich. It was in this very hotel; on 4 Mar 1993 Tiger Memon shared with three of his closest deputies his full plans for serial bombings. Analysts are persuaded to believe that Memon had a sentimental fondness for Taj as it was the only one among Mumbai's key land marks not chosen for attack/destruction. At two later meetings there on 9 and 10 Mar, 33 men were assigned their largets and told how to go about bombing them.

Muslims had reacted passionately, often violently to the demolition of the Babri Masjid on 6 Dec 1992. Violent reaction in Mumbai resulted in serious communal riots there—among India's worst ever. Muslims suffered more. "Soon after the killings began, Dawood Ibrahim called several key Mafia leaders, including Yakub Memon, Ayub Memon, Dawood Mohd Phansemiya and Mohd Umar Dossa, to Dubai for discussions.

There are three versions of what transpired at Dubai:

- Dawood was, insiders claim, against his own better judgment, pushed by Tiger Memon and other furious lieutenants into authorizing the use of the Mafia to avenge the communal violence.
- Others claim that pressure from the ground—from inner-city Muslims who had long believed Mafia promises to protect them against Hindutva violence—compelled Dawood to act.
- Still others insist that initiative for the action come from the ISI.

What ever the truth, a plan for terrorist in Mumbai was in place at the end of the discussions n Dubai. Consequently, on 9 Jan 1993, well before the communal killings in Mumbai had ended, the first consignment of ISI-supplied weapons landed on a beach near the village of Dighi, on the Raigad coast. Dossa bribed customs officials and policemen to ensure that the consignment went passed on to Mumbai safely. Indeed, the weapons traveled under the personal escort of Customs Inspector Jaywant Keshav Gaurav. The police intercepted the consignment at Gonghar Phata, near Shri Vardhan, and then let it pass after accepting a bribe of Rs. 700,000. Between 2 and 8 Feb 1993, Phansamiya delivered more weapons, and the RDX eventually used in the bombing, on the Shekhadi coast.

Tiger Memon personally met with customs officials at the Big Splash Hotel in Raigad to ensure these consignments also reached Mumbai safely. Investigators later found that Additional Collector of Customs Somanath Thapa responded to specific intelligence warnings on the landings of the explosives by asking his staff to keep a watch on a stretch of the coast he knew the Mafia would not use.

Even as the weapons and explosives were landing on the Maharashtra coast, Tiger Memon had begun sending Mafia members to Pakistan to learn to use these resources. At least 27 men, according to the testimony of two among them, Usman Ahmad Jan Khan and Mohd Umar Khatab, traveled to Dubai, using documents identifying them as workers for legitimate businesses with links to Dawood Ibrahim. From there, they were flown to Islamabad on Pakistan International Airlines, using visas provided on plain paper, to avoid detection. At an ISI-run training camp, the men learnt how to assemble explosives, use assault weapons and throw grenades.

Raw, India's external covert service, succeeded eventually in ripping the veil off the ISI's exertions to conceal the men's travel to Pakistan by obtaining passenger manifests documenting their arrival in Islamabad. Forensic evidence also emerged proving that the grenades and detonators had been manufactured at Pakistani military-run facilities. At the time, though, no one in India's intelligence community knows what was going on.

Maharashtra's police authorities, for their part, had chosen not to keep key members of the Dawood gang under close surveillance, a monumental omission yet to be accounted for.

Now the final act of meticulous preparation. Late on the might of 11 Mar, Tiger Memon met with his key aides for a last meeting at the Al-Husseini Apartments on Dargah Street in Mahim. In a garage downstairs, bombs were being fitted into jeeps and scooters purchased for the attacks. Tiger Memon and his family left for Dubai early next morning and then flew on to Pakistan where they joined Dawood Ibrahim.

Most of the other key figures who planned and organized the bombings followed in their wake. The mafia foot soldiers who physically executed the bombings dispersed within India, confident that their role in the terror strikes would never be detected. It was a cardinal mistake—the one the ISI made sure was never repeated. In bombing after bombing since, terror outfit have made enormous efforts to ensure that the foot soldiers, the perpetrators, are out of the reach of the Indian investigators within hours of the strike.

Successive Indian Governments have handled the hunt for Dawood Ibrahim and Tiger Memon in a rather casual way. One analyst is rather harsh, accusing the Indian authorities of sleeping over the issue in the manner of Abdul Gani Turk, one of the chief wreckers. "I slept", Turk had said in response to a question about what he did after planting the bomb that alone claimed 113 of the 227 people who died in the Mumbai serial bombings.

The authorities may not have slept over the issue of extradition of the key perpetrators of the serial bombings, but the lax and slip shod policy in this context needs immediate and serious reappraisal. Can it be denied by any unbiased analyst of this tragedy that India made little serious effort for extradition of the major culprits from Pakistan after 1994, even when credible evidence of their presence in Pakistan surfaced. Initial error of judgment – may not be of the official level but at the political level—was not to make a demand on Islamabad for extradition of these Indian citizens who had committed a heinous crime on the Indian soul in 1993.

But this error was corrected when India demanded extradition of 20 terrorists in the wake of the 2001-02 military face-offs with Pakistan. The names of the main culprits of the 1993 blasts figured in the list of the 20. True to its lackadaisical ways, India relapsed into pattern when "calls were dropped once peace talks resumed."[16]

Now the goodly Prime Minister of India, Man Mohan Singh, has announced his intention (late Sep 2006) to push Pakistan to hand over figures like Dawood Ibrahim to India under the yet-to-be concretized joint mechanism agreed in Havana on 16 Sep 2006! Without meaning any disrespect to him, it is fair to say that the 'Innocent' doctor is expecting too much and hoping too high. Letting India to question Dawood Ibrahim, who knows too much about Pakistan's covert intelligence services, is for more dangerous than giving a chance to the American to walk all over AQ Khan. Indian's are far from getting a measure of Islamabad's duplicitous diplomacy and clever ways.

Pakistan to Focus on Jammu and Kashmir: 14-15 Nov 2006 Meet

Ahead of foreign secretary-level talks on 14-15 Nov 2006, Pakistan said it hoped to finalize a number of CBMs, including on reducing risks of nuclear accidents, besides a treaty on prevention of incidents at sea. But it insisted "Kashmir will remain the central issue."

10 Kg Heroin Seized from Pak Nationals: 5 Dec 2006

On 5 Dec 2006 BSF constable Ram Asre Yadav, guarding border pillar 112/14 area from Border Outpost (BOP) Jagdish along the Zero line of Indo-Pak border in Ferozpur sector, at 3.15 A.M, spotted three Pak nationals throwing something across the cobra fencing near pillar 112/14, 400 mtr from his BOP. He immediately alerted his colleagues at the company headquarters, BOP.

Meanwhile, Pakistani nationals started firing with 7.63 mm Chinese-made pistol which was returned by the BSF men. A Pak national was killed in the firing. The remaining two, giving covering fire to the slain smuggler, escaped in darkness and fled back into the Pak territory.

As the nearest Pakistani BOP Akbarwala is only 500 mtr. from the site of incident and is manned by 11 Wing of Pakistani Rangers, their complicity in the smuggling attempt could not be ruled out, confided officiating commandant Kailash Chander Jha, 7 BSF' who briefed the press later.

When the BSF men recovered the body after the incident, they also found eight packets of heroin each weighing 1 Kg lying near the fencing on the Indian side. Two more packets were recovered from the body of the killed.

During their inspection of the area at 6.30 AM, the BSF officials spotted the foot prints of two persons on the Indian side of the Colera fencing. BSF sniffer dogs, pressed into service to track two Indian smugglers who had come up to the fencing to receive the consignment, found the foot print missing near the Dhussi Bandh. The officials also recovered three cartridges and some empty shells of 7.63 mm pistol from the spot of incident.

Heroin packets bore the mark of Pak Company in Urdu characters identified as "Marvel Ittifaq Company, Meer Agency, No 50/50."

At the subsequent meeting with the Rangers, the BSF officials protested the smuggling attempt.

Pak National with Indian Currency held: 18 Dec 2006

The Nepal police arrested a Pakistani national at Kathmandu's Trivubhan International airport with Rs 1.1 million in Indian currency.

Hassan Alam was intercepted on a tip off and arrested, with the money (in Rs. 500 and 1,000 denominations) when he was about to board the Delhi flight.

Indian Concerned for Terror Bases in Pak, Bangladesh, Nepal: MHA Report

In a status report on Internal Security "presented to the Parliament last week" and whose details were carried by the dailies in their 3 and 4 Dec 2006 issues, Ministry of Home Affairs (MHA) is unambiguous in declaring that terror infra-structure in "Pakistan and POK is yet to be dismantled" and that the "LET and JEM use the territory and elements in Bangladesh and Nepal for movement of terrorists and finances.

Indian youth is recruited by outfits like these two and trained in Pakistan and POK and subsequently are re-launched into India for sabotage and subversive activities.

Terrorism Fomented by Pakistan

The detailed document says the terror infrastructure in Pakistan is alive and kicking. While this is not new, what is, is that it comes in the form of an official announcement from Home Ministry, which confirms yet again that Prime Minister Man

Mohan Singh strayed too far from the assessment of his own government when he, on the sidelines of NAM Summit (mid-Sep 2006,) agreed to Pakistan's favorite alibi about anti-India jihadi gangs acting independently of ISI.[17] The Report, in fact, nails the ISI for using terror groups, like JEM, LET, Al-Badr and HM, it has reared and armed to target India. Centre has also acknowledged the new challenge in the form of terrorists' ambition to take the proxy war beyond Kashmir and into Country's hinterland.

The continued training of Indian youth in Pakistan came to light in the investigations into the Mumbai suburban train blasts when many accused confessed that they had been taken to Pakistan for training.

Even as the security forces combat the Kashmir-centric terrorism, it is the gradual movement of subversion to the hinterland and the increasing use of locals—a worrying new development—which has sent the alarm bells ringing in the top echelons of the MHA and among the security think-tanks. The probe into the blasts at Varanasi Sankat Mochan temple and the attack on the Ayodhya complex, too, had found that Pak—Bangladeshi terror groups had used locals to carry out subversive acts.

The recent arrest of two Pakistani youths in Mysore, belonging to Al-Badr, blew the bid on the new strategy.

The two had liaised locally and received finances to set up terror infrastructure in the South. Malegaon and Mumbai blasts, besides the huge haul of explosives in different parts of Maharashtra, confirmed that terror was moving beyond the known hotspots.

Indians must take note of what the status paper says about one of the most important paragraphs with serious implications for their security interests:

> "The current strategy of these groups is to maintain a continuous flow of finances to sustain terrorist network, target vital installtions and economic infrastructure, recruit and train local modules, attack soft targets like market places, public transport system, places of worship and congregations. (It is) to provoke communal tensions to create

a wedge between communities. And to supply hardware through land and sea routes."

The four terror outfits mentioned, and particularly the LET and JEM, "are well-organized and inter-linked, have the latest hardware and communication equipment", the report highlighted.[18]

Making Bangladesh and Nepal Partners in Crime

ISI is always known to open new fronts against India in pursuit of its plan to "bleed India through thousand cuts." After having used the western border for years, Pakistan-based outfits like LET and JEM have opened new fronts for India to guard against, using Bangladesh and Nepal as launching pads for its cadres.

The two outfits, guided by the ISI and Bangladesh's DGFI, have forged a relationship with Bangladesh's Harkat-ul-Jihadi-Islami (HUJI) to which many recent terror attacks, notably the one on Varanasi historic Sankat Mochan temple, have been traced.

The Report highlights the nexus and the consequent emergence of Bangladesh as the new entry point for subversive elements into India.

The candid tone of the report contrasts sharply with the reluctance the MHA showed till as recently as the last meeting of the DGPs in naming the countries hosting anti-India terror gangs. The report says: "LET, JEM use territory and elements in Bangladesh and Nepal for movements of terrorists and finances."

The consequence of the (Pakistan's) ISI's exertions in this field that Bangladesh and Nepal have been turned into bleeding grounds for terrorists activities against India—a kind of terrorism—generating facilities for export to India.

Advice/instructions to States on Counter-Terrorism Measures

The State governments are regularly sensitized and specific intelligence inputs are shared with them by the central agencies about the plans and designs of the terrorists in order to meet the challenge posed by these outfits.

The Centre has also asked the state governments to over haul the intelligence gathering mechanism as the same acts as a force multiplier and holds the key to prevent terrorist activities.

Promising financial and technical help to the state governments in strengthening special branches of their police, the Centre has issued a six-point advisory for police modernization. The recommendation include:

1. Recruitment of additional manpower with competence and a mandatory 5-year posting with the Special Branch.
2. Introduction of incentives and disincentives
3. Appointment of a dedicated staff for intelligence gathering upto the police station level.

Central funds are also provided under the police modernization scheme, and security-related expenditures.

The Ccentre has also the state government to set up well-equipped and specially trained police units to deal with the acts of terrorism.

Besides, two new initiatives including mega-city policing, were launched under the police modernization scheme in the current fiscal (2006-07). Mega policing for the seven cities of Hyderabad, Ahmedabad, Delhi, Bangalore, Mumbai, Chennai and Kolkata aims to strengthen policing with emphasis on intelligence gathering. Desert policing will be applicable for desert areas of Gujarat and Rajasthan.

Cross-Border Terrorism: India Faces New Challenges

Students of continuing, decades-long terrorism in India discerned certain changes during 2006 in the operational patterns followed by the jihadist outfits active in India.

"In 2006, Pakistan sponsored jihadi terrorism in India under went several significant changes that is bound to define the terror strategies of different groups inimical to India and its national interests."[19]

The most significant indicator of the changed scenario is the growing alliance between *jihadi* outfits operating from Pakistan (LET) and Bangladesh (Harkat-ul-jihadi-al-Islami-HUJI) with ideologically extreme groups in India like SIMI. In specific terms, groups like LET are tying up with smaller and diffused groups of extremists with the primary objective of hitting at India's 'core' values: open, democratic polity; secularist traditions; and pluralism in the characteristic multi-religious, multi-cultural, multi-linguistic, multi-ethnic society. This development signals a new phase of terrorism in India, more dangerous in its intent, striking at its vitats and its intrinsic, innate strengths.

Another visible change over the past some years has been the conscious attempt on the part of the jihadis to expand their anti-India theatre of operations beyond Jammu and Kashmir. Different parts of the country, particularly in the West and the South, are increasingly coming under their gaze. Most of the states in North and North-East of India are already experiencing different shades of insurgent and terrorist violence. In all likelihood, the North-East, especially Assam, already facing serious secessionist threat from the long years of illegal immigration from across the border, will come under even more virulent threat from Islamist terrorists operating out of Bangladesh. New terror bases have been discovered in Madhya Pradesh, Karnataka and Kerala.

Third point of concern is the changing profile of terrorists. They are no longer necessarily bearded, *madrassa*-educated jihadis. A sizeable number among them are well educated—doctors, engineers and even computer and IT savvy—and adept in exploiting latest communication technologies like Internet, e-mail and satellite phones. These men are also trained in explosives by experts in Pakistan. Their expertise and ingenuity is reflected in the use of locally available material like pressure cookers and mixing ammonium nitrate with explosive for maximum damage to men and materials.

They use computer-aided tools like e-mail (processing data through draft Bolders in e-mail accounts) with equal felicity to plot and execute terrorist acts. Their skill sets in IT enable them to tap into the world wide web (www) of terror which has not only become a virtual university of *jihad* but also an overarching umbrella of faith, bringing all the faithfuls together on a single cyber platform.

All that leads to the fourth point. A large number of local recruits are influenced not by any ideological convictions or concerns as such but by, what they perceive or are made to perceive as, communal hatred and injustice inflicted by certain sections of society. A best example to illustrate this particular development in the Indian context is the large number of CDs, books, magazines, and pamphlets highlighting the Gujarat riots and some other incidents that portray "victimization of Muslims at the hands of the Indian state".

Although India has witnessed communal riots since Independence, it was the demolition of the disputed mosque in Ayodhya "which drove a deep division between the two communities, bringing to the fore, perhaps for the first time since partition, the clash between the majority community and the minority community on a pan-India scale. For the Muslim community as a whole, this incident raised the specter of being to tally subjugated in a nation of their choice."

Exploiting this communal frenzy and hate-filled propaganda, outfits like SIMI stoked the fires, supported in no less measure by the ISI and various groups in West Asia, creating the first groups of home-grown *jihadis* who wanted avenge the demolition of the mosque by inflicting death and pain on the majority community and on what they perceive to be a "Hindu state." The ISI has been playing—more appropriately, perhaps 'preying'—on the fears of the common Indian Muslim (which is no different for members of other religions in an impoverished country struggling to make progress) to create dissensions and communal disharmony within the wider Indian society.

The aim obviously is not only to foment social disharmony and even animosity among different sections of society—essentially between the Hindus and the Muslims, but also sow seeds of political division. If a Muslim-dominant district was created in Kerala in far less acrimonious times some decades back, there is a move afloat presently, aggressively instigated by the ISIS, backed LET in the recent past, to create a separate Muslim state carved out of the moth state of Uttar Pradesh. Mere division of UP to create a Muslim state in India is a minor worry for the Indian security establishment, compared to the creation of a Muslim enclave in the country. How? An added dimension to the growing secessionist threat is the increasing ability of Muslims to voice, and often broadcast widely, dissent and thus break down the walls of perception and communications among different groups within community. Terrorist groups like LET (and in the near future, Al-Qaeda) are beginning to exploit this to destabilize India and carve out an exclusive Muslim conclave within, which will then become the critical bridge between Islam in the West and its proponents in the East. Several Indian Muslim organizations are not using cyber space to articulate views on issues that had hitherto remained confined to mosques and drawing rooms.

Of the multiple objectives the masterminds behind the terrorist attacks seek from their violence, one is least articulated and understood. It is the hate that is created within the community as a result of mass (and often mindless) arrests of Muslims, following the blasts most of them innocent, ordinary citizens, their harassment and torture as police routine; and worst of all, stereotyping and demonizing the community by parading bearded accused before the media even before the investigations have been completed—often even before they have begun in right earnest. When groups like the LET plan their terror attacks, they are well aware of this cycle of terror and hate. They have also perfected their plans to harvest this hate for furthering their own cause: youths so harassed and tortured fall easy and willing prey to their machinations. They join the terrorist outfits without too much questioning and doubts. They obviously carry a hurt in their minds. This is sixth and penultimate point in the list.

This is about the postulation the Muslims, whether in India or elsewhere, are radicalized by reading Quaranic verses on jihad or listening to speeches on the theme. This argument is fallacious. The radicalization of the community, at least some sections of it, needs to be studied in the context of political events and processes, changes at the social, economic and religious levels, especially in a country like India which has a sizeable share of world's Muslim population. Analyzing religious beliefs in isolation is not enough to understand why and how sections of a particular community, in this case Muslim, are prone to get radicalized and take up arms against the state in the name of religion.

It is perhaps time to sound a warning here. There are various reasons why India should be prepared for renewed cycle of terrorist violence, and an increase in its frequency and intensity. Unfortunately, these reasons and causes mostly lie beyond India's borders. First set belongs to Pakistani state: Given Pakistan's own internal sectarian dynamics, unsatisfactory internal security situation and failing polity; rise of fundamentalism and extreme radicalization of sections of society, particularly in border areas contiguous to Afghanistan, as illustrated by Lal Masjid fiasco and consequent violence in July 2007, rise of religious parties led by the MMA; Gen Musharraf's failure to extract a "solution" of Kashmir issue from India as he has repeatedly promised his countrymen; and growing clam our from numerous jihadi outfits for liberation of Kashmir are bound to result in increased terrorist attacks and consequent communal disharmony, tension and acrimony within India in the coming months and years. Secondly, increasing and incessant terrorist violence in the world, including Iraq, Afghanistan and West Asia is bound to affect Muslims in India, and in turn the Indian polity. Thirdly, exertions of extremist groups like SIMI are bound to aggravate the communal situation in India.

In sum, it is time India put in place a well-considered counter-terrorism policy to face the serious situation, created by the Islamist extremists in and around India.

ISI Cells in UP? There is Evidence

Interrogation of two persons, arrested by the Directorate of Revenue Intelligence (DRI) at Indira Gandhi International

Airport on 28 Feb 2007 in a fake currency smuggling case, has yielded important on a number of ISI-operated sleeper cells based primarily in Hapur and Bulandshahar in western UP.

Officials of the DRI and other security agencies jointly interrogated a 22-year-old Hapur resident; Mohad Shame at the DRI HQ at New Delhi till late on 1 Mar. Shame had received a consignment of Rs 10 lakh in fake currency brought in by 77-year-old women, Laiquen, on a Pakistan International Airlines (PIA) flight from London.

Both Shame and Laiquen were remanded to judicial custody by a local court on 2 Mar. Shame's interrogation yielded vital leaders on other gangs which are in touch with operatives across the border. Women revealed that she was taken to a warehouse in Lahore by her ticket sponsors and kept there for a couple of days to "get acquainted" before boarding the PIA flight. While boarding the flight, she was given a "dinner set" by those people to be delivered to the person who came to receive her.

This is the first time in recent years that a person coming from Pakistan on its official airline has been caught with fake currency. It is known that "Pakistan has been sending fake currency and other contraband but that always came via Dubai-Sri Lanka or Dubai-Bangladesh route. Though couriers were used in the past, the consignment always came through the land route, either using the Samjhauta Express or smuggled in by the infiltrators through the porous borders.

"We would not give up Kashmir": Pak President: 25 Mar 1957

(A page from the history)

The following news story is reproduced from the *Deccan Chronicle,* dated 25 Mar 1957, as published in the *Asian Age* of 25 Mar 2007 under the headline '50 Years Ago':

- "Karachi: Pakistan President Gen Iskander Mirza today warned that Indo-Pakistan relations would be further embittered if 'India continues to be unreasonable on Kashmir'.
- "In a nation-wide broadcast on Pakistan's first republic anniversary, President Mirza said, 'our most vital problem continues to be that of Kashmir. Pakistan's relations with India depend solely on the issue of Kashmir'."

Three Lashkar terrorist held at Indo-Bangla Border: 1 Apr 2007

The BSF confirmed on 2 Apr 2007 that three of the four

foreign nationals apprehended on 1 Apr at the Indo-Bangla border in Petrapol, North 24-Parganas, belonged to the terrorist outfit LET.

The incident brings to fore how West Bengal has become a corridor for international terrorist movements.

The four foreign nationals were intercepted by the BSF intelligence personnel as they were trying to enter the Indian Territory at Petrapol border on the morning of 1 Apr.

After a prolonged interrogation at the BSF's Haridaspur camp (193 Battalion), which continued overnight and the next day (2 April), the BSF authorities suspect that the four had sneaked into India to carry out subversive activities.

The four were identified as:

1. Sheikh Shamim.
2. Sheikhh Abdullah.
3. Muzzafar Ahmad Khan.
4. Mohammad Younis.

Notes

1. Samudra Gupta Kashyap, *Indian Express*, 7 Dec., 2006.
2. *Ibid.*
3. *Ibid.*
4. The Item under "50 Years ago in *Deccan Chronicle*" of 5 Apr 1957, reproduced in *Asian Age,* 5 Apr., 2007.
5. Hindustan Times,12 Jun, 2007.
6. It is not difficult at all to know the state this senior and distinguished bureaucrat is chary to name. It is, for certain, West Bengal. His reason to be Coy on the issue is simple: all bureaucrats want to ensure their future.
7. S G Kashyap, *Indian Express,* 16 Jul, 2007.
8. *Indian Express,* 25 Jul, 2007.
9. *Ibid,* 8 Aug, 2007.
10. *Asian Age,* 17 Apr, 2007.
11. The Seventh India-EU Summit is being presently (Oct 2006) held at Helsinki.
12. B. Raman, *Pioneer,* 19 Dec, 2006.
13. Iftikhar Gilani, *Daily Times*, 21 Jan, 2006.
14. Nirupama Subramanian, *Hindu*, 6 Jun, 2006.
15. Praveen Swami, *Frontline,* 6 Oct, 2006.
16. *Ibid.*
17. *Times of India*, 4 Dec, 2006.
18. Rakesh K. Singh, *Asian Age*, 3 Dec, 2006.
19. Wilson John, *Pioneer,* 3 Jan, 2007.

13

PAKISTAN : THE CHIEF INSTIGATOR

PAKISTAN CONTINUES PLAYING CLEVER GAMES ON INDIA: APR 2007

Pakistan's bid to wash its hands clean of the Dawood Ibrahim smear was foiled mid-Apr 2007. An Indian daily claims in a lead story that because of on alert sounded by it, the UN Security Council put his Pakistani address back in the Interpol files.

To begin from the beginning, Interpol records had two Karachi addresses, detailed below, listed as Dawood Ibrahim's possible shelters:

1. House No NU-37

   30 street, Defence Housing Authority, Karachi
2. White House near Saudi Mosque, Clifton, Karachi

This was seen as clear endorsement of India's instance. India had supplied these addresses to Islamabad while demanding the extradition of this outlaw after the 1993 serial Mumbai blasts.

In a Special Notice issued in Apr 2006, Interpol had listed these two Karachi addresses as Dawood's possible hide-outs.

Pakistan has been persisting stubbornly with the UN Security Council that "Dawood Ibrahim is not present on its territory." It vigorously lobbied the Interpol headquarters at Lyon, France during June-July 2006, asking it to strike off the Don's Karachi addresses from the Special Notice.

Surprisingly, its efforts paid off even though the solid body of evidence about Dawood's presence in Karachi has got even stronger. With the US also designating Dawood a global terrorist, Islamabad, already staggering under the perception of being the nursery of the world terrorism, has been becoming even more anxious to have the embarrassing link erased.

Pakistan's success in getting the Interpol's records—Special Notice—airbrushed of any reference to Karachis as the possible hideouts of Dawood, "since designated global terrorist," would have caused a major set-back to India, which has consistently maintained that Dawood is being hosted by ISI.[1]

While Pakistan had pulled off a coup of sorts by getting the international police body to buy its protestations of innocence— "Dawood is not present on our territory—the UN Security Council [acting in response to query from this daily] has ensured that Interpol continues to regard Pakistan as the country in which the fugitive Don could be holed up. The daily in question opens its story on the subject in a self-congratulatory tone in its issue dated 16 Apr 2007: "New Delhi; acting on the basis of a Times of India alert, the UN Security Council has frustrated Pakistan's attempt to get Interpol acquiesce to its claim that it was not sheltering India's most-wanted Don, Dawood Ibrahim."

The expunction of the two addresses at a time when all evidence strongly points to the continued presence of the Don in Pakistan could have turned the situation to Islamabad's favour.

UN Security Council (UNSC) came to India's by ensuring that one of the two addresses [White House, Clifton] was put back on 13 Apr 2007. The UNSC had confirmed the "glaring change" to the daily which had alerted its panel—Committee 1267—to the missing Karachi addresses. Committee 1267 is entrusted with the task of listing people aligned with Al-Qaeda and Taliban.

In was a 'close shave', in a manner of speaking, as the Interpol, for reasons best known to itself, suddenly found merit in its disclaimer and expunged both the Karachi addresses from its Special Notice.

It may be worth while to comment upon the (lackadaisical?) functioning of the UN and its agencies. The daily in its issue of 16 Apr 2007 writes: "while Interpol is yet to respond to an email from TOI alerting it of Pakistan's shrewd move to get two Karachi addresses as possible hideouts of underworld don Dawood Ibrahim removed, the UN panel (Committee 1267) acted promptly and took up the matter with the world police body."

Consequently, by 13 Apr 2007 the White House address was back on Interpol's Special Notice for Dawood.

Thanking the daily for sounding alarm bell, the committee 1267 sent an email to it: "We have looked into this matter and have discussed it with relevant authorities at Interpol. It appears that there has been a problem, but this is now being resolved.

Both the Karachi addresses of Dawood were part of Interpol-UNSC 'Special Notice' issued in Apr 2006. Since it was the first – ever official disclosure of Dawood's Pakistan addresses and possible location, it had obviously caused a lot of embarrassment to Islamabad, which had, even after this confirmation from a UN body, continued to feign ignorance over Dawood's where-about.

While the UN committee has done its part, now it is the responsibility of Indian's CBI leadership, which represents the India chapter of Interpol, to find out how Pakistan almost succeeded—coming so close to getting its denial endorsed by the international police body. Were the Pakistanis too prompt and too skilful, or were the Indians too lazy and too smug?

A word on Special Notice. One is pending against Al-Qaeda Chief Osama bin Laden, and so are several against Taliban leaders. When a person is covered under this notice, no Interpol member country (obviously including Pakistan) is expected to allow travel of such a person within its territory and let their financial transactions take place in the country.

Besides disclosing Dawood's addresses for the first time in Apr 2006; the Special Notice had also put details of 11 passports and 16 aliases used by him during his foray into the world wide terror syndicate of Osama bin Laden while traveling to Bahrain, Kuwait, Qatar, Saudi Arabia and Oman.

This detailed treatment of the issue should end with an easy summary:

- In a Special Notice issued in Apr 2006 (first-over of its kind), Interpol lists two Karachi addresses as possible den/hideout of India's most wanted fugitive outlaw.
- Pakistan lobbies hard (June-July 2006) with Interpol that it is not sheltering the by-now designated international terrorist and gets both the addresses expunged from the Special Notice.

- Alerted by a daily, UNSC takes up the issue with the Interpol and one of the two addresses is back on the Special Notice by 13 Apr 2007.

ISI Creating Trouble in India's North East: Stratfor: Apr 2007

From time to time, various authorities in the United States, like the White House staff, the State Department, the Congressional Committees, and even the leading newspapers like the *New York Times* and the *Washington Post*, have come out publicly with the reports of Pakistan continuing to foment terrorism in India. Some are sanguine that President Musharraf's repeated assurances to India since Jan 2004 notwithstanding, Pakistan has not changed its policy of making use of cross-border terrorism against India as an instrument of its foreign policy.

Latest to join the list of such entities to warn and caution India is the US news intelligence service Stratfor. It says: "Pakistan's Interservice Intelligence (ISI) is working with Bangladesh's intelligence agencies to facilitate cooperation between north-east militant groups like ULFA and other jihadi outfits in the South-Asian region, besides Tamil rebels in Sri Lanka." A PTI report in a daily of 24 Apr 2007.

In its latest forecast titled "India: The Islamisation of the northeast", it observes that there is a growing Islamisation in the region—spurred by the ISI and instability in the neighboring Bangladesh which is giving foreign (China and Pakistan) a gamut of exploitable secessionist movements to use to prevent India from emerging as a major global player.

Stratfor says that there exists a strong nexus between the ISI and Bangladesh's intelligence agencies. There are growing indications that these two agencies are working clandestinely in Bangladesh to bring all north-east-based insurgent outfits and jihadist elements under one umbrella. "The ISI has facilitated cooperation between ULFA and other northeastern militant outfits with the Liberation Tigers of Tamil Ealam in Sri Lanka, Islamist militant groups in Jammu and Kashmir, Islamist groups in Bangladesh and a growing number of Al-Qaeda-linked jihadist groups operating in the region", it adds.

Pak Army Officer Arrested in Kashmir: A first: June 2007

Shahzad Khan, an ex-captain of Pak Army who had fought in the Kargil conflict as a subaltern and was arrested on 22 June 2007 from the outskirts of Srinagar, was considered to be the "most wanted" militant commander in the valley since LET's top commander Salahuddin alias Bilal left for PoK in 2006.

His arrest, the first of a former Pak Army regular in the Valley, is the result of a concerted police effort to close in on key strategists behind the militant outfits in Kashmir today.

Police had been keeping a close watch on Sahazad alias Abdullah Omar who was in the process of shifting his base from Bandipore forests to another "safe zone".

A month ago, police had credible reports that the former Pak Army captain was regularly visiting a family staying in rented accommodation in Syed Colony between the Hobak crossing and the Zakura crossing in the outskirts of Srinagar. A police party reached there and arrested Shahzad. In his late 20s, he is lean and sports a stubble. Aware that he was trapped, he showed no resistance.

He told his interrogators: He belongs to Punch district across the LOC and was actively involved in Kargil war as a Second Lieutenant in the Pak Army. He claimed to have won a gallantry medal.

The police moved him to an "undisclosed camp" for comprehensive questioning and even denied his arrest. Sources revealed that he claimed to be a close relative of Lt Gen Mohd Aziz Khan, Musharraf's pointsman in Kargil and said he had links with PoK Prime Minister Ateeq Khan a well.

These claims are yet to be confirmed. Interrogators also are in the dark about the circumstances of his leaving the Pak Army: Did he leave voluntarily, or was he dismissed?

Shahzad's arrests comes at a time when the police are keeping a watch on several top militant Commanders. On 19 Apr the police successfully encircled another top militant and Pak national, Khalid, who is believed to direct militant operations in central Kashmir, especially Srinagar. Spotted in a house in Harman, the police cordoned off the house late in the evening. Khalid opened fire and escaped. Police suspect Khalid too could have links to the Pakistan Army.

PAKISTAN'S ANTI-INDIA ACTIONS : A TRADITION

The country came into being riding on the wave of anti-India sentiments. Ever since then, this sentiment has not only grown stronger, but in fact has been converted into anti-India hatred, if we go by the assertions of some analysts.

No Pakistani leader can afford to be seen even mildly pro-India in his pronouncement or policy decisions. In fact, the political leaders often vie with each other to gain popular ratings through their anti-India slogans and speeches. Some of these are mentioned here in the succeeding pages.

ISI Activities

The ISI could not have been unaware of Dr. AQ Khan's nuclear proliferation activities. The disgraced scientist could not have sustained his international operations without prior permission from various regimes in Islamabad—forget about mere 'prior knowledge' or 'tacit approval'. The ISI should have been privy to the entire operations, and possibly a useful link between the Pak government and AQ Khan on one hand and AQ Khan and his customer-clients on the other—given its extensive spy network the world over.

Given the AQ Khan saga, some linkages between Pakistani scientists and the terrorist groups can be easily imagined. Thus it came as a no surprise when the *Washington Post* (12 Dec 2001) disclosed that two senior retired Pakistani nuclear scientists—Sultan Bashiruddin Mahmood and Abdul Majid—had met Osama bin Laden in 2001 to conduct "long discussions about nuclear, chemical and biological weapons." This news has direct implications for India as Pakistan has been targeting India for years through vicious cross-border acts of terrorism. Even more sinister is the fact that Osama has added India to his list of enemies, next only to Israel and America.

From the time of the Soviet presence in Afghanistan, the ISI has had direct contacts with Al Qaeda. Declassified US Defence Intelligence Agency (DIA) documents from Oct 2001 indicate that the Al Qaeda camp targeted by American cruise missiles in 1998 was funded and maintained by the ISI.[2] The *New York Times* in a front page story in October 2001 argued that

Pakistan's ISI even used the Al Qaeda camps in Afghanistan to train terrorists for covert operations in India. The American fears over the ISI's dealings with the Kashmiri militant groups and the Taliban were such that the US Secret Service opposed a plan by the then President Bill Clinton to visit Pakistan in 2000. According to American officials, the ISI's reliance' on bin Laden's camps for training came to light in August 1998, when the US launched a cruise missile attack against Al Qaeda terrorist camps near Khost, Afghanistan, in response to the bombings of two American embassies in East Africa. The casualties included several members of a Kashmiri militant group supported by Pakistan who were believed to be training in the camps.[3]

It was strongly believed that sympathetic ISI officials "may even have provided shelter to Al Qaeda cadres in both Pakistan and Kashmir.[4] Again, the ISI might have orchestrated Al Qaeda's shift into South Waziristan in 2002. Washington DC, 8 May 2002. Two analysts have argued that the Taliban was part of a much wider radical Islamist network in the region, whose true centre was Pakistan, not Afghanistan. Al Qaeda, the Taliban, the Pakistani Deobandis and "all of these groups" are based in Pakistan, which continue to serve as the regional hub for Islamist movements and their terrorist offshoots.[5]

The terrorist groups in Pakistan have been systematically carrying terror acts in the Indian states and have now shifted their attention to urban infrastructure. The 11 July 2006 serial bomb blasts targeting the railway network in Mumbai had connection with Pakistan-based terrorist groups.[6] The Mumbai police stated on 30 Sept 2006 that Pak ISI had conceived and executed the carnage through the LET and JEM, using the SIMI and other modules. The principal conspirator of the attack has been identified as a top LET functionary, Azam Cheema, who runs a terrorist training camp at Bahawalpur, Pakistan's Punjab, and his three executive planners in India were Faizal Sheikh, Kamaluddin Ansari and Ehtesham Siddiqui. LET's presence in the attack was revealed after a LET module was neutralized in Mumbai in July 2006.[7]

Testifying before the Senate Foreign Relations Committee in Oct 2003, Assistant Secretary of Defence Peter Rodman said: "There are elements in Pakistani Government who we suspect are sympathetic to the old policy of before 9/11", adding that there still existed in north-western Pakistan a radical Islamic infrastructure that "spews out fighters that go into Kashmir as well as into Afghanistan."

Narcotrade in Afghanistan and Pakistan also has implications for India. 70 per cent of narcotics production in Afghanistan is trafficked through Pakistan.[8] The drug trade nurtures a network of smugglers, traffickers and terror groups in a 'vicious cycle of conflict.' The underworld don Dawood Ibrahim, an Indian fugitive and the mastermind behind the 1993 Mumbai blasts, has linkages with terror and Islamist extremist groups. Despite the denials by Pakistan, the press has confirmed his presence in Karachi—flashing a picture of his house with a door plate bearing his name.[9] New Delhi's claims pertaining to Dawood are largely shared by the US government. According to a 2003 US Treasury Department Report, the Karachi-based criminal "has found common cause with Al Qaeda, sharing his smuggling routes with the terror syndicate and funding attacks by Islamist extremists aimed at destabilizing the Indian government. He is wanted by India for the 1993 Bombay Stock Exchange bombings and is known to have financed the activities of (egregiously anti-India) Lashkar-e-Tayyaba."[10] Dawood and his associates reportedly facilitated the transport of several Ahmedabad residents recruited by Jaish-e-Mohammed to Dhaka and then to Karachi in 2001 and aided the transit of another group of terror recruits through Bangkok.[11]

Consequent to these findings Washington has officially designated Dawood Ibrahim as a terrorist supporter.[12] Likewise, the US had signaled increased pressure on Islamabad in Oct 2003 when the Treasury Department designated the Pakistan-based Al Akhtar Trust as a terrorist support organization under Executive Order 13224.[13] Notwithstanding all this, Pakistan has not only not taken any action against Dawood but has also cavalierly dismissed India's demand for his extradition to bring him to justice for crimes committed in India.

This brief review of some past incidents between India and Pakistan is essential to see if Pakistan could be trusted to deliver when the two countries start working jointly to fight terrorism in the region, as agreed upon in September meeting at Havana between Prime Minister Singh and President Musharraf. There are analysts who seriously doubt any positive outcome from the Havana agreement, since Pakistan is behind most of the terrorist acts in India, they argue. The other side argues Pakistan must be given a chance to prove its sincerety and not condemned with a trial.

Peace Process: Hiccups in the Way

Ever since the peace process was set in motion, the tensions in Kashmir had been on the downswing. There was certain hope in the air. But the calm stands shattered with the recent (May-July 2006) bloodletting of tourists, political rallies and politicians in Kashmir. Bloody encounters are also back, claiming the lives of Armymen including officers and militants.

The recrudescence of violence is always omenous. If the 1993 Mumbai blasts had derailed peace-talks, so have the 11 July 2006 serial rail blasts the Indo-Pak composite dialogue 2004, the chief mechanism of the peace-process. The third round of this dialogue was to be rounded up by 20-21 July 2006 Foreign Secretary level talks between India's Shyam Saran and Pakistan's Riaz Muhammed Khan. If the serial rail blasts of 11 July rendered that meeting doubtful, Pak Foreign Minister's insensitive remarks sealed it fate. While Musharraf condemned the Mumbai terror attacks, Kasuri added a smart one liner—linking the attacks/blasts to the lack of resolution of disputes between India and Pakistan. In an interview with the Reuters, Kasuri said: "I think the Mumbai incident—however tragic it may be and it is undoubtedly very tragic—underlines—need for two countries to work together to control this environment, but they can only do so if they resolve their disputes".

Till Kasuri's indiscretion, the Man Mohan government had been resisting the temptation to see the usual 'Pak hand' behind the blasts. With another round of Foreign Secretary level due before the end of July, New Delhi seemed keen to give the 'usual suspect' the benefit of doubt. That was, perhaps, why Home Secretary VK Duggal refused to see a link between Mumbai blasts and attacks on Bengali tourists at five places in Srinagar the same day.

Exercising restraint was indeed a bold decision, since the main opposition party BJP has been blaming the UPA government of adopting a soft policy towards Pakistan and terrorism unleashed by it. Worse, some analysts feared Shiv Sena staging a repeat of the communal revenge of 1993.

But Kasuri's thoughtless remarks undid all this. Duggal was upset enough to say "the purpose behind both incidents is common and so are the people working behind them. Their objective is to destabilize the country."

Foreign office also dropped a few veiled threats of taking a retook at some of the CBM and thinking of postponing the Secretary – level talks. The MEA spokesperson Naviej Sarna made following points:

- Kasuri's remarks are "appalling", as they suggested Pakistan would cooperate with India against cross-border terrorism only if disputes were resolved. This was unacceptable.
- "We urge Pakistan to take urgent steps to dismantle terrorist infrastructure on its side, take action against those responsible for violence and fulfil its solid commitment in the Indo-Pakistan Joint Statement of 2004."

Kasuri, ironically got a drubbing for his remarks, while he is criticized in Pakistan being soft on India. Kasuri, incidentally, has often scoffed, of course, in private at India not having a Foreign Minister for him to talk to Musharraff may now be regretting for having a Foreign Minister, one who is too voluble for diplomatic niceties.

Political leaders in Pakistan, however, condemned the incident and called for the two nations to fight the terrorism jointly. They hoped history would not repeat itself. December 2001 bombing of its Parliament had compelled India to move its troops to the borders, with Pakistan following suit. There was usual Pak rhetoric and sermons: The two countries should not repeat the old mistakes. Placing two countries, one aggressor and other victim, on equal footing is not being naeve but igenious. "Such incidents must not hamper the peace process", advised Saddiqual Farooq, a senior leader of the PML(N). Secretary General PPP Raja Parvez Ashraf felt it was the duty of Pakistan government to make India realize that working together was the only option to cope with the menace of terrorism.

Regrettably, on the Indian side, barring the BJP, no one was telling Pakistan what to do under the circumstances. Indians generally are given to self-flagellation, and equally often, bashing their own government. Majority of the Indian political class, driven by vote-bank politics/compulsions are either mushy or soft on Pakistan. Majority of analysts, journalists, and academics follow the political class to project and preserve their 'liberal' and 'secular' credentials.

If India is frustrated with the increased level of violence in Kashmir and other parts of the country, Pakistan may be peeved with the lack of substantial movement on the 'core issue of Kashmir'. It feels India is minimizing the significance of peace talks by keeping it at the Foreign Secretary level.

May be, Musharraf has personal interest in seeing some so-called movement on Kashmir issue to enable him to garner some additional support during the polls due in Pakistan in 2007.

One must appreciate the Pakistani journalists* for espousing their country's line on all issues and even offering rationalization to their presidents, even the ones in uniform. Here is one instance:

> "The uprisings in Balochistan and Afghanistan have added to the frustration. The upsurge in Kashmir violence and outrage in Mumbai could well be the reflection of that frustration."

This is exactly the Kasuri line, in fact this goes beyond that. He postulated that if Kashmir is not resolved, there will be 11/7 Mumbais. This Pakistani journalist says if Pakistan faces frustration in Balochistan, they will take it on India by staging train blasts in Mumbai. He goes still further: if they face troubles even in Afghanistan, they will still take it on India through acts of terrorism—the art which the ISI and LET has mastered to perfection. If the mushy, nay namby pamby Indians, do not understand the implications of this explicit postulations, Pakistanis can't be blamed for it. The blame will rest on these Indians for refusal to see the writings on the wall.

---

*It is Tariq Bhat with Shahzad Raza (Islamabad), The Outlook, 23/7/06.

It was general perception that New Delhi was getting a little soft on the Musharraf regime, whatever their reasons. But the conduct of Pak-inspired gangs in Afghanistan had convinced New Delhi that Musharraf was not keen on hunting down groups like the LET. India is seen as having failed to convince Pakistan/ Musharraf about he Pak role in the terrorist violence in India, whatever direct or indirect evidence the latter might have adduced. Now Kasuri has provided just that.

The rising public outrage impacted the Parliament's monsoon session that started on 14 July and government came under pressure to adopt tough policy towards Pakistan.

India had been providing Pak authorities the Karachi address of the much-wanted don Dawood Ibrahim. To avoid any further embarrassment to Pakistan, he was reported to have shifted base to NWFP, where Osama too is under hiding. If that be the case, the Don is in safe haven as in these areas inhabited by the tribals, Musharraf's writ, or that of the Pak Army state, hardly runs. Subsequent by both were rendered beyond the reach of Army/state when Pakistan struck a deal with the North Waziristan tribes to discontinue all operations there and with her Army from there. This shows the true colours of Bush's valuable ally in his war against terrorism (The subject is discussed in fuller detail, later).

There were other disturbing reports and development in Jammu and Kashmir :

- Ever since the 2005-06 winter season was over, there has been increased infiltration in Gulmarg. Army Chief JJ Singh said (June 2006) "nearly 1,500 militants were operating in Kashmir at the moment."
- Securities agencies disclosed 200 militants have infiltrated Kashmir and made Bandipore in Baramulla mountains their base.
- Most of militants are from the banned LET. Salahuddin. LET (Kashmir) Chief, is behind the spurt of attacks in Kashmir. The police has put a Rs. 5 Lakh reward on his head. Mudasir, another LET commander, also has a similar prize on his head, and he was allegedly behind the attack on 21 May Congress rally

in Srinagar and grenade attacks on many places in Srinagar on the tourists.

The militants have innovatively resorted to outsourcing the grenade attacks to young boys with no police records. IGP SM Sahai disclosed at Srinagar: "The planners first distribute grenades to a group who carry it to their conduits in the city. The conduits hire youngsters who carry out the attacks." Most of the grenade attacks have been on the tourists; six between 24 May—the last day of the second round table conference—and 24 June 2006.

The terrorists achieved a conspicuous success when they attacked a Congress ralling on 24 May 2006 which was to be addressed by Prime Minister Manmohan Singh. The attacks on political parties pitted political rivals against each other. When the NC leader and former minister Sakeena Itoo was attacked, its President, Omar Abdullah implicated the PDP for the outrage, going to the extent of giving a clean chit to the HUM. The PDP threatened to sue Omar if he did not apologise for the allegation.

It is a tribute to the common man in Jammu and Kashmir, and a well-deserved one, that he has the courage and gumption to stand by the democracy and attend the political rallies of his party, braving the terrorist's bullets and grenades for his beliefs.

It was necessary to paint a broad picture of Kashmir mid-2006 to understand the ground realities. And it is not a happy picture. The world, and Pakistan in particular, must understand that India cannot discuss Kashmir issue, the so-called 'core issue' for Pakistan, with a neighbour as the latter holds a gun to its head. It is equally important to understand that peace in the Valley must precede the success of Indo-Pak peace process. If Pakistan will use terrorism in Kashmir as a policy option to 'force' India to accept its stand on this issue, peace process is bound to take a knock. It is again important to understand that the peace process was predicated on Musharraf dismantling the terrorist infrastructure which exist in Pakistan and PoK. The composite dialogue, the Chief instrumentality of peace process, itself was predicated on Pakistan honouring its word given in the January 2004 Joint statement of Islamabad that he would not allow any anti-India terrorist outfits on its soil. With Pakistan defaulting on its pledge, peace process is bound to be derailed. Some more of the Mumbais and Malegaons, the peace process will stand buried, fathoms deep.

TERRORISM IN INDIA, JIHADI WARRIORS AND PAKISTANI ROLE

Pakistan was born in sin as for as India is concerned. Not only some extremist elements among the Indian Muslims broke it in 1947 and got a so-called homeland for themselves, they persisted in continuing scheming and plotting against India even after achieving their desideratum. A democracy, a republic and a secularism-practicing state on their borders was an anathema to the bigots. India was and remains a pet hatred for Pakistan from day one and there was never a let-up in their determined endeavour to undermine its integrity and so vereignty. In this unholy scheming, Pakistan never baulked from trying one conspiracy after another, including the use of subterfuge, half truths and force.

It started with 1947 aggression, and continued through 1965 testing of waters in Kachh, Gujarata and a fresh full-fledged war forced on India in Jammu and Kashmir in August/September, ending with fourth aggression in 1971 when it destroyed itself losing its Eastern half. One had reasons to believe that this fatal blow of consequences of the 1971 war would have chastened that nation—rather whatever was left of it. But that was futile hope. Pakistan mounted another aggressive mischief in Kargil, plotting to block the Jammu-Srinagar-Leh National Highway and strangulate the Indian forces in Ladakh confronting the Pakistani and Chinese troops. So anti-India strategy and visceral hatred are not only intact but even more potent and vengeful for one obvious evidence: Pakistan has not only not dismantled the anti-India terror infrastructure including camps but also not stopped cross-border terror attacks. In fact there is empirical evidence to show that Pakistan has upgraded the level of this low-cost aggression both in frequency and virulence.

Another important aspect of Pakistan's anti-India venture needs attention. It has always calculated that it would be in a position to enlist the support of Indian Muslims in its evil designs because of reasons of religious affinity if possible, and through persuasive Goebbelsesque propaganda, if necessary. It is a matter of history that Pakistan had planned 1947 and 1965 aggressions under the assumption that as soon as its soldiers entered/landed in Jammu and Kashmir, the local Muslims would rise as one man to welcome them and subsequently support their subversive operations in India. No such thing happened and to Pakistan's utter chagrin, the Muslims in Jammu and Kashmir, including the Valley, extended all necessary help to the Indian troops to defeat the enemy.

But things underwent a slight change in the last two decades or so. Pakistan succeeded in planting some operatives of the ISI and agents on Indian soil, in the first place. Secondly, and more unfortunately, its constant and rabid anti-India propaganda barrage on grounds of religion and jihadi extremism did affect a very small number of Indian Muslims—perhaps not more than a miniscule percentage. With the help of these converts to jihadi terrorism, Pakistan was able to create a number of terror modules and sleeper cells in some Indian states, whose active help has been enlisted by Pakistani intelligence agencies to stage violent jihadi incidents in India during the last couple of decades, seriously threatening its national security and sovereignty.

What follows is a detailed/critical examination of Islamist extremist role in terrorism inflicted on India during the last two decades or so—going no further back. It will unavoidably involve the discussion of role of Pakistan—the source of India's major terrorist troubles.

Islamisation of Terrorism in Mid-1990s

An Indian journalist saw the Islamisation of terror in a news story written for 15 May 1994 issue of a fortnightly, which is paraphrased here:

> The facts that establish the depth and dimensions of the foreign-inspired anti-Indian conspiracy—led, of course, by Pakistan—are not just in the secret files of Indian intelligence agencies. Unless dissuaded by international pressure, Pakistan's ISI is expected to orchestrate a host of pan-Islamic organizations into launching another aggressive mission from across the border.

Hundreds of veterans of Afghan War, of different nationalities, are waiting to pour into the valley. In the rest of the country, communally-sensitive areas are being targeted by the ISI for triggering of riots. The proxy war is now entering the home stretch. It started in 1987, phase I when the first batches of JKLF volunteers were trained at four abandoned Afghan camps and sent to India. Phase II began in 1989 when systematic Islamisation of the military with the induction of graduates from the 500-odd *madrasas* run by *Jamaat*. They promote the fundamentalist and pro-Pakistan Hizbul Mujahideen. Phase III was the internationalization of the Kashmir issue. Phase IV, extending a religiously motivated militancy among the Muslim population in the rest of India, has begun now (Apr 1994).

The Pakistani game plan has a steel-edged logic:

- Escale trouble in Kashmir and force Indians to hit back hard.
- Convince the Islamic world that a Hindu government is persecuting a Muslim population.
- Simultaneously exploit the insecurities and anger among the Indian Muslims by creating communal incidents.

  Apply the same Kashmir 'formula' elsewhere whenever the state machinery hits back.

The above story written in 1994 was revisited by its author in the same magazine's 18 Dec. 2006 issue. Adding some "Behind the scene" material to this story, the author says "Osama bin Laden was a mostly unknown Arab in exile in Sudan or there abouts in 1992-94 when this investigation, which mentioned him for the first time in Indian Media, was carried". In his reporting career no other story matched this one in its geographical spread or in the complexities and dangers involved. "Our own security agencies had only now started seeing some evidence of the pan-Islamisation of terrorism which, until now, was considered indigenous to Kashmir. Its wider link to the 'university of jihar' on the Pakistan-Afghanistan border was still unclear." The story took the authors to Kabul, Peshawar, Karachi, Washington, London and Moscow. "Finally we had the leads that tightly into a picture that surprised even our own security establishment which still saw Kashmir insurgency as mostly indigenous.

The author[14] of that important 1994 news story thus ends up his reminiscences: "My favourite memory of that story is a meeting with former ISI Brigadier, Mohd Yousuf (author of *Bear*

Trap) at his Karachi house ... and he even mentioned his golden handshake: 5000 acres of land in Sindh. 'No big deal', he said, 'much of its is not irrigated'. I reeled with shock and surprise."

This anecdote, directly related to a mere Brigadier serving the ISI, is indicative of the power and influence wielded by this intelligence agency—the chief organizer and sponsor of anti-India terrorism—in the Pakistani military and polity.

Indian Muslims Unaffected by Extremism: Was it a Myth?

Following the terrorist strikes of 9/11, American scholar Richard Hass, who quit the Bush Administration primarily because of his opposition to any invasion of Iraq, warned against stereotyping Muslims worldwide, as being sympathetic to terrorism. He noted India could be proud of the fact that none of its Muslim citizens responded to Osama's call for an international Jihad against the "Jews and crusaders" He asserted that a pluralist democracy was the best anti-dote against terrorism. Indians rightly felt proud of their fellow Muslim citizens.

Smug with this thought, many ignored a series of events in India that should have rung alarm bells in the minds of the cognescenti: a chain of terrorist attacks in urban centre like Delhi, Ayodhya, Mumbai, Malegaon, Bangalore and Hyderabad in which the motivators may have been sitting across the borders but the perpetrators were Indian nationals.[34] Obviously, some Indian Muslims indeed were being converted by the jihadi propaganda.

Most Indians were rudely shaken out of this comfort when highly qualified Indian nationals hailing from the IT city of Bangalore were found involved in acts of terrorism and suicide bombing in London and Glasgow in early July 2007, and consequent arrest of Indian nationals in the UK and Australia. Such happenings could no longer be brushed under the carpet for considerations of "political correctness." Whatever possessed that well-qualified and well-to-do Indians to indulge in such murderous crimes that brought disgrace to India and created circumstances that are going to be severely damaging for Indians seeking employment and residence abroad? Are n't Indians now going to be subjected to the same humiliations and suspicions that visitors from Pakistan face at immigration counters and among local communities abroad?

Most analysts assert that there is no justification to kill innocent people, and any attempt to justify terrorism is direct encouragement to the crime. Even then, there are apologists who keep doing it day in and day out. If apologists attribute 1993 Mumbai bomb blasts to the destruction of the Babri Masjid in Dec 1992 and the consequent rage among sections of Muslims due to it and likewise some recent acts of terror in India can be attributed to the communal killings in Gujarat, but what motivated Kafeel Ahmed to blow himself up in Glasgow when the British had not done him or his countrymen any harm? Is it justifiable for an Indian nationals to disgrace his country (and his community) merely because he feels strongly about American and British actions in Iraq and elsewhere. That way, some Indians can take it upon themselves to avenge the perceived wrongs of the Indo-US civil nuclear deal by killing their fellow Indians.

Yet agains, how will the apologists justify the continued acts of terrorist violence—the latest being Hyderabad-II of 25 Aug 2007?

Original sin was committed as far as present-day terrorism is concerned by the Reagan Administration in 1981 deciding to threat the opposition to the Soviet occupation of Afghanistan as a jihad. The organizations opposing the Soviet occupation were ideologically motivated and funded by Saudi Arabia. Wahhabi Islam, consequently gained a toehold in the Sub-Continent. The Saudis sought an obliging Gen Zia-ul-Haq to nurture and strengthen the influence of Wahhabi organizations in Pakistan.

Saudi Arabia was one of the only three countries in the world that recognized the Taliban regime in Afghanistan. But Saudi Arabia soon became the target of its own erstwhile protégés-Osama and the Taliban, who objected to the presence of American forces in the desert Kingdom. Further, by 1993, Wahhabi-oriented groups were used by the ISI for its jihad in Jammu and Kashmir.

When an Indian commentator G Parthasasathy an IFS-Retd officer and a former Ambassador to Pakistan—proudly asserted that Indian Muslims strongly opposed Pakistan's jihad in Kashmir, the Pakistani interest in undermining communal harmony in Indian was made known to him forcefully through a strong riposte from a former DG, ISI: "Your will see. We will soon make the Kashmir issue an issue of faith amongst your Muslims."

There is evidence galore that in the recent years assiduous efforts have been made by Pakistan to radicalize Indian Muslims in Saudi Arabia and UAE by attempting to poison their minds about alleged injustices that Muslims faced from people practicing other faith across the world. The Lashkar-e-Tayyaba, which has played a prominent role in the endeavour, openly proclaims that "Hindus, Jews and Christains are enemies of Islam." It is well-established that Wahhabi-oriented groups now spreading their wings in India like the SIMI, the Jamat-e-Islami, the Tableeghi Jamat, and the Jamat Ahle Hadise draw their ideological inspiration from Whahhabi groups of Saudi Arabia.

It, of course, would be wrong to assume that there is a unified, world wide, or monolithic Islamic ideology. The Shia-Sunni cleavage (rather enmity) is as old Islam itself and is evident presently not only from development in Iraq, but also from the Iranian-Arab divide. Interestingly, "the Al-Qaeda works against the Shia Hezbollah by strengthening its Sunni rivals in Lebanon and has been noticeably silent of American pressures to force Iran to end its nuclear enrichment programe."

In view of the facts mentioned above, and to keep a cautious eye on the anti-India exertions by some Islamist formations to entice Indian Muslims into their fold, New Delhi must strengthen its intelligence surveillance in Gulf countries like Saudi Arabia and the UAE. For similar reasons, India must keep a watch on infiltration from Bangladesh and Nepal by members/ activists determined to build local assets to carry forward their agenda of disturbing communal harmony in India.

While the external challenge can be suitably addressed, it is the internal challenge posed by the London and Glasgow events that require careful and sensitive handling. Sadly, the approach to promoting communal harmony has become an issue of political football and vote-bank politics in India.

The jihadi terrorism the world over has an intra-Islam dynamic: ideological clash between the extremist, fundamentalist and moderate Muslims. A major anti-terrorist victory will be achieved only if the moderate Ummah unitedly prevail on the extremist fringe to give up violence and adopt peaceful means as prescribed by the Quaran. It will, of course, be a long drawn battle.

As an immediate first step it is imperative that political parties across the country should unite in getting together with leaders of the Muslim community, to agree on measures that community leaders should take to ensure that pernicious Wahhabi indoctrination does not lead to misguided youth turning to violence. This should be the soul subject for a serious discussion in a special meeting of the National integration council, suggests a diplomat. Secondly, the intelligence surveillance on the disruptive outfits named above should be enhanced. If credible evidence surfaces, such organisation should be banned.

Investigations into terrorist attacks should not be hampered by political interference.

Is Congress Politics Hampering Anti-terrorism Battle?

It has been discussed earlier, al be it in brief, that certain political parties, the Congress included, are practicing vote-bank politics to get the Muslim votes in the hustings. A critical look on this aspect and related issues is called for as it inolves the national security issues.

Prime Minister Manmohan Singh's anguish and loss of sleep over the arrest of some Indian Muslims for suspected Al-Qaeda links are not difficult to understand by any proud Indian. Similarly, the latter would understand his statement that, being a Sikh, he particularly understands the implications of community being tarred with the charge of terrorism. The Prime Minister was roundly criticised for saying he "could not sleep the night after seeing the photograph of a...," because as his critics said, he never lost a night's sleep over the plight of the victims of terrorist attacks, nor the families of the soldiers and policemen who fell fighting the murderous terrorists whether in Kashmir, or in Akshardham or in Parliament attacks, nor for that matter for the miserable Kashmiri Pandits who have been rendered homeless refugees in their own country What is unfortunate is his selective sympathy for victims of terrorism. Unfortunately, with such an approach, he lets himself open to the charge of practicing vote-bank politics.

But where it hurts every Indian, whatever his religion, is that it—the above-noted arrest of Indian Muslims—dents the one claim we have been so proud of since 9/11: When so many Muslims have been caught or identified the world over for links with pan-Islamic terrorism, not a single one was from India, when its Muslims count some 15 crore. This significant phenomenon has been analysed in great detail and generally credited variously to Indian democracy and secularism as also to the unique fact of Indianism, where national, ethnics, regional and linguistic identities often transcend or mask those of religion. "Just a few arrests here or there, and that too in an isolated case now, says this senior journalist, do not change the picture." But these raise some other questions that even the Prime Minister needs to answer, and also must ask his government and its allies.

While profiling of any community is bad, it should equally be imprudent to profile one for being a permanent victim. In the business of democratic secular and one-law-for-all system of governance, all citizens and communities must be equal and innocent unless proven otherwise. Or, to put it even more, simply: Just because you cannot simply presume a person to be a terrorist because he belongs to a particular community, you cannot presume a suspect to be innocent just because he happens to come from 'a' particular community. The question that the Prime Minister needs to ask/answer is: Has his government—and, even more precisely, the political formulation that keep it in power—been true to this test?[16]

It is indeed a cruel question to ask of a government which has a record of complete, total failure in cracking any of the major terrorist attacks that have taken place on its watch in three full years. Not in one single case—including the most significant and horrendous one of the 2006 serial Mumbai train bombings—has this UPA Government been able to catch any suspects and charge them. Even by the usually dismal standards of Indian policing, this record indeed is remarkable. Terror attacks in Malegaon, Jama Masjid in Delhi, Mecca Masjid in

Hyderabad, Ayodhya, Samjhauta Express, Sankat Mochan Mandir in Varanasi, the Indian Institute of Science, Bangalore, Sarojini Nagar in New Delhi have all gone fully unresolved. And these were no minor attacks, which have claimed nearly 300 lives in what is generally considered a phase of India-Pakistan thaw.

The UPA has often accused its predecessor, the NDA, of communalizing the phenomenon of terrorism, of tarring one community and victimizing a citizens belonging to it. But has the UPA itself not been guilty of the same charge, but in reverse? Has it served itself, and India, well by communalizing the very approach to fight terrorism? Ask the police forces in Karnataka, Maharashtra and Hyderabad, the counter-terror veterans in intelligence agencies and even the army, and the answer will stare you in the face. After the attacks they faced in the first flush of the Mumbai rail attacks for 'targeting' Muslims and the hurry in which they were forced to call off the searches and interrogations have put the fear of God in the minds of security men. They do not understand the politics of fighting terrorism in such a situations. And, not surprisingly, they think it is better to play safe, do the minimum to avoid making any political mistakes, and go for the next posting/promotion. In the given situation, taking risks is no wisdom.

This reverse-communalization of the fight against terror and the responsibility for this lies not so much the security machinery, or the Union Home Ministry which controls it, as it does with this peculiar minorityist politics Congress has been playing for long, and has assumed sinister shape under the influence of the communists who are supporting the UPA from outside, that is, wielding power without accountability and/or responsibility. So the Prime Minister must be asked this question: if it is wrong and unfair to profile any community as terrorist, must you always consider a suspect innocent just because he belongs to 'a' community, and if so, is the motive just fair, constitutional secularism, or a misplaced quest for vote banks?

Senior Congress ministers are both embarrassed and concerned, realizing fully that they have allowed their allies, particularly the Left, to 'secularise' the agenda of governance so aggressively that it has now become communalism in reverse and both the Congress and India will be made to pay for it. Nobody today even claims that any of these attacks were the handiwork of anybody but ultra-Islamic groups, howsoever small and miniscule. And ultimate result? A few more such attacks, God forbid, a soft, this kind of politically loaded approach towards them, along with issues like Afzal's hanging, will be seen to be a repeat of the old "biryani for terrorist" story.

Needless to say, the Congress is going to be the sufferer. As popular insecurity grows, with unresolved terror attacks and increasing Naxal mayhem, the mainstream (as different from the majority community) Indian voter will blame the Congress party. But so stifling is the compulsion to sustain this government for two more years, come what may, and so compelling the nostalgia for Muslim votes, that nobody is willing to question this at the party's top forum. No wonder, as a result of this obsession to remain in power for the next two years, the Left is dictating terms to the Congress—and often humiliating it. The best example of it is the presidential election where the Left rejected on flimsy grounds one leader, Home Minister Patil he is close to Satya Sai Baba—after another, Karan Singh, as he heads Viraat Hindu Samaj. And Congress pocketed all this humiliation.

The Congress-led UPA has to choose between retaining the power for two more years or fighting terrorism effectively. It is unable to go after the terror suspects because of fear of public threats and demonstrations by influential Muslim outfits and their leaders. The country will be the ultimate suffer because of this namby pamby policy on fighting terrorism.

Pakistan's Long Arm of Terror and 'Invisible' Hand

(Brief History of Lashker)

Pakistan fomenting and sustaining terrorism in India has earlier been discussed. Now some additional information on specific cases and terrorist outfits.

Even as Pakistan's armed forces massed the formations that would spearhead the Kargil war, the Lashkar-e-Toyyaba's over all military commander, Zaki-ur-Rahman Lakhvi, proclaimed the opening of a second front against India: "To set up Mujahideen networks across India is our one target. We are preparing the Muslims of India, and when they are ready, it will be the start of the disintegration of India." Lakhvi was talking (to *The Nation*—of Pakistan) on 9 Apr 1999.

Seven years after the Lakhvi delivered this open threat, India was finally waking up to its seriousness with the 11 July 2006 Mumbai serial bombings. While mass of evidence emerged on the Laskhar's role in this bombing, Indian investigators continue to search for clear answers to the two most important questions:

1. What exact strategic purpose was this bombing intended to serve?
2. Is the regime of President Musharraf an enemy of the Lashkar's jihad—or, in fact, its author?

When India's Foreign Secretary Shivshankar Menon met his Pakistani counterpart Riaz Mohd Khan in Nov 2006, the two finalized the shape and constitution of Joint Anti-Terrorism Mechanism. In the first meeting of this Mechanism in early 2007, India's covert services, in an effort to find answers to these two questions, sought information on the "stocky, middle-aged Bahawalpur resident, Cheema who was believed to be the most important custodian of the secrets of the Lashkar's jihad in India."[17]

Mohd. Azam Cheema has long been called "Baba" by his students and among them are the men who bombed Mumbai in July 2006. Born to a lower-middle class Punjabi family in 1953, Cheema went on to teach Islamic religious studies at the Government Municipal Degree College in Faislabad. During his stint there, Cheema came into contact with a circle of theologians at the Department of Islamiat in Lahore's Engineering University.

What were these theologians/scholars engaged in at that time? Hafiz Mohd Saeed, Hafiz Abdul Rehman Makki, and other scholars linked to the ultra-conservative Jamaat Ahl-e-Hadis sect were busy setting up what was then called the Markaz Dawa Wal' Irsha. Sited on a 160-acre campus near Lahore (at Muridke) donated by Gen Mohd Zia-ul-Haq, the Markaz was a platform to draw recruits for the anti-Communist jihad in Afghanistan. Aided by generous contributions from the ISI, the

CIA, and Osama bin Laden's close aide Abdullah Azam, the Markaz soon set up the foundation of its new armed wing—the Lashkar-e-Tayyaba.

After 1989, and the Islamist triumph in Afghanistan, the Lashkar's energies and gaze turned eastwards. The Lashkar's strategic goal, the scholar Yoginder Sikand has observed, was "to extend Muslim control over what is seen as having once been Muslim land, and, hence, to be brought back under Muslim domination." It must be given to the Lashkar that from the very outset, its objectives were clear.

By 1993, the Lashkar had put in place the requisite infrastructure to realize its ideological goals it had deliberated upon for long. Even as it carried out its first major military operations in Jammu and Kashmir, the terrorist group demonstrated its desire to act on a larger stage. To wit, on the first anniversary of the demolition of the Babri Masjid, Lashkar operatives Jalees Asnari, Azam Ghauri, and Abdul Karim 'Tunda' carried out a series of bombings across north and west India.

Working under the command of Lakhvi, Cheema is believed to have been assigned charge of enhancing the capabilities of these networks. His efforts, however, came to little. In July 1998, the Delhi police arrested Abdul Sattar, a resident of Pakistan's Faislabad district who had set up a covert terror cell in the town of Khurja. A year later, the Jammu and Kashmir police broke up a Mumbai-centred cell run by another Pakistani, Amir Khan. Also arrested was Mohd Ishtiaq, the son of a shop-keeper from Kala Gujran in Pakistan's Jhelum district who had risen to become one of the Lashkhar's top operatives.

Despite its grand polemic, then, the Lashkar's jihad came to little. After 1999, the outfit came under intense pressure. The newly formed Jaish-e-Mohammad, whose leader was released on the last day of 1999 in exchange of the passengers of the Indian Airline's hijacked Kathmandu-New Delhi flight, and with which Lashkar had to compete for both cadres and resources, won applause among Islamists with a series of increasingly spectacular strikes, culminating in the 13 Dec 2001 attack on Parliament House. In sum, Cheema had expended the enormous assets at the Lashkar's command, and failed—having little to show for all that . Pakistan was forced to proscribe the

Lashkar-e-Tayyaba in the wake of the Indo-Pak military crisis of 2001-2002. But for the outfit, it was not the end of the road. Its patrons in the ISI ensured that the outfit's assets and infrastructure were left untouched. More importantly, the ban did not apply to the PoK. Given these two factors, the Lashkar was up and running again within six months of the ban. All it had to do was to rename the Markaz as Jamaat-ud-Dawa, which was obviously advertised as an organization for charity and proselytisation, but had no problems whatsoever in continuing raising funds for the Lashkar as heretofore.

It is learnt from the interrogation records of Abdullah Mujahid, a terrorist arrested from Afghanistan in July 2003 and presently held in Guantanamo Bay, that the Lashkar reached out to its friends in Al-Qaeda for help. At a Feb 2003 meeting in the Lashkar's Muridke Headquarters, Mujahid was appointed chief of operations against India. But he was arrested in Afghanistan by the US before he could take up this new assignment (in India).

New names had to be searched for Lashkar's renewal—Mohd Muzammil—if that is indeed his real name—and Abu Alqama, who is still known only by his chosen alias, were selected to lead the new phase of jihad as promised, but not fulfilled by Cheema. Both were the battle-hardened veterans of the jihad in Jammu and Kashmir.

So, Muzammil and Alqama had, unlike Cheema, seen real fighting in Jammu and Kashmir. More important, they had demonstrated their ability to work in an environment where the Lashkar had no overground network or mass support—the real problem that had confronted Cheema, and led to the failure of his mission. In Pakistan, the Lashkar had drawn on the resources of the Jamaat Ahl-e-Hadis cherical order. But while the Jamaat's presence in Jammu and Kashmir date back to at least 1923, the ultra-conservative organization had few followers. Its assaults on traditional religious practices even provoked a hostile backlash. "Several Ahl-e-Hadis activists were physically attacked," Sikand has recorded, "a social boycott was instituted against them; they were turned out of their localities, and, being branded as apostates, they were refused entry into the mosques."

Overcoming this considerable handicap, or may be in spite of it, the duo of the new leaders succeeded in leveraging the

Lashkar's military resources in Jammu and Kashmir to consolidate and accelerate its pan-India jihad. In Sep 2002, Muzammil supervised the storming of the Akshardham Temple in Gandhinagar. Among his best-known ambitious operations was a June 2004 plot to assassinate Union Home Minister, LK Advani. Investigations into the 2005 serial bombings in New Delhi demonstrated similar networks at work. Alqama tasked a Bandipora-based commander code-named Abu Huzaifa and his immediate subordinate, Abdul Rehman 'Mota' (=fat) to excute the strike. Tariq Ahmad Dar, a Srinagar-based pharmaceuticals salesman, was then charged with its physical execution.

Cheema has not been a total failure. It is now clear that he kept alive his SIMI-linked networks in India. Members of the Mumbai-cells, investigators have been able to establish, began to train in Bahawalpur from as early as 2001, slowly acquiring the multiple skills that were demonstrated in the July 2006 Mumbai bombings. For his part, Cheema built up bases in Bangladesh and Nepal, using them as launch pads for major actions in much the same fashion as Muzammil and Alqama had done from Jammu and Kashmir.

Back to the important questions. Were the 2006 Mumbai serial blasts Cheema's doing to show that he could do better than Muzamil and Alqama? And did the ISI initiate the enterprise or just turned a blind eye to it?

The answers can only come from the Joint Mechanism meetings. But if the first ever meeting under the Mechanism is any indication, it is a vain hope. As an analyst writes: "Unless this Mechanism succeeds in putting pressure on Pakistan, credible answers may never emerge. The probabilities are sadly." After all, a confidential research paper prepared by the UK's Defence Academy in mid-2006 asserted that "Pakistan (through the ISI) has been supporting terrorism and extremism—whether in London on 7/7 or in Afghanistan or Iraq."

Only Pakistan's covert services could help fill in the blanks—if they choose to do so. In mid-Oct 2006, Pakistan's Additional Advocate General, Mohd Hanif Khatana, failed to defend the continued detention of Lashkar Chief Saeed in the Lahore High Court. Khatana refused to present in open court the facts that led to Saeed's detention soon after the London Underground bombings, saying "it is not in the public interest." Saeed was released on 19 October, and promptly described India as "an eternal enemy of Pakistan." A simple question raises its head: "Was this (refusal to present the facts) a deliberate move by Pakistan's Government to engineer Saeed's release"?

In view of such acts of authorities, can India expect anything from the Joint Mechanism? Optimists can still suggest that India wait for its second meeting—at the very least. As for the realists, they were against this Mechanism, ob initio. The Pakistani Government may indulge in equivocation, even obfuscation, but its terrorist outfits have no doubts about the future course of action. The Sep 2006 issue of the Markaz magazine *Majallat al-Dawa* threatened to "butcher every Hindu." Should anyone take such hate-filled blood-curdling assertions/pronouncements dismissively? That will be foolhardiness. Some can already be heard saying: "They are already doing it in India through their selected operations/activists/murderous terrorists/puppets and also local sleeper cells composed of some misguided Indians."

It should not be forgotten that behind this "butcher every Hindu" hate polemic lie both demonstrated hostile intent and capabilities.

"Like audience of the Indonesian Wayang Kulit theatre, we have been following the story of the Lashkar jihad in India only through the shadows its puppets cast. Prime Minister Manmohan Singh in Oct 2006 called on Pakistan to "walk the talk on terror." So for, there are no indications of Pakistan doing so —the institution of Joint Mechanism notwithstanding.

Indian investigators will inevitably be frustrated while tracking the cross-border terrorism perpetrated on Indian soil. They known the several marionettes enacting the jihadi death dance orchestrated by several Pakistan-based terrorist outfits but the men who hold the string are out of their reach.

To conclude, by now it is clear that the boast of a former DG, ISI was not an empty rhetoric. Pakistan indeed has succeeded in making Jammu and Kashmir problem into an issue of faith, as far as good number of Valley Muslims are concerned. More than that, Pakistan in concert with international jihadi organizations has succeeded in radicalizing the Indian Muslims. Their number could range between .001 per cent and .01 per cent of 15 crore Muslims in India, which will translate into any figure between 1,500 and 15,000. Unless India, even at this stage, crafts an effective declaratory counter-terrorism policy, Pakistan could exploit these radicalized Indians to cause disintegration of India—a goal long cherished by many Pakistanis. In realizing this dream, the Muslim majority Assam districts bordering Bangladesh, will come handy to Pakistan. After all, as some claim, Ummah for an overage Muslim is more important than their country.

As for the Indian Muslims are concerned, their loyalty to country remain unshaken, barring the miniscule minority which seems to have been radicalized. Indians can still be proud of the fact that its Muslim population remains unaffected by the Al-Qaeda and Jihadist ideological extremism.

All said and done, India needs to be on guard against terrorism—a scourge afflicting the entire world from East to West and North to South, with nary any exception.

JOINT INDIA-PAKISTAN ANTI-TERROR MECHANISM

Indo-Pakistan Joint War on Terrorism: Joint Mechanism

The Manmohan Singh-Musharraf agreement in Havana in Sep 2006 has been subject of intense discussions. In fact, it has evoked more criticism than support in India. There are doubts, suspicions, occasional praise and some self-goals too by Indians. All of these are discussed here.

The Joint Statement Issued in Havana

Here is the text of the statement: "The two leaders met in the aftermath of the Mumbai bombings. They strongly condemned all acts of terrorism and agreed that terrorism is a scourge that needs to be effectively dealt with. They decided to put in place an India-Pakistan anti-terrorism institutional mechanism to identify and implement counter-terrorism initiatives and investigations."

Prime Minister Defends Joint Mechanism

Notwithstanding reports about the increasing activities of Pakistan's ISI in India, Dr. Manmohan Singh on 24 Oct. 2006 fiercely defended his decision to set up a joint mechanism with Islamabad to fight terrorism.

Describing it as a "trial and experiment", he said the two countries had to talk and explore all possible means of finding a peaceful solution to their mutual problems.

"Since we are not at war with Pakistan, we have to talk and explore all peaceful possibilities," he told reporters after the swearing-in ceremony at the Rashtrapati Bhavan.

The decision to set up the joint mechanism to fight terrorism has come in far sharp criticism both from the Opposition and the security establishment who believe this would prove to be a non-starter given Islamabad's role in encouraging cross-border terrorism.

The Prime Minister was also on backfoot regarding the controversy fuelled by his National Security Advisor (NSA) MK Narayanan's recent remarks that India did not have a "clinching evidence" about Pakistan's involvement in the Mumbai train bombings (of July 2006). Dr Singh said there was "credible evidence of Islamabad's hand in the Seven—Eleven attack case, but refused to comment on the contradictory statements emanating from the government on this issue.

After the embarrassing comment by the NSA, the Home Ministry let it be known that it has not merely clinching but "solid evidence" to nail Pakistan's ISI in the Mumbai train blasts case.

Backing the move for joint mechanism, External Affairs Minister Pranab Mukherjee said its success would depend upon the information "we get from Islamabad," and added India will share information with Pakistan about the Mumbai blasts and await its response.

Brickbats from Harsh Critics

No amount of ham-fisted spin-doctoring can take away from what is becoming a open secret: Prime Minister's laughable attempts at diplomacy. "The evidence is there in full public gaze. It has taken not even a fortnight for the contrived Havana bon homie with Pakistan to be overwhelmed by the slippery General's cigar smoke. Even if there are some missing links in the Mumbai Police Commissioner's assertion that the 11 July blasts were the handiwork of the Pakistan-based LET and local traitors, the implication of his charge that the whole massacre was conducted under the benign supervision of the ISI is grave." This comes from a critic on 8 Oct 2006.[18]

If the ISI stands indicted, its chief patron Gen Musharraf cannot be exculpated. It is obvious that the preliminary findings of the Mumbai police inquiry were available to the Prime Minister and his NSA when they arrived at the Non-aligned Movement summit. Even then, the analyst says, it is surprising that the Prime Minister chose to sign the joint mechanism agreement with a man he knew was the chief patron of terrorism. This seems to be inexplicable.

There simply is no basis for separating and delinking President Musharraf from the ISI. Responding to the growing disquiet in the West over the ISI's complicity in the Taliban's resurgence in the eastern provinces of Afghannistan too (which are incidentally contiguous to Pakistan), Musharraf defended his so-called state within-a-state aggressively. He told BBC's *News night* that the ISI was a disciplined force. When it was pointed out that a leaked Ministry of Defence (MOD) reported advocated that a future civilian Government should send the Army to the barracks and disband the ISI, Musharraf retorted angrily that the MOD should disband itself first.

Big refusing to perpetuate the fiction that the ISI is somehow an autonomous cabal, Musharraf was, somewhat uncharacteristically, not being economical with the truth. However, by choosing to point Pakistan as a co-victim of terrorism, the Prime Minister and his Foreign Secretary have compromised India's diplomatic offensive against terrorism. The logic of Havana agreement was rather queer: The terrorist and his victim must conduct joint whodunit.

And why blame Pakistan's Foreign Ministry for dismissing the Mumbai investigations as preposterous. If Pakistan is the victim of terrorism, how can it be accused of masterminding terror? This agreement has dug India into a foxhole.

Another harsh critic of Gen Musharraf is the famed KPS Gill. What he says on 28 Oct., 2006 about the General is paraphrased below:

1. It is truly astonishing that a man who has lied so often and so obviously on the subject, should still be

constantly sought out for his opinion and assessment on the course of terrorism in Sough Asian region and, in fact, the world.

2. It is incomprehensible that the world leaders still tolerate, acquiesce in, and even encourage this man's continuous mendacity, his baseless boasting and his incessant and false posturing.
3. Gen Musharraf must be one of the few dictators in the world who has made such an utter mess of his country, and of regions well beyond, during his tenure, and still gets such an excellent Press globally, and constant support and praise from leaders of the free world in public.
4. In return, Musharraf harangues and threatens the very leaders and nations that support him and his perverse regime and its monstruous intelligence wing, the ISI, claiming that the West would be 'brought to its knees' by terrorism, if Pakistan and ISI did not support the 'Global War on Terror'.
5. Gen Musharraf is, in fact, the most effective agency of Pakistan's propaganda machine, and his relentlessly propagated fabrications and half-truths, largely or entirely unrelated to the situation on the ground, and that prey on public, western—and particularly—American ignorance.
6. The sheer brazenness of these fabrications, and Pakistan propagandists' strategy of the offence being the best form of defence, is illustrated by Gen Musharraf's recent riposte to Indian allegations of Pakistan's role in terrorism: "There are 21 such places in India where violence continues. The situation in Assam is also visible. So New Delhi must first correct its own matters and then talk to Pakistan.

Then KPS Gill gives reasons for this brazenness, which is directly related to India's failure to expose Pakistani propaganda, and to adequately demonstrate to the world Pakistan's continuing role as source of Islamist terrorism in India and internationally, and support to terrorist groups across India's North-East. This is despite the immense volume of hard evidence that is available in terms of arrested cadres from Pakistan and their narratives of Pakistani military and intelligence involvement in their recruitment, training, arming and deployment; the thousands of clearly identifiable weapons and tonnes of RDX, detonators, communication equipment and other materials, overwhelming proportion of which could be traced back to Pakistan with sufficient forensic attention and international cooperation.

In effect, India is part of the conspiracy of silence and appeasement that has allowed Pakistani deniability and falsification to flourish. Through the current "peace process and the charade of the "joint mechanism" for counter-terrorism, India continues to provide international legitimacy to a terrorist state and Gen Musharraf's criminal regime.

These are the circumstances—our ignorance, our indifference, our pusillanimity, our inability to understand and neutralize the strategic intent of Pakistan's propaganda and terrorist machinery—that creates the enveloping ambience which allows Pakistan to remain the principal breeding ground of Islamist terrorism in India/South Asia. India's security forces are constantly upon to make sacrifices for the defence of the country against the Pakistan-backed terrorism; and thousands of security personnel and even larger number of innocent civilians have lost their lives in Pakistan's covert war against India. To continue to give Pakistan and its leadership the latitude it currently enjoys is nothing less than criminal complicity in this enterprise of terrorism. India's political leadership and the higher echelons of its policy establishment are squarely guilty of this complicity.

There can be no bigger condemnation of India's innocent hope of securing Pakistan's cooperation than this assertion of its complicity in Pakistan's anti-India games.

Pakistan's Double Standards

It is instructive to study the attitude of successive Pakistani leaderships—military or political—to the question of counter-terrorism cooperation with other countries. This can be discussed under two heads:

1. Counter-terrorism cooperation with countries other than India.

2. Counter-terrorism cooperation with India.

Pakistan has generally cooperated with other countries, provided such cooperation was perceived by its leadership to be in its national interest. This cooperation has been in the following forms—arresting and handing over to other countries terrorist suspects wanted by them for investigation and allowing foreign investigating officers to interrogate suspects held in Pakistan custody. Such cooperation has been extended irrespective of the religion of the suspects, and irrespective of the fact whether there was an extradition treaty with the country seeking custody of a suspect. In fact, the Pakistani authorities generally follow the practice of informally handing over a suspect to a foreign country without showing his arrest on paper because if he is shown on record as arrested, the Pakistani judiciary comes into the picture and its order had to be obtained before handing him over.[19]

Some examples of such informal handing over are cited here:

1. Ramzi Yousef, wanted by the US in connection with the New York world Trade Centre explosion of 1993.
2. Abu Zubaidah, Ramzi Binalshib, Khalid Sheikh Mohd, Abu Faraj al-Libi and others associated with al-Qaeda
3. The brother of Hambali, the leader of the Jemmah Islamiya (JI), wanted by the Indonesian authorities.

Some examples of foreign investigating officers being allowed to question suspects in Pakistani custody are of Pakistani nuclear scientists Sultan Bashiruddin and Abdul Majid, suspected of contacts with Osama bin Laden.

However, there are two categories of cases where the Pakistan Government has refused to cooperate or avoided to cooperate with even other countries. The first category relates to cases where Pakistani authorities fear that cooperation with other countries might result in self-incrimination, that is, the Pakistani state incriminating itself in wrong-doings. The examples would be its refusal or reluctance to hand over Omar Sheikh, involved in the murder of Daniel Pearl, to the US. AQ Khan, the so-called father of the Pakistani atomic bomb, to the International Atomic Energy Agency (IAEA) in Vienna and Rashid Rauf, arrested in August (2006) in connection with the plot to blow up US-bound planes, to the UK.

Its reluctance to hand over Omar Sheikh is due to the fact that he was reported to have told Pakistani police during his interrogation that during a visit to Kandahar before Nine-Eleven he had come to know of al-Qaeda's plans for the Nine-Eleven terrorist strikes in the US and had passed on the information to Lt Gen Ehsan-ul-Haq, the then Pakistani Corps Commander in Peshawar. The Pakistani authorities are afraid that if he is handed over to the US and repeats this statement to that nation's interrogator, this could implicate the state of Pakistan in the Nine-Eleven terrorist strikes by raising questions as to why the information alleged given by Omar Sheikh was not immediately passed on to the US.

Its reluctance to hand over AQ Khan is due to fear that he might tell his foreign interrogators that the political and military leadership was aware of whatever he did and he had their approval. Fear of public demonstrations in Pakistan, where AQ Khan is a national hero, is another factor behind Pakistan's reluctance.

The reluctance to hand over Rashid Rauf was due to his association with the Jaish-e-Mohammed (JEM), whose Amir Maulana Masood Azhar is related to him by marriage, and his three-year stay in Bahawalpur where part of the training infrastructure of the JEM and the Lashkar-e-Tayyaba (LET) is located and where according to Mumbai police, some of the perpetrators of the 11 July Mumbai bombings were trained. The Pakistani authorities worry that he might tell the British about the activities of the JEM and LET directed against India.

The second category relates to cases where Pakistan perceives that is would not be in its strategic interest to cooperate. The most important example of this is its non-cooperation with the Hamid Karzai Government in Afghanistan in the arrest and handing over of the Pakistan-based leaders of the neo-Taliban. Pakistan vehemently denies their presence in its territory.

In the case of India, Pakistan's cooperation has been limited to handing over non-Muslim suspects; Muslim suspects—both Indian and Pakistani—found safe haven in that country. Even in case of non-Muslim suspects, there has been only one instance of cooperation where Pakistan, after having informed the Indian authorities, pushed across the border four Sikh deserters from the Indian Army, who wanted to join the so-called Khalistan movement.

In fact, Pakistani leaders, including Musharraf, have made public declarations: Even if we get a fool proof evidence against a Pakistani citizen, we would not hand him over to India! He will be tried in Pakistan and dealt with under Pakistani laws. No Pakistani leader can afford to be seen 'bowing' before India under what soever circumstances. It is a settled policy. India may keep sending any list of 'wanted persons', like the one sent earlier with twenty names on it, the answer will be unrelenting, "They are not on Pakistani soil. Please knock at some other door."

Self-Goal by MK Narayanan, the NSA

In an interview to a news channel on 22 Oct., 2006—a month after the Manmohan-Musharraf accord at Havana—the National Security Advisor answered some of the questions which had been raised by sceptics regarding the feasibility of the idea of an India-Pakistan joint anti-terrorism mechanism.

Whether he succeeded in answering the doubts and suspicions of the doubters/cities/sceptics is debatable, but his scoring a self-goal against India is beyond any doubt. He famously—rather infamously pronounced that India does not have a 'clinching' evidence about Pakistan's involvement in 11 July Mumbai train bombings. This flew right in the face of Mumbai police's claim to the contrary. Not only the Union Home Ministry but even the Prime Minister had to contradict the NSA publicly on the issue, without, of course, naming him—as has been detailed earlier in this section itself. Politicians are known to suffer from this foot-in-the-mouth syndrome, it is incredible that a nation's chief security advisor could ride so brazenly rough shod over his nation's national interest.

As for the joint anti-terrorism mechanism, it has not shown any promise of achieving its aims, even months after the first India-Pakistan confabulations were held under it in March, 2007 at Islamabad. Given Pakistan polity's track record so far, it may not be realistic to expect any results from this mechanism.

Of course, this accord has a limited value. Like the 'peace process', it is one more avenue for two countries to negotiate, sitting across a table. It definitely makes Western powers—especially the US and UK—happy. As cynics would suggest, it is better that the two 'hostile' neighbours fight their battles across the negotiations table than across a battle field which they have done so often in the past.

Too Many People Doubtful, Some Even Cynical: Joint Mechanism

Looking at the history of relations between India and Pakistan during the past 60 years, it is not easy to be optimistic about any new peace initiative between them. In fact, not one accord or agreement has brought them closer. In fact, it should be no surprise if some people even display signs of cynicism over the latest move at harmony and improving mutual understanding between the two nations. One analyst says: "Thaw and freeze work so seamlessly between the sub-continent's big two that it is t-ough not to be a shade cynical about news of a fresh breakthrough in Havana. Such bonhomie and making of common cause at the top leadership level is not unprecedented."[20]

After all, any number of political agreements and truces have been signed since January1949 agreement that established ceasefire between the two nations after the first war between them over Kashmir. Pakistan's fixation with Kashmir has been the stumbling block, India feels. But the peace process over the last three years seems to be making some headways, with some people-to-people CBMs institutionalized under it working well. But this can be an exception to the rule. India-Pakistan relations are generally marked by tensions.

As for these occasional accords signed by the top leaderships of the two countries, what has happened more often, unfortunately, is the rapid dissipation of concord once leaders have departed from summits, and the resumption of discord. The difference this time, it is claimed by some authoritative sources, is that two countries will be on the same team against the terror anywhere in the sub-continent; and for that purpose, they decided to establish a "Joint Anti-Terrorism Mechanism." This, obviously, is some achievement, knowing that India has been a victim of cross-border terrorism sponsored and supported by Pakistan's ISI for decades. That its chief tormentor of long years will be India's ally to fight terrorism jointly might beat one's imagination, and round too good to be true, but is probably the right ring to things. Just consider the possibilities:

- Pakistan extraditing Dawood Ibrahim, red-flagged internationally as a terrorist.
- Will Islamabad arrest the likes of Maulana Masood Azhar and Syed Salahuddin for their covert and overt support to violent acts of terrorism on Indian soil?
- Will it now take a fresh look at the most-wanted list presented to Gen Musharraf by the NDA government which Pakistan has never really responded to with any credibility?

Answers to the three propositions mentioned above will be emphatic 'no', if the past is any guide. The reasons are only too many, ranging from unresolved attrition over Kashmir, which has driven Pakistan to several military and guerrilla misadventures, to Islamabad establishment's proven inability—admitted public by no less a person than Gen Musharraf himself—to control religious extremists and ideological fanatics that work within and outside the State.

The Kargil intrusion-aggression will be a more accurate description of this bold military adventure—happened mostly unknown to Prime Minister Nawaz Sharif, if are to exclusively go by his version. If Gen Musharraf as Army chief could hoodwink his Prime Minister, is he getting paid back (hoodwinked) in the same coins by his own subordinates ? It is believed in some circles that ISI's collusion with Taliban in Afghanistan and its continued support to anti-India terrorist outfits like the LET, JEM and even JUJI(B) is in direct defiance of Musharraf's orders. In a manure of speaking, the ISI and terrorist outfits like LET, JEM and HM are mocking the General's vision of creating a modern State (of Pakistan modelled on the lines of Kemal Ataturk's Turkey.

But this picture of a helpless Musharraf may be overdrawn by motivated journalists or critics impelled by their ideological inclinations. It is difficult to see Musharraf as a Nawaz Sharif of 2006! Until, of course, he wants to stick to power at any cost.

It is more likely that he is playing this game of 'apparent helplessness' to suit his political and personal agenda.

It suits him to appear a victim of helplessness, and under that garb, let his cronies do the things exactly the way he scripted them. It was this "helplessness act" that persuaded Manmohan Singh to dub Pakistan, an exporter of terrorism, a victim of it. He may be fighting terrorism as front-line ally of the USA, but by making the MMA, fundamentalist Muslim party, a member of his ruling coalition, he has given a fillip to extremism in Pakistan. The things are obviously not as they seem to a casual observer of scene in Pakistan. There may be, indeed are, layers and layers of obfuscation and duplicity. Some analysts go to the extent of doubting his claims of three assassination attempts against him? Nothing can be straight and uncomplicated as for as Gen Mussharraf is concerned.

Given the above, it is amusing to have some analysts writing: "Pakistan is not an easy plate to possess. It was probably a clever 'come hither' ploy to set Musharraf as a terror victim as a preface to set up the joint counter-mechanism." Has it he not escaped three assossination bids? Does n't he remain a target of forces ranged against the US-led war against terrorism? But then, can India expect help from Musharraf even if he genuinely wants to extend it?

The above is an interesting line: Musharraf genuinely keen to help India but unable to have his way against his own minions! A roaring line failing to discipline his progeny. This linc of logic deployed by some Indian journalists of a particular ideological bend is rather ingenous. It is well known to all those interested to know the facts that all the top positions in the Pakistani Army are held by generals personally picked by Musharraf. A hamstrung and helpless Musharraf against his own minion does not convince. It is time that analysts/ journalists, who purvey such ill-conceived frames, realize that Musharraf of, a consummate player of politics, is enacting a charade!

Most Indian commentariat remain sceptical about the prospects of thaw, trust and transparency becoming the essential descriptors of relations between India and Pakistan. Prime Minister Manmohan Singh perhaps put things in a perspective when he said matter-of-factly: "The new mechanism will be made or unmade by how Pakistan exhibits its determination to contain and fight off terrorism at home and on Indian soil."

Before finishing with this piece, it is rather important to state an apparent conundrum: who enticed, coaxed or tricked whom into this accord? Each side is claiming victory for pushing the other into this Joint Mechanism pact! At least, this is the impression created by the media of the two countries. It will certainly need some doing, and a lot of time, to sort this riddle out.

Indo-Pak Joint Anti-terrorism Mechanism: Naivety or Masterstroke

There has been news in the air about India making an agreement with Pakistan on jointly fighting terrorism. But the feasibility of the proposal was often greeted with scepticism, and even outright disbelief. How could India even think about such a pact when Pakistan was the source of much of terrorism on its soil? Was it optimism run amock? Or, there was some grand design up its sleeve? The analysts were unable to make up their minds, either way. There was passionate argument between the doubters and some believers ranged on the other side of the fence.

Then it happened at Havana where Prime Minister Manmohan Singh and President Musharraf had gone to attend the Non-Aligned conference in Sep., 2006.

Arguments Against the Agreement

Some journalists even discerned certain luke-warm attitude in Musharraf's postures immediately after the signing ceremony at Havana. One[40] of them needs quoting in extenso:

> As PM Manmohan Singh read out the joint statement committing India and Pakistan to a new joint mechanism to address various aspects of terrorism, beside him sat Pakistan President Gen Pervez Musharraf, wearing a stiff and formal smile. Later, when Indian journalists asked him if he was satisfied with his meeting with Manmohan, Musharraf put a finger to his lips, indicating he was to keep quiet-odd for a man who is usually garrulous, especially in such settings where he can indulge in grandslanding.
>
> But the media persisted. Finally, he opened his mouth. "Usually, I enjoy talking to the media but this time I have

decided not to say anything," he said, adding, "whatever needed to be said has been said in the joint statement." *Outlook* prompted him: "Are you going to call the beginning of this new chapter of India-Pakistan dialogue, 'Mohabbat zindabad?"

"Yes, Mohabbat Zindabad", he replied without much enthusiasm. Irritation was writ large on his face, as if he had been compelled to do something he did not want. This was surprising, considering that Pakistan had, in the past, offered to cooperate and jointly investigate acts of terrorism in India. Example: Blasts in Delhi on the eve of Diwali 2005.

Musharraf's reticence was just an aspect of the mystery surrounding the decision to establish a joint mechanism to deal with terrorism. On the flight back from Havana to New Delhi via Frankfurt, the PM, the NSA Narayanan and Foreign Secretary-designate Shiv Shankar Menon: Was Musharraf not duping India once again? With the real genie of terrorism in Pakistan being the ISI, how could it cooperate with RAW on terrorism? Was this joint mechanism practical? Would it work. The PM exuded confidence in his replies but even four days after his return to Delhi, reactions in the higher echelons of the government ranged from disbelief to cautious optimism. This largely stems from the fact that few in the governments on the either side know the precise contours of this mechanism. "These are early days. We do not know what each side promised the other behind closed doors", said a source. Excluding the PM, the NSA and FS-designate, everybody else, including the back channel, is currently out of the loop. Nor has the PM briefed his cabinet colleagues. This is expected to happen some time next week (after 1 Oct., 2006), and should hopefully unravel the mystery.

Partly, the prevailing confusion is due to the PM himself sounding tentative on the flight from Havana. He told the media on the flight, "I hope it works, but if it does not work, then also we have to deal with the consequences" Was it an expression of his lack of conviction in Musharraf fighting terrorism?

This reporter, besides being a journalist, seems to be equally well-versed with the art of reading body-language of Musharraf. Some may find this reporter displaying pre-conceived disposition towards Indo-Pak understanding on anti-terrorism mechanism.

But for sake of balance, the picture painted by him even if a little over drawn, should not be dismissed out of hand.

If Musharraf wanted to remain reticent about his reaction to the joint mechanism, Manmohan was tentative. These uncertainties are understandable as both countries are treading the untrodden fields, not sure of each other's intention. Given the unhappy history of their relations, it is an uphill task for India and Pakistan to build trust capital in their diplomatic interaction which is presently known for its deficite.

To start with, operative part of the Havana statement: "The two leaders met in the aftermath of the Mumbai blasts (July 2006). They strongly condemned all acts of terrorism and agreed that terrorism is a scourge that needs to be effectively dealt with. They decided to put in place an India-Pakistan anti-terrorism institutional mechanism to identify and implement counter-terrorism initiatives and investigations." (In Havana, some analysts felt, Musharraf was apparently stiff due to the Mumbai reference in the statement).

On board the aircraft the journalists learnt India had been trying to get the Pakistanis to agree to this (joint) mechanism for the past two years. The Prime Minister said on the plane: "The mechanism is yet to be worked out...It must be credible, and inspire confidence in both our countries." He was, obviously, cautious.

Ironically, it is Pakistan which has been publicly expressing its willingness to cooperate in investigation into bomb blasts in India. Besides 2005 Delhi blasts, Musharraf personally offered cooperation in July 2006 Mumbai blasts: "If Indian side has any concrete information, it should be shared with Pakistan instead of casting aspersions on it, even before the process of gathering evidence about the incident begins." A joint effort would compel India to measure it words, Pakistan presumes.

Senior official sources, however, stress the idea of a joint mechanism is India's, that is well-thought out, a result of exchange of several ideas between Manmohan and Musharraf through their emissaries. Menon is believed to have long been on the mechanism that could provide a platform on which Pakistan's bluff could be called.

Even if the counter-terrorism initiatives under this mechanism are yet to be worked out, some officials suggest there is no harm in sharing with Pakistan, for instance, the frequencies on which the militants communicate. Given this information, anybody can tune in and verify for themselves the terrorist chatter. A concerned official asked: "Why can't we furnish some explicit details about Pakistani infiltrators who are routinely killed in Kashmir? We can, even, produce some of these people and present them to the Pakistanis." After all, LET publications routinely provide the details of their cadre killed in Kashmir and the government had begun an exercise of matching the details of the dead Pakistanis with the printed details. Critics within the government are not so sure. They are against sharing operational intelligence with the very people who are controlling levers of terror. It is from the ISI-controlled ware-houses that explosives and weapons are supplied to infiltrators, who are entities that retired Pakistani Army personnel train. In the past, it was not a happy experience to share radio frequencies, infiltrator routes and militant camps with a third country, as these were passed on to Pakistan. Consequently, the frequencies used for conducting communications among terrorists were promptly changed, as were the infiltration routes and the camps.

These critics have a point: "Even if evidence on cross-border infiltration is furnished to Pakistan, they would have a rejoinder ready. 'We are trying our best but these fellows still manage to sneak across. Don't you have a fence now that is supposed to check them? How is it they are able to get past that and all the 7 lakh soldiers you have deployed in Kashmir?"

Intelligence officials are understandably against sharing intelligence with Pakistan, given their past experience. They cite the Kargil example. In May, 1999, RAW had taped telephonic conversations between Gen Musharraf, who was then visiting Beijing, and his Chief of the General Staff Lt. Gen Mohd Aziz in Pakistan. These topes nailed the Pakistani lie that its troops were not in the area. It was a telling point made by India, but Pakistanis, warned of the leak, quietly changed the frequencies on which the two generals were communicating—and which had yielded rich intelligence. India was the ultimate loser, as not a squeak came its way on these frequencies subsequently. An intelligence officer put it bluntly: "There is no sense in compromising your intelligence for the purpose of indulging in a process that will essentially be a dialogue of the deaf."

"It is question of intention," said another intelligence source familiar with the issue, "if its intentions are true, then there is no need for another body." Some nations with which India does not have a joint working group on terrorism have supplied practical and useful intelligence. "It is a question of political will; Pakistan's intention is clearly malafide", he persisted.

Critics are amazed at Menon describing Pakistan as a victim of terrorism. In doing so, India has conferred a moral equivalence to a state sponsor of terror. Pakistan, indeed, is a victim of terrorism but most of it is either sectarian or emanates from Al Qaeda because of the Musharraf policy of being a front-line ally of the US in its war on terror. They assert: The joint mechanism will not help India. "Rather it will now provide Pakistan a legitimate platform to it to voice its allegation that India is sponsoring some of the violence in Sindh, Balochistan and other place. It is going to degenerate in to a farce", predicts one to them. Also, Pakistan can cite the joint mechanism to claim that Islamabad and New Delhi are together fighting terrorism, blunting India's diplomatic offensive against its neighbour.

But senior officials counter this line of argument: The PM deliberately kept out of the debate the quality and nature of terrorism that Pakistan and India faced, that no moral equivalence has been consequently conceded to Pakistan. And yet, they contend, this should not gloss over the reality of Pakistan being a victim of terrorism as well.

An important if telling question is: "Is Musharraf as concerned about the terrorism racking India as he obviously is about that which targets him or his country, and the West?" Not even once, say the critics, has Pakistan shared any information or intelligence that would have helped prevent an act of terrorism in India. On the other hand, India had, on two previous occasions, passed actionable intelligence on bids to eliminate Musharraf. Here, a caveat needs to be made on behalf of Pakistan. India doing a good act in this field will earn it immediate kudos. But equivalent act by Pakistan will only reinforce the contention that Islamabad has much more information than it chooses to share with India. Even if not spoken in so many words, any prior information by it to India will only prove its culpability as far as terrorism in India is concerned. Whether it acts one way or the other, Pakistan has a lot to ponder over it!

Critics go beyond such theoretical arguments. They contend the joint mechanism also conveys the impression that Pakistan is neither directly or indirectly controlling the levers of terrorism directed at India. The defenders of the proposed mechanism deny it, saying it gives no clean chit to Musharraf whose Jan 2004 commitment to prevent acts of terrorism emanating from Pakistani soil has been largely observed only in the breach. Majority of officials feel that sharing of actionable intelligence, especially on a live, unfolding scenario as it indeed happened in Kargil, is a risky proposition. They argue that Pakistan will use the interaction to enhance the deniability quotient which is already substantial.

They cite the example of Shoaib Hassan from Lucknow, and Mahaboob Mandal from 24 Parganas districts, who were picked up in connection with the blasts at the Varanasi railway station and the Sankat Mochan temple in Mar 2006. Their interrogation revealed they had gone to Bangladesh on Indian passports. A Pakistani minder met them there, provided Bangladeshi passports to them and took away their Indian ones. They were flown on Bangladeshi passports to Karachi, and then to Balochistan for arms training. Subsequently they returned to Dhaka where their Bangladeshi passports were taken by their minder. They returned to India on Indian passports. Had India confronted the Pakistanis with this damning, incriminating information, they would have demanded proof, of which there is none. Their counter would be simple: This information has been extracted from the two using third degree methods and, hence, not credible.

It would not be sagacious for Indian intelligence to share active telephone numbers and the like with the Pakistani intelligence. One, they know the numbers any way. Two, once they become aware of the numbers India knows of, they would switch them off. An official, who wants to be unnamed, described the last round of Home Secretary—level talks, where terrorism was discussed, thus: "We presented evidence, they trashed it."

Beyond the questions of intelligence sharing and related issues, this agreement also need to be examined in the context of wide ambit of India-Pakistan relations.

One analyst wrote, in the context of India signing 16 Sep 2006 agreement at Havana, "In four months, Pakistan has changed. If not Pakistan, at least India's view of Pakistan has. From an exporter of terror to a victim of terror."[21] After all, on 17 May, while releasing the joint doctrine of armed forces, the then Defence Minister Pranab Mukherjee had said: "No evidence is available to suggest that Pakistan has taken measures to completely dismantle the terrorist infrastructure within Pakistan and PoK."

This new joint mechanism is a far cry from Musharraf's earlier proposal to jointly patrol the LOC, but much wider in its ambit-embracing the entire Sub-Continent. But there are doubts. He has already signed a truce with pro-Taliban tribals in FATA, enabling him to shift bulk of his army to Balochistan, and also to curry favour with the MMA hardliners whose support he will need in the 2007 polls. As such, he would not find it hard to sell the 'peace victory' to his people but Manmohan will find it harder to self it to Mumbai blast-shocked India.

The main opposition, the BJP, whose Prime Minister had extracted a promise from Musharraf in Jan 2004 to dismantle terror infrastructure in Pakistan, is crying hoarse. Its General Secretary Arun Jaitley said: "After (July) Mumbai blast, Manmohan said the terrorist modules are instigated, inspired and supported by elements across the border without which they can not act with such devastating effect....." Then came the loaded question, "Has Pakistan destroyed the terror camps in its territory?" The BJP, nurturing notions of being a sole political custodians of national security, seems determined to make a heavy weather of this agreement.

A number of national security brain-banks too did not take kindly to what they call Havana shift in India's Pakistan policy. "It is wrong to reclassify perpetrators of terror as victims of terror," said Lt Gen (Retd) Vijay Oberoi, former Vice Chief of Army Staff (VCOAS) and Director, Centre for Land Warfare Studies, an Army think tank. "Definitely, we are not in the same boat."

The Foreign Office has not come forward with any details of the new deal. The only explanation has come form the Prime Minister who said in his on-board press conference, mentioned above: "Gen Musharraf has assured me that Pakistan has no hand in perpetrating this [terrorism in India]. He said, 'let us work together in the future'."

Are not the Indian leaders trusting too much? They should not be blamed for nurturing unhappy memories of a similar promise, on a far more important issue, made by ZA Bhutto to Indira Gandhi in balmy climes of Shimla in 1972. Musharraf has proved even more of slippery customer than Bhutto as is obvious to Pakistanis within his country, and Afghans and American beyond.

The fact is that the Indian polity, and even the strategic establishment, are yet to learn to trust Musharraf, who is yet to even respond to the six-year-old demand for extradition of the 20 'devils', including the Lucifer among them, Dawood Ibrahim.

Record of Pakistan under the General is hardly re-assuring. It is widely believed that the loud claims notwithstanding, Pakistan has not done anything substantial to dismantle the terror infrastructure on its soil. On the contrary, the 28 June 2006 meeting, coordinated by the MHA and chaired by the COAS Gen JJ Singh, had also noted that there had been "increased reports of infiltration and spurts of grenade attacks in and around Srinagar, mainly aimed at soft and vulnerable targets."

In fact, Army sources said infiltration across the LOC has gone up in 2006. An officer in the operations room said : "Figures available with us show that 169 persons infiltrated from January to June 2006, up from 91 during the equivalent period last year (2005)".

Havana Accord has earned praise from abroad. Former US Assistant Secretary of State Strobe Talbott described it as statesmanship of the two leaders. But security experts do not see it that way.

- Maj Gen Sheru Thaplial who commanded a division in Siachen, said: "We should not make such unilateral concession. Pakistan is getting the impression that if they trigger an attack, we would rush to the negotiating table."

- Another General points out: Pakistan has been telling the world that but for Kargil attack, India would never have recognized the centrality of Kashmir to the peace process.

The signals coming from the MEA are that unlike in the case of 1993 Mumbai blasts, India can no longer squarely establish the hand of Pakistan government or its agencies behind the bombs exploding all over the country. But an MEA official on record takes a tougher stand: "As the Prime Minister explained, if the joint mechanism does not work, we will give it up. There is no commitment to go ahead with it till kingdom come. After all, we have suspended the composite dialogue process many times in the face of provocation. We can always do that."

Brig Gurmeet Kamal, Senior Fellow at the Center for Air power Studies, adds a touch of realism in his comments : "The optimism displayed at Havana is not reflected on the ground. On the contrary, terrorism has picked up on the ground. Yet, it is necessary to continue to talks. Dialogue process should not be subjected to the nature of public statements."

The Positive Side of Joint Mechanism

Official may not be able to look at the issues of immediate concern to them in the wider context of their political significance and diplomatic implications. Intelligence officials may find it counter-productive to share evidence with Pakistan and they have their past experience to reinforce their stance on the joint mechanism. But any agreement that widens and deepens the peace process going over the past nearly four years (since 2004) is a welcome step. If India has certain misgivings on the joint mechanism, so must be Pakistan. The entire peace process is meant to create trust between the two long-time adversaries. If this mechanism strengthen that process even in a little measure, it should be welcome.

Peace process may not have yielded any spectacular results so far, but certain ideas have come from Pakistan which India has agreed to look at. Pakistan has accepted certain Indian postulates on Kashmir issue, like the one of its aversion to redrawing of boundaries. The international community has expressed satisfaction that the two are engaged in serious negotiations, 4th round being in progress currently (May 2007 onwards). In any case, as the cliché goes, talking is better than fighting. Reverting to the joint mechanism, it is too early in the day to be pessimistic about it as yet.

Another major criticism likely to surface in the days to come will be: New Delhi has finally accepted the US line that Musharraf is the best bet to save Pakistan from the stranglehold of fundamentalists, and the world from terrorism. The US perception may be the result of what we in India call TINA (there is no alternative) factor. Talbott, who was in Delhi-India when Havana agreement was signed, said: "Bush had been coming on him like a ton of bricks on supporting the Taliban...The US has also discouraged the attempts on Kashmir. Let us not write off Pakistan as a Taliban country." Sage advice from a well-meaning outsider—a senior American figure. But many leaders and security experts do not have the inclination to take his exhortation at its face value as being nearer the scene, they have a less optimistic view about Pakistan's future for a variety of reasons, not discussed here.

Supporters of the Havana line, seeing India as a world power in not too distant a future, want India to display strategic self-confidence to accept such diplomatic risks. Talbot reinforces the postulation: "India has had great leaders who did not give up their efforts even in the face of criticism."

Some analysts puts the debate in stark choices: Is the Havana line reflection of a boldness in trying new approaches or a simple capitulation before the terrorism? An unnamed officer from the MEA puts it in undiplomatic bluntless, from behind the veil of his anonymity: "The proof of putting will be in eating. Bombs may continue to go off in India, but if Musharraf cooperates in getting them investigated, and getting culprits nabbed, he would have earned his clean chit. Till then he would have to tame his 'famous' military temper, be it over Siachen, Sir Creek, or Kashmir."

Realism in analysis of such situations is a necessary tool. Musharraf has made no secret of his guiding policy related to

Fallout

No dramatic statements, but progress on CBMs and dialogue process till Mumbai blasts force India to postpone dialogue.

16 Sep. 2006: Havana

(On the Sidelines of the NAM Conference)

The Setting

Dialogue process remains suspended, especially after Pakistan Foreign Minister Kasuri linked the blasts to lack of resolution of disputes.

Joint statement says

"The leaders agreed that the peace process must be maintained and its success was important for both countries and the future of the entire region...They directed their foreign secretaries to resume the composite dialogue at the earliest possible.

Fallout

Joint mechanism on counter-terror faces domestic criticism in India. Dialogue process to restart.

Anecdotal

Musharraf, apparently, redrafted the prepared speech made before the UN General Assembly on 19 Sep., 2006, after 16 September meeting with Manmohan in Havana.[42]

India has Several Joint Working Groups Accords on Counter-Terrorism

1995	Egypt
1997	Canada
1998	Germany
2000	UK and USA
2001	France and EU
2002	China, Israel, Kazakhstan, Russia and Croatia.
2003	Uzbekistan, Thailand, Turkey, Singapore, Australia and Tajikistan
2004	BIMSTEC, Mauritius, Indonesia, Myanmar and Poland
2005	Japan and Canada
2006	Pakistan

11 JULY 2006 VERSUS JOINT ANTI-TERRORISM MECHANISM

Signed a little more than two months after the gruesome 7-11, the Havana accord on the Joint Mechanism between India and Pakistan to fight terrorism in the Sub-continent seems to have a relevant connection with it. More so because the Havana joint statement "has specifically condemned the Mumbai blasts" and for New Delhi that is the may to test Islamabad's sincerity. It was because of this specific reference to 7-11 that, as analysts/journalists present on the occasion noted, President Musharraf wore a serious visage during the time Prime Minister Man Mohan Singh was reading the Joint Statement on 16 Sep. 2006 and in the subsequent joint press conference–barring a few moments when he permitted himself a formal, diplomatic smile!

In the phraseology of India's neighbourhood diplomacy, "putting Pakistan on notice" and "exposing Pakistan's duplicitous double standards" in the context of cross-border terrorism, have been reduced to an over used, miss used or even abused rhetorical flourishes. Will it really happen this time? This is the leading question that is reverberating in the diplomatic and journalistic/academic circles, now that more and more evidence that Pakistan's ISI masterminded the 7-11 bombings in Mumbai that cost 187 Indian lives.

Even before the offspring of the Havana truce, the Joint Mechanism, had come out of the incubator, the Prime Minister made certain observations on his way back from South Africa, laying bare his intent on the issue and his expectations from it:

> "Pakistan's cooperation in bringing the perpetrator's of the Mumbai blasts to book would be the acid test. We will test it. We have set up this mechanism. How else can we ask for information except through a mechanism like this? I think Pakistan will have to walk the talk."

Armed with adequate evidence, or so India thought, it was planning to pursue the issue through diplomatic channels. Realizing the desirability and importance of building up a strong case and presenting credible evidence, Home Secretary V.K. Duggal and Foreign Secretary Shiv Shankar Menon met on 4 Oct 2006 to coordinate their responses. India plans to "raise the issue at the forth coming foreign secretary level talks." Subsequently, New Delhi will do the same when the structural details of Joint Mechanism would have been finalized and put in place by the two countries.

It was with this in mind that Indian Prime Minister had remarked: "We will share the information with Pakistan and ascertain how sincere they are in carrying forward the commitment."

Pakistan's past record on cooperation with India on terror has been ridden with arguments and debate. In fact, some analysts argue, Pakistan's records on dismastling terrorist infrastructure is based more on convenience and political considerations than on conviction and India's concerns. When it is cornered or finds it in national interests, it delivers. 'It is well-known that "it has handed over close to 700 Al-Qaeda suspects including the big ones like Khalid Sheikh Mohd, Abu Zubaida to the US and, by Musharraf's own admission, been handsomely rewarded for it. But, on the other hand, it has not delivered even one of India's large list of 37 suspects. It bears emphasis that not to speak of big fish like Dawood Ibrahim, Masood Azhar and Tiger Memon, Pakistan has not handed over even unknown culprits on that list. Yielding to India even on such inconsequential issues is unthinkable for any Pak ruler, and for Musharraf it is absolute "No, no". Pakistan polity survives on shrill anti-Indianism. There will the strong reaction from the street, if not from the intellectuals and the cognescenti, if any concession or consideration is given to India's view point.

This is one reality of Pakistan in its relationships with India that Indians will do well to remeber. For Islamabad, the US and India do not belong to the same league: one is a superhuman and a milch cow, the other were an 'equal', 'Hindu' neighbour despite the huge disparity of sizes in their areas, populations and economies. Indians must understand that Pakistan has its political compulsions while dealing with India. At a more mundane level, can India ever mach the US munificence for Pakistan?

But for the time being, the only issue of immediate relevance to India is extradition of India's "most wanted." That includes the hijackers of IC-814 who melted in the crowds on the

Kandahar airport on 31 Dec 2000 and subsequently located themselves on Pakistan territory and got active in training their cadres for terrorist attacks on India. Azhar is the chief of the JEM ever since the raised it in Pakistan/PoK after his release on that fateful 31 December. Wherever India asks for it, Islamabad has a proforma reply: "These suspects are not in Pakistan. They never were." It is now a pattern that has resulted in a belief —at once logical and empirically true—that Islamabad will never deliver.[43]

Pakistan has consistently —and persistently –ignored all appeals by India to come clean on terrorism. For instance, though Gen Musharraf gave a solemn assurance to India on 6 Jan 2004 that Pakistan will dismantle the infrastructure of terrorism it has remained a promise till date. It is common knowledge that the ISI continues to fund and sponsor terrorist camps.

In this limited aspect of Pakistan's stand vis-a-vis India, it is fair to concede a point to Pakistan: In spite of all the fullsome praise for Musharraf in public by the highest US officials, President Bush downwards, there is an under-current of unhappiness, even serious reservations and resentment, about Pakistan's commitment to fighting terrorism as the "front-line" ally of the US. Not only the Bush administration in private and in confidential letters keep criticising Islamabad for "not doing enough" in this field, even the think-tanks in the US and Europe keep publishing reports that show the photographs of the infrastructural terror training facilities but also the experts and analysts suggesting Pakistan's continued support for pro-Taliban elements into its areas bordering Afghanistan and across it as a policy option not only against Afghanistan of Karzai but also against its eastern neighbour India. Indians should be under no illusion that as soon as the US attention is diverted from Iraq and Afghanistan, Pakistan will be reverting to its policy of having Afghanistan as its strategic backyard and re-adopting openly the cross-border terrorism against India as an instrument of its foreign policy. It is for this very policy considerations that Pakistan will never allow a let up in its cross-border terrorism against India, nor will it allow any vital presence of India in geo-strategic sense or India–created industrial or commercial entities in Afghanistan.

It is not that Indian security establish ment is not aware of these realities of Pakistani real politik. Even then it has decided to play along for policy considerations. In any case, in the present world situation, negotiations is the only accepted way for resolution of disputes. India's readiness to sign a truce at Havna should be seen in this light, even if there is strong opposition to it within the country.

Understandably, besides the domestic opposition to the Joint Mechanism, even the two principals have signed it for their own respective reasons and interests. While India believes that the joint institutional mechanism will help it put pressure on Pakistan and it can bring international pressure to bear on its adversary if the latter Chickens out and fails to abide lay the truce provisions, Pakistan feels India has conceded it the moral equivalence of being an equal victim of terrorism. In addition, Islamabad also sees the mechanism as providing it an opportunity of painting India in lurid colours as instigator, supporter and even sponsor of the anti-Pakistan violence in Singh and insurrectionary movement in Baluchistan. So, as the critic see it, the talks under Joint Mechanism will be reduced to a wordy duel, with each blaming the other for terrorists attacks and violence within its borders.

The critics further aver that India already had a mechanism of cooperation with Pakistan on the issue of terrorism at the home secretary level. So, how will this Joint Mechanism created at Havana mark any difference? Even within South Block (read, MEA), there is some disagreement on the mechanism. Such reports are floated merely, some would suggest, to assert that the truce and consequent mechanism were pushed through by the PMO and the NSAI.

A senior MEA official put it this way: "Earlier too, at the highest level, Pakistan had promised that they would end terrorism and cooperate with us, but they have not followed it with any action on ground. This Mechanism will make Pakistan a stake-holder in the fight against terrorism." But by not defining the parameters of the mechanism, it has left it open to interpretation — a potential opportunity for mischief-makers to exploit for their partisan aims.

But the shape of future things can be seen from one development concerning a single incident of the 7-11 terrorism act. Surely, it can not be a matter of an inconsequential coincidence that "out of the 15 people arrested in connection with the Jul 2006 Mumbai blasts, 11 are Pakistani nationals,"[44] and the accused were trained in the LET run schools/camps in Bahawalpur , home to many other terrorist outfits like the JEM. But Pakistan still continues to remains in the denial mode. When the Mumbai police blamed ISI for the blasts, Pakistan came out with a set-piece, routine statement : "This (Indian) statement, like those made immediately after the Mumbai blasts, contains unsubstantiated allegations, which Indian officials and media keep making for propaganda purposes." Worse could not be expected from our neighbour.

While intelligence-sharing is an integral part of agreements against terrorism, and Havana one is no exception, many serious hurdles can be seen on the issue. Dowe hare a guarantee that the intelligence offered will not be misused? Even more importantly, will it be prudent and discreet to share a actionable intelligence with a country with whom trust-deficit is a glaring fact of life and whose past actions did not generate confidence and future intent suspicious. Now the final blunt question : Can Indian covert services meaningfully and unhesitantly discuss terrorism with Pakistan's ISI, a well-spring of anti-India terrorism for decades and continues in its determined may, notwithstanding the nearly four-year-old solemn assurances given by the Big Boss himself to a believing/trusting Indian Prime Minister in Jan 2004 to stop/discontinue it?

The supporters of the Joint Mechanism feel its critics are too harsh, and too early in the day. Surely, India and its leadership must have seen some merit in it. Reason demands that it be given a fair chance. A pre-mature burials of such agreements is not an act of statesmanship, or even mature diplomacy. After all, only one meeting between the officials of two nations has taken place so far. The next quarterly meeting is yet two months away. A little more patience is required to work such accords than its critics seem to be willing to grant it.

So, the real test of Indian diplomacy will be to make sincere effort to make the Joint Mechanism work and ensure that India's concerns on terrorism are addressed, including and particularly the ones emanating from the cross-border terrorism. That will be the barometer—the single, sole test—to judge the success or otherwise of Man Mohan Singh's Havana diplomacy; else this joint anti-terrorism mechanism of the two countries will be yet another meaningless exercise destined to go nowhere. Or, to put it in historical perspective, yet another Indian Prime Minister would have been led up the garden path or down a slippery slope by yet another shrewder Pakistani leader!

There is indeed, no case for being judgmental on the issue in a hurry. The realities might surprise the inveterate critics on either side!

"India Would not Share 'Hard Evidence' with Pakistan"

Days before the first meeting of the Joint Anti-Terrorism Mechanism scheduled for 6-7 Mar 2007 at Islamabad, "India has decided not to share "hard evidence" about terror attacks with Pakistan". Although New Delhi will provide Islamabad "enough details" pinpointing the role of Pakistan-backed terrorist outfits in carrying out blasts on this side including the ones in Samihauta Express and the Mumbai suburban trains, India feels that "hard evidence" in the hands of intelligencies agencies of the neighboring country could be misused or tampered with.

"There is always a chance of tampering with the technical evidence (intercepts) which points fingers at terrorist outfits across the border. Concrete details comprising outfits phone numbers and web server data can be changed any time to suit the perpetrators' claims" said a senior officer who has been part of a high-level team working to finalize the agenda for the forthcoming meet. Additional Secretary (International Organizations), MEA, will be leading the Indian delegation at this (6-7 March) meeting.

Referring to the internal meetings held in the past one week on the agenda for the first meeting, government sources said on 2 March 2007[45] "Since the Mumbai police has already filed the charge sheet in the Mumbai blasts case, India would share a bit more information with Pakistan indicating involvement of Pakistani citizens in planting the bombs in the suburban trains.

Besides discussing the terror incidents, India will also try to impress upon Pakistan the need to explore the option of signing a Mutual Legal Assistance Treaty (MLAT) between the two countries which may eventually lead them to sign an extradition treaty.

"Though Pakistan is not going to take up these proposals kindly at this stage, we hope to initiate a dialogue over such issues which are quite important for investigation as well as deportation of criminals from each side", said an official, adding that the possibility of taking up matters relating to Interpol references may be fruitful only if Pakistan agrees to a legal assistance treaty referred to in the preceding paragraph.

India-Pakistan: First joint meeting on Anti-Terrorism: March 2007

The two countries hold their first ever meeting of the Indo-Pak Joint Anti-Terrorism Mechanism (JATM) at Islamabad on 6-7 Mar 2007. During this meeting, "India and Pakistan made conceptual progress on fighting terrorism together, but operational progress, if it comes about, is still in the womb of time."[46]

Conceptually, the two countries decide on three things, noted below:

1. They mutually agreed to increase the size of the body (JATM) from three members, including the head (as decided earlier), to five members from each side. This was done to have larger number of players on board for the sensitive talks. The revised composition will have two displomats and three spymasters from each side.
2. They agreed to have an institutionalised arrangement of quarterly meetings for exchanging specific information and helping investigations on terrorist acts related to either side.
3. They agreed that instead of finger - pointing in the event of a terror incident, the two would immediately get in touch with each other by using JATM platform. Importantly, this could be done even during the inter – session period of JATM meetings.

During this meeting, India presented evidence of the involvement of Pakistan's ISI in several high profile incidents in India like Mumbai, Ayodhya and Bangalore. The Indian side also gave photographs, telephone numbers and addresses of some of the wanted terrorists in these incidents who were Pakistani nationals. India also provided information to Pakistan on several wanted men based in Pakistan against whom Interpol has issued red-corner alert notices.

On its part, Pakistan assured India of aiding and abetting terror acts in Baluchistan both sides agreed to disagree on this crucial operational question.

The Pakistan delegation was led by Tariq Osman Hyder, Additional Secretary, and Ministry of Foreign Affairs. His Indian counterpart was Mr. K.C. Singh, Additional Secretary, MEA.

Being an important document, the full text of the Joint Statement issued after the first meeting of the India – Pakistan Anti-Terrorism Mechanism is reproduced below in toto:

> "In pursuance of the decision taken during meeting between the President of Pakistan and Prime Minister of India in Havana, Cuba on 16 Sep. 2006, the first meeting of the Anti-Terrorism Mechanism was held in Islamabad on 6 Mar 2007. The Pakistan delegation was led by Mr. Tariq Osman Hyder, Additional Secretary (UNEC.), Ministry of Foreign Affairs. The Indian delegation was led by Mr. K.C. Singh, Additional Secretary (IO), and Ministry of External Affairs of India.
>
> "The two sides discussed the Parameters of the Anti-Terrorism Mechanism and agreed that specific information will be exchanged through the Mechanism for (i) Helping investigations on either side related to terrorist acts and (ii) prevention of violence and terrorist acts in the two countries.
>
> "It was also agreed that while the Anti-Terrorism Mechanism would meet on a quarterly basis, any information which is required to be conveyed on priority basis would be immediately conveyed through the respective heads of the Mechanism."

It is a brief Joint Statement on the usual and expected lines. The meeting had spilled over to 7 March. The official (Indian) spokesman read the Statement to the press at Islamabad.

Equally expected were some 'awkward' questions asked and diplomatically skirted round by the spoken man. The questions are given below:

- There were reports in Pakistani press that Pakistan has presented evidence on the alleged Indian role in Balochistan and also the operation of Indian Consulate in Afghanistan.
- I understand that five or six names of people who have red corner notices against them were handed over to Pakistani side.
- There are PTI reports that the Indian side presented some photographs of the Pakistani suspects involved in some of the blasts.
- How cooperative has the Pakistani side been?

Notes

1. Vishwa Mohan, *Times of India*, 16 Apr, 2007.
2. Sajit Gandhi (ed) "The September 11th Source Books", *National Security Archives Electronic Briefing Book* 97, 11 Sep., 2003 at http://www.gwu.edu/-nsar-chiv/NSAEBB/NSAEBB 97/indcx.htm
3. James Risen and Judith Miller, "Pakistani Intelligence Had links to Al-Qaeda, US officials say," *New York Times,* 29 Oct, 2001.
4. Philip Smucker, "Al-Qaeda Thriving in Kashmir", *Christian Science Monitor,* 2 Jul 02; and Leon T. Hadar "Pakistani America's War against Terrorism: Strategic ally or Unreliable Client?", Cato Policy Analysis No. 436, Washington DC, 8 May, 2002.
5. Mariam Abou Zahab and Olivier Roy, *Islamist Networks: The Afghan-Pakistan Connection,* Columbia University Press, 2004.
6. Lisa Curtis, Three steps to improve counterterrorism cooperation with Pakistan, Web Memo, No. 1197,The Hesitage Foundation, Washington DC, 18 Aug, 06.

7 Kanchan Lakshman, "The ISI hand in 7/11 Mumbai blasts, say police", *The Hindu,* 1.10.06; Anand Giridharadas, "India's police say Pakistan Helped plot", *New York Times*, 1.10.06.

8 "70 per cent Afghan Narcotics Move through Pakistan", *Daily Times* (Lahore), 21 Mar 2005.

9 Pramod Kumar Singh,"Quiet goes the Don to new Karachi den", *Pioneer*, 28 Oct, 2003.

10. "Keynote Address of Assistant Secretary Juan C. Zarat", Office of Public Affairs, The Department of Treasury, 1 Feb, 2005, at

    http://www. ustreas.gov//press/releases/js 2225.htm. Also see "US Designates Dawood Ibrahim as terrorists supporter : Indian Crime Lord has assisted Al-Qaeda and supported other terrorists in India,"16 Oct, 2003, at.

    http://www. ustreas./gov/press/releares/js 909.htm.
11. Praveen Swami and Anupma Katakam, "Breedom Ground", *Frontline*, 20 May-2 Jun 2006, 23 (10).
12. United States Treasury, n. 29.
13. "US Designates Al Akhtar", US Treasury Department Press Release, 14 Oct 2003; United States Treasury, n. 29.
14. Shekhar Gupta, *India Today*, 18 Dec, 2006.
15. G. Parthasarathy, *Tribune*, 12 Jul, 2007.
16. Shekhar Gupta, *Indian Express*, 7 Jul, 2007.
17. Praveen Swami, *Hindu,* 23 Oct, 2006.
18. Swapan Dasgupta, *Pioneer*, 8 Oct, 2006.
19. B. Raman, *Pioneer*, 26 Oct, 2006.
20. Sankarshan Thakur, *Tehelka*, 30 Sep, 2006.
21. Alok Mehta, *Outlook*, 2 Oct, 2006.
22. R Prasannan, *Week*, 1 Oct, 2006.
23. *Week*, 1 Oct, 2006.
24. Saurabh Shukla, *India Today*, 16 Oct, 2006.
25. *India Today*, 16 Oct, 2006.
26. Vishwa Mohan, *Times of India*, 3 Mar, 2007.
27. Rajeev Sharma, *Tribune*, 9 Mar, 2007.